Italy, Piedmont, and the War of the Spanish Succession 1701-1712

Ciro Paoletti

'This is the Century of the Soldier', Fulvio Testi, Poet, 1641

Helion & Company

Helion & Company Limited
Unit 8 Amherst Business Centre
Budbrooke Road
Warwick
CV34 5WE
England
Tel. 01926 499 619
Email: info@helion.co.uk
Website: www.helion.co.uk
Twitter: @helionbooks
blog.helion.co.uk/

Published by Helion & Company 2021
Designed and typeset by Mach 3 Solutions Ltd (www.mach3solutions.co.uk)
Cover designed by Paul Hewitt, Battlefield Design (www.battlefield-design.co.uk)

ISBN 978-1-913336-49-3

British Library Cataloguing-in-Publication Data.
A catalogue record for this book is available from the British Library.

For details of other military history titles published by Helion & Company Limited contact the above address or visit our website: http://www.helion.co.uk.

We always welcome receiving book proposals from prospective authors.

Contents

List of Acronyms

ASR	Archivio di Stato di Roma
AST	Archivio di Stato di Torino
ASV	Archivio di Stato di Venezia
ASVa	Archivio Segreto Vaticano – Roma
AUSSME	Archivio dell'ufficio Storico dello Stato Maggiore Esercito – Roma

Foreword

The War of the Spanish Succession was fought to decide possession of Spain and its European and overseas empire. Though waged primarily in western and southern Europe, the conflict involved operations elsewhere, notably North America where is was known as Queen Anne's War, as well as running in parallel to Rákóczi's Rebellion in Hungary (1703–11) and the Great Northern War (1700–21). For most English-speaking readers, the war is mainly associated with John Churchill, Duke of Marlborough, and his famous victories over the French, particularly Blenheim in 1704. The Anglophone view generally narrows the conflict to Flanders where Marlborough fought most of his campaigns, as well as shortening it to the dates of Britain's entry (1702) and exit (1713) from the war. Ciro Paoletti's excellent book expands our view to the war's full duration (1701–14), as well as drawing attention to the fighting in Italy.

Spain's Italian possessions were extensive, populous, rich and collectively formed one of the chief objects in the war. The Spanish succession was the most pressing international issue in Europe since the 1640s when it appeared that the Spanish branch of the Habsburg dynasty was on the verge of extinction. This appeared ever-more inevitable with the accession of Charles II in 1665 whom most contemporary observers felt was incapable of fathering an heir. The Austrian Habsburgs and French Bourbons both claimed the succession, while England and the Dutch Republic, allied since 1689 as the Maritime Powers, were determined to ensure than neither claimant secured both Spain's European and overseas possessions. Once it became clear by 1700 that the compromise option of devolving Spain to the Wittelsbach family would not work, partition increasingly looked the likeliest outcome. It was here that Italy's significance emerged, since Emperor Leopold I, head of the Austrian Habsburg line, was primarily concerned with securing Spain's Italian lands in Lombardy and despatched an army under Prince Eugene of Savoy to secure Milan, thereby opening the war in May 1701. Not only was possession of Milan considered vital to Austria's security against France, but it was central to the continued defence of imperial jurisdiction across most of northern and central Italy, as well as acting as the main gateway to the south and, with that, to the control of Spain's other territories in Naples, Sicily and Sardinia. Leopold and his successors were far more interested in securing these than conquering the Spanish Netherlands which, while also populous and rich, were strategically vulnerable and distant from Austria. Thus, supporting Marlborough's campaigns in Flanders was something Austria did out of duty to its British and Dutch allies, whereas for those powers, ejecting the French from the Spanish Netherlands was a primary goal.

As Paoletti shows, Italy posed a very different set of operational challenges than Flanders, or indeed also the Rhineland and Spain itself. Like the Nine Years' War (1688–97) which also saw heavy fighting in northern Italy, the conflict was waged by rival coalitions, neither of which had sufficient troops in the theatre and depended on local allies and hired auxiliaries, as well as reinforcements brought in by sea. Both sides relied heavily on locally-sourced supplies and transport, as well as substantial financial contributions to sustain their operations. Crucially, as Paoletti argues, though Italy was a battlefield, the Italians themselves were active participants in the conflict. Foremost among them was the grand duke of Savoy whose support for the pro-Austrian coalition was fundamental to its eventual success against the French and Spanish Bourbon forces. The duke's reward was a royal title that signalled Savoy's rise to a middle-ranking power and which represented an important step towards its eventual dominance over Italy. Savoy's armed forces are covered in detail in the book, but attention is also given to the papacy which fought its own, unsuccessful war against Austria in 1708–9 to limit the Habsburgs' dominance over central and southern Italy.

The book offers a wealth of detail, much of it fresh from Italian archives. It is written with the author's characteristic verve and wit and deserves our attention as a valuable account of this important but neglected conflict.

Peter H. Wilson
Chichele Professor of the History of War
University of Oxford

Introduction

Readers, including me, normally jump over the introduction, thus I will try to make it short. The War of the Spanish Succession is supposed to be rather well known. Unfortunately it is not so. English speaking readers know it to have been fought, have plenty of accounts about when, and how Lord Marlborough did this or that, thanks to the good work of people like John Lynn they know almost everything about how the French acted and reacted to the British in Flanders and Germany, and … stop, the other fronts basically do not exist, even if, sometimes, one remembers Spain, mostly due to that boring cry: "no peace without Spain".

Well, there was also another front, and it was quite more important than anybody may think now. It was so important that the French considered it as important as the German front, and committed there their best generals. It was so important that King William III considered it to be far more important than Spain. It was so important that, in spite of having no British army there, after King William's death London committed to it 1/10 of her war expense. It was so important that the Emperor sent there his best general. In case you think I exaggerate, read, first, and then see whether am I wrong or not.

If it was so important, why does nobody recall it now? Simply, because a very few people can read Italian – first – and because a lot of people make no actual research, and simply "copy" what the previous generation of historians wrote.

Last: the reader who by chance bought my previous book about the Nine Years' War, must honestly be told in advance that he, or she, will find here and there, many parts from that book – about logistics, Piedmont in general, and Piedmontese army. I had to use them as they were, for nothing changed during the five years between the end of the War of the League of Augsburg in 1696, and the start of the War of the Spanish Succession in 1701. I beg your pardon, I'm rather sorry, but, especially when writing in a foreign language, it is almost impossible to say the same things in a different way.

Part I

THE WAR WITH THE FRENCH

1

The European and the Italian Situation

I: The Italian States in 1700

On the eve of the eighteenth century, Italy was a mosaic of States. The Italian peninsula, as it is well known, takes the shape of a boot, and politically was more or less divided in three. The south and two of her three major islands – Sicily and Sardinia – and the most of her small islands were under the rule of Spain. The north was under the formal authority of the Holy Roman Emperor. The Papal States lay in between.

Italy had a homogenous cultural entity dating from the end of the collapse of the Roman Empire. Roman Catholicism was dominant. Religion and laws derived from the Roman system and a common art and culture unified the peninsula. The Italian language, a derivation of Latin, was spoken since at least the seventh century and written since at least the twelfth in a way that is still possible to easily and fully understand. Despite these commonalities Italy was not politically homogenous. A Frankish invasion in 774 led by Charlemagne established Italy as a separate kingdom from the Holy Roman Empire. After Charlemagne's death in 814, however, northern and central Italy became part of the Holy Roman Empire, except for Venice, Genoa, and the Papal States.

In the eleventh century the Normans conquered southern Italy, and expelled the Muslims from Sicily. Then their new kingdom of Naples was recognised by the Pope as a feudal dependency on the Roman Church.

In subsequent centuries Italy became increasingly important as a commercial hub. Her States grew in wealth and her banking system emerged, and expanded throughout Continental Europe. The wealthier Italy became, the weaker the authority of the Holy Roman Emperor. And when Frederick I "Barbarossa" (which in Italian means "Redbeard"), tried to reassert his authority in Italy, the cities – the commons as they called themselves – formed an Italian League, and defeated him at Legnano in May 1176. This was a turning point in Italian political history. The following peace of Constance, signed in 1183, confirmed the autonomy of the Italian commons, supported by the Pope, and by the King of Naples.

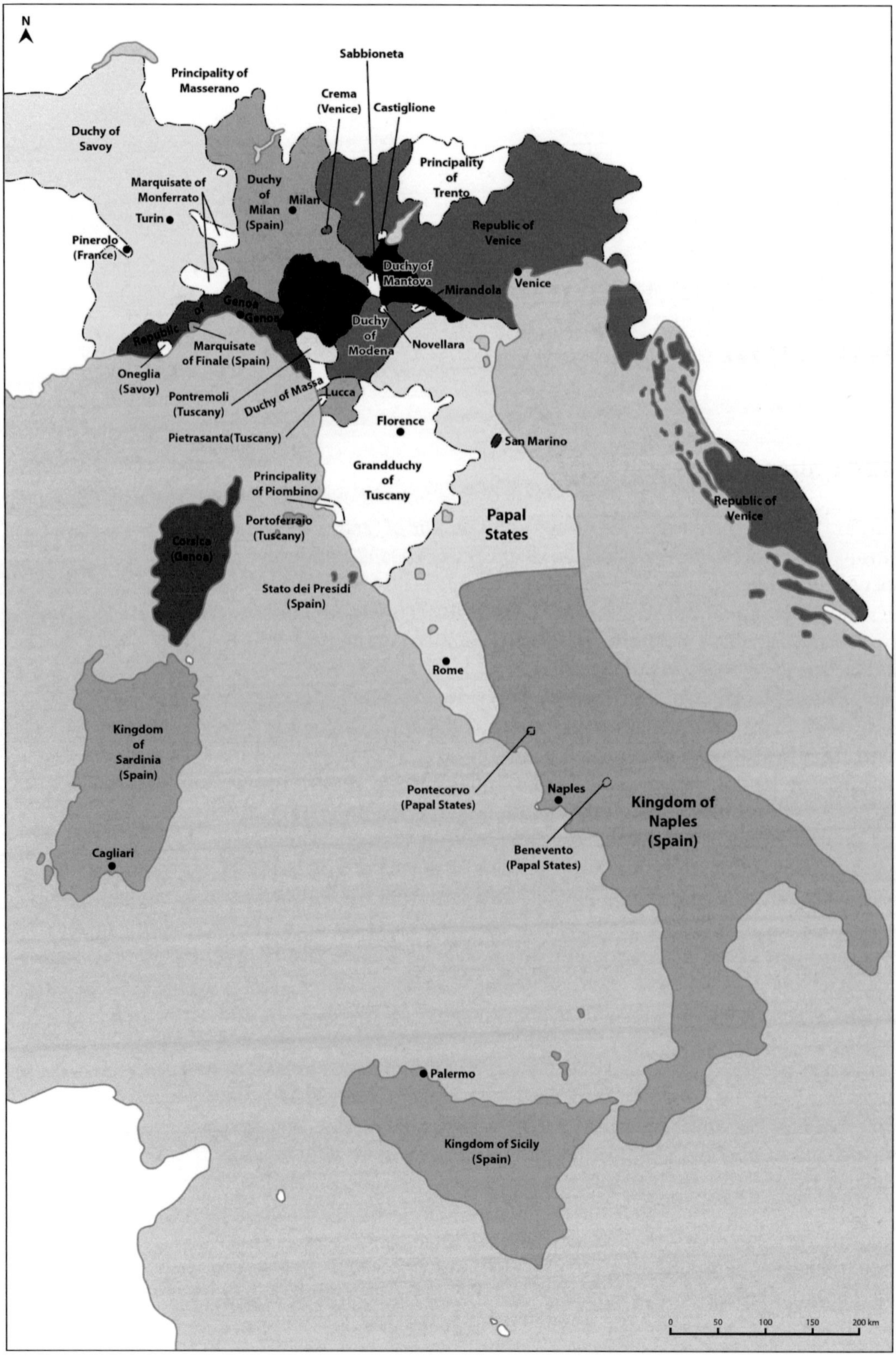

Map of Italy, 1696.

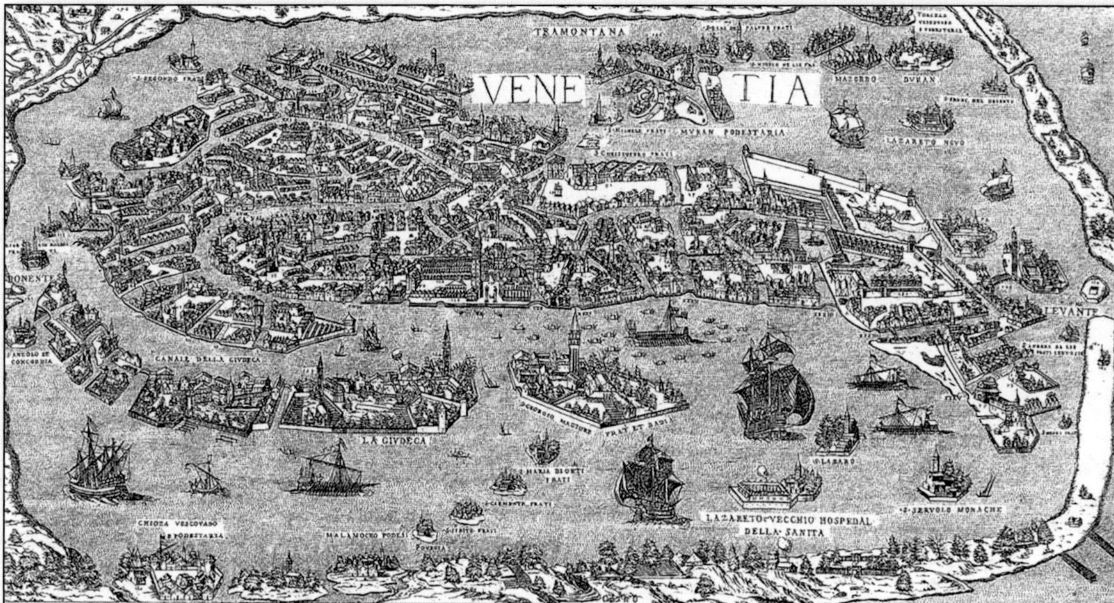

Plan of Venice.

The political system, composed of small scattered commons, and lordships, was economically strong, but politically and militarily weak, Moreover weddings, inheritances, and treaties created over four centuries a complicated web of interests, and rights, which by the end of the fifteenth century allowed both the king and queen of Aragon and Castile, and the King of France, to claim some rights allowing them to intervene in Italy. Thus the long Spanish–French clash started for Italy, and ended by the mid sixteenth century with a total Spanish victory. The Spaniards held huge portions of the country and kept them for the following century and a half, no matter what the French tried to do. So at the end of the seventeenth century Italy was still divided. There were the four kingdoms of Corsica, Sardinia, Sicily, and Naples. The first was held by Genoa, the others by Spain and ruled by a Spanish viceroy each. There were five republics: Venice, Genoa, Lucca, and San Marino on the Italian mainland, and Ragusa in Dalmatia.

There were some small principalities in Piombino, Monaco, and Masserano; the Grand Duchy of Tuscany; the Duchies of Savoy, Modena, Mantua, Milan, Massa and Carrara, Parma and Plaisance, Guastalla and, the smallest, Mirandola.

The Habsburgs of Austria controlled the Trentino, the Upper Adige that they called South Tyrol, and the cities of Gorizia, Trieste, and Fiume.

However, many Italian States held territories outside the peninsula. The Duke of Savoy possessed in Italy the principalities of Piedmont and Oneglia, and the Marquisate of Saluzzo, and west of the Alps the French-speaking Duchy of Savoy and the Italian-speaking County of Nice. Venice owned Dalmatia on the Eastern coast of the Adriatic Sea and since 1699 ruled the Peloponnesus, that is to say half of Greece, and many Greek Islands. The Pope owned the city of Avignon, and the Venassine County in France. Malta belonged to the crown of Sicily, but the Knights Hospitallers of Saint John had held it since the first half of the sixteenth century. They were in fact independent, but presented each year a falcon as feudal tribute to the King of Sicily. Lastly, just to make things easier, some States had territories within other States. Mantua had the Marquisate of Monferrato between Piedmont, owned by the Duke of Savoy, and the Spanish-held Duchy of Milan. The Savoy-owned principality of Oneglia, facing the sea, was completely surrounded by the Republic of Genoa. The Pope had the two principalities of Pontecorvo and Benevento in the Kingdom of Naples. The Duchy of Milan – or rather, the Cathedral of Milan – still owned the small town of Campione in the Swiss-owned Tessin.

Thanks to their common language and culture, and although they referred to themselves as Florentines, Lombards, Venetians, Genoese or Neapolitans, when relating themselves to outsiders such as Turks, French, Germans, and Europeans in general, the people of the Peninsula and her dependencies self-identified, and were identified by the others as "Italians".

As said, the whole northern part of the Italian peninsula between the Alps and the Papal States, except for the Republic of Venice formally belonged to the Holy Roman Empire.

So the small duchies of Modena, Parma, Piacenza, Ferrara, Guastalla, Mirandola, and Mantua, and the bigger duchies of Milan and Tuscany, as well as the Republics of Genoa, and Lucca, and the Principality of Piedmont, were officially under the Holy Roman Emperor's rule, no matter what they thought and preferred. Except for the two Republics, whenever the sovereign died, his successor had to ask for Imperial consent and investiture within one year and one day since the death of his predecessor. In the past many of the duchies, for instance those of Modena, and Parma, had been accepted as feudal subjects by the Pope, thus according to the legal rules of that time they were included within the Church's authority and hence subtracted from the Imperial one. But the Emperor never accepted it. After the Legnano defeat he remained silent during the Middle Ages, the Renaissance, and the whole sixteenth century, that is to say while he was weak. But in 1690 things started changing. The end of the War of the League of Augsburg rendered the Holy Roman Emperor, who was now Leopold I of Habsburg, stronger than in the past.

Emperor Leopold I.

The Italian campaigns during that war saw Imperial troops return to Italy for the first time after 1629, and these troops had to be lodged and fed. According to Imperial laws it was up to the princes of the Empire to do it. Or rather: every prince of the Empire had to cooperate with the wars of the Empire, no matter whether in money, or men, or both. Hence, since 1690, Leopold wanted his rights back, or rather wanted back the money linked to the Imperial rights, and demanded his Imperial subjects in Italy pay. It was a matter of millions. The order was not happily greeted, but unfortunately Imperial troops were on the spot and were ready to enforce the Imperial demands, thus the Italian princes could do nothing but pay. There were only two exceptions: Savoy, because she was engaged in the war, and Venice, because she did not belong to the

Empire, and the Emperor knew it was better not to try any trick against her; but all the others had to pay during the war, and at the end of the war.

In fact, when in 1696 the Nine Years' War ended on the Italian front, Leopold stated that the Italian princes and the Republics of Genoa and Lucca, had to pay to the Imperial troops' wages, and their travel back to Austria, that is to say 300,000 doubles. Once more there was not that much that could be done. Those were the Imperial rules, and the Imperial Army could enforce them. Tuscany paid 75,000 doubles; the Duke of Modena 40,000. Ferdinando Gonzaga paid 40,000 as the Duke of Mantua, and 25,000 as the Marquess of Monferrato. The Duke of Parma gave 36,000; the Republic of Genoa 40,000; the small and wealthy Republic of Lucca 30,000; and the Pope voluntarily contributed with 40,000.

This greed by the Austrians caused bad consequences in a few years, and worse consequences within less than a generation. But the 1696 payment was not a lone event: there was a further attempt in 1697, which came immediately after the huge payments already imposed. It came when Italian pockets were empty, and it was not welcome.

II: The Twilight of the Spanish Habsburgs, and Charles II's Last Will

The affair of the Spanish succession is well known, thus it is not necessary to go deep into details.

Charles II of Habsburg, King of Spain, had no heirs. Initially he was in favour of the Austrian branch of his family, but then changed his mind; it happened due to a couple of major mistakes by the Emperor in the 1690s. The first occurred in Spain. When, during the Nine Years' War, the French entered Catalunya and threatened Barcelona, the Austrians were literally begged by the Spaniards to commit an expeditionary force to relieve the city, and protect the region, but the Emperor refused, although using a lot of nice words.

Charles II of Spain.

Now, Spain was supporting the Great Alliance with tens of thousands of men in Italy, on the Pyrenees and on the Rhine, with hundreds of thousands of scudi funding the Italian front, and with millions spent to sustain the war. Obviously Spain did it in her own interest, to protect her properties; nonetheless now, just when Imperial support looked important to protect Catalunya, an important portion of Spanish homeland from the mutual enemy, the Emperor – a relative, a cousin, and a brother in law of the King of Spain – refused it. There were many reasons, they said in Vienna. The most important was the lack of men, for the Empire had to fight in Hungary in the Balkans, and on the Rhine, and had just

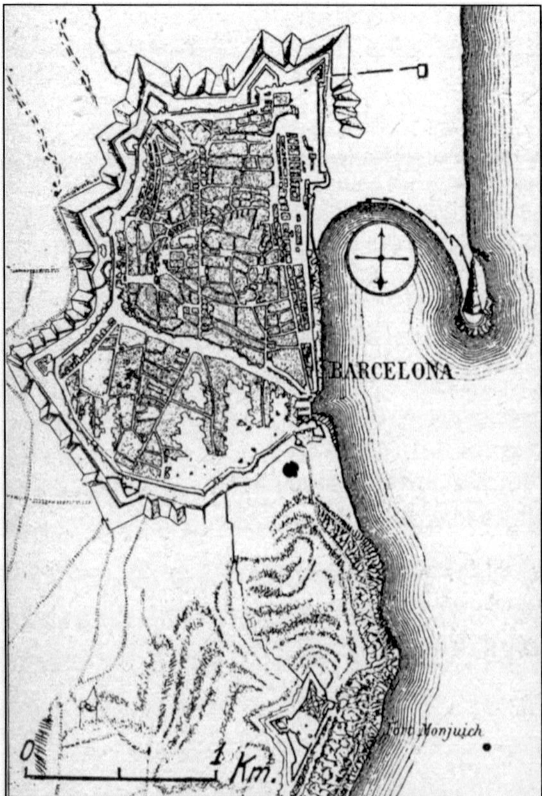

Barcelona in the Seventeenth Century.

committed five of its best infantry regiments to Lombardy to protect the Spanish-held Duchy of Milan against any French threat. And even if soldiers could be found, there were no vessels to ship them to Barcelona, and, thus, in Vienna everybody was so sorry, but unfortunately by now nothing could be done to relieve Spain.

This did not change Charles II's mind, who was still in favour of his relatives, the Austrian Habsburgs, but it deeply changed the Spaniards' minds, who began looking at the Austrians as selfish and ingrate, as by the way they were. This was not too important, yet, when in early summer 1697 the new Imperial ambassador, Count von Harrach, reached Madrid. The King, the Queen, and the most important ministers were all still in favour of an Austrian heir.

The King felt relatively well, and still hoped to have children. But the French siege of Barcelona was going on, no Imperial soldier was in sight and, as the Queen told Harrach, the good opinion Spain's highest ranks still had of Austria could vanish soon if no help came. And no help came, at all. And the Spanish noblemen, and this time the King too, would remember it.

III: The Troubles of the Italian Princes and the Rumours About the French Heir

There were many reasons for the Emperor not to look for further engagements, in Spain or wherever, other than those he already had. In the last days of the seventeenth century the Holy Roman Empire had many troubles along all its borders. There were concerns in the south after the recent War of the Holy League, due to the attitude of the Turks defeated by Austria, Venice, Poland, and Russia. There were concerns in the west, due to France, and there were problems in the north beyond the borders, across the borders, and within the borders. Beyond the borders the ongoing Northern War between Saxony-Poland and Sweden was not an immediate concern, but could perhaps affect the delicate situation within the Empire. Then there was a big problem involving Denmark, and the northern German princes just across that border, and, within the Empire, there was a political clash whose consequences went as far as Rome.

It all started when due to William III of Orange the House of Hannover obtained, at least in perspective, the ninth Electorate of the Holy Roman Empire. The Protestant/Catholic ratio became 4 to 5 electors to the Catholics, instead of 3 to 5 as in the past. The Pope perceived this as a threat to Catholicism in the Holy Roman Empire and protested, and a diplomatic

The Diet of the Empire.

storm arose also among the German Princes. It widened when the King of France intervened due to his position as a German Prince, the Duke of Burgundy. Only after a long series of acts and laws was the situation kcpt more or less as it had been in the past, but the solution took a long time, and only in 1706 would George Louis of Brunswick, Duke of Hannover, be admitted as an Elector to the Diet of Regensburg. But, meanwhile, between 1695 and 1700, Rome was the recipient of a bad surprise from Emperor Leopold: he accepted a Protestant as the ninth elector due to pressure from the King of England, who was a Protestant Dutchman, and this meant that Leopold had a remarkable dependency on English and Dutch – thus on Protestant – money, and interests. Today a ninth elector, and what about tomorrow? From the Roman Catholic point of view, Leopold was unreliable.

On a lower, and more local Italian political level, additional troubles were caused by Leopold and his men to the Pope as an Italian prince, and to all the other Italian States. And this was the second big mistake the Emperor made after that in Spain. Since 1691 Imperial policy in Italy had been anything but nice and friendly, thus it had been just what was needed to push all the Italian princes onto the opposing side, no matter whether French or otherwise. Apart from the money repeatedly demanded by the Imperial generals from the Italian States during the Nine Years' War, just after the end of that war a Viennese lightning bolt fell on Italy. On 9 June 1697 (officially issued on 29

April) the Emperor's decree concerning the Italian fiefs was published. It had been suggested by the Imperial ambassador in Rome, Count George Adam von Martinitz, a selfish and arrogant nobleman who, in a few months, had fully succeeded in clashing with everybody in Rome, including the Pope. The decree said that every Italian feudatory had to gather documents proving his rights on the fiefs he retained, and to show them within three months to the Imperial Chancery in Vienna, or the Imperial War commissioner Count Maximilian Breiner, or to Count von Martinitz in Rome. There were fees to be paid, huge fees, and, in the case of doubt or competition, the first claimant who arrived got the fief, no matter whether he was already the feudatory or not. A lot of additional clauses and threats followed, and basically it was a wonderful way to raise money from Italy. One could say that it was simply a matter of respecting the Imperial rules, and of enforcing those rules after a long time, but in fact it was a big political problem, and in policy a problem may easily turn into a mistake: this was the case. There were a lot of Imperial fiefs in Italy. Of course there were the major feudal lords, the Dukes of Tuscany, Parma, Modena, and Mantua, and so on, but there were also a lot of noblemen – hundreds, if not thousands – who were subject to this or that Italian sovereign but held also a fief of the Empire. The worst situation was probably in the mountains between Piedmont and Genoa. On a map it looked like a fully Genoese-owned area. In fact it was a dangerous situation, a quantity of small, and very small Imperial fiefs, normally owned by noblemen belonging to the Genoese aristocracy. Each of those small Imperial fiefs was legally outside the Republic's authority, and had extraterritoriality, and many other rights, often including minting too. Many of them had been purchased or obtained in other ways by their ruling families very long ago, centuries ago, and it was anything but easy to provide documental evidence of their uninterrupted legal ownership. For instance, could everybody provide documental evidence that his ancestors paid the succession fees, and had the related investiture, since, let us say, the thirteenth century? Hardly, and every gap had now to be filled by money.

The situation in the Genoese Apennines was probably the most grievous, but the same happened in the whole of northern Italy, and there could also be some Imperial fiefs in what was now comprised within the Papal States. What was certain was that many fiefs were retained by people who were not Imperial subjects, but Papal, Neapolitan – thus Spanish – and Venetian subjects, or worse, Genoese, Sabaudian, Tuscan, and so on. Thus the payment had two terrible consequences. It was a drain of resources because every lord concerned suddenly had to pay a dramatic amount of money, which he could not have at hand, thus needed time to find it, no matter under what conditions. But it was also a political earthquake, for such a direct payment to the Emperor by itself legally weakened the previously uncontested submission that the local owner had toward his Italian sovereign. Why be loyal to a duke, and pay taxes to him, and also to the Emperor if one could rely directly on the Emperor, and pay taxes only to him? It would be cheaper.

The Italian reaction was quick. On 17 June 1697, eight days after it had been issued, the Holy Seat officially cancelled and annihilated the Imperial decree in, and out the Papal territories, as if it had never existed. Then the

Pope asked the King of France for a help in case of trouble – which was immediately, happily, and graciously granted – and sent two letters: one to all the Italian Princes, and one to the Emperor. Leopold realised what a storm was gathering, and how it could weaken the Imperial position during the ongoing Rijswijch talks, thus he humbly answered to the Pope, and stopped the whole procedure. But the mistake had been made, and the Italian States were now more suspicious than ever. The Emperor was threatening what they cared most: their liberty, and their money. It would not be a good idea to let his authority be enhanced. It had to be stopped, no matter how.

Then, in late spring 1700, news of the partition of the Spanish domains among France, Britain, and the Netherlands trickled out. According to this news, it was expected that Italy would fall into French hands.

The King of Spain protested, but nobody in London, Versailles, and The Hague cared about him. He was too weak, for Spain was too poor to be considered a consistent military threat. The Emperor was invited to join the pact within three months, but remained silent for a long time.

Things went neither fast nor smoothly during that summer. News and rumours spread everywhere. All the ambassadors in all the capitals plotted, asked, acted, discussed, listened, and immediately reported to their masters.[1] An impressive quantity of reports flooded all the chanceries, and slowly a portrait of the situation started being drafted, and was day by day enhanced by details.

As soon as 2 July 1700 the Venetian Ambassador in France, Ser[2] Alvise Pisani, told the Senate that in Paris the Spanish Lords were known to accept a French ruler, if this meant the Spanish crowns not to be shared among different princes.[3] On the following day Ser Niccolò Erizzo wrote from Rome that letters from Spain reported both the aristocracy and people – that is to say the middle class – to be ready to sell all the silver and gold from the churches and to give until the last drop of their blood to avoid the dissolution

1 The best overview from an Italian point of view can be obtained through the Venetian ambassadors' reports, for Venice intended to be neutral and was the Italian State with the most articulate diplomatic net. The reports are all filed in the Venice State Archive (hereafter ASV), in *Dispacci degli ambasciatori al Senato*. Files are divided according to the country the ambassador wrote from, and further divided according to the year. In some cases, they were fully published, as happened for the sixteenth-century reports. Concerning the eve of the Spanish Succession, a good but very partial and decidedly swift survey is provided by the reports gathered in the three big volumes edited by Fausto Nicolini as *L'Europa durante la guerra di successione di Spagna* (Naples: 1937–1939). Unfortunately it focuses only on the 1700–1703 period and only on the reports from some European and Italian capitals, that is to say Paris, Vienna, Madrid, Milan, Naples, Rome and Florence.

2 The "Patrizi veneti", were – and still are – the members of the Venetian patritiate. They were listed in the Venice Golden Book. They had the right to accede to the Senate, and to obtain administrative, military, diplomatic, and governing positions, had no title but "Nobil Homo e patrizio veneto" – Nobleman and Venetian patrice. They were addressed as "Excellence" by those who did not belong to the patritiate, and "Ser" by peers, being Ser – pronounced as "Sar" in English – a shortened version of "Messer" (My Lord) and just the same as "Sir" in Britain.

3 Pisani to the Senate, on 2 July 1700, from Paris; it is the first of the two reports sent on that day, in ASV, *Dispacci degli ambasciatori al Senato*, Francia, Archivio proprio Francia, 5 bis, filza 194.

of the Spanish monarchy.[4] Thus the Spaniards did not want their territories to be shared. That was something, but additional rumours, which time proved to be right, started dropping here and there about the next king of Spain. It is impossible to discover now whether they were rumours, or information from really well-informed people, and it is hard to know how reliable they were considered by the notable sovereigns at that time. What is certain is that, from the begining of July, the first news about the Duke of Anjou being the next king of Spain appeared. On 14 July the Venetian resident in Milan, Vendramino Bianchi, notified the Senate that someone had written from Spain that the King had chosen the Duke of Anjou as his heir.[5] This may have been the first news about that issue, but, as we shall see, it was not the last they got in Venice, and long before the death of the King.

Meanwhile, all the sovereigns of Europe were asked by the French, more or less kindly, whether or not they would consent to the French–British–Dutch partition agreement of the Spanish domains. And the weaker the sovereign, the ruder the question. It was cautious and very kind to the Emperor, kind to Venice, friendly threatening to the Duke of Savoy and, when Genoa was asked by France, a big French fleet appeared in front of the city, and remained there until the Republic's acceptance of the partition.

Swiss Guards, Lucca.

The Italian princes were quite unhappy, and really worried. To be under French influence was not nice, but cheaper than to be under Imperial authority. But as things were, a clash between Versailles and Vienna was as likely as having Italy as their battlefield. The Italian Princes silently discarded the suggestion by the ambassadors of the Duke of Savoy about an Italian League to support Italian autonomy, and liberties, and tried to find a successful way to avoid trouble. There was not that much choice about what to do: Venice had a big fleet, 14,000 foot, and some 6,000 cavalry, but half of them were in Greece, and in Dalmatia. Genoa could pay a lot of men, but found it too expensive to keep a big permanent army, thus on the paper she could field perhaps 2,900 men, but probably in fact no more than 1,800 on the ground, and 500 of them garrisoned Corsica. Modena had 1,500 men. Parma had a bit more than 3,300,[6] Lucca only 800, the Pope 4,500 and six galleys, Tuscany 3,000 and half a dozen galleys; the Duke of Savoy could have 10,000.

4 Erizzo to the Senate, on 3 July 1700, from Rome, in ASV, *Dispacci degli ambasciatori al Senato*, Roma, Archivio proprio Roma, 18, filza 214.

5 Bianchi to the Senate, on 14 July 1700, from Milan, summarised in Nicolini, op. cit., p.50. In this case one must rely on Nicolini's summary: the original, once in ASV, *Dispacci degli ambasciatori al Senato*, Milano, Archivio proprio Milano, 3, filza 148, was destroyed along with the whole filza 148 and 149 by the Germans in Naples on 30 September 1943, as a retaliation before leaving, on the last day of the four-day-long victorious anti-Nazi popular insurrection that succeeded in expelling the Germans from the city one day before the entrance of the Allies, on 1 October 1943 at 09:30 a.m.

6 There were 166 different guards (31 archers, 68 German horse guards, 39 German halberdiers, 28 Swiss guards), 283 men serving into the fortresses, and, only due to the expected war, in February 1701 the Duke organised 28 infantry companies composed of professionals, totalling 800 pikes and 1,600 arquebusers, plus 767 men belonging to the Companies of the Gates (300 in Parma and 467 in Plaisance).

Papal Troops Parading in Bologna in 1700.

This meant that all the Italian Princes had in theory 46,000 men, but 10,500 were overseas, many others were household or garrisons, thus the most the Italian Princes could field did not exceed 22,000 men: nothing, especially in comparison to the French–Spanish alliance.[7] Moreover, on the Papal southern border was the Spanish-held Kingdom of Naples, Venice was between the Emperor and Spanish-held Milan, Savoy was locked between France and Milan, and thus, in the case that an Italian league was organised, her first task would have been to face a strategic nightmare, with her uncoordinated or hard to coordinate armies having the belligerent armies between them – Milan – or just along all the borders.

So, no surprise if Venice did not answer the Sabaudian proposal, and declared she would welcome whatever agreement could keep peace in Italy. The Grand Duke of Tuscany said more or less the same, and was followed in a few days by the dukes of Parma, Mantua, and Modena.

7 Of course they all had a militia: Venice had 24,000 men belonging to the Cernide ("selected" troops) Parma had 38,000 militiamen, Lucca 2,700, Modena 18,000, Genoa listed probably 4,000, the Papal militia around 1701 listed up to 65,000 men – more or less 47,000 foot and 17,750 horses – and Tuscany 60,000, but most of them, as in Parma, were simply registered as militiamen, had no weapons, and never drilled or were poorly drilled.

The Kingdom of Naples.

But nobody knew what the Emperor would answer, and everybody saw how feverishly the Spaniards were arming. Madrid asked for Papal consent for taxes on the clergy,[8] then cut pensions and ordered the purchase of new vessels, and the capitulation – the contracting – or organising of new regiments. When French ships were reported to be about to leave Toulon, the viceroy of Naples gathered money, raised new regiments, and looked for additional ships.

The Spanish garrison of the Presidii, the small and important Spanish-held group of walled coastal towns in Tuscany, was improved. The Galley Squadron of Sicily gathered in Messina. The governor of Milan, the Prince of Vaudémont, from Lorraine, raised money, looked for new regiments to be capitulated in Switzerland, ordered the arsenal in Pavia to cast new cannons, and went there to oversee the casting of the first six. In September he committed 200 Spanish foot to Finale to strengthen that port, a landing point on the Genoese coast strategically vital for getting reinforcements from Naples and from Spain. Although, as was later reported by General Colmenero to the French, even if on paper in December 1700 the Milanese garrison was 14,400 men strong,[9] supported by 20,000 militiamen, in fact the whole Duchy could field only 6,340 foot, and 3,140 cavalry. Their artillery listed 50 field guns, but they had no horses or oxen to pull them,[10] and, according to the Governor, a war would cost 150,000 Milanese scudi per month: three times the monthly cost during the previous war. In the case of an Austrian attack, it was more than doubtful that they could hold.

8 Erizzo to the Senate, on 10 July, 1700, from Rome, in ASV, *Dispacci degli ambasciatori al Senato*, Roma, Archivio proprio Roma, 18, filza 214.

9 There were 8,500 foot, 3,700 cavalry, 235 artillerymen, 15 engineers, and 1,900 foot and invalids used in garrisons. Officers were 1,000. The ratio between non-Italians and Italians was 3 to 2. Non-Italians came from different Spanish-ruled lands, mostly Flanders. Italians – 40 percent – were 5,000 Lombard (1,213 foot, 290 guards, 800 dragoons, 1,421 feudal militia curassieurs), and 800 Neapolitan infantrymen, cfr V. Ilari, G.C. Boeri, C. Paoletti, *Tra i Borboni e gli Asburgo: le armate terrestri e navali italiane nelle guerre del primo Settecento (1701–1732)* (Ancona, 1996), p.46.

10 The French minister of war, Louis-François-Marie Le Tellier, Marquis de Barbezieux, to Marshal Count de Tessé, from Versailles on 25 December 1700, reported in François-Eugène de Vault, *Mémoires militaires relatifs à la Succession d'Espagne sous Louis XIV, extraits de la correspondance de la cour et des généraux par le lieutenant général de Vault*, ed. Jean Jacques Germain Pelet-Clozeau (hereafter de Vault), 10 vols. Paris, Imprimerie Royale, 1835–62, vol. I, Part II, p.198.

IV: The Troubles of Savoy

The last Italian State in real trouble was Savoy. Traditionally the Duke of Savoy benefited from, or rather survived, thanks to having opposing powers as neighbours, as Duke Victor Amadeus II recently did in the recent War of the League of Augsburg. But if Spain were allied to France then Victor Amadeus would be trapped, and could only hope for a rapid and decisive Austrian intervention.

The Emperor made great promises, and great plans, but lacked money, and men. On the other hand Louis XIV was heavily pushing for Savoy to join France. Savoy was important to France due to both her geographical and political position. Being across the Alps, between France and Milan, the Duchy commanded the future French logistical route to Italy. Then, according to Philip IV's last will, Victor Amadeus was a possible heir of the Spanish realms. It was not that much, nonetheless it was something, and Louis XIV believed it was better to have an agreement with him too.

During summer 1700 Savoyard ambassadors went here and there, discussed, and tricked, plotted and manoeuvred, for their master was looking for even the smallest room he could find to get something, to avoid damage, and, above all, not to lose what he had gained in the previous war. His ambassadors started trying to organise the League of the Italian Princes for mutual defence and to keep strangers out of Italy. When, very soon indeed, it was clear that no Italian state wanted to be involved, they started negotiating on different tables. Victor Amadeus knew that clashes among the major powers normally involved the small states, and were easily solved at their expense. The problem now was to gather intelligence in order to get all the necessary information to avoid mistakes, for a diplomatic mistake in such a suddenly changing situation could be a final, and fatal one. But the Savoyard ambassadors' tasks were not easy, due to foreign attitudes toward Savoy.

William III was still upset due to the 1696 "betrayal", when Victor Amadeus played in advance to the Maritime Powers the same trick they were going to play on him: he signed a separate peace with France just before a similar separate peace could be signed by William and Heinsius, leaving Savoy alone at war in front of France. Nonetheless, the King of England had conceived a deep esteem, and a good opinion of the Savoyard agent, President de la Tour, so when the latter was sent to him anew, William was less cold than he could have been.

The Emperor too was suspicious after 1696, and did not trust the Duke of Savoy, but Leopold, as William, was also too fine and experienced a politician to not know how to forgive the past in order to gain something now, and in the future. On the other side of the barricade, Louis XIV also did not trust Victor Amadeus, but preferred to be on good terms with him, because the Duke commanded the Alpine passes the French troops had to cross to go to the next-to-be Philip V's new Italian domains. Hated by everybody, and trusted by nobody, what could Victor Amadeus do? Nothing; but things suddenly changed on 30 July 1700, English Old Style – which in the rest of Europe except Russia was 9 August – when the 11-year-old William Duke of Gloucester died. He was the sole son and heir of Anne Stuart, and this caused a terrible problem for the English and Scottish successions. William and Mary had no children, and the Duke of Gloucester was the sole heir to the crowns of England and Scotland. After his death Anne was next to be queen of England, but she had no other child, so if she died who would be the next king of England? The dethroned 67-year-old King James II? His son Prince James Stuart, who would later be known as the Old Pretender? Or? Who else could be called to the thrones of England, and Scotland, no matter the Bill of Rights issued in 1684? There were only two possible heirs: Sophia Electress of Hannover, mother of the future George I of England, and Anne-Marie d'Orléans, Duchess of Savoy, the wife of Victor Amadeus II, who in May 1699 had just had her first male son. Suddenly, more or less one year before the Settlement Act, thanks to his wife, the Duke of Savoy and his son came incredibly close to the crown of England. Victor Amadeus could not be considered as a real clamant. Sophia's son, George, already had a 17-year-old son, the future George II, thus the Protestant succession of the House of Hannover was assured. Nonetheless, when a child or a teenager Victor Amadeus had as few possibilities to be called to the crowns of Spain as he had now to be called to the crown of England, and even then the death rendered him one of four possible heirs of the Spanish Empire. George of Hannover was in good health, and his son too, but according to the thinking of that time no possible heir could be completely neglected, for nobody knew what the future could bring. William III had that mentality, and this was a good reason not to dismiss Victor Amadeus. The other good reason was a strategic one: Piedmont could be used as the base for attacking southern France, just as in 1692.

Victor Amadeus never thought seriously of the British crowns. He was a Catholic, but even with Henry IV of France as one of his ancestors, he did not think London "to be well worth a Mass", as his grand-grandfather stated about Paris.[11] Nonetheless, he did not neglect his wife's rights, and ordered to prepare a protestation to be submitted to the British Parliament, just in case. Thus on 6 April 1701 de la Tour submitted his master's protestation – in Latin – against the just stated English succession, received a kind answer meaning nothing and the issue ended this way.

In fact during summer and early autumn 1700 Victor Amadeus went on looking for every additional opportunity – if there was any – to get not Madrid, but Madrid-owned Italy, that is to say Milan, Naples, and Sicily, and, in case – why not? – Sardinia too. It is useless to see in depth all he thought, planned, tried, and attempted. France suggested to Britain that it accept Victor Amadeus in order to exchange Savoy, and Piedmont – to France – for Naples, and Sicily. William III rejected it at first, but the more time passed the more he thought of it, and considered it as a real possibility, as he wrote to Lord Portland.[12] The problem was if, and how much Victor Amadeus could

11 Henry IV's daughter Christine – Chrestienne de France – married Duke Victor Amadeus I, whose surviving male son was Duke Charles Emanuel II, Victor Amadeus II's father. Christine was five years younger than her eldest brother Louis XIII.

12 William III to Lord Portland, 14-24 April 1698, reported in Baron Carl Frederik Sirtema de Grovestijns, *Histoire des luttes et rivalités politiques entre les Puissances Maritimes et la France*

be aware of it, and agree about it, but no matter: Victor was the owner of a small state, and could not react.

It is enough to say that Victor Amadeus was ready to give Savoy and Nice in exchange for Milan, but all his attempts ended in nothing. He succeeded in offering his youngest daughter to the Duke of Anjou, who needed a wife, for Spain needed a queen. Actually, the House of France had not that much choice. No Spanish princess existed, an Austrian princess was impossible, and a Portuguese one – if there were any – too. Other Catholic rulers included at that time only Savoy, Tuscany, Parma, Modena, Bavaria, and Saxony-Poland, and, at the end of the story, Savoy was the only viable solution. But this proved soon to be a non-existant result, because the young king and queen of Spain were strictly controlled. They could say only what Louis XIV stated, and could only act accordingly.

The problem was the stubborn Imperial attitude versus the English–French–Dutch partition agreement. Day by day summer 1700 changed into autumn, and when the leaves fell it was clear that if things remained so – and there was no reason to think they would change – as soon as the King of Spain died, a war between France and the Empire had to be expected shortly. What was still unclear to Victor Amadeus was: what would the Maritime Powers do?

On the one side Leopold I promised this, and that; on the other side Louis XIV softly threatened this, and that. Leopold offered 30,000 men to be deployed in Piedmont to stop any French attempt on Milan, and the Marquisate of Monferrato, an Imperial fief assigned to the Duke of Mantua, who clearly leaned towards the French. Louis … well, Louis was more direct, and above all faster.

In Versailles, throughout the whole summer Savoyard ambassador Count di Vernone made a skilful diplomatic skirmish with French minister Jean-Baptiste Colbert, Marquess de Torcy, and at least got a result: Savoy and some more lands across the Alps could go to France in exchange for the Duchy of Milan. This was reported to the Duke[13] on 19 October.

---

durant da seconde moitié du XVII Siècle (Paris, 1853), vol. 7, p.151.

13 Vernone to the Duke, from Paris, on 19 October 1700, reported in Domenico Carutti, *Storia della diplomazia della Corte di Savoia* (hereafter "Diplomacy"), 7 vols (Turin: 1879), vol. 3, book IX, p.284.

2

A Small State

I: The Importance of a Small State

The reason why Savoy was so important to France lies in strategy. The Duchy of Savoy was a small state, of course, but it was on both the sides of the Western Alps. Its dukes belonged to the oldest ruling house of Europe, but, being locked between the two most powerful crowns of their time – France and Habsburg – during the seventeenth century they had been reduced to mere clients of Louis XIV's France, and got back their full autonomy only due to their successful participation in the Nine Years' War.

Savoy occupied in Europe a prominence altogether out of proportion to its small size and its resources. For this, it was chiefly indebted to its geographical position. The dukes of Savoy were the gatekeepers of the Alps. The eastern part of their states gave access to Italy, the western to France, the northern to Switzerland, thus their alliance was constantly of vital importance to their more powerful neighbours, and the dukes always balanced themselves in between.

On the eve of the eighteenth century, the Duchy was actually a mosaic of different smaller states on both the sides of the Alps. Victor Amadeus was the Duke of Savoy, and the Count of Maurienne, and the Count of Nice, on the western side of the Alps, but also the Prince of Piedmont, and the Count of Aosta on the Eastern side of the Alps; more he was the Prince of Oneglia, the small coastal city not far from Genoa, enclaved in the Republic of Genoa's territory, because his ancestor Duke Emmanuel Philibert purchased it in 1576.

Last, according to some well-founded dynastical pretensions, he was the king of Cyprus and Jerusalem too. However he was known as the Duke of Savoy, and the ensemble of his domains was known as the Duchy of Savoy, or as the States of Savoy, and that is why we shall speak of Duchy of Savoy.

Cyprus and Jerusalem were too far, but all the other domains were close, and still locked between France and the Habsburgs of Spain, and needed protection. Protection meant an army, and money to feed it. So, a standing army had existed since the second half of the sixteenth century and it proved not bad during the recent War of the League of Augsburg, also known as the Nine Years' War or the War of the Great Alliance, and it was to be thanked too if in 1690–1696 the young Duke Victor Amadeus succeeded in regaining the independence his ancestors lost, and the first step toward the unification of Italy was made under his House.

Being locked between France and the Spanish-owned Lombardy, the Duchy could always be attacked by one of the major powers of that time. The French were on the other side of the Alps, and the Alps were hard to cross, nonetheless they could be crossed. Milan was on the other side of one border on an open, flat, easy to cross plain. Thus in the last quarter of the sixteenth century Emmanuel Philibert ordered a ring of fortresses built in Piedmonth, having that of Turin as its centre. Had the French crossed the Alps in spite of all the opposition by Savoy's army, the fortresses would be the next obstacle and they could hold as long as needed to get reinforcements from Milan. Vice versa, had the Spaniards attacked from Milan, the ring could hold as long as needed to allow French allies to cross the mountains; for Emmanuel Philibert knew that he must not trust either enemies or friends, and who is a friend today, can easily be an enemy tomorrow.

Victor Amadeus II, Duke of Savoy, in the 1690s.

The army could be used for defence and for attack, supporting foreign policy. And Emmanuel Philibert had a clear political programme: his dynasty had to increase her power, and this meant they had to get more territories. Expansion was impossible on the western side of the Alps, because France was too strong, but it was still possible in a politically fragmented Italy, hence the House of Savoy started looking at Italy as the ground of her next expansion. The process was stopped during the period of the Thirty Years' War. Italy was heavily affected and involved in that conflict and, when it ended, Savoy was reduced to a client state of France. Fifty years later Victor Amadeus, thanks to long and bloody participation in the War of the League of Augsburg, in 1697 succeeded in regaining his full independence. Nonetheless, the Duchy could be locked again. The northern borderers were the Swiss, who were officially neutral. The western borderer was France. The Republic of Genoa was in the south, and was a close ally to Spain, because it served as the bank of the Spanish crowns. And Spain herself directly ruled the Duchy of Milan, in the East, but now Milan could become French; with Piedmont in between.

The only possibility Victor Amadeus had to not be back in the condition of a client state was to have a Habsburg ruling Milan, no matter whether as a winner of the competition to the Spanish crowns, or as direct supreme master of that part of Imperial Italy. The problem was that there was nothing Victor Amadeus could do in that period to help such a change occur. He could only wait, and at the same time prepare to join the Imperial side as soon as a possibility appeared.

II: The Duke, His Wife, and Their Daughters

Victor Amadeus was born on 14 May 1666, and was just a little more than 34 years old when Charles II died. Due to a complex political situation, when still very young he had been forced to accept as wife a princess chosen by Louis XIV. She was Anne Marie d'Orléans, a niece of Louis XIV, the daughter of his brother Philip Duke of Orléans, and of Philip's first wife, the wonderful and charming late Henrietta of England.

As said, that marriage rendered Victor Amadeus a first cousin of both Mary, the wife of William of Orange, and of William of Orange himself, the queen and king of England, and of Anne Stuart, who now was the heir to the crown of England in one of the most important periods of the history of England herself and of the whole world.

Anne d'Orléans was pretty, mild and clever. He was handsome, tough, and clever. He was pretty lucky with his wife. She was not that lucky with her husband. He was always respectful, but had so many mistresses that she certainly did not have a really happy life. Nonetheless it was also, if not mostly, thanks to her, and to her relatives on her mother's side, that he got his royal crown in 1713 and the House of Savoy started a long alliance with England, which lasted with no interruption until World War II. This may seem excessive, but it was not so. Not only did all sovereigns have the utmost care for questions related to family links, but Queen Anne was perhaps more careful than the most of the others. When she ordered in her instructions to the English envoy extraordinary in Turin in 1703, "particularly you shall give the Duchess the real assurances of our kindness as to one so nearly related to us in blood".[1] she was writing what she really felt, not what was polite to say, and to do.

When the seventeenth century ended, Victor and Anne had only two daughters: due to the recent peace treaty with France, the eldest married the young Duke of Burgundy, the eldest son of the Grand Dauphin, who after his father was expected to succeed to his grandfather Louis XIV on the throne of France.

The other, well, we shall see which kind of future the other daughter was going to have.

III: Victor Amadeus II's State

The state Victor Amadeus ruled in 1700 was in fact a mosaic, and still a weak one, even if stronger than 10 years ago. It was a mosaic for it was composed of different peoples speaking different languages. The people on the other side

---

1 Anne R[egina], *Instructions for our trusty and well-beloved Richard Hill, Esq.re whom we have appointed our Envoy Extraordinary to the Duke of Savoy. Given at our Court, at Windsor, the 26th day of July, 1703, in the second year of our Reign*, in W. Blackly, *The diplomatic correspondence of the Right Hon. Richard Hill (L.L.D., F.R.S., &c., &c.), envoy extraordinary from the Court of St. James to the Duke of Savoy, in the reign of Queen Anne: from July 1703, to May 1706* (henceforth "Hill – *Letters*") (London: 1845), part I, p.2.

Drawing of Nice .

of the Alps, the loyal and faithful Savoyards, spoke French and in fact were French, even if they disliked France and did not feel French at all. France had heavily influenced also the language on the Italian side of the Alps, thus the inhabitants of Piedmont spoke a half French and half Italian dialect, but those in the County of Nice and in the Principality of Oneglia spoke a Ligurian dialect, quite closer to what was spoken in the Republic of Genoa than to the language commonly used in the other parts of the Duchy.

After the end of the previous war almost all the inhabitants of Piedmont were now subject to the Duke of Savoy. Some of them, as in some upper alpine valleys, were ruled by France, whilst others, as in Monferrato, were ruled by the Duke of Mantua, and a portion, living on the western bank of the Ticino river – the future border with Milan – were ruled by Spain.

How big was the state? After the previous war a bit less than 35,000 square kilometres – as big as Moldova, or 50 percent more than Wales – and it was still inhabited by no more than 1,200,000 people, the newly born having been balanced by the huge number of civilians dead in the previous Nine Years' War. The Duchy of Savoy covered 10,786 square kilometres and had more or less 300,000 inhabitants. The County of Nice was 3,600 square kilometres with 70,000 inhabitants, whilst Oneglia was 146 square kilometres and populated by some 15,000 people.

The Duchy of Aosta was 3,260 square kilometres, but had no more than 5,000 inhabitants. All those areas did not suffer that much during the war. The same could not be said about the last part, the Principality of Piedmont: it suffered heavily, at least in its western part, during the seven years of fighting from 1690 to 1696. It was now bigger than in 1690, but still smaller than in the following centuries, for the future wars reconquered, or added, some areas Victor Amadeus did not rule at the beginning of his reign. Piedmont, thanks to what had been obtained after the Nine Years' War, was now a bit more than 16,000 square kilometres and populated by some 800,000 people.

The economy was not healthy. The annual total income of all the inhabitants was evaluated to some 50,000,000 liras and heavily relied on agriculture. The commons were poor, or at least could always resent the result of a bad harvest. According to accurate studies, 4/5 – or 8/10 – of the overall income came from agriculture and only 1/10 was originated by commerce and industry, the remaining tenth coming from real estate rents. The main exported product – 2/3 of total exports – was raw silk, the result of a long agricultural process, which could easily be affected and stopped by weather and by war.

Overall the situation in Victor Amadeus' states was not that good, also because the Spanish succession crisis began four years after the end of the previous war, the damage from which was not yet completely repaired. This complex situation also heavily influenced the policy of the Duchy. Every town and every common had some privileges and kept them as firmly as possible, for a reduction of privileges could make the difference between survival and starvation, due to excessive tax pressure. If the commons were not happy with the ducal rule, they could, in theory, ask the Emperor for justice, or, more concretely and quickly, rebel.

In such a doubtful situation the state relied upon only two pillars, the aristocracy and the army, and both had been successfully tested during the last war. When Victor Amadeus took power, his first problem had been how to enforce his rule on his states, a problem he could consider solved by the end of the War of the Great Alliance.

Turin, Capital of the States of Savoy.

Victor Amadeus II, Duke of Savoy Portrayed when a Teenager, Probably at the Age of 16.

One thing must be said now: no matter which theories or schemes historiography created, especially in the twentieth century, it is absolutely useless to try to plug the Savoyard State in any of them. Theories are recent, but people lived in that time, long before theories, and did not act according to theories.

Victor Amadeus was an absolute monarch. He perceived and ran his state just as the owner of a private firm or a big real estate property. Of course he was not the owner of everything, but almost. Everything depended on him, and it was up to him, and only to him, to manage his state.

State management was centralised, and decision-making processes were firmly in the Duke's hands. He had to think of how each decision could influence, or affect, or dictate, every aspect of his state and his subjects' lives. Our minds, influenced by our way of thinking, consider ruling as a process made by people acting with a certain degree of decisional autonomy, and later reporting to the chief of the state, who purposely delegated them an authority and a power to achieve some goals. For instance, in military terms, we think of an army as something commanded by a chief of staff, who is delegated by the chief of the state; and nobody since the second half of the nineteenth century onward expects the chief of a state to be the commander on the ground. But, even if in the seventeenth century it could be so – for example, Louis XIV in France, the Emperor, or the Kings of Spain – Victor Amadeus did not act that way. He was the one who managed foreign policy according to the means he had, or supposed to be next to have. He commanded his army in the field, and used it as a political tool. He decided how big the army could be according to the taxes and revenues he could get; and he imposed taxes and revenues according to the funds he was supposed to be able to get from his subjects, or donors like Spain and the Maritime Powers during the Nine Years' War, or the Dutch and British during the War of the Spanish Succession, or to borrow from bankers or commercial companies. Taxes and revenues had to be calculated according to the economic situation the Duchy was facing, and the Duke knew that he could not squeeze his subjects beyond a certain point, otherwise the result could be only a total collapse. In other words: he knew how many golden eggs his goose could lay, and knew that he could not force her to go beyond, otherwise she would die from exhaustion. This balance had to be kept day by day, compensating as much as possible the problems and lack due to unpredictable events. For instance an excessively rainy period, or frost, as it happened in winter 1708–09, could affect agriculture, reducing the harvest. If so, the food and fodder price rose, and more money was needed to feed both the army and the subjects, who had to produce whatever the army needed, including manpower, that is to say recruits. Improving agriculture meant reducing recruits and weakening the

Giovanni Battista Gropello, Count di Borgone.

army. A weaker army could be reinforced by enrolling or contracting foreign professionals, but this too needed more money, hence one had to find it, asking donors, or borrowing, or imposing new taxes. New taxes could cause reactions somewhere and somehow, and this could have a domino effect, which had to be carefully considered. So, Victor Amadeus had to think of waging war, managing foreign affairs, managing state affairs, thinking of how to get money, and taking care of all the mutual influences and interactions required in order to keep all in balance, and let his state survive.

Clearly he could not be wherever needed and whenever needed, so he relied on some ministers whom he deeply trusted. At the eve of the War of the Spanish Succession, they were basically only two: Giovan Battista Gropello, an attorney recently ennobled as the Count di Borgone, and Filiberto Sallier de la Tour, Baron de Bordeaux, still his personal envoy to William III and the States General, as he had been during the War of the League of Augsburg.

A third was Giuseppe Carron, Marquess di San Tommaso. His father had been Victor Amadeus' first secretary of state, and minister, a skilful one, but the old Carron died soon after the end of the War of the League of Augsburg and left the "survival" of his post to his 27-year-old son.[2] So, it was Giuseppe who had to manage the affairs related to the War of the Spanish Succession, but it was too demanding a task for him.

The War of the Spanish Succession tested both the Sabaudian bureaucracy and its men by iron and by fire. When tested, San Tommaso did not succeed that much. He lost a portion of the Duke's consideration, who, on another side, found two new aces among the cards he was playing with: Prié, and Mellarède. Prié was the Piedmontese shortening of the lordship of Ercole Turinetti, Marquess di Priero, who already played, and in 1700 was still playing an important role in Vienna as Victor Amadeus II's ambassador since 1691. Pietro Mellarède di Bettonet was an attorney from Savoy, who proved himself well in Nice between the two wars, and arrived in Turin as a refugee when the city was threatened by the French in 1703. He was later employed as a diplomat, and the Duke was so happy with the results that Mellarède soon became one of the most important figures of the Duchy. Then Victor Amadeus, who was always looking for skilled, loyal, and faithful officials, no matter whether noble or not, found some few others that he deeply trusted. They provided the facts, figures, and information he needed. They acted according to his orders, but Victor Amadeus was the only one who evaluated, decided, and commanded, and it was a very heavy burden, to be carried day

2 The "Survival" – Sopravvivenza – in Piedmont was the possibility to pass one's own post to his heir. Other than the French "inheritance", the "survival" normally was conceded by the Duke (and rarely sold to the person who asked for it) as an award for the good job made in the state's service, and could be transmitted only from father to son, and only through one generation. This avoided all the problems related to the longlasting and purchasable French "inheritance".

by day. Now the burden was heavier than ever, due to the gathering storm. The Duke of Savoy realised how dangerous his position was, and that, in the case of a war, it would render his states a likely battlefield, thus he started increasing ordnance, and troops: 12,000 more cannonballs were stored in his military harbours of Nice, and Villafranca, new horses had to be purchased in Switzerland, and money was raised. Then two expected, and feared pieces of news spread: both the Pope and the King of Spain were dying.

3

The Death of the Pope, the Death of the King, the Birth of the Storm

I: An Advice, a Codicil and Two Deaths

Pope Innocent XII, born in Naples as Antonio Pignatelli, and a subject of the King of Spain, was old, and very ill. In the past he strongly opposed Louis XIV's demands, and attempts, and fought against French overwhelming preponderance with all means. But now, in summer 1700, when the Emperor's pro-Protestant attitude was greatly displeasing him both as the chief of the Church, and the sovereign of the Papal States, he was privately, and officially, asked a very serious question: who should be the heir of the Spanish realms? And the question was asked by the King of Spain in person, through his special ambassador the Duke of Uzeda, and with the deepest secrecy.

Charles in Madrid had asked a special commission, chaired by Cardinal Portocarrero, to decide who should be his heir to the Spanish crowns, according to Spanish law. In the summer the commission had declared in favour of the Duke of Anjou. Charles was surprised: of course, he was a relative, but he was not a Habsburg: was such a decision right? Thus Charles asked the Pope for advice. Innocent summoned a specially tasked congregation composed of three cardinals[1] and charged it with discussing, assessing, and providing him an answer about the Spanish succession. The cardinals discussed, and concluded in favour of a French heir, if the two crowns of France and Spain remained separated. France was less threatening than the Emperor, and to have the whole of Southern Italy, Sardinia, the

1 The Roman Catholic Church relied on these special commissions. Their name was "Congregazioni particolari deputate" – specially tasked congregations – and they were consulting bodies organised from time to time at the Pope's demand. They were composed of a variable and small number of cardinals, chosen by the Pope one by one. Their task was to assess a situation, and give the Pope a written and signed opinion, providing one or more possible solutions. Then it was up to the Pope, and only to the Pope, to decide what to do. The three cardinals asked to assess the Spanish Succession were Fabrizio Spada, Giovan Battista Spinola, and Giovan Francesco Albani, who was later elected Pope Clement XI.

Presidii, and Milan directly in Leopold's hands was decidedly dangerous for the Church's religious autonomy.

This was what the cardinals assessed, and this was what Innocent accepted, and on 6 July from his Quirinal palace wrote to Charles, and Charles acted accordingly. As soon as he received the Papal answer, he made a new testament, or rather made a change to the old one, at least so they said. According to Ser Alvise Mocenigo, on 26 September 1700 Charles II made a new codicil. Only Cardinal Portocarrero, and two or three amongst the most important noblemen knew it, but, we can add, at least one of them did not keep the secret, for the news immediately spread in Madrid that Charles had declared the Duke of Anjou his universal heir.[2] Sabaudian ambassador Operti[3] immediately notified the Duke of Savoy. Imperial ambassador Count von Harrach was furious – Venetian ambassador Mocenigo wrote – and declared that neither Louis XIV, nor Britain, and the States General would ever accept such an arrangement, which clashed with their partition agreement.

Pope Innocent XII.

On the next night, 27 September, Innocent XII died in Rome and this opened the Papal succession. Letters were sent to the cardinals all around Europe, and as soon as they received them they started leaving for Rome, but nobody dared to notify Charles II, for everybody feared the news would kill him.

In fact Charles was worse. By mid July, due to the lack of success of the Spanish doctors, a famed Neapolitan physician, Donzelli, had been called to Madrid. He arrived at the start of September, but, after a long visit could only state that the King will not recover. In the very best case he could survive a little longer, but not that long.

The King still demanded to rule, but he was too sick and weak, thus affairs were delayed, and problems remained unsolved. On 28 October Mocenigo reported how bad things were. Castile and Aragon were doing whatever they wanted. Portugal was in arms and seemed ready to seize Galicia and Estremadura. Naples and Sicily looked for autonomy. Milan, Flanders, Navarra and Catalunya depended on foreign, thus unreliable, viceroys. The Spanish ambassador in Paris reported that Louis XIV was preparing three armies to be committed to Italy, Spain, and the Rhineland, and that his son, the Dauphin, was ready to leave for Naples to be crowned king there as

2 Mocenigo to the Senate, on 1 October 1 1700, first of three messages on the same day from Madrid, in ASV, *Dispacci degli ambasciatori al Senato*, Spagna, Archivio proprio Spagna, 1, filza 135.

3 Frà Costanzo Operti, knight commander of the Order of Malta, cfr. Carutti, "Diplomacy", cit. p.287.

Louis XIV Allows Philip of Anjou to Accept the Spanish Legacy.

Archduke Charles of Habsburg when a child.

soon as Charles died.[4] The Spanish army and the fleet were weak, and an empty treasure could not enhance neither them nor the Crown.

On 1 November 1700, on All Saints Day, Mocenigo sent an express: two hours after midday, Charles II had died. The State Council immediately gathered and the King's testament was opened: the first heir called to inherit the kingdoms depending on the crowns of Spain was Philip of Bourbon, Duke of Anjou, and Louis XIV's second grandson. Second in line was his youngest brother, the Duke of Berry, Louis XIV's third grandson. In case he too refused, or died, the third was to be Emperor Leopold's second son, Archduke Charles. The fourth and last possible heir was Victor Amadeus of Savoy.[5]

The news reached the European and Italian capitals at a courier's speed, that is to say slowly,

4 Mocenigo to the Senate, on 28 October 1700, from Madrid, in ASV, *Dispacci degli ambasciatori al Senato*, Spagna, Archivio proprio Spagna, 1, filza 135.

5 Mocenigo to the Senate, express sent on 1 November 1700, from Madrid, in ASV, *Dispacci degli ambasciatori al Senato*, Spagna, Archivio proprio Spagna, 1, filza 135.

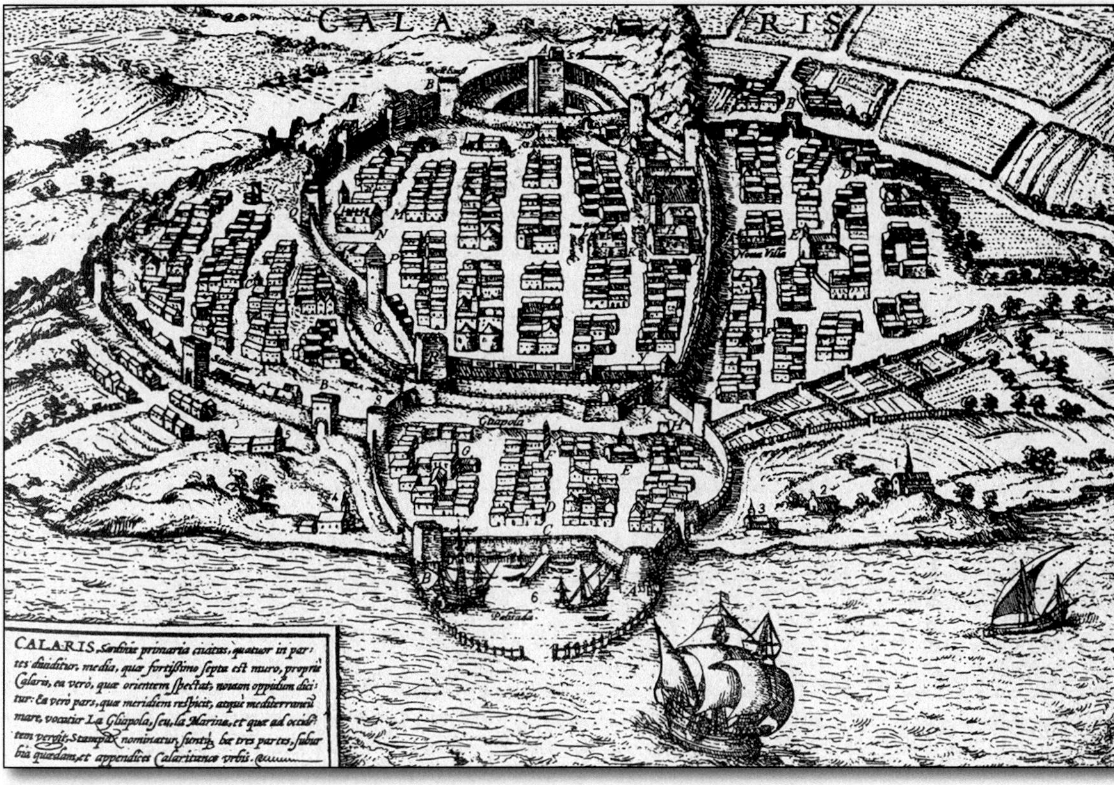

View of the Street Layout of Cagliari.

and gave room to a macabre situation. On the 2 and 3 November, while Charles' body was publicly exposed in Madrid, people in Naples and Milan were rejoicing due to the just-received letters from Spain, dated 20 days ago, saying that the King was better. Whilst on 5 November Charles II was buried, feasts and special lightings occurred in Naples, and on the 6th, though his grave was already closed, Charles' 39th birthday was happily celebrated in Naples, and Milan.

On 7 November Louis XIV was notified. Tears filled his eyes – or so it was said – and he still had tears on his face during the public lunch in front of the foreign ambassadors, as Ser Alvise Pisani saw, and reported.[6]

Louis received the testament and gathered the council, and on 16 November 1700, soon after the "lever", called into his cabinet the Spanish ambassador, and, immediately after, the Duke of Anjou. Then the ambassador came out, and, in tears, announced to the court and the foreign ministers the Duke of Anjou to be the King of Spain, and that he had just had the joy to be the first to take the oath of loyalty to the new king.[7] Just in that moment came in, by chance, the Imperial ambassador. He had to announce to the King of France the birth of Leopold's grandson, and had the worst possible surprise.

6 Pisani to the Senate, on 12 November 1700, from Fontainebleau; it is the first of the two reports sent on that day, in ASV, *Dispacci degli ambasciatori al Senato*, Francia, Archivio proprio Francia, 5 bis, filza 194.

7 Pisani to the Senate, on 16 November 1700 at 10:00 p.m., from Paris, in ASV, *Dispacci degli ambasciatori al Senato*, Francia, Archivio proprio Francia, 5 bis, filza 194.

Italy was still late on the news. The Venetian courier from Spain bringing Mocenigo's report written on 1 November arrived in Milan only on the 17th, the day after Louis XIV's acceptance, and reached Venice the next day. The Prince of Vaudémont had stopped him. Only after Resident Bianchi's intervention did he allow the courier to proceed to Venice. Then, in tears – everybody easily melted into tears in those times – Vaudémont summoned the top officials of the Duchy and told them the news, issuing orders to keep the Duchy secure, and militarily safe. The same news needed five more days to reach Naples,[8] and a longer time to reach Palermo.

Spanish viceroys in Palermo, Naples and Cagliari, and the governor of Milan immediately accepted Philip V as their legitimate king. Half of Italy now was under Bourbon rule, and the Habsburgs were cut off.

II: The Emperor's Fury

Leopold I received the first alarming news of Charles' death, and of a French heir, only on 19 November from his ambassador in France, Count von Sinzendorff.

The war was practically already on. The Marquess de Villars, the French ambassador in Vienna, and soon one of the smartest and best French generals in the forthcoming war, told his Venetian colleague Loredan that 20,000 French were already marching to Italy.[9] But the Imperialists, too, were on the move: 20,000 men had to march to the Rhine, and 20,000 to Italy. The Markgraf – Marquess – of Baden, and Prince Eugene of Savoy had respectively been chosen as commanders, also if the Emperor preferred not to have Eugene versus his cousin Victor Amadeus.

This preference recalled information the Venetian ambassador in Rome, Erizzo, provided to the Senate in the summer. At the end of July Ser Nicolò had reported rumours about an Imperial expedition to Northern Italy to be led by Prince Eugene, adding that, if that was true, it would mean a secret agreement existed between Victor Amadeus of Savoy, and the Emperor.[10]

Anyway now, in the second half of November, Vienna enhanced the ongoing negotiations to get men and money from the German Princes. The Elector of Brandenburg was said to have been offered with the Imperial acceptance of the self-imposed title of king, passing from King "in" Prussia to King "of" Prussia in exchange for sending 12,000 fully equipped and paid men to the Emperor, as well as further units were expected to be given by the Duke of Hannover, the promised Ninth Elector. The Austrian military administration looked for horses, and for cavalry and infantry recruits.

8 Venetian Resident in Naples Francesco Savioni to the Senate on 22 November 1700, in, ASV, *Dispacci degli ambasciatori al Senato*, Napoli, filza 107.

9 The ambassador in Vienna Ser Francesco Loredan to the Senate, on 20 November 1700, from Vienna, in ASV, *Dispacci degli ambasciatori al Senato*, Germania, Archivio proprio Germania, 11 ter, filza 183.

10 Erizzo to the Senate, on 31 July 1700, from Rome, the first of the two reports sent on that day, in ASV, *Dispacci degli ambasciatori al Senato*, Roma, Archivio proprio Roma, 18, filza 214.

Emperor Leopold I.

Prince Eugene of Savoy, in a Print after a Portrait by Kneller.

Louis, Marquess of Baden.

As Napoleon one century later said, Austria was always one army, one year, one idea late, and so it was now. Whilst the Emperor was organising his army, the French were already on the move. Whilst Imperial diplomacy was arranging a way to stop the French, the latter were already influencing, negotiating or blackmailing everywhere. Regarding Italy, on 20 November Ser Francesco Loredan was fully right when writing to the Senate that, as things were, the French would be in Lombardy in a few weeks. If so, they would prevent the Imperialists entering Italy through the classical Swiss route of Valtellina, and Lake Como, thus the Emperor would commit his army to pass across the Venetian Terraferma (the so called Mainland State): a forthcoming disaster for the Republic.[11] By the way this was just what the Imperial troops were expected to do. Resident Bianchi announced too,[12] and repeated,[13] that the Prince of Vaudémont expected the Austrians to cross the Venetian Terraferma.

Only, such an expedition needed money to pay the army, and everybody knew how poor Austria was. In the best case, Leopold could field 50,000 men, whilst Louis XIV 200,000. No competition seemed possible.

III: The Maritime Powers' Position as it was Known in Italy

Whilst the storm was gathering, the Italian Princes tried to discover what could it be expected from the Maritime Powers. Did Britain and the Netherlands intend to support the Emperor or to accept the Spanish succession falling to the Duke of Anjou? Had they supported Leopold, the war was completely

11 Loredan, cit.

12 Bianchi to the Senate, on 18 November 1700, from Milan, resume in Nicolini, op. cit., pp.182–183, for the original report was in the destroyed abovementioned filza 148

13 Bianchi to the Senate, on 24 November 1700, from Milan, resume in Nicolini, op. cit., pp.194–195.

certain, for it could be funded by London and The Hague. Had they accepted the succession as it was, there was a significant possibility not to have a war, or, at least not to have a long one, for the Emperor's military strength was by no mean comparable to the French one, and Austria had no money.

The first Dutch reaction had been harsh, but in December a Dutch embassy to Versailles presented Their High Powers' compliments to the new king of Spain in such a flattering style that everybody thought the States General preferred not to be involved in a clash with France, but in fact it was not so. As the Italian diplomats realised immediately, and reported to their masters, this happened because the Netherlands relied mostly on the English attitude, which in early December was still unclear. Thus the English attitude was the core of the situation. King William had supported the Partition agreement but British public opinion, and hence the Parliament, were not happy with the treaty and were fully against it. According to the British public the agreement warranted too many advantages to France, especially in the Levant. The public reaction against it had been so strong that the Duke of Portland, considered to be the main person responsible, and the author of the treaty, had to flee to Amsterdam, whilst King William in July decided to leave to Holland earlier than planned. Actually the court of Vienna was suspicious about the Maritime Powers, even if some Viennese ministers thought William to have made, and then published, the Treaty with France because he hoped to trigger a harsh public reaction against it, and against France, in order to ease a declaration of war on France in the future.[14]

William III.

The Venetian ambassador in Vienna explained it when reporting why could the Emperor still have a chance.[15] According to the English constitution, King William decided whether to declare war or not, but, according the laws, it was up to the Parliament to decide year by year whether to give him the needed money or not. In theory, had the Parliament refused, the King could manage the war he declared, but only relying on his own personal money, which was unlikely, for no royal personal treasure was as rich as that needed to sustain a conflict. Hence, the Parliament had a significant role to play, and no war was possible without its consent.

The Emperor's position was not exactly that of the English Parliament, but in general they had a mutual task. The Emperor wanted the whole Spanish

14 Loredan to the Senate, on 3 July 1700, from Simmering, second of the two messages sent on that day. This idea was reported by Ser Francesco as circulating again in Vienna, in his report from Kaiser-Ebersdorf dated on 9 October, 1700. Both the reports are in ASV, *Dispacci degli ambasciatori al Senato*, Germania, Archivio proprio Germania, 11 ter, filza 183.

15 Loredan to the Senate, on 11 December 1700, from Vienna, first of the two messages sent on that day. Ser Francesco had already explained the constitutional rights of both the King and the English Parliament in his report to the Senate on 28 August 1700 from Wienerisch-Neustadt (now Wiener Neustadt). Both the reports are in ASV, *Dispacci degli ambasciatori al Senato*, Germania, Archivio proprio Germania, 11 ter, filza 183.

succession to be inherited by his younger son; the Parliament wanted France to get less than the Partition agreement left her, which by the way, was far less than the whole Spanish succession. Succession by a French prince was absolutely to be rejected by Britain, and the point shared by England and Austria was: whatever the deal, eliminate the French first.

The Dutch knew the differences existing between William and the Parliament, so in fact they simply gained time through their December embassy to Louis XIV. Had England chosen not to make war, a flattering embassy would avoid any possible trouble with, and threat by, France. Had England decided to fight, the General States would share her views, just as they did during the creation of the Partition Agreement.

IV: The Attitude of the Italian Princes

The Italian states preferred neutrality, but it was quite difficult to keep it. Mantua, Parma, and Modena were officially members of the Holy Roman Empire as lying in Imperial Italy, but how could they act against the French? They were too weak, and small, and, whilst Leopold was shouting, and threatening, a French army led by the Marshal de Catinat crossed the Alps, passed through Piedmont, and was happily greeted by the Prince de Vaudémont in Milan.

Nicolas Catinat de la Fauconerie.

Vaudémont provided Catinat with whatever he needed. For instance: the French lacked cannons, but did bring gunners, and the Spaniards lent the French 50 guns from their arsenals. Food? The French paid, and got plenty. So, the French were in Milan, and were strong. They were on the left embankment of the river Po, where Mantua too was, whilst Parma, Modena, and the Papal Legation of Ferrara, were just on the right embankment of the same river, thus they had the French very close. At the same time the Imperialists were very far away, in Trento, and from the Swiss border to the Adriatic Sea, the Republic of Venice's Terraferma was between them, and Lombardy. How could an Imperial army reach Milan? And how could an Italian prince react in arms against the French without Imperial military support? There was no way, but … how many Italian princes really disliked this situation? The French did not ask them for money, and did not enforce Bourbon rule. On the other hand, joining the French could mean to be charged, and prosecuted for a felony in a trial by the Diet of the Empire, and when found guilty be deprived of one's own duchy. But joining the Emperor meant to be invaded by the French, and deprived of one's own duchy. No matter which side one joined, the result would be the same. So, what? Neutrality, was the smart answer. Parma immediately announced it was under the protection of the Roman Catholic Church. The Duke raised the Papal flag in his capital, received a Papal legate followed by General Paolucci with 1,200 men from the garrison of Ferrara, and sent ambassadors to the French army. The Duke of Modena did the same, but he was closer to the next-to-be war theatre, and had to expect far more damage, no matter how neutral he could claim to be.

Rinaldo d'Este, Duke of Modena.

Mantua too tried to do the same, but as we shall see, the French prevented her doing it and seized the city.

Genoa felt well protected. Lombardy on one side of the Po, and Parma and Modena on the other side were between her and the Imperialists; and behind Lombardy and Parma there were mountains to cross. So Genoa could easily keep neutrality. Had an Imperial army arrived, well, one could see what to do. The same happened to Tuscany, thus Florence too remained neutral, as Lucca did. The Pope did not belong to Imperial Italy, but his neutrality brought different problems. Officially, he was the feudal sovereign of the Kingdom of Naples, and nobody could be recognised as the King of Naples unless invested by him. Now the two most important and powerful Royal Houses of Catholic Christendom claimed Naples – and much more – and both demanded their candidate to be recognised as the legitimate king of Naples by the Pope; and both more or less clearly threatened the Pope with the ghost of something which could also be a schism, and the organisation of a national church. What to do?

Venice, too, was in trouble. If the Republic had ever been subject to an empire, it was the late Eastern Roman Empire, which was heavily weakened in 1304 also due to substantial Venetian help, and disappeared in 1453. In the eighth century Charlemagne had tried to make Venice submit, but had been rejected, thus nobody in Vienna could claim Venice belonged to the Holy Roman Empire. Now, if Leopold wanted to see his army entering Lombardy he had to cross Venetian Terraferma, for Venice owned all the territory between the Duchy of Milan and Austria. There was a route from Lake Garda downstream to the Mincio river to Mantua, but it was cut because, as said,

Genoa and its Fortifications.

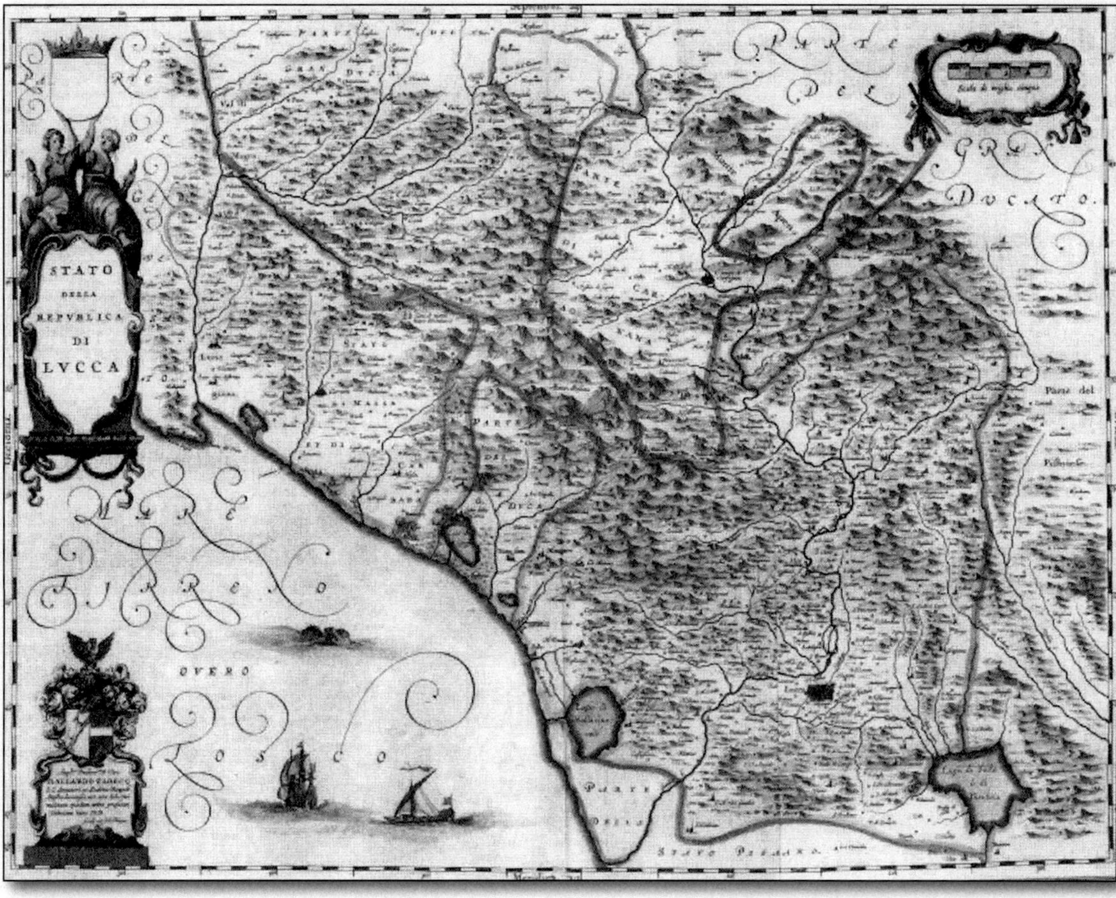

The Republic of Lucca.

that city was quickly seized by the Bourbons. Besides, the Senate was warned in November 1700 that the Emperor was planning to sent his troops to Italy through Venetian territory.[16]

The Austrians then requested from Venice permission for transit. Leopold hoped Venice would join the anti-Bourbon coalition. The Holy League established in 1684 against the Turks technically linked Venice and Vienna, even if that alliance was dedicated solely against the Turks.

The Venetian government had a difficult task to determine its position in this conflict. France and the Ottoman Empire were clandestine allies since the early sixteenth century, thus allying with Austria against France could lead to a renewed war with the Ottomans. The results of the previous war of the Holy League in 1684–1699 demonstrated that Austria could provide military support in the Balkans, but no help at sea, and was not so reliable as an ally in peace negotiations for she thought a bit too much of herself. So, what if the French Mediterranean fleet moved into the Adriatic, joined the Turks and attacked Venetian possessions in Dalmatia and Greece? Likewise,

16 The ambassador in Vienna Ser Francesco Loredan to the Senate, on 30 October and 20 November 1700, both from Vienna, in ASV, *Dispacci degli ambasciatori al Senato*, Germania, Archivio proprio Germania, 11 ter, filza 183.

the Austrians may intend to use the Venetian Terraferma as a bastion against France. If so, Venice could suffer to Austria's advantage and without a gain.

A Franco-Venetian alliance was not advantageous either. Venice and Austria shared a long common border in Italy and an even longer one in Dalmatia. Venice would withstand the worst of an Austro-Imperial offensive into Italy before the Emperor's army reached Milan. Indeed, the Turks could profit significantly in Dalmatia and Greece if a break occurred in Austro-Venetian relations. History illustrated that in this case, Venice could not count on French aid. Hence the Senate chose neutrality, because Venice could face one powerful enemy with allies, but she was not so fool to believe she could fight two powerful enemies without allies.

V: The Enforced French–Piedmontese Military Alliance

Louis XIV.

The arrival of the new French ambassador Phélipeaux in Turin proved how hard the situation could become. The French wanted Victor Amadeus on their side, for free, or almost.

Actually the Duke volunteered as soon as he realised how bad things could turn, and far earlier than any proposal by Louis XIV. The latter was quite pleased, but being pleased did not mean he intended to give the Duke whatever he liked. This was soon clear. As early as 4 October 1700 the ducal ambassador in Paris, Count di Vernone, reported that Louis XIV refused to give Victor Amadeus Lombardy as a payback for his participation in a possible war on the French side, lest he become "a too powerful prince in Italy".[17]

This was the premise, thus no matter which offers and negotiations could be later suggested, for they were swept out in advance by this French statement which, within a month, was further supported by Charles II's last will.

Negotiations between Versailles and Turin had an indirect result. The Maritime Powers and Piedmont went back to talking terms after a four-year freeze. If the strategically relevant Piedmont had talks with France, and if de la Tour was in Holland, and Victor Amadeus was still a possible heir to the crown of England, well, it was better not to neglect him any longer and at least talk with him. Who knew? Things could turn interesting.

In a few weeks they did turn interesting.

Three days after Charles II's death, when the news was not yet known either in Paris or in The Hague, nor, of

17 Vernone to the Duke, from Paris, on 4 October 1700, rep. in Carutti, *Diplomacy*, p.282.

course, in Turin, William III also agreed to see Victor Amadeus exchanging Savoy with Milan, thanks to the work of President de la Tour. Filiberto Sallier de la Tour had reached William as early as August. As said, Victor Amadeus chose him for he had been his personal envoy to William III and the States General during the Nine Years' War. Both the Dutch and the British had a very good opinion of him, and he had been greatly appreciated by William.

Now de la Tour summed all the information he had, melted them with his master's tasks, and step by step obtained the result. On 4 November 1700, whilst Charles body still lay publicly exposed in Madrid, de la Tour notified Victor Amadeus[18] that King William did not object to giving Savoy and some other lands across the Alps to France in exchange for giving the Duchy of Milan to Piedmont. Then the news of Charles' death came, and the chaos started in The Hague too, whilst William left for London.

Only a final remark: in this long diplomatic comedy, all the negotiating parts were aware of Charles II's last will since at least the end of the first week of October, but nobody mentioned it, and all acted as if the testament simply did not exist, also as if everybody knew the others to be aware of it.

Thus it was war, probably, once more, less than five years after the end of the last one, and the most concerned Italian State was Savoy, trapped between France and French–Spanish-held Milan.

It was immediately clear that Turin could get nothing from France now.

On 13 November Phélipeaux told the Duke that the Sun King had to keep intact his grandson Philip's inheritance, so any further talk about Milan, as well as, of course, Naples, Sicily and Sardinia, was impossible. But at the same time a bigger portion of that same inheritance, the Low Countries, was presented by France to Victor Amadeus' cousin, Max Emanuel, elector of Bavaria.

Maximilian Emanuel of Bavaria

So, the rule worked for Piedmont and did not work for Bavaria, an attitude towards Italy that France constantly kept over the next three centuries, and which would badly affect French–Italian relationships also in the European Union.

Seen that he could get nothing but damage from the French alliance, Victor Amadeus started looking at the Empire and the Maritime Powers.

Two years later he wrote that after Philip V's accession to the Spanish throne and the fall of Milan in Bourbon hands, "I found myself, due to this widening, in a condition far more dangerous than when France had Pinerolo, Casale and the same Marquisade of Saluces ... The union of the two Crowns, so dangerous to the whole Europe, put me suddenly in a complete servitude ... I was encircled by all the sides."[19]

18 De la Tour to the Duke, from The Hague, on 4 November 1700, reported in Carutti, op. cit., p.286.

19 Rep. in Carutti, *Diplomacy*, p.300, note 1.

Ercole Turinetti, Marquess of Priero, Known as the Marquess of Prié.

Victor Amadeus of Savoy. Portrayed in 1700, but probably looking as he was at 14 years old.

That is why on 16 January 1701 he wrote to his ambassador Priero in Vienna, that he preferred the war to start, for it was the only way he had to free himself due to support by the Emperor or negotiation with France and Spain. Thus suggestions had to be made to Imperial ministers, just as Priero was wondering about a possible alliance Victor Amadeus was not yet thinking of.[20]

Meanwhile, Louis XIV suspected the accession of his grandson to the Spanish throne would lead to hostilities, but believed the Emperor to be too weak to challenge the Bourbon succession. Leopold possessed merely 42,000 men, while Louis had 200,000 and could deploy no less than 75,000 men in Northern Italy, including Spanish and Piedmontese forces. Anyway Louis was careful, and the reports from Italy by Tessé about the information gathered from Vaudémont rendered him more careful: it was better to commit troops to Milan, just in case.

That is why on 26 January Victor Amadeus was notified by Torcy that the French forces were to enter Piedmont, to proceed to Lombardy. They consisted of 48 cavalry and dragoon squadrons and had to cross the Alps from the end of February, whilst Infantry had to be shipped from Toulon and Antibes to Vado, Alassio and Finale in Liguria. It is unclear whether Victor Amadeus knew or not that in the early days of February Tessé had suggested Louis XIV send a second expeditionary corps to Piedmont, to besiege Turin from April 1701.

What to do? As things were, nothing but accept the enforced French alliance, because no Imperial soldier was in sight. The Emperor in Vienna was still wondering, thinking, discussing, arguing, wishing and planning, whilst Louis XIV was making profit from the strategic situation. And what could Victor Amadeus do but say yes? Thus he said yes, and in Turin on 6 April 1701 signed the treaty of alliance.

Five days later, on 11 April, he wrote to Priero to explain the situation and to tell him how to present it to the Emperor: "At last, after managing with dexterity for five months, no more attempt

20 Rep. in Carutti, op. cit., pp.301–302, note 1.

could be made and it was necessary to come to the point … We could no longer delay to accept the will of the Most X.an King to sign a treaty of league…"[21]

Victor added that France would never accept him remaining neutral and, in the unlikely case that it was accepted, the French would surely demand Piedmont disarm, provide an expeditionary corps to be used in Flanders, and let the French troops enter the main Piedmontese fortresses "… and about this point you will be allowed, when you'll think it to be doable safely, to tell the most confident among the ministers [Harrach] or His Caesarean Majesty alone, our sincere desire to have on one day the route opened to join the Caesarean Majesty."[22]

Six weeks later, on 31 May 1701, Victor Amadeus added to his ambassador:

> You'll have to organise in the utmost secret the way and the manner to keep an occult and impenetrable correspondence with the Lord Count of Harrach as much as it is needed between you two in a way it can never diminish … Lord Prince Eugene neither must have with us occult dealing, to make us any proposal, nor must have with us any negotiation…[23]

Because, as he wrote, Eugene was too much under the eyes of everybody, because he was considered the natural channel between Savoy and the Emperor. No, the only connection between Victor Amadeus and Leopold had to pass through Priero and Harrach. It was safer, but the future would reveal it to be not safe enough.

According to the alliance treaty, Louis XIV appointed the Duke of Savoy "generalissimo"[24] of the Most Christian, and of the Most Catholic kings' armies in Italy, also known as the Army of the Two Crowns.

There was a financial problem. In 1700 Victor Amadeus' military budget absorbed 2,750,000 liras[25] and was not enough for a war. Thus the Treaty granted him 600,000 French écus yearly in funding. It meant 1,800,000 French liras per year, in 12 monthly instalments of 150,000 liras each,[26] to be paid 15 days before the end of every month. The first month had to be paid

21 *Idem.*

22 Rep. in Cautti, op. cit., p.302.

23 Rep. in Carutti, *Idem.*

24 This word exists in Spanish "generalissimo", French "généralissime" and Italian. Literally it means "the most general", that is to say "the top general", the supreme commander.

25 Prato, "Il costo della guerra di successione spagnola e le spese pubbliche in Piemonte dal 1700 al 1713", in *Le campagne di guerra in Piemonte 1703–1708 e l'assedio di Torino del 1706*, 10 vols (Turin: 1903–1908), vol. X, p.260.

26 Given the écu/lira ratio, the treaty clearly speaks of French currency. Since 1697 one needed 12 French liras to get a golden pistole – the common name of the golden "old" Louis of France whose legal change in Piedmont was 15 liras of Piedmont. Every Pistol equalled four French écus , thus an écu – écu means "shield", due to the coat of arms minted on the coin – equalled three French liras. Now, 600,000 écus equalled 150,000 French pistoles, which on the other hand equalled 2,250,000 liras in Piedmontese currency. One needed 20 soldi to get a lira of Piedmont, and four liras and six soldi of Piedmont, or 86 soldi, to get a Piedmontese silver scudo, also called a white scudo, thus 2,250,000 liras of Piedmont equalled 523,255 white scudi of Piedmont. Seeing that a golden Louis, or pistole, was less than a contemporary English pound, for it equalled – in contemporary English currency – 17 shillings and 6 pence, a French franc

in advance. It seemed a lot, but soon this funding proved to be not enough, for in 1701 the Piedmontese military budget absorbed 4,738,341 liras,[27] and the French funding covered only 47.48 percent of the budget, less than a half.

That money had to be used to feed a Piedmontese army composed of 8,000 foot, 2,500 cavalry, including the Duke's household, and six field cannons. In the case of a siege, it was up to the Duke to provide the siege artillery, whilst France and Spain would refund him the price of ammunitions and gunpowder.

Basically, to match the Treaty, the Duke had to commit his entire army. Due to such a sudden engagement, the Treaty admitted that not all the corps could be combat-ready on the spot, so, whilst enlisting the missing soldiers, Victor Amadeus could send 5,000 foot, and 1,200 to 1,500 cavalry and dragoons at the beginning of the campaign, promising the others would reach the Allied army within the end of next August.

Clearly, the command had to be in French hands whenever the two armies operated jointly and their commanders' rank equalled. But what was the army we are speaking of? And how did it move, live and fight?

equalled 1 English shilling, and 5½ pence, hence 15 liras of Piedmont equalled 17 shillings and sixpence. A double of Savoy was 15 liras and 15 soldi and equalled roughly 18 shillings.

27 Prato, op. cit., p.260.

4

Early Eighteenth-Century Warfare in Italy and Abroad[1]

What in English is known as the early modern era, and in Italy is simply known as the modern era, or Baroque era, had some commonly shared military characters, but in other respects they were peculiar, due to some local influences and evolutions.

The battle of San Quentin, won by Victor Amadeus' and Prince Eugene of Savoy's great-great-grandfather, marked the triumph of regular fire, and that of manoeuvre and interaction between cavalry, artillery, and infantry, which prevailed on the static column formations. It was an actual but unconsidered turning point in Western military art. What happened on the ground on that 10 August determined a good portion of following century's warfare. A further improvement occurred when the Swedish troops entered Germany during the Thirty Years' War. Gustav Adolphus' systems became the new and more recent milestone of the art of war. They were imitated, developed, and also opposed by other very good commanders, the best of whom were mostly French and Italian, such as Turenne and Montecuccoli.

Here is a point we must immediately make clear. If we want to understand how and why the European generals, and the princes of the House of Savoy in particular, fought in a certain way, we must remember that, until Napoleon, there never was a military science as it was conceived since Austerlitz, and Clausewitz. There was a way of waging war, the background of which was mutual to all the European military leaders, and each commander later developed this background according to his personality and experience.

There were many texts of military art. There was a collection of examples and studies of how to organise the movements and the armies, and these books presented also tactical examples or strategic principles. But ignorance was so widespread that only a few officers cared to read them. At that time, apart for some schools for young gentlemen, providing also a sort of rudimental military training, the practice of arms was the only actual school.

1 The reader should be aware that this chapter was already published, with very few changes, in the author's *William III's Italian Ally*, published by Helion & Company in February 2019.

And the practical school educating the young and noble volunteers had at least a main, if not only one, common ground, the war against the Sublime Porte: the campaigns opposing Venice, the Empire and Christendom to the Ottoman advance in Eastern Europe.

French, German, Danish, Italian, Spanish, Portuguese, Polish, Bohemian, Hungarian, Swedish, Walloon, and Flemish volunteers systematically enlisted under the flags of Saint Mark and of the Habsburgs. They fought on land in Hungary and in the Balkans in the Imperial army, and at sea on Venetian ships and islands against the same enemy, using the same weapons and in the same way. They met, established contacts and made friends. Then they returned home and served in their respective sovereigns' armies. The common preparation they received in the Levant and the Balkans was completed by the European wars they were involved in. And often they found in the opposing camp some old comrades-in-arms from the campaigns against the Sublime Porte of Happiness.

It was during the wars between Europeans that they quickly learned the systems used by their respective armies: the employment of cavalry and infantry, siege techniques, how to advance and withdraw, the importance of foraging and of warehouses, of reconnaissance to spot enemy supply lines, and the need for short marches. All these things, due to the different environment, had to be performed a little differently than how they had learned them against the Ottomans.

The young officers passed through some dozen campaigns, half a dozen wounds, some pillages and then were army-command ready. The most cultured among them could have learned as much Latin as needed to read Plutarch, Cesar, Livius, Tacitus, and Sallustius. Then they could try a comparison between the learned theory and the daily practice. If they were skill and lucky, they survived and their career went on, otherwise they simply died. The smartest among them had a good imagination, good practices and a certain knowledge of the enemy commander's mentality, an enemy commander they often met in their youth, when they fought together in the same army against the Ottomans.

Their commanding action was limited only by their sovereign's orders, but in Victor Amadeus' case, he was the sovereign, so he had no limit. Well, actually he too had some: supplies.

Every army relies on two basic things: firing and eating, and supplies are never plentiful for either of these things.

Let us start with food. Until the early seventeenth century, armies ate what they found in the countries they crossed or they stayed, and often that meant to starve. To avoid such a situation, during the last quarter of the seventeenth-century armies established a supply service. It had to find, keep, and distribute food and forage, but it had to provide also uniforms – whose first use is documented in Italy since the last quarter of the sixteenth century – gunpowder, bullets and weapons.

Some civil contractors gathered all these materials from a widespread network of small producers, and poured it into the warehouses. Then, the military administration or the contractor forwarded the supplies by water or by land to other warehouses, closer to the troops in the war theatre. If the system did not work, or did not work as much as needed, the army raided the neighbouring area and pillaged whatever it could find: food, forage, carts, and animals, not disdaining money, of course, with some rapes and tortures here and there, just for the soldiers' amusement. If the supply system worked, the army could be fed without requisitions in the operational area, but depended almost entirely on the presence of warehouses and on its link to them.

The maximum autonomy – and consequently the widest range of action – an army could have was dictated by the quantity of food the soldiers could carry. It was certainly not that much if the famous 'five-marches system' invented by Frederick the Great was greeted as brilliant. Since the mid eighteenth century that system allowed the troops with nine rations – three in their bags and six in the following wagons – to march ahead during three days and then return to the camp, whose stocks would provide the evening meal of the sixth day. But at the end of the seventeenth century this was still a dream. Thus the generals tended much more to destroy enemy communication lines and warehouses than the enemy army, for a field clash would cost, in men and weapons, much more than a raid against a supply centre. Moreover seizing a supply centre necessarily enforced the enemy to withdraw to his surviving stores, further but still intact, whilst a battle could not always force the enemy to withdraw. And that is why many generals said it was possible to win a war without fighting too much or, as the Marshal of Saxony said in the eighteenth century, with no fight at all.

Campaigns were therefore rather slow and the battles relatively scarce. On the other hand, there were a lot of marches.

Fighting occurred mostly in spring and summer. Autumn always slowed down war activity, for the first rains rendered the roads muddy, so the supplies needed for major operations could not be moved and this hindered the movement of troops. Thus, the armies left the theatre of war and lodged close to their warehouses, getting so-called winter quarters. Winter quarters had to be paid for by the sovereign, but almost often he mostly graciously gave such a honour to the commons, whilst the commanders-in-chief returned to the Court, reported about the just-finished campaign and prepared the next. Before the next spring the army was reassembled. Gaps due to dead, wounded, prisoners, sick and, in large part, deserters were filled and troopers were re-equipped and rested.

But only the major operations were suspended. At least in Italy small operations continued as long as possible. It was so, for instance, in Piedmont during winter 1690–91. It was so in Lombardy in winter 1702, during the Spanish Succession, when Eugene of Savoy tried to seize the city of Cremona, the enemy headquarters.

A winter battle was an exception and a surprise, and there were very few before the War of Spanish Succession. This depended mainly on the lack of ammunition during the poor-weather season, due to the bad state of the roads, and to the great variety of firearms, and consequently of calibres and projectiles.

The problem affected infantry and, much more, artillery. Infantry had up to two or three different types of individual firearms. Since contemporary technology allowed only an approximate uniformity of the barrels and, therefore, of gauges, the soldier at the camp looked for bullets in a pile, chose some balls, tested to see if they entered the barrel and, more or less, he found always enough bullets to feed his weapon.

Artillery had a completely different and more complicated situation. Guns were classified according to the weight of the projectile – usually an iron ball – they shot. Thus their variety was wider than infantry weapons and changed according to the army. For instance, in 1713 there were 13 types of guns officially listed in the Imperial army, whilst the Piedmontese had a dozen and the French no more than seven or eight.

During the seventeenth century the technological evolution of the gun carriages led to their progressive lightening and consequently to a decrease of the horses, or oxen, needed for towing. Besides, at the end of the seventeenth century and the beginning of the eighteenth one still needed a dozen horses to tow a 33-pound gun, eight horses for a 24-pound gun, six for the 12-pounder, and so on.

The ordnance – ammunition, gunpowder, tools, and equipment – in the Piedmontese army were carried by the convoys of the so-called artillery train.

It used four-horse wagons, whose loading capacity went from 500 up to 800 kilogrammes.

Each gunshot could need from two to 18 pounds of gunpowder, being a pound some one third of a kilogramme. The gunpowder, whose grain varied according to the type of firebox to which it was intended, was usually stored in barrels. A barrel's weight went from 100 kilogrammes – for the bigger guns – down to 50 kilogrammes for the smaller guns. Thus, a wagon could carry from five to eight big barrels, or from 10 to 16 small barrels. This allowed the firing of some 16 shots with a big gun, or around 50 with a small one.

Field Cannon.

A large-calibre gun could safely fire up to 50 shots a day, thus its gunpowder needed to be carried by three or four wagons, that is to say by 12 to 16 horses, and three or four coaches; and this was what the daily activity of a single gun needed only in gunpowder, not considering the balls.

On the other hand, there were many different projectiles: free balls, enchained balls, shells, hollowed grenades, canisters and so on. They were carried by other wagons; and usually no wagon could load more than 30.Then it was necessary to provide the gunpowder for the fuses, which needed a finer grain. This kind of gunpowder

A 24-Pound Cannon Ready to Move.

Mortar Battery.

was in 25 kilogramme boxes. And then the wagons had to carry the additional equipment: brushes, shovels, spoons, fuses, flints, and so on.

In principle, we can therefore calculate at least six wagons needed for the daily and non-intensive activity of each big calibre gun. And that was just the minimum needed.

It is recorded that in the previous war the 20 Piedmontese mortars battering Pinerolo during the 1693 siege required 10,000 bombs and 2,500 carts. And we are informed that, when the siege began, 100–150 wagons left Turin every day just to feed the mortars. If we calculate no less than four horses for each wagon, we have a total of 400–600 animals daily employed only for feeding siege batteries.

Soldiers at rest, playing cards.

During the Spanish Succession, the French had similar problems when besieging Verrua in 1705, and Turin in 1706.

The horses needed to rest, thus they needed to be changed, and had to be fed. Their fodder had to be carried by further wagons, pulled by further horses, which also has to be fed. Then, food, ordnance, tools, and spare parts had to be provided to the soldiers; and the wounded had to be evacuated. And it was necessary to feed the cavalry; and the horses of the artillery in front of the city.

Moreover Pinerolo was a lucky case, because that city was very close to the main ordnance storage and Arsenal in Turin and there were no marches. Had it been a normal campaign, it would have been necessary to use between two and 10 times the number of animals, men and wagons, depending on the distance from the supply base.

For instance, when in July 1708 Eugene of Savoy and Marlborough moved to the siege of Lille, they needed 16,000 horses to tow the wagons and, when moving, their "grand convoy" carried to Lille 100 siege cannons, no less than 40 mortars and their ordnance, using 5,000 cars, wagons and chariots, and the convoy resulted 25 kilometres long.

The logistics problem caused by this large quantity of vehicles and animals was increased by other militarily useless people: the families of officers, non-commissioned officers and soldiers, with servants, clients, boys cellars, prostitutes, jugglers and receivers, who "composed an army of almost innumerable rascals".[2]

Reliable studies about the Imperial army in Italy during the War of the Spanish Succession since 1701 until 1706, calculated these people to be as many as the fighting personnel. And, when considering the French, Piedmontese and Milanese (in Spanish service) armies in eastern Lombardy in 1701–1703, we find an army-related people to local population ratio from a maximum of three military-related to one local, to a standard minimum of two army-related to one local. All this mass of people had to move whenever the army moved. Hence, the marching unit had to carry its heavy quantity of baggage, plus the personal effects of officers, soldiers and their families; and that slowed the movements of the whole army.

The army's overall figure and how it affected military movement was a serious problem, especially when considering how strategically important the march was. Generally a march was done in short stages, in daylight, sunshine to sunset. Security was impressive. Troops were detached ahead, on the flanks and to protect the back. Light cavalry was sent far ahead, along with the commissioners, who had to choose the camp location and find all, or at least a portion, of the supplies needed for the incoming army.

When on the spot, the chosen place was inspected, and if all was fine, cavalrymen went ahead to check if any enemy in sight. Meanwhile, commissioners requisitioned everything they could find, and demanded what was missing, sometimes threatening local people with pillaging. If people gave them what they asked for, the commissioners promised to pay, a promise they sometimes did not keep, especially if they were penniless Austrians. When the army arrived, usually a few hours later, the soldiers put up their tents where ordered.

During a march, every evening the camp had to be assembled, and every morning had to be dismantled. In between, soldiers had to think of getting dinner. Usually this meant that, if what the commissioners had found was not enough, the army had to send out infantry and cavalry detachments looking for food, water and fodder, losing additional time to be subtracted from the march.

All these operations did not leave that much time for marching from one place to another. Thus it is not surprising that until the Napoleonic era the standard march did not exceed a dozen kilometres per day (three leagues, or about seven miles). The troops marched in column, but generally not in order, on narrow roads. As a consequence, it was not rare to have an army whose head began setting up the arrival camp, whilst the rearguard was still disassembling the departed one.

Actually, marches were said to be short, but here too there is some evidence of this "tradition" to be wrong or to have, at least, some remarkable

2 Anton Domenico Rossi, *Ristretto di storia patria ad uso de'Piacentini* (Plaisance: 1832), vol. 4, p.272.

The Duke of Marlborough.

exceptions, at least on the Italian fronts. What in 1700 was a recent case occurred in July 1692. The Allied army moving from Piedmont to Dauphiné did not keep to the schedule of three days marching and one resting, according to the general rules described by Perjés, which so many authors think to be the absolute standard.[3] Actually the troops did a two-day march, followed by a one-day stop, and then by a five-day uninterrupted march, followed by a three-day stop, which was a fake one, because they stopped to seize a city, thus to fight, not to rest. Thus they covered 148 kilometres in only seven days, thus a daily 21 kilometres average, that is to say at least five kilometres per day – if not nine – more than the "rules", and, moreover, climbing the mountains. This should be enough at least to start questioning all the authors blindly supporting Perjés as an absolute rule, which in this case was not followed; and this case is not an exception in Italian campaigns between 1690 and 1748. Actually during the Spanish succession crisis Eugene of Savoy's march to Turin in 1706 was quite fast, as we shall see, as was Eugene's and Victor

3 Geza Perjés, 'Army Provisioning, Logistics and Strategy in the Second Half of the 17th Century', in *Acta Historica Academiae Scientiarum Hungaricae*, T. 16, No. 1/2 (1970), pp.1–52.

Amadeus' march to Toulon in 1707, whilst in the following years we have at least two more remarkable cases: the Piedmontese march from Palermo to Syracuse in 1716, and Charles Emmanuel III of Sardinia's march from the Adriatic coast to the Western Alps in 1742.

Anyway, no matter how short it could be, the march was really fatiguing. Troopers had only one uniform, the winter one, but they marched and fought in summer, and used that same uniform. In that case, when marching and whilst in camp, they could remove their overcoat, but if we think of a poorly fed soldier, marching in summer, carrying 30 or 40 kilogrammes total weight, dressed in winter clothes, with an external temperature that, in Northern Italy and Southern France could easily be between 25 and 30, and perhaps 35 centigrade, we shall not be surprised to discover that the casualties due to marches were high. Reports and diaries between 1688 and 1748 give a bleak overview. The only exceptions appear to be Marlborough's supplies in 1702–1710, and the logistics organisation of Charles Emmanuel III of Sardinia, Victor Amadeus' youngest son and heir, in 1733–38 and 1741–48.

Complaints of desperate generals and cries of pain by looted and mistreated civilians reported by diaries and chronicles arose to heaven everywhere. Therefore there was a harsh friction between the marching or encamped troops and the local population. Civilians reacted as they could. They concealed or consumed all the food and fodder they had. So, the army needed much more time for finding food, and slowed down its movement. The other civilian reaction was violence. Peasants looked for isolated soldiers or small detachments, and attacked and massacred them without mercy.

This happened in Lombardy during the Spanish Succession and regularly happened in Piedmont when invaded by the French or by the Spaniards. At the beginning, in the sixteenth century, these were isolated initiatives, easily broken. But during the seventeenth century resistance became harsher and more organised, also thanks to the militia established by Emmanuel Philibert and enhanced by Charles Emmanuel I. Its military relevance increased so much that during the War of the Grand Alliance it became a relevant factor, even if its best performances were in the next century, against the French in 1702–1707, 1742–1748, and 1792–1796.

Military counter-reactions were as usual: looting, and then hanging – when the enemy was humane – all the people suspected of resisting, or to have resisted, a looting.

Local chronicles from the period of the War of Spanish Succession, provide plenty of details about these cases, and the results of those clashes filled the underground of the Po Valley, where, still in the late nineteenth century, at least in the Province of Brescia, it was possible to run into mass graves of Imperial soldiers massacred by the angry population between 1702 and 1706.

Anyway the major obstacles for a seventeenth and eighteenth-century army, the hardest to overcome, were the cities, the walled ones, of course. If a city was not immediately seized, it had to be besieged; and this generally required a lot of time, because a ring of fortifications and siegeworks had to be built around its walls.

And all these fieldworks had to be held by a substantial number of soldiers, which was very difficult to get in a period when 15,000 men composed a

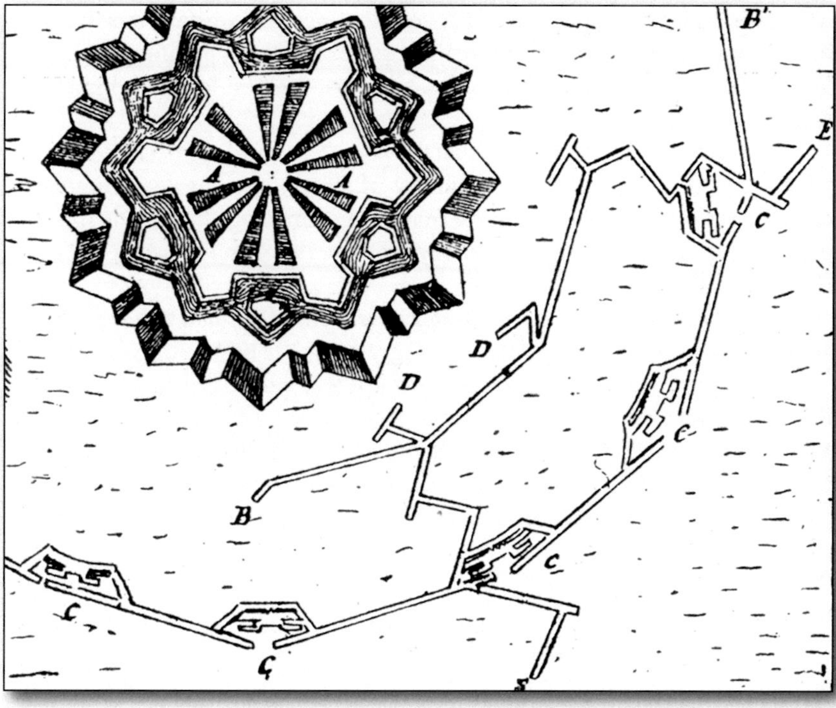

Example Plan of a Siege.

good army and the King of France's 200,000 men was considered an amazing figure, hard to be equalled and, above all, dramatically expensive.

It is true that the sieges could be planned well enough, but it is equally true that they only succeeded if the besieging army had safe and continuous supplies.

We must underline a problem here. The literature in English during the twentieth century focused only on war theatres where the British fought, mostly Flanders. In some case this was due to a logical and reasonable interest on one's own country or culture. In other cases this happened because the authors read and understood only English, thus were unable to read diaries, journals and accounts written in languages other than English. No matter the reason, this left many people making two remarkable misunderstandings. The first was – and still is – to consider the valuable Geza Perjés' work as absolutely valid, and a set of rules good for explaining logistics on every war theatre of every war prior to Napoleon, whilst Perjés himself clearly said he was speaking about the sevententh-century Hungarian and Eastern European war theatre alone. A focus on different war theatres would provide evidence of differences between some aspects underlined by Perjés – mostly relying on sources concerning Hungarian campaigns – and the contemporary eyewitness accounts from other war theatres and other wars.

The second misunderstanding was to consider sieges as the main kind of warfare of that period, and to think of the seventeenth- and eighteenth-century generals as focusing on sieges and thus relatively neglecting battles. This is a fallacy, a real mistake, bigger than blindly considering Perjés' work as always good despite the period, location, and circumstances. It comes, normally, from a wrongly overstressed application of the concept of 'reason'.

Being the eighteenth, the Age of Reason, that period's warfare was 'rational', hence logical, thus planned, and the best example of planning was siege warfare, thus siege warfare had to be, and was, the best loved and practised warfare of that period.

Actually, nobody would deny that the sevententh and eighteenth centuries were marked by an enormous quantity of sieges, but due to a completely different reason. Logistics was the main issue, and logistics needs free and protected connections, that is to say, in that time, roads, waterways and related facilities.

Cities commanded roads and waterways, hence they had to be seized and kept. If this could be done without a siege, it was the best option for all.

Marlborough always did his best to cause a battle and to avoid sieges. Eugene of Savoy undertook only two sieges during his life, from 1690 to 1736 – Lille and Belgrade – and, at the end of the story, the first had no real consequence on a strategic level, whilst the result of the second was overthrown just one year after Eugene's death. On the other hand, Eugene definitely swept out – and forever – the enemy from the theatre winning three battles: Zenta in 1697, Turin, and Oudenaarde during the Spanish Succession, whilst Marlborough and he did the same at Blenheim.

Sieges worked well in the Rhineland and Flanders, where the plains, the dense network of canals and the wide range of rivers including the Rhine itself, allowed regular and copious amount of supplies. But if one looks at war reports from theatres other than Flanders and the Rhineland, finds the trend of the operations to worsen according to the roughness of the ground. In central Germany they did not go that well, and the more one proceeded eastward, the less sure the result of a siege became. In Italy, due to the Alps, there were two possible results. The besieger from across the Alps immediately won, in a very few days, or, and that was the most likely case, his siege took longer than expected, went very badly and often had to be interrupted. Thus, generals disliked cities – and sieges – just due to the risks involved. Every trick was good to seize a city: heavy shelling, mines, climbing, underground digging, underground fights with poisonous smoke, starvation, bribery, poisoning, and very favourable surrender conditions offered to the defenders. Everything was good to seize a fortified city, but no general of the late seventeenth and eighteenth centuries really loved sieges, except Marshall de Saxe, who seemed to have found the secret to undertake and win whatever siege in a few days.

Sieges went always the same way. They began with the incoming army blockading the city, or the fortress, by distributing its troopers around it.

Then, the besiegers' commander decided the main attack approach and its scheme, and gave the order to 'open the trench'. This meant the digging of the siege trenches. It could be carried out both by the soldiers of the besieging army and by ad hoc civilians. It was not a very long story, even if it was dangerous and complicated, and the duration of the siege was calculated from the day they started opening the trenches, i.e. from the first day of the excavation, no matter how long the excavation could last.

Once the trench was made, the army could start the real siege. Its schedule was dictated by the structure of the fortress and by the practice.

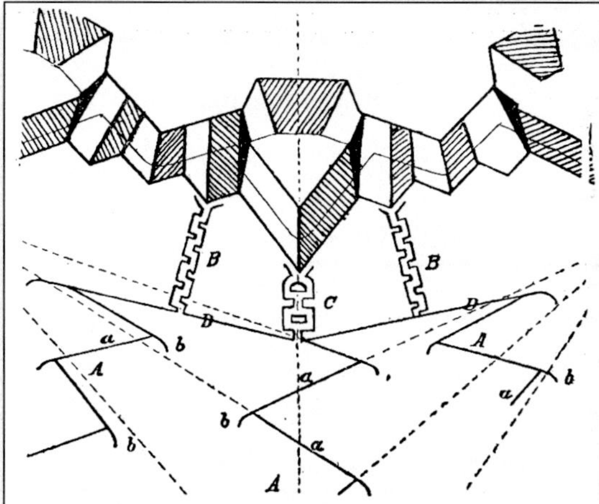

Approcci verso una piazzaforte: *A*) Zig-zag; *B*) Trincee trasversali; *C*) Raccordi; *D*) Parallele; *a*) Fronte; *b*) Incroci.

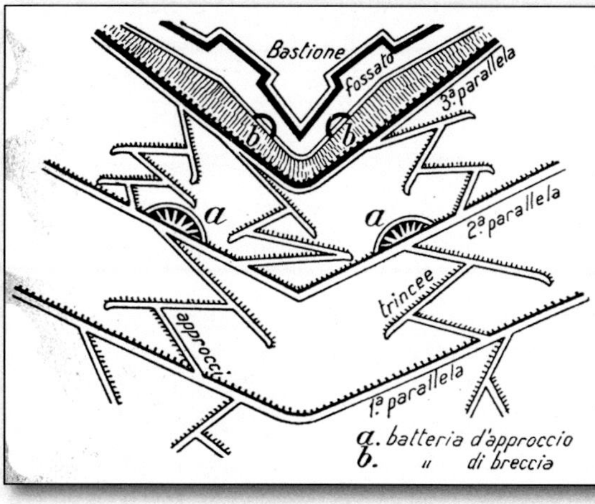

Left: Diagram of a Siege: Approach.
Right: Diagram of a Siege: Attack.

First of all it was necessary to overcome the defensive positions out of the walls. This was not easy, as some European fortresses had a defensive mine system. Mines were fired and exploded under the feet of the besiegers, causing terrible casualties. Turin was one of the best-protected cities in Europe. Its underground network included tunnels and mine stoves and, after the improvements made by Victor Amadeus II, it was organised on three underground levels, totalling some 10 miles.

Besiegers had to neutralise mines with countermine works and, if all went well, they could then storm the external defensive positions facing "only" the enemy artillery and riflemen.

Then there was the attack to the counter-scarpe and to the scarpe, that is to say, the seizure of the outer edge of the moat, the descent into the moat itself and, if possible, the attack on the walls. The next step was always considered so important that special messengers were chosen among the high-ranked or noblest officers to inform the sovereign. It was the conquest of the covered road. It had this name because it was 'covered', that is to say protected, by the fortress artillery. It was the internal road behind the defensive wall, allowing the defenders to move along the inner part of the walls; this seizure was actually anything but decisive.

Once the covered road taken, it was time to break through the fortifications with all available artillery. Assuming that the besieged troops did not dig mines under the siege cannons, making them blow, as the Piedmontese did in Turin against the French in 1706, and assuming that their sallies were always repulsed, the day came when a breach was opened in the walls. Its width was measured in 'men on front', that is to say the number of infantrymen who could enter it marching side by side.

Now, if it was a matter of a fortress, at this point the garrison received a demand to surrender. Usually, in order to complete that task, the besieging commander granted to the besieged one not only the honour of arms, but even permission to withdraw with all his men, a small number of guns (usually no more than half a dozen of light guns), playing their fifes, rolling their drums,

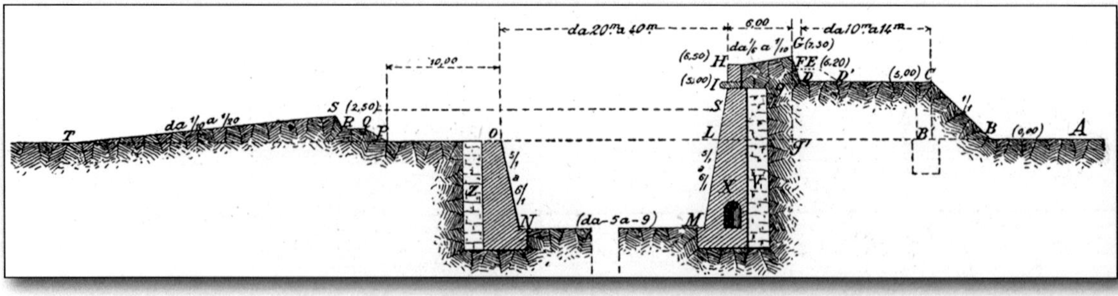

Diagram of a Bastion.

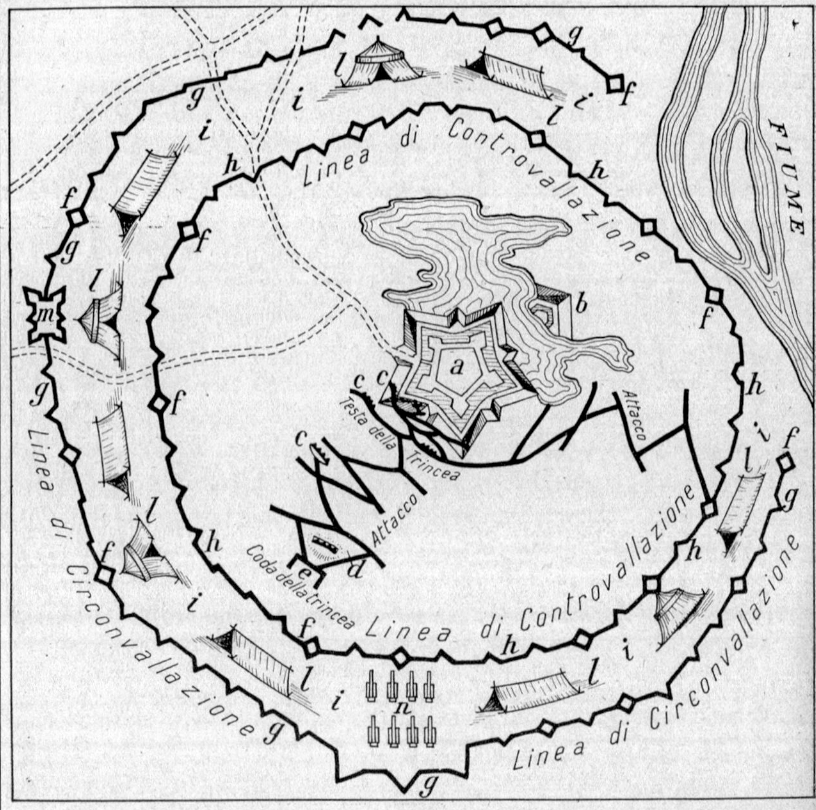

Linee di Circonvallazione e di Controvallazione intorno a una piazzaforte assediata (secolo XVII): *a*, piazzaforte; *b*, mezzaluna; *c*, batterie dell'attaccante; *d*, idem; *e*, *f*, ridotte; *g*, fossato della linea di Circonvallazione; *h*, fossato della linea di Controvallazione; *i*, campo; *l*, tende; *m*, deposito viveri; *n*, parco d'artiglieria.

Diagram of a Siege: Circumvallation.

waving their flags and bringing their wagons along. The besieged had only to promise not to fight again before a certain term was up. The same could happen in battle, if an army surrounded so a big enemy unit that waging a negotiation seemed easier than a further bloody assault.

If he was – or was supposed to be – still strong enough to negotiate, the besieged commander discussed the capitulation, then ordered the drummers to 'roll the surrender'[4] lowered the flag and came out of the walls bringing

4 If the besieged commander asked for surrendering before being demanded by the enemy, he ordered the drummers to "roll the call".

what was permitted according to the capitulation, that is to say the written text listing the surrendering conditions.

But if a city was besieged, things went in a completely different and much more annoying way for the besiegers. A city always had its own fortified citadel, where the garrison withdrew every time they saw a breach opened in the walls. Then the besieged commander gave the city delegates the permission to negotiate with the besiegers, whilst he retired into the citadel with the garrison and arranged to hold it. Hence the unlucky besieger had to start a new siege, for the capitulation often concerned only the city.

Meanwhile, a relief army could come. If so, it was rare to see a besieging army keeping the siege and, at the same time, turning against the relief army and defeating it. Eugene of Savoy destroyed the incoming Ottoman relief army whilst he was besieging Belgrade in 1717, but usually the besieger packed his tents and left swiftly, so as not to be surrounded and defeated in turn.

It could happen that every surrender demand was rejected. If so, the garrison could later surrender only 'at discretion' of the winner.[5] Thus if the garrison rejected any negotiation, it could not be sure to be taken prisoner of war when the city fell. If the city was seized, or, as they said, was "taken by assault", that is to say stormed, looting and massacre were certain. This explains why until Napoleon so many cities surrendered after sieges so short that they looked like a pure formality.

In most cases the generals were much more willing to fight the enemy in the open field. They did not consider it as their best choice, but the battle could be regarded as a colossal duel. And if they were forced to do it, since no gentleman refused a duel, they deployed their respective troops and made them fight.

The armies clashed with remarkable ferocity and enormous difficulties. This was mostly due to the individual and corps weapons. Not all the armies of that time were organised in the three branches of infantry, cavalry, and artillery.

In the past, the battle of Saint Quentin had destroyed both France, and the myth of the infantry's invincibility by less well-considered corps as cavalry and artillery. To cope with the threatening preponderance of the former, based on speed and impact, European armies quickly and widely adopted portable firearms to damage the charging enemy cavalry before being engaged. On the other hand, they improved guns, looking to render them lighter and lighter, easier to handle, and capable of a firing high rate.

---

5 Surrendering could be, "with quarter", "without quarter" and "at discretion". In the first case the winner promised to pay for the prisoners' lodging and food, and hoped to be repaid – with interest – when getting the ransom. "Without quarter", or "no quarter", meant simply that the prisoner had to pay for his own lodging and feeding once captured. "Discretion" meant that the winner could do whatever he wanted with the prisoner. Troopers normally charged screaming: "quarter", "no quarter" and "discretion" because, in a period of professional armies, professional soldiers on both sides found it correct to let the enemy know in advance what could they expect. It was just to let the enemy evaluate whether it was more convenient to fight or to surrender, the latter option being discarded in the case of the fourth and most feared of all the cries: "no mercy".

On the eve of eighteenth century the remarkable development which marked weapons evolution in the seventeenth century were achieved. Troops now used the flintlock musket or the flintlock rifle.There was a difference in Italy between the two: the rifle had a longer barrel than the musket, thus infantry long-barrelled weapons were called rifles, whilst the cavalry's relatively short-barrelled weapons were muskets.

Technical improvements in infantry firearms made infantry white arms, especially pikes, decrease. Pikes disappeared and the socket bayonet, to be put on the barrel thanks to a ring, by 1701 was widely used by all the armies.

Triangle-shaped, looking like a sort of mason's trowel, lighter and longer than the previous plug-in bayonet, the new bayonet allowed the rifle to shoot and be reloaded. The firing rate was therefore higher, although its precision remained somewhat approximate.

The flintlock rifle, adopted by all the armies at the end of the seventeenth century, was smoothbore. Therefore it was neither accurate nor did it have a long range.

The first inconvenience could not be solved. The second was solved by making rifle barrels longer. Thus rifles became as tall as their owners. But this was a new problem. Since the weapons of the time were almost all muzzleloaded, infantrymen had to put the rifle's stock on the ground. Then, holding the barrel, the soldier had to put the gunpowder and the ball in. It was a long process, it took time, and during that time the soldier was at the enemy's mercy and could react only using his own white arms.

Therefore, to protect each other, to ensure an uninterrupted firing and to better withstand the attacks by the enemy cavalry, infantry manoeuvred on the battlefield in squared order, divided in several lines, one by one, moving

Cannons in an Artillery Battery.

Batteria di cannoni (secolo XVII)
A) B) C) D) cannoni in batteria; E) F) G) servizio delle polveri; H) magazzino di polvere; I) sentinelle

relatively quickly also under the enemy fire. This meant that in a battle, whenever they were commanded, troopers advanced towards the enemy having the captains and lieutenants marching before them continually checking the ranks did not tumble into disorder. It was not a rare situation. Lines could be disordered by the ground, but the main risk was artillery fire.

There were too many unpredictable factors the commander had to face, and no theory, and often no plan, could be kept in an actual battle. Ground, fortifications, enemy cavalry and artillery, weather, time ... everything had to be evaluated moment by moment, without prejudice. In fact every general, and every colonel decided on the spot how to manage the situation, according to the ground and according to the kind of units he had at hand and in front of him.

Regiments were the core of armies, and every regiment had a different kind of soldier. Fusileers had to hold the front. Grenadiers were used for attacks and protection whilst retreating. There was normally a grenadier company in each battalion, supported by the sappers. Sometimes, at least in the Piedmontese army and at least until the Napoleonic Wars, regimental grenadiers were gathered in occasional battalions or regiments, to be used during the fight.

Bandsmen were employed to play music on march and in battle – which gave the troopers the marching cadence and contributed to keep the lines in order – but were also employed for gathering the wounded and to bury the dead. The regimental provost and his soldiers, usually still called 'archers', were the military police, and were often supported by dragoons.

Weapons and clothes differed according to the soldier's specialisation. All dressed in a wide coat, basically an overcoat. Fusileers now normally used the normal tricorne, and had a bayonet, a rifle, or musket, and a short sword to be used during a hand-to-hand fight. Actually there is a remark to be made: the tricorne was used by the armies dressed according to the French fashion, but not all the European armies' clothes were so. For instance, the Papal army in 1700, or at least the garrison in Bologna, according to contemporary picture was still dressed as in the mid seventeenth century, even if by 1708 its uniforms reached the European "French" standard. The Imperial army also looked still quite old-fashioned, much closer to the second half of the seventeenth century than to the first years of the eighteenth.

Grenadiers had the same weaponry as the fusileers, but with a huge quantity of hand grenades, to be launched on the enemy from a short distance.

This affected their hat and rifles. To launch their grenades, they had to put aside the rifle. This was dangerous, so they soon started applying a belt to the rifle, to hang it to their shoulders whilst throwing the grenades. Musket belts became the distinctive sign of grenadiers' weapons, but they had another problem. It was not easy to wear musket belts having on the head the wide tricorne of that time, hence the grenadiers started using in battle their freetime cap, the nightcap, which had to be worn only in the barracks or in camp.

Then they added to the nightcap a cardboard frontal plaque, which became taller and taller, and in Continental European armies south of the Rhine was later covered with fur.

The Huge Difference Between the Papal Army's Old-fashioned Uniforms, and the Civilians' Updated Clothes, in a Ceremony Held in Bologna in 1700.

Sappers had to act as pioneers during attacks, digging, opening a way through enemy trenches, and quickly preparing field fortifications. Thus they were usually dressed like the grenadiers, but they had a big axe, no rifle, and a wide leather apron.

Piedmontese line infantry since the War of the League of Augsburg was flanked by irregular units, composed of Waldensians. the Protestant population of some alpine valleys close to the French border. They were a useful mountain light infantry, and, in a certain sense, the ancestors of the Italian Alpine troops established in the last quarter of the nineteenth century.

The Waldensians fought in scattered order. Grenadiers attacked in column, opening their own way with hand grenades, whilst fusileers held the line and fought in line.

Cavalry was divided into heavy and light cavalry. There were dragoons too, but they were quite distinct. As in other armies, in Piedmont too dragoons were mounted infantry, and in the Piedmontese army they were an élite corps. Being infantry, they had their grenadiers, used rifles instead of muskets, and did not have boots. They used the so-called *bottine alla granadiera* ("grenadiers'gaiters"), made of leather.

After the War of the Grand Alliance, Piedmontese cavalry still relied mostly on dragoons, and actually as later in the Italian army – its first four and oldest regiments were, and are, dragoon regiments.

There were also heavy cavalry regiments, tasked to charge and crash the enemy lines.

Cavalry patrolled, performed long and short range reconnaissance, escorted convoys, raided, protected withdrawals, attacked by surprise, disturbed and opposed the advancing enemy, or pursued them when retreated.

Cavalry was employed in battle mainly to crush infantry. Artillery had not yet a long range fire, at least at the end of the seventeenth century. Cannons were used all at the same time against all the targets in sight. Fire was not concentrated, and the projectile was shot to a longer distance by simply increasing the launching charge. This made the barrel suffer a big strain and a quick overheating. There was no solution but to use the cannon until it broke, or exploded, and try to refresh it using buckets of water.

The most used firing technique was that used mainly by the French, and which had been used by the Portuguese navy at least since the sixteenth century.

The cannons fired their balls at a relatively close range, in order to let them bounce many times – as flat stones on the water – until crashing against the enemy men and horses.

Howitzers appeared by the first time during the Nine Years' War and were now widely used Artillery usually included the military engineers corps.[6] At that time engineers dealt both with machines and civil construction, hence the officers composing the engineer corps were all military architects and, at the same time, able in dealing with every kind of machine, whilst weapons and ordnance were normally reserved to the artillery officers, whose scientific background was basically the same.

Engineers had to draw maps, direct road and fortification works, and direct the sieges. Directing a siege meant planning the fire sector of each battery, planning and overseeing the excavation of trenches and mine galleries, and taking care of the technical side of the attacks on the besieged fortress.

Infantry, cavalry, and artillery too, had to keep their lines in battle, thus a strict discipline was enforced, and it had to be kept every time and everywhere. Penalties were hard. A Piedmontese soldier guilty of *lèse majesté*, betrayal, cowardice in front of the enemy, complaint or protest against a superior whilst in rank, atrocious blasphemy, aggression to members of the clergy, sorcery, desertion, blackmail, or insubordination was sentenced to death. Normal swearers and people acting against the Roman Catholic faith were sentenced to prison the first time; to the stocks the second time, and the third time to have their tongue pierced. Minor faults were punished by *strappados*, by the stake, by passing through the bars – in infantry – and through the sticks in cavalry.[7] These punishments kept

6 It must be underlined here that whilst in English the word "engineer" means both the man dealing with engines, and the person having a master degree in engineering or in architecture, in Italian – and in French – the man dealing with engines is called a *macchinista*, and the word "engineer" means only the person who has a master degree in engineering.

7 'Passing through the rods' or 'through the bars', or 'through the sticks' meant that the punished soldier had to walk step by step between two rows of comrades – usually his whole company, or two companies – each of them armed with a rod, or with the rifle ramrod – which in some

more or less in order a heterogeneous, mostly illiterate, and superstitious troop, largely composed of people released from prisons or sometimes who had been forced to enlist. Ruined peasants, dismissed servants, men with no family, artisans who lost all, people unemployed and looking for adventure, booty, or even daily food and a roof, both national and foreign subjects, were trained by corporal and noncommissioned officers, under the control of the officers, until their discipline and the habit of executing orders were so automatic to allow them to advance in open field, in close order, at a speed of about 80 steps per minute[8] without even attempting to shield themselves from enemy bullets.

Obviously, as soon as the opportunity came, many soldiers deserted. There was little chance for them: enlist in another army, or turn to brigandage, with the threat of the gallows for desertion and a reward on their head. The best opportunities generally came after a battle; but the battles were few due to supply problems.

But when there was no other solution and it was necessary to fight, armies faced each other in open field with remarkable ferocity. Movements were not very fast, at least compared to the wars of the following centuries, simply because ranks and close order had to be kept. It was not that easy, due to smoke. The first volley produced so thick and stagnant a curtain of smoke that nobody could see through it. Therefore, after an initial exchange of shots at a very close distance – usually some tens of steps – the armies engaged in the hand-to-hand fight.

An additional problem came now. Uniforms looked practically the same in all the armies, and since the most internationally used colour was grey – later, in the eighteenth century, different shades of white – it was very hard to know who was the friend or who the enemy; nor could one succeed in hearing the enemy speak, because every commander enlisted foreigners, no matter whether they were single deserters or whole units of mercenaries, volunteers or prisoners. So it was very easy to find people of the same origin or nationality under opposing flags.

The only sure distinctive mark was a badge. In a short time it became the cockade, worn by each soldier at least in battle on the left side of his hat, and whose colour varied, but with little imagination, according to the sovereign[9] Only, it was not always possible to see it in time. So it was better to hit first, and then make one's own deductions.

Casualties were huge. The number of dead was often very high and few wounded survived the clash. No medical service existed, for there were only a few surgeons. In general, only at the beginning of the campaign the military administration organised a field hospital by contract. The field hospital

---

armies was wooden, but in others iron. Each of them had to hit the punished soldier when he passed In front of him. Some men died before the end of the punishment.

8 This is the ordinary and parade cadence of the Italian alpine troops even now.

9 Spaniards and Neapolitans had a red cockade; the Piedmontese and the Venetian had a blue one; the Papal troops used a yellow and red cockade, the French usually had white ones but sometimes also black. Black was used by Prussians, the British and, from a certain period, by the Austrians. The latter, however, when fighting as Imperial troops, that is to say always except for the 1741–1745 period, wore an oak twig on the hat: the badge of the Empire.

followed the army with ambulances, servants, nurses, surgeons and doctors, who were considered civilians in all respects.

Many of the wounded by a gunshot died within hours due to wound infection and blood loss. Moreover, given the size of the bullets of that time, if limbs were concerned, the physical damage was often so terrible that one could do nothing but amputate.

The biggest concern armies had was disease. Military physicians and surgeons[10] had good practical experience. They knew what happened, but did not know why. Studies were going on, but an additional and remarkable result appeared in 1700, when doctor Bernandino Ramazzini first published his *De morbis artificum diatriba* – debate on workers' diseases – a milestone in the history of medicine and the starting point of occupational medicine.

Ramazzini examined in Chapter 40 of his book *de Morbis Castrensibus*[11] what he called, according to contemporary use, the 'camp diseases' whilst the term 'camp disease' is now a synonym of typhus. Ramazzini remarked how the lack of care during winter quarters weakened and sometimes definitely handicapped, or killed, the men wounded during the previous campaign. It was rare not to have battalions devastated by diseases, and the whole army stopped by an epidemic.

According to Ramazzini, the worst was what were called "camp fevers". The first occurrence seems to have been in the Imperial army during the 1566 Hungarian campaign. It was a consequence of the rotten food and waste water, even if their effects were enhanced by concomitant causes as excessive labour, lack of sleep, rain, excessively cold or hot weather, fear, and "a thousand further uncomfortable and noxious things".[12] But, Ramazzini underlined, the worst came from how filthy camps were, and, he added, this was because people simply did not take care of where and how they left their faeces. Whilst the Hebrews – according to the Bible – and the Ottomans used latrines, that is to say holes dug in the soil far outside the camp, and covered them after use, European armies – as he saw in Imperial winter quarters in 1690–96 in Northern Italy – did not, and left everywhere within the camp their "production", "the work of the body", as the medieval Italian language said.

The first consequence was a terrible stink, and if the results were terrible for men of the late seventeenth century, accustomed to living among stinks that men of the twenty-first century simply do not imagine, we can easily understand how hard that had to be.[13]

10 We must always remember that surgeons and physicians were two different kind of medical doctor, the latter often considering the former as culturally inferior because they were not doctors.

11 Bernardino Ramazzini, *De morbis artificum diatriba* (first edition, Modena, 1700); here the Venetian 1743 edition is used.

12 Bernardino Ramazzini, *De morbis artificum diatriba* (Venice: 1743), p.221.

13 Ramazzini mentioned the works by Dutch physician Raymond Minderer (1570–1621) on military medicine, by Swiss physician Heinrich Screta (1637–1688), and by the Neapolitan physician Luca Antonio Porzio (1637–1715), but he got also much important information by the first physician of the Duke of Hannover, Doctor Georg Heinrich Bernstorff, during the Nine Years' War winter quarters of the Hannoverian troops in Modena.

The result was dysentery, typhus, and "evil fevers", which were probably mostly malaria,[14] normally spreading among the troops during the end of summer. Their symptoms were headaches, fevers, deliria, convulsions and diarrhoea, alone or all together. Suggested drugs and cures seemed to be not that useful, even if, when speaking of malaria in another part of his book, Ramazzini was among the first who suggested and supported the use of chinchona, a quinine-rich flowering plant from South America, no matter how toxic many contemporary physicians claimed it to be.

The sick and wounded were less fortunate than prisoners. Prisoners were robbed immediately after, if not already during, the battle. The same occurred to the dead, who were stripped of everything, and left literally naked on the ground. It was the fastest way to remedy the shortcomings of military supplies, and the eternal lack of money of the privates, although every camp had receivers who bought everything.

Moreover when losing their uniforms, the enemy suffered an economic loss, for his administration had to fully re-equip its own men once released due to an exchange of prisoners.

Last, another serious problem was the slowness and approximation of information. Normally a mounted messenger needed at least a quarter of hour to reach the army commander from a sector. Assuming that he got an immediate answer, he who had sent him asking for instructions received the answer not earlier than half a hour, or perhaps never if the messenger had been wounded or killed when going or coming back. This meant that usually most of the orders were issued according to outdated information, thus they were hopelessly useless, and the situation could be solved only thanks to the sector commander's experience and skill, and to how good in holding the line his regiments were.

Army commanders tried to solve this problem staying where they could see the whole battlefield, and delegated the command of the different sectors. More exactly: the army commander decided the battle plan, told it to his subordinates in a council of war, and assigned and explained to each of them what he had to do, and the respective tasks. Everyone had relative autonomy during the action and only the general direction and management of the battle remained in the commander's hands. Traditionally there were six subordinated commanders: one for each wing and for the centre on both the first and the second line. It was their ability, precision, smartness, skill, experience and constancy which dictated the result of the battle.

This was the European armies' warfare in the Baroque or early modern era, according to very precise rules and conventions. Such warfare was basically the same from the end of the Thirty Years' War until the early Napoleonic campaigns. And that was the way Victor Amadeus' army had to fight.

14 Malaria is an Italian combined word, literally meaning "evil air".

5

The Duke of Savoy's Army[1]

I: Infantry

Victor Amadeus' father, Duke Charles Emmanuel II, reorganised his army between 1660 and 1664. In 1655 he introduced bayonets, to be plugged in the musket barrel, and, following the wave, in 1672 the Arsenal of Turin standardised some 18,000 muskets. In 1674 calibres were determined to be equal to a heavy lead bullet, whose weight was an ounce of Piedmont, that is to say 30.7 grams, or 1.22 British ounces, and between 17.3 and 17.5 millimetres in size.[2]

Charles Emmanuel II, Duke of Savoy.

Five years before, in 1669 Charles Emmanuel declared six infantry units to be "order" regiments, that is to say six "standing" regiments, described that way for they had to keep the "order", or the ranks of the army's core in battle. However the army had standing units since long before. In 1619 was established the Savoyard Regiment du Cheyne, which later evolved into the Casale Infantry Regiment. In 1625 was raised the Fleury Regiment of foot,[3] later known as Catalano Alfieri Regiment, after his commander's name, and then as the Piemonte Infantry Regiment and at last as the 3rd and 4th Piemonte Infantry Regiment. The

1 This chapter was also already published in the author's *William III's Italian Ally*, published by Helion & Company in February 2019, though this one has some changes in all the paragraphs, and includes a totally different paragraph about artillery. In five years the army had no time to change that much. Artillery alone changed thoroughly, thus here there are some things differing from the similar chapter in the other book, but not that many.

2 See Francesco Sterrantino, "L'esercito del Duca di Savoia", in *La guerra della Lega di Augusta fino alla battaglia di Orbassano* (Turin, 1993), p.217.

3 In 1619 Charles Emanuel I appointed Jean Wilcardel – or Villecardel – de Fleury, Fresne e Sandreville, lieutenant in his son's – Prince Thomas of Savoy – company of cuirassers as the Marquess of Mortigliengo, and the new Marquess raised and commanded the regiment.

An Officer's Pike Dating from Victor Amadeus' Time.

Savoy Infantry Regiment – later 1st and 2nd Savoia Infantry Regiments in Royal Sardinian Army, and then "Re" – the King – Infantry Regiment in the Royal Italian Army – was originally raised in 1639. Prior to 1660 some more units were organised: the Guards,[4] Nice and Monferrato Infantry Regiments.

Victor Amadeus enhanced the military organisation. In 1685 he established grenadier units after the French example. Meanwhile he slowly increased the quantity of infantry regiments up to 10, enlisting Croce Bianca,[5] Saluzzo, della Marina[6] and Chiablese, and in 1690 he ordered the troopers to abandon pikes, leave the musket and use the new flintlock rifle. So, by 1690 ducal infantry included 14 regiments, that is to say: Guardie (Guards), Savoia (Savoy), Monferrato, Piemonte (Piedmont), Aosta, Mondovì, Nizza, Croce Bianca, Saluzzo, La Marina, Chiablese, Fucilieri, La Trinità, and Artiglieria (Artillery), which included the whole artillery, listed within the infantry.

By the eve of the eighteenth century the "order" infantry regiments Guards and Savoy had two battalions, whilst the other regiments had only one.

Each battalion was composed of 10 companies.[7] The Reggimento – literally meaning in ancient Italian "the government", or "the rule" – was also called *colonnello* – "colonel" – or *colonnellato*, which could be translated as "domain of the colonel", for it was supposed to compose a "colonna" – a column – and that was why it was commanded by an officer called a "colonel", which meant something like 'the columner'. The colonel commanded at the same time his

4 Officially the Guards are said to have been established as late as 1659, but the present author is rather doubtful. The year was decided in the nineteenth century due to a levy order issued on 18 April 1659, but I found different documentary evidence in Turin. The Turin State Archive has in Materie Militari, Ordini e Regolamenti, Mazzo 2, number 1, an order issued on 22 April 1617 by Duke Charles Emmanuel I, printed by Luigi Pizzamiglio "ducal printer", and entitled *Ordine del Duca Carlo Emanuele I per la levata delle Compagnie di Soldatesca ivi espresse per il suo Reggimento delle Guardie* ('Order of the Duke Charles Emmanuel I for the levy of the companies of soldiers within expressed for his Regiment of the Guards'). The text provides evidence showing that it did not speak of the Duke's Household, but of a regular and normal infantry regiment.

5 The Croce Bianca ['White Cross'] Regiment was so-called due to its officers being all Knights of Malta, whose coat of arms was a white cross. Actually the white cross on scarlet shield was also the coat of arms of the House of Savoy. Originally Savoy's coat of arms had been a black eagle on a golden shield, but when the Duke of Savoy was appointed Imperial Vicar of Italy, his House received the Imperial Vicar's coat of arms: a white cross in a red shield.

6 The Reggimento La Marina or della Marina – "The Navy Regiment", or "the Navy's Regiment" – belonged to the infantry and normally fought on land, for the navy included only three galleys based in Villafranca, but it was supposed to serve on board too. That is why it was later dressed in red and green, red coat and green cuffs and breeches, even if during the Nine Years' War it was dressed in grey and green. Red was the distinctive colour of military personnel serving on galleys in all the Italian fleets (whilst who served on vessels was dressed in blue), and green was – and still is – the distinctive colour of the Order of the Saint Maurice and Lazarus, committed for the war against the Unfaithful – the Moslems – and hence responsible for the navy. No real marine corps existed in Italian independent States, because Venice used its infantry both on land and sea, as did Genoa, Tuscany and the Papal states; so, Savoy's La Marina Regiment was the only one specifically established to serve on ships.

7 Regiments hardly respected rules, hence they could have from 16 up to a maximum of 25 companies, depending on the cases and on the periods. Companies could differ depending on the case and on the period, from 90–100 men in the Guards down to 40 in the Savoy Regiment.

regiment and a company, named after his rank as the *compagnia colonnella*, the "colonel's company".

In hierarchical order, under the colonel there was a lieutenant-colonel – literally meaning "the one who keeps the colonel's place" – and the *capitano maggiore* – meaning the "most important and oldest (in the sense of oldest ranked) captain" and shortened to *maggiore,* hence the English spelling, "major" – who respectively commanded the 'lieutenant-colonel's company' and the "major's company". All the remaining companies were commanded by normal captains. No matter how many battalions existed – one or two – all the captains depended directly on the colonel, and each of them was (or was supposed to be) supported in his company by a lieutenant – literally meaning 'the one who keeps the place' – an ensign, a lodging marshal and by the sergeants, who were the platoon commanders. Each platoon was divided into *squadre*, literally "teams", and each team was commanded by a corporal. This system did not differ from that used in other Italian armies of that period.

As it happened in many European armies and still happens in Brazil, soldiers usually served under a "war name", a nickname they chose when enlisting. War names normally indicated a feeling as "l'allegranza" – "the glee" – or were flowers one, as "La violetta" – "the violet" – or indicated the holder's geographical origin.[8] It was normal to have the same war name used by many different soldiers belonging to the same company or squadron. The company roll then reported one by one each private's basic data: specialisation – fusileer, drummer, grenadier, fife, sapper, nurse – name, family name, war-

8 Apart from L'Allegranza (the Glee), other very used war names were, for instance: La Grandur (The Greatness), La Giunezza (The Youth), La Rigur (it can mean The Strictness, as well as The Accuracy), La Regiovisanta (The Rejoyssance), Sanfason – from French "sans façon" – (Easygoing), La Speranza (The Hope), Sant'Amor (Holy Love), Passepartout (in English it means the master key, but in French and in Piedmontese dialect it literally means "the one passing through everywhere"), or locations, as for instance could be Verceli (the city of Vercelli, indicating the origin of a private). Please note that the article too was written with an initial capital letter, for it was a full part of the war name. The latter being a personal choice, it was rather common to find many privates and corporals in the same company holding the same war-name. People using their family name as their war name seem not have exceeded 10 percent of the total. War names in Piedmontese armed forces were used until after the Napoleonic Era. For instance, when a Royal Sardinian Navy conscript in 1833–34, Giuseppe Garibaldi chose "Cleombroto" as his war name. Privates seem to have chosen their war name not only the first time they enlisted, but also when re-enlisting. The present author gained this impression from research on the 1774–1775 rolls of the La Marina Regiment. The privates had the normal variety of war names, but the corporals were listed only by their family name, or by war names other than those indicating a location. Now, a corporal was a private who served no less than 10 years, often no less than 12. The normal professional term did not exceed 8 years, thus a private had to re-enlist at least once before becoming a corporal. Thus, if the corporal served a first term as private, but no corporal held a location-related war name, being at least unlikely that corporals were appointed only among who had other than location-related war names, it is clear that the private could change or leave his war name at least every time he re-enlisted. The war names I found in use in 1774–75 rolls were the same used during the Spanish Succession, as proved by the list of the soldiers dead during the siege of Vercelli in 1704, reported by Giovanni Faldella in his *Gesta ed Eroi del tempo antico* (Turin, 1910), pp.82–84. Lastly: among Italian troopers at least until the last quarter of the twentieth century it was normal to address each other – especially if one did not remember or know the other's family name – using the respective city or region of origin, saying for instance: "Hey you, Sicily", or "Milan, come here".

name and age. Then the roll said if the soldier was completely illiterate or was able to read and to write, or to read only, when did he enlist the first time, if he had been in other corps, and how many times he had re-enlisted. Last, the roll said whether the soldier had a wife or not, and how many children, if any, and his wage: the longer the service, the higher the wage.

The colonel had also a staff, including himself, the captain-major,[9] the adjutant-major, the quartermaster, the surgeon-major, the chaplain, the drum-major, the sergeant-major, the corporal-major, and the sergeant-provost.

The adjutant-major was an officer and in fact the colonel's secretary. The quartermaster – usually a lieutenant – was responsible for regimental lodging, feeding and managing materials. The surgeon-major, the *chirurgo maggiore*, was the surgeon and usually had some nurses, called in Latin *fratres* – 'brothers' – helped by the bandsmen, because, as said, the bandsmen had to gather the wounded after the battle. The drum-major was the chief of the bandsmen, and he was especially important because the drummers rolled the signals during the day, and above all in battle. The sergeant-provost was the Regiment's constabulary, and his soldiers – the archers – were the regimental military police and executioners. The sergeant-major, who was considered an officer whose rank equalled that of the captain-major,[10] was the chief of the sergeants.

The corporal-major was the chief of the corporals, but was considered a corporal as all the others. Last, the staff could include also a carpenter and a *armaiuolo*, literally a gun-maker, who actually was a gun-repairer. He was always quite busy, because every Savoy's soldiers had firearms, whilst officers and sergeants still used sword, and, respectively, spontoon and halberd.

As all the Italian princes, the Duke of Savoy too kept foreign professional regiments in his pay, but this will be seen when speaking of the war. Besides, Swiss and German infantry units served practically under every colour in Italy from the sixteenth through to the eighteenth centuries.

II: Militia

As all the Italian States, the Duke of Savoy maintained local militias, which were employed as an additional military organisation to be called upon in case of war.

Militiamen were globally grouped into the so-called Battalion of Savoy and Battalion of Piedmont. Both the battalions could serve as reserve to the "order" Regiments, but could also develop local units – battalions or

9 Who successsively lost the command of a company and obtained that of the sole staff, which in Italian was and is called *Stato Maggiore*.

10 A comparison between the ransom to be paid for a sergeant major in 1690 and those for the comparable ranks in infantry and cavalry provides evidence that the rank of a sergeant major equalled that of infantry captains, for their ransom was far higher than a sergeant's, as shown in the *Traité d'échange, et rançons des prisonniers de guerre faits par les troupes de Sa Majesté Très-Chrétienne, et celles qui composent l'armée de S.A.R. monseigneur le Duc de Savoie, et de ses Alliés, tout en deçà que delà des monts*, in Solaro della Margarita, op. cit., vol. II, p.132 and following.

regiments – named after the city they came from. Militiamen generally had to drill once per season using their own firearms, and only when called they could be organised into infantry regiments. Militiamen had some benefits and privileges. Emmanuel Philibert granted some when he established the militia.

Until the previous war, militia had included both infantry and cavalry, but at the beginning of the Nine Years' War the Duke ordered the cavalry militia to be gathered into newly established cavalry regiments, and after the war so remained the situation, thus in 1701 militia included only infantry, normally grouped in battalions and regiments.

An exception was provided by the Protestant inhabitants of some Piedmontese valleys, the Waldensians, who composed relatively small and scattered bands, especially suitable for mountain warfare.

This system proved quite useful and effective in both Savoy and in Piedmont, from the Grand Alliance onwards, and now was going to be of basic importance in 1703 to relieve the territory from the French immediate threat

III: Cavalry

Cavalry in Europe was generally divided in light and heavy regiments, and dragoons. The latter were actually mounted infantry even if they were often employed as cavalry instead of infantry.

In Piedmont the cavalry included the *Guardie del Corpo*, literally "the bodyguards", that is to say the Duke's household, and two cavalry regiments – Savoia and Piemonte Reale – resulting from grouping during the Nine Years' War pre-existing Gendarmerie companies, and three dragoon regiments, known as the Red, the Green and the Yellow Dragoons, due to their uniforms: the Red Dragoons were actually His Royal Highness' Dragoons, and wore a red coat with blue cuffs. The dragoons of Genevois[11] – the County of Geneva, owned by the Dukes of Savoy before the Calvinist reformation – were originally dressed in green with red cuffs, whilst the dragoons of Piedmont originally had a yellow uniform with black cuffs, changed to a red coat and pearl-white cuffs by their new colonel in 1691. Cavalry regimental organisation was just like in the infantry with a few differences: trumpets instead of drums, brigadiers instead of sergeants, 'appointed', instead of corporals, swords and pistols instead of rifles, whilst the dragoons, being mounted infantry, had also grenadiers, drums, and hautbois instead of infantry fifes, which the cavalry did not. As said, after the previous war there was no more cavalry militia. Cavalry and dragoons were completely composed of standing regiments, and included both professionals and conscripts. The former could engage up to 10 or 12 years, the latter normally served from two up to four years, except in case of war. During the Spanish Succession crisis cavalrymen were retained

11 According to tradition, originally the regiment was raised by Giuseppe Maria Manfredo Scaglia Count di Verrua, who in 1689 levied a dragoon regiment of 400 men divided into eight companies, each 50 men strong.

in active duty up to seven years, only the time needed to defend Piedmont. The personnel were almost completely national, that is to say from the States of Savoy. Foreigners – which meant also Italians from other Italian States – could be admitted, not exceeding a five percent ratio. Wages were higher than in the infantry, and fees too were larger. A cavalryman received in theory 135 liras per year, but up to 36 were retained to pay for his equipment, and up to 54 to pay for his weapons and horse in case a change or a repair were needed. Thus in fact he received no less than 45 liras. But if he maintained his assets well clearly the fees were smaller, and he could get more than the 45 liras minimum. Dragoon wages were lower, only 117 liras per year, and were affected by the same fees. The Duke's Household – the Guardie del Corpo – was inserted into the cavalry, but its wages were higher, because its men were higher ranked. Each of them was a nobleman and hence in fact an officer, and their officer's rank was much higher than the similar rank in the cavalry or infantry.[12] Hence their wage was 376.10 liras for the Guards belonging to the 1st Company – the best qualified and skilled – and 335.8 for the Guards in the other three companies. Each company included 50–60 Guards.

Wages in cavalry were paid every 10 days, that is to say on the 1st, 11th and 21st each month. All the money was managed by the captain commanding the cavalry squadron, or the dragoon company, and that money was increased by a daily six soldi per horse average to pay for the horseshoes and the blacksmith. Squadrons and companies were eight to 10 per regiment, and each included 60–70 men.

IV: The Artillery, and the Engineer Corps

Soon after the end of the War of the League of Augsburg, the Sabaudian artillery was fully reorganised. Until 1696 it had been considered a civilian-composed corps under the control of military officers, as the Engineer Corps was. But on the day of Saint Stephen, 26 December 1696, the Duke told the Ufficio del Soldo – the Wage Bureau – what he had decided about the artillery and its wages,[13] and the artillery became a fully military corps. It received a staff, a gunner battalion composed of six bombers' companies, one miners' company, one Maestranze[14] company, and the "servants" in the places.[15] The battalion had a uniform, and was dressed completely in dark blue with golden

12 A household captain equalled a 1st Field Marshall, a lieutenant equalled a 1st Field Master, a hornet equalled a lieutenant colonel, cfr. also the Order issued on 18 June 1698, in AST, Sezione 1, Impieghi militari, mazzo 1, n.91.

13 *Stabilimento dell'Artiglieria e del Battaglione di Cannonieri, Maestranza e Minatori*, issued on 26 December 1696, rep. in Carlo Montù, *Storia dell'Artiglieria Italiana*, vol. 1 (Rome: 1934), pp.716–717.

14 In origin "Maestranza" meant the ensemble of the master craftsmen, that is to say the ensemble of the specialised workers who had proved their skill, thus had been declared "masters" of their art. Actually in subsequent times the term, which was officially used in the Piedmontese Army and then in the Italian Royal Army until World War I, was progressively used simply to mean "workers".

15 Although the term may appear odd and misleading, in Italian a servant was simply a man providing a manual service, thus the men attending the guns-related service, were – and still are

buttons and laces. It absorbed the pre-existing three separate artillery corps of Piedmont, Savoy and Nice. Thus in 1697 artillerymen were grouped into a regiment, included in the infantry. On the battlefield the artillery had still to be protected, following the French example, by the Fusileers Regiment, established on the eve of the previous war as a dedicated although separate unit.

The corps was still commanded by an artillery 'great master', who had under him the staff, the companies and the few artillery servants existing in 16 places.[16] The gunner companies were in six places.[17] The Maestranze and miner's companies – only 24 and 25 men strong, respectively – were in Turin.

Each company was commanded by a captain, supported by a second captain, and comprised by a lieutenant, an ensign, a sergeant, two corporals and 50 gunners, including a drummer. Each captain received 961 liras per year and a daily allowance of two bread rations. The second captain received 600 liras per year, the lieutenant 400, the ensign 350, the sergeant 300, a corporal 240 and the gunner 180 liras each, that is to say 10 soldi per day, reduced to 7.5 "after taxes", whilst the soldiers of the Maestranza, being more specialised, got 15 soldi per day, reduced to 12.5 after taxes.

The artillery staff included the 'great master', who received 7,000 liras per year; three lieutenants, who in fact were lieutenant colonels, two being paid 1,550 and the third 2,000 liras per year; a general intendant and controller, 1,500 per year; a major, 1,152 per year; and 12 other people in charge of technical or administrative tasks. Overall in 1697 the corps included only 452 men and needed 123,477 liras for wages and bread allowance, but it was very expensive, so the following year each gunner company was reduced to 40 gunners. In 1699 a further reduction to 28 was decided on, but probably not made.

In 1700 a further change was made. The wages increased: the "great master" was raised to 10,000 liras per year, and the "lieutenant" just under him in the staff was converted into "colonel", with a 3,006 liras yearly wage. Now the staff included new features, as a major, an adjutant-major, a surgeon-major, and a chaplain; but the most important change was the bombers' company, differing from the gunners, for the bombers were specialists of bombs and grenades, and were paid as much as the miners and the Maestranze, that is to say 30 percent more than gunners.[18]

Engineers in fact depended on the artillery, even if they were no longer listed with them. All the artillery officers, as well as those of the Engineer

---

in the Italian artillery – "Serventi", whose best translation in English is "servant", or in this case, "servers".

16 Places having artillery personnel were: Turin, the citadel of Turin, Verrua, Ivrea, Susa, Vercelli, Asti, Cuneo, Mondovì, Demonte, Fosse di Ceva, Castle of Nice, city of Nice, castle of Villafranca, the Holy Hospice of Villafranca (which was a fortress), and Montmélian.

17 The 1st company was in the city of Turin, the 2nd company in the citadel of Turin, the 3rd company in Vercelli, the 4th in Cuneo, the 5th in Nice, the 6th in Montmélian.

18 *Paghe dell'artiglieria*, handwritten copy in Archivio Ufficio Storico Sato Maggiore Esercito [Archive of the Historical Bureau of the Army Staff] (henceforth AUSSME), L 3, XI, *Stati italiani preunitari, Regno di Piemonte e Sardegna*, Studi particolari, cartella 6, ex original in AST [Turin State Archive], Ms. 129.

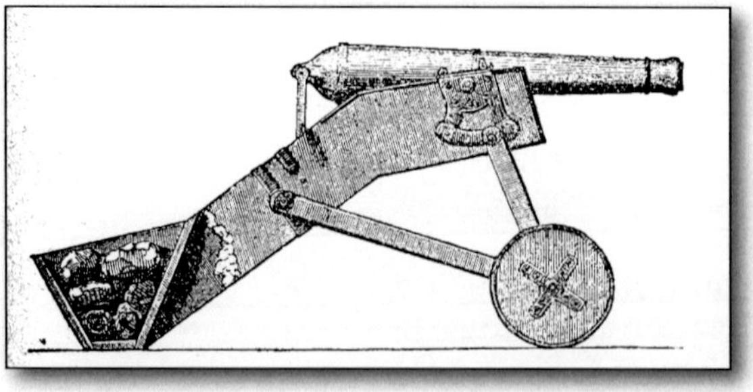

Light Mountain Cannon of the Piedmontese Infantry.

Corps, could get their commission through an exam, no matter whether they had been educatd and trained in the Royal Academy, established in 1667, or not.

The artillery and ordnance administration was under the responsibility of the Artillery Council, chaired by the "great master", and including the three colonels, the artillery superintendent, the artillery controller, the treasurer, and the secretary, This composition changed many times during the war, until 1711, when the Artillery Administration was established.

The Council was responsible of the whole artillery administration, from the provision of wood – normally elm, to be used for gun carriages – and saltpetre, to be collected also in the interior of private houses, to the payment for lost cannonballs that people retraced in the fields and gave back.

The artillery's needs determined a major change in the Piedmontese army, as elsewhere, due to the increasing need of gunpowder, balls, and related materials and tools. Cannons and mortars in ducal fortresses were 449 in 1667, and a bit more in 1690. Standards, as said previously, were a dream. During the Spanish Succession crisis the Piedmontese artillery had 13 types of guns, divided into "mortars" and 12 kinds of cannon. The former included six different calibres, the latter 39, totalling 45 different calibres for the whole Piedmontese artillery.[19]

The increasing use of firearms – as said, Savoy's army was among the first, if not the first, to provide its soldiers exclusively with firearms – included an equally increasing need for transport. Artillery and its ammunition needed carriages and horses. Year after year, logistics became a growing concern, and supply, march and communication routes became more important too.

19 This is the list of the kind of guns existing in Turin in 1706, but we cannot take it as comprehensive, for we are not sure of what could have existed in other fortresses before or after the 1706 siege. As all armies, Piedmontese artillery used whatever it could find, no matter where it was from. This was normally done by every army in Europe, and that is why one finds cannons made in Italy in the seventeenth or eighteenth century not only in Europe, but in North Africa, the Middle East and South America too, where some seventeenth-century Italian-made cannons are in Rio de Janeiro. Anyway, as said, Piedmont had mortars and cannons. Cannons were divided into: sagri, quarters of cannon, half-cannons, colubrines, cannons, cannons Curtò, newly invented cannons, disassemblable cannons, falcons, falconets, smerigli, and the small metallic guns called "organs". Their calibres were listed according to the weight in pounds of the fired ball, and were: sagri, 4 pounds, 4.5 pounds, 5.5 pounds, 6 pounds, 8 pounds, 9 pounds, 10 pounds; quarters of cannon: 11 pounds, 14, 15, 16 and 18 pounds; half-cannons: 21, 30, 32 and 35 pounds; colubrines: 38 pounds; cannons: 40, 50, 55, and 60 pounds; cannons curtò: 4, 11, 16, 20 and 45 pounds; newly invented cannons: 4 and 6 pounds; dissasemblable cannons: 12 pounds, falcons: 2, 2.5, 3, and 3.5 pounds; falconets: 1 and 1.5 pounds; smerigli: 6, 9 and 10 pound. The calibre of the "organs" is not known, but they were small guns. Mortar calibres were in inches and the different calibres of the Piedmontese mortars were 6, 8, 9, 12, 14, and 18 inches. The curtò cannons were the guns called "cortana" – which we could render as "shortened" – in Medieval Italian artillery and can roughly be considered as howitzers, for they fired straight forward at short range.

6

Piedmontese Logistics[1]

As in the rest of Europe, operations in Italy began in early spring. Major operations were routinely conducted during summer and first months of autumn, generally until the end of October. Armies entered winter quarters in November as bad weather and mud caused by rain and snow made routes impracticable and often impassable, especially to heavy carts.

The consequence could be a reduction, if not an interruption in supplying and each army halted operations until the following spring. Only limited operations made mostly by cavalry or, rarely, by some infantry companies, were carried out for purposes of foraging or reconnaissance. Foraging, that is to say supply on the field, was vital for every army.

More than the previous War of the Grand Alliance, the War of the Spanish Succession marked the culmination of a surge in the size of the armies, and this was especially right for Victor Amadeus' army. His father's army had been small. Its aims were those of a small client state enchained between two powerful neighbours, and watched by one of them from inside.

For an entire generation, nobody thought seriously of a war against France. One could think of waging some operations against the Spaniards in Milan, but, of course, with substantial French help, or, as happened during Charles Emanuel II's reign, against a small enemy such as the Republic of Genoa, but France was completely another issue. When that issue became real between 1690 and 1696, Piedmontese logistics were tested and proved sound.

European standing armies had been relatively static in numbers, between 20,000 and 50,000 since the eve of the seventeenth century, even if sometimes, exceptionally, in Italy they could rise to bigger numbers, as it happened in 1629, when 100,000 men gathered around Mantua, or in the 1640s during the Castro War between the Pope, on one side, and Venice, Modena Tuscany and Parma on the other.

Louis XIV's standing army was credited to be 200,000 strong. Nobody opposed it, or, rather, succeeded in opposing it, but now, since 1701, all the German States, no matter how small they could be, gave the Emperor money

1 The reader should be aware that this chapter – and this is the last – was already published, with some changes, in the author's *William III's Italian Ally*, published by Helion & Company in February 2019.

and men, as Britain, and the Netherlands, and also Spain did, and suddenly the armies on the field once more rose in size, and easily reached a 100,000-man force.

All these king's horses and all these king's men had to be dressed, be paid and be fed. The supply of these unexpectedly big armies by pre-industrial states caused real troubles. Provisioning had been a major concern of warfare, but now it became the major concern. Provisioning needed money, a lot of money, and now it needed much more money than in the past, and not that many states had it.

Leaving aside the general European situation, the Duke of Savoy had a problem. No matter against whom he had to hold, he needed money to do so, and money could be found, somehow. But, as the previous war proved, he needed also men, many men.

His military organisation in theory could allow him to field a consistent army, just calling the militia to arms. But there was a direct ratio between military and civil manpower he had to respect. The former could not exceed two percent of the latter, otherwise the lack of manpower would affect agriculture. In a pre-industrial age, the harvest depended on the weather and on the number of workers. You could have the best possible weather, the weather of your dreams, but if manpower was lacking, nobody worked the ground, and the result was no harvest, thus no food.

The Dukes of Savoy, and later their descendants, the kings of Sardinia, knew that in case of emergency they could call every man to arms, but they knew very well that this meant to win the war within a campaign, or to starve in the following year, hence they never declared a general levy.

What to do? Luckily for Victor Amadeus, at the eve of the war the fighting occurred in eastern Lombardy, where the Sabaudian army committed an expeditionary force as part of the Spanish-French-Sabaudian Army. Thus Piedmont was safe, did not need too many troopers, and the standing army was enough. When in September 1703 the situation changed, and Victor Amadeus was attacked by the French before he could change alliance, his army suddenly faced a dramatic lack of well-trained professionals, thus he needed men, no matter they were from, and money to pay and feed them.

As in 1690, also now, and since 1701, Victor Amadeus was considered a key ally by William III. In William's mind, Piedmont had to be secured first, and then had to be used as the base for attacking southern France just as happened in 1692. William of Orange was too experienced a soldier to believe that such an action could solve the war. Everybody knew that the Spaniards invaded Provence from Italy in the sixteenth century and it did not work. Paris was too far, and Provence too wide to be permanently occupied, but, as in 1692, such an invasion would attract French troops from Flanders: an important result for the Allied armies there. Hence, Savoy had to be supported in men and money. When William died, his strategic vision was kept alive by Marlborough and the Dutch Grand Pensionary Heinsius, so, after autumn 1703, Victor Amadeus once again received money and infantry units directly funded by England.

Baroque era armies were composed of professionals, hence they were quite expensive and hard to keep. As said, a 15,000-man army was decent, a

Antonie Heinsius, Grand Pensioner of the Republic of the United Provinces.

25,000 one threatening, a 60,000 one enormous and a 200,000 one – the maximum reached by Louis XIV's France – hard if not impossible to be equalled, won and paid, in the literal sense of the word. Victor Amadeus' problem was how to get a credible military result having only the money he had, or could be given.

Resource optimisation was the first step. Since 1688 he concentrated military administration into the *Contadoria Generale* – General Accountancy – and in 1692, appointed a first secretary of war, who was responsible for general affairs, personnel and transmitting orders.

In order not to waste money, Victor Amadeus had to see how much he spent for every soldier in terms of weapons, clothes, lodging, wage, equipment, recruitment, drilling, ordnance, general logistics and general administration. Hence he started from wages and regulated them differently,[2] depending on when they were paid, and on the rank of the man. It was during the War of the League of Augsburg that the ducal administration made comparisons between the food prices in different parts of the Duchy,[3] and between different cities, just to discover how much did troops' staying cost. As a consequence it was decided how much every Common had to pay in case soldiers were lodged within its limits.[4] Clearly all the commons complained, especially if they suffered due to the war.[5]

Gathering all the available data, facts and figures, the Duchy produced a scheme showing that the annual cost of an infantry company[6] composed of three officers and 50 men equalled the cost of an artillery company, composed of 35 men, or of half a cavalry squadron three officers and 32 cavalrymen

2 See for example AUSSME the *Paghe dell'artiglieria dal marzo 1699* [wages of the artillery from March 1699] ms., copy ex AST, Ms. 129; then the *Paghe e spettanze dell'artiglieria*, del 1708, ms. in AUSSME, L 3, XI, *Stati italiani preunitari, Regno di Piemonte e Sardegna*, Studi particolari, cartella 6; *Paghe e spettanze di pace e di guerra*, del 1701–1713, in AUSSME, L 3, VIII, *Stati italiani preunitari, Regno di Piemonte e Sardegna*, Studi particolari, cartella 8: *Parallele de la paye en temps de paix et de guerre*, ms AUSSME, ex A.S.T. – Ufficio del Soldo, 1701–1713.

3 For example the *Raffronto fra i prezzi delle derrate ad Aosta e a Torino – Tassa del prezzo delle Vettovaglie che si vendono nella valle d'Aosta*, del 1691 [comparison between the prices of foods in Aosta and Turin – tax of the price of the foods sold in Aosta Valley, of 1691] ms. in AUSSME, L 3, 11, *Stati Preunitari – Piemonte*, cartella 7, number 4, showing that the same quantities of the same foods were cheaper in the Valley than in the city of Turin.

4 For example the manifesto issued on 21 November 1691, starting with "The continuation of the war brings with itself the need for supplying the Troops in Winter", signed by Victor Amadeus II, Bellegarde, Granerij, and Marelli, printed in Turin, by Antonio Valletta H.R.H.'s and the Most Excellent Chamber's printer, 1691.

5 For instance the *Rimostranze della Città di Vercelli con sue risposte, toccante il quartier d'Inverno del 1695* [Remonstrations of the city of Vercelli with its answers, concerning the 1695 winter quarter] ms, in AST, *Imprese Militari*, Mazzo 8 d'addizione.

6 All included, a company needed a standard of 9,400 liras of Piedmont per year.

strong. Hence, the administration knew that a cavalryman's or a dragoon's cost was as much as 4.2 foot soldiers, or 2.1 artillerymen, and, knowing how much money was available, it was easy to know how many infantry, dragoons and artillery companies, and how many cavalry squadrons one could field keeping a certain ratio among them.

As last, Victor Amadeus kept the *deconto* – "detraction" – that is to say the money the administration retained: 20 percent from each soldier's wage to pay his uniform, ordnance and equipment, according to an old decree issued by Emmanuel Philibert, who, when speaking about soldiers who enrolled and did not own weapons, had said: "…we shall provide to those who will not have weapons, with a two-year time for paying them, and they must not miss it, for that is our mind."[7]

Wages – more or less five soldi per day[8] per foot soldier, plus a daily bread allowance of 24 pounds in peacetime[9] – were paid every five or every 10 days.[10] There was a further 20 percent deduction by the captain commanding the company, to pay for the goods whose distribution he was responsible for. Hence only three out of five soldi per day were received by the private. On the other hand, this money was traditionally increased by some fringe benefits, and, in wartime, by additional assets and food, such as meat and wine, and the Duke carefully regulated them too,[11] as well as he thoroughly considered transport.[12]

Armies spent most of their time in camp. In Piedmont, "to camp" often meant to be in a fortress, a town, sometimes in a city. The armies encamped only in case of an expedition further than the standard marching range from their departure base.

As said, during the Baroque era few camps were more than 12 to 16 kilometres – or seven to 10 miles – apart, because this was the most that

7 Rep. in Edoardo Scala, "Intendenti, commissari ed amministratori egli eserciti sabaudi", in Edoardo Scala, *La guerra del 1866 e altri scritti* (Rome, 1981), p.23.

8 As said before, a soldo was 1/20 of a lira, thus it equalled less than an English penny: 0.7 penny, that is to say less than three farthings. The soldi were minted using a silver-copper alloy, and were equal to 12 denari. The denari were made of copper alone and one needed 240 denari to get a lira.

9 See *Parallele de la Paye en temps de paix et de guerre – Infanterie – Ordonnance* [comparison of the wage in peacetime and wartime] in AST, *Materie Militari*, Ufficio del Soldo, mazzo 3. The private received four soldi and eight per day in peacetime and a bit more than eight soldi per day in wartime.

10 This timing passed into the Royal Italian Army, no matter if the wage was paid by the army, instead of the captain. It was used for a long time during the twentieth century too, and was called "cinquina", substituted sometimes by the payment every ten days, which was known as "decade".

11 See the *Regolamento delle piazze di Quartiere d'inverno, di quali gioiscono gli Uffiziali di fanteria regolati a ss 10 caduna ed a R 1 di fieno caduna il giorno, come anche del contante che godono li Bass'Uffiziali e soldati come infra*, [Rule of the places of winter quarter, enjoyed by the infantry officers regulated by soldi 10 each and by 1 rubbi of hay each per day, as well as of the cash enjoyed by the Deputy Officers and soldiers as – (it is said) – inside,] issued on 12 December 1701 and the *Regolamento stabilito da S.A.R. per le tappe*, issued on 3 August 1700, handwritten copy in AUSSME, L 3, VIII, *Stati italiani preunitari, Regno di Piemonte e Sardegna*, Studi particolari, cartella 8.

12 Cfr. the manuscript, *Treno di provianda: schema cronologico dei provvedimenti presi*, [Supply train, chronological scheme of the rules decided] in AUSSME, L 3, VIII, *Stati italiani preunitari, Regno di Piemonte e Sardegna*, Studi particolari, cartella 8.

an army could comfortably travel in daylight, even if there is evidence that in Italy this rule had very often remarkable exceptions. Anyway the Piedmontese army relied on an effective system established long ago. In 1591 Victor Amadeus' great-grandfather, Duke Charles Emmanuel I, issued a decree[13] and organised the marches. The standard *tappa* – "the trip" – was, by decree, 10 miles long, no more and no less. The common – the town – had to provide men, animals and four wagons to each company of the incoming troops when they entered the common's limits, until they left it. Colonels and soldiers were strictly prevented from keeping animals and carts after 10 miles, the former under penalty of "losing our favour", the latter under penalty of "three rope-tractions", or, as it was said in England at that time using a Spanish word: *strappados*.[14]

The common was repaid by the ducal administration, according to the season and the kind of animals used. When no agricultural work was in progress, that is to say from 1 December until the end of February, the owners received "four florins and half for each wagon with two oxen every 10 miles, during the whole other time seven florins and, where there will be four oxen, one third more."[15]

The 1591 rule and the others issued by Charles Emanuel I were still used when Victor Amadeus became duke, and had no substantial change all along neither his reign nor the first part of his son's, that is to say until the 1730s.

Actually the *Ordine delli 13 agosto 1620* – "Order of 13 August 1620" – by Charles Emanuel I confirmed the existing rules, simply reducing to only one per company the number of wagons to be used to carry sick and wounded.

On 18 February 1622 another order by Charles Emmanuel had divided Piedmont – "the whole State on this side of the mountains" – into 12 trips,[16] that to them meant provinces, declaring that all the troops' baggage and whatever military load had to be equally shared among the commons of the provinces according to the rules.[17] Lastly, in 1651 an additional rule ordered

---

13 *Stabilimento delle Truppe, passaggi & Alloggiamenti, Ordine del 23 novembre 1591*, [Establishing of the Troops: passages and Lodgings. Order on 23 November 1591] in AST, *Materie Militari*, Ordini e Regolamenti, Mazzo 2, *Ricavo d'ordini Militari per il buon regolamento delle Truppe de'duchi di Savoia dal 1591 al 1682* [List of military orders for the good rule of the Troops of the dukes of Savoy from 1591 until 1682].

14 The Italian term is "tratti di corda" – rope-tractions – the well known torture. a man whose hands were tied behind his back was lifted by a rope linked to the hands, thus dislocating his shoulders. it was not deadly, but very painful. The word "strappado", clearly from Spanish, is provided as the translation in English – thus it was currently used in that time English – by the first Italian/English dictionary – *Dizionario delle lingue italiana ed inglese di Giuseppe Baretti, al quale è preposta una grammatica delle due lingue/A Dictionary of the English and Italian Languages by Joseph Baretti, to which is prefixed an Italian and English Grammar*, whose "*new edition corrected and improved by F. Damiani*", published in London in 1798.

15 *Idem.*

16 Actually the word used was "tappa", whose translation is "staging point", but, as we shall see, the word "tappa" in fact meant – and still means also – the trip to be made from a staging point to the next, that is why the word "trip" seems more appropriate.

17 *Ordine del sud. Duca per cui ripartisce tutto lo Stato di qua da Monti in 12 Tappe, o sia Provincie; con dichiarazione che tutte le Moggiate della Soldatesca, ed ogni altro Carico Militare si debba frà tutte le terre d'esse Provincie ripartire egualmente, nel modo, e sotto le regole ivi espresse* [Order of the aforesaid Duke for he shares all the State on this side of the Mounts in 12 Trips, that is to say Provinces, with a declaration that all the Burdens of the Troop and every other military load

the commons to provide to the general ammunitioner with as many carts and wagons as might be needed each time.[18]

This was valid only for a company's baggage, but in the case of war the army needed much more, and the state found one, or more, civil firms providing animals, wagons and coaches and guaranteeing their activity to be continued also across the border, that is to say where subject commons did not exist.

March routes in Piedmont had been quite well known for a couple of centuries, due to the long war periods between 1534 and 1544, again from 1592 until 1601, and last from 1613 to 1656, and from 1690 to 1696.

Especially after the last war, every road, every bridge, every ford was in the officers' and soldiers' minds, as well as how many houses every village and every town had, and how much food, and which commodities could be offered. So marching in Piedmont was rather a simple affair, except for the threat provided by the enemy.

Just before the crisis of the Spanish Succession, Victor Amadeus made some changes in logistics. On 3 August 1700, he issued the new rules about the tappe – the trips. He confirmed that the wagons had to be provided by the communities, but added details about lodging. The commons had to prepare a housing list, according to the room available in each house. The list had to be given to the war commissioners, who, as soon as the troops arrived, distributed the troopers in the houses accordingly. The war commissioners had to pay to the landlords an indemnity for the lodging provided. It ranged from one lira of Piedmont per day – lodging the colonel commanding the Regiment of the Guards, or a colonel commanding a cavalry regiment – down to 10 denari per day for each private.[19] In case the town could not host all the soldiers, a camp had to be organised on the outskirts. No private was allowed to go further than a rifle shot from the camp, or from the town, and the corps commander had to mark that range clearly. Military personnel were forbidden to take or damage fruits, or vegetables, or animals, or any other private property, and had to pay for whatever they wanted to take.[20] This was because, whilst in a town, the military personnel had to live on their own money, thus the commoners had to sell them all they needed at a price not exceeding the price on the day before their arrival.

Before leaving, the corps had to purchase bread, no less than a four-day allowance. If the march was supposed to last more than four days, they

must be equally shared among all the Lands of those Provinces, in the way and under the rules there said], in AST, *Materie Militari*, Ordini e Regolamenti, Mazzo 2, n. 15.

18 *Obbligo alle Comunità di provvedere li carriaggi al Munitionero generale* [Enforcement to the communities to provide carts to the General Ammunitioner] on 17 July 1651, in AST, *Materie Militari*, Ordini e Regolamenti, Mazzo 2, n. 22, *Ordini Militari dell'A.R. di Carlo Emanuele II dall'anno 1648 à l'anno 1674*, folio 17.

19 The commissioners paid 15 soldi per day for a cavalry lieutenant colonel, for the lieutenant colonel of the Guard or for an infantry colonel, 10 soldi for an infantry lieutenant colonel, seven for every cavalry major or captain, as well as for the same rank of the Guards, five for each infantry major or captain, three soldi for every lieutenant or ensign, no matter his corps.

20 *Regolamento stabilito da S.A.R. per le tappe* [Rule established by His Royal Highness for the trips] on 3 August 1700, handwritten copy in AUSSME L 3, VIII, *Stati italiani preunitari, Regno di Piemonte e Sardegna*, Studi particolari, cartella 8.

could take more bread, or the commissioners could arrange a further four-day bread provision somewhere along the route. Again, the price had to not exceed the price paid on the day before the arrival of the troopers.

How did Piedmontese logistic organisation work before Victor Amadeus, and, above all, how did its transport system work? Quite well, indeed.

Contemporary reports and thus successive accounts normally do not speak of transport, or make just a quick mention, but the recent War of the League of Augsburg provides evidence.

When in 1692 the Allied army crossed the Alps and raided France, the logistics systems proved quite good. They worked well, fast and safely, and allowed good power projection and sustainability. Thus, after such a recent experience, there is no doubt that it could work at its best also during the Spanish succession crisis. Was it so? Presumably yes, at least as far as we know.

The Piedmontese army followed the French system, which included up to three carts and up to 40 pack animals available to each general and colonel. Several pack animals and two four-horse carts for the *vivandiere*, the food provider, of each infantry battalion and, ultimately, according to fairly reliable calculations, one could get to 1,000 wagons and some thousands of mules for an army of 50 battalions and 50 squadrons, that is to say for an army composed of about 25,000 foot and 2,500 cavalry. The whole organisation was called by the French a "train", which in Italian was rendered with the phonetic spelling of *trèn*, hence the word *treno* simply meant and still means "train".

The transport system had to supply both ordnance – weapons, gunpowder and ammunition – and food supplies. The Piedmontese private of the Spanish Succession period received a two pound, equal to 738 grammes, daily ration of wheat bread and rye; a pound – that is 369 grammes – of meat, and a pint and a half – two litres and five centilitres – of wine.

The horses had to get not less than one *rubbo* – equal to 9.2 kilogrammes – of hay, and a measure – two litres and 87 – of oats a day, or, alternatively, two measures, that is five litres, and 74 of *biada*, a dry fodder mixture composed of oats, rye, barley, farro, broad beans, and vetch.[21]

It must be said that the rations did not always reach their destination, so the soldiers provided by themselves, requisitioning, that is to say often robbing the peasants. Apart from such, not a small detail, the general intendant of the army, as during the previous war, had to feed and supply about 20,000 men including foot, cavalry, artillerymen and sappers belonging to the field army and to the garrisons, no matter whether national or foreign professionals, and at least 10,000 horses. It meant preparing every day the movement of over 90 tons of hay, 28 tons of oats, seven and a half tons of bread, three or four of meat and more than 40 tons of wine, that is, as we shall see, about 160 tons of food, because the animals were moved to the troops and slaughtered

21 Biada is a dry fodder mixture composed of oats, rye, barley, farro, broad beans and vetch. This can't be properly translated into English. According to the first Italian/English dictionary, the already quoted *Dizionario delle lingue italiana ed inglese di Giuseppe Baretti/A Dictionary of the English and Italian Languages by Joseph Baretti,* (London: 1798) I used, the contemporary translations of Biada – see op. cit., volume I, ad vocem – were "*corn*", or "*standing corn*", or "*any corn reaped except wheat*", and also "*oats, a kind of corn*", thus I left the original Italian word.

on the spot. Then, tons of gunpowder and ammunition had to be carried in variable quantities, according to operational needs.

As we said when speaking of logistics in general, the average of a contemporary wagon was between half a ton and a maximum of 800 kilogrammes. Thus daily supply of only the troopers would have required at least 200 wagons, if not 300.

But such a calculation however had several variables: the bread was not distributed every day, but usually every four, so the tons to be transported went up to 30, but to be moved only every four days. On the other hand it was necessary to transport flour and yeast to the ovens, where the *Munizionieri* – ammunitioneers,[22] that is to say the supply corps, composed of civilians – were preparing the bread. When baked, the bread was loaded onto the *provianda* – provision[23] – carts attached to the convoys of the ammunitions, or the artillery train. But even so, one cannot even make a calculation, because, in order to simplify and speed up the distribution, in May 1692 a bread-baking test was made using experimental mobile ovens. Their baked bread resulted in loaves as good as the usual ones, and Victor Amadeus ordered the army to go forward with that new system, hence there was a substantial reduction of carts used for bread.

This is a general overview, but what about the Spanish succession war? From a logistical point of view, Piedmontese participation in that war must be divided into three parts, each presenting a different operational and logistical situation. In the first period, from the beginning of the war until autumn 1703, the army of Savoy was included in the Bourbon one and – as far as one can implicitly realise after the alliance treaty – shared the French logistics system, relying on supplies and food purchased in Lombardy.

Then, from September 1703 until September 1706 all the operations occurred in Piedmont and the army faced a terrible period, mostly defending fortresses one by one, thus the logistical problems were relatively easy in term of distance between the troops and their supply bases, but very hard in terms of money, men and assets to be gathered and distributed.

During the third period, from September 1706 until the end of the war, operations were relatively scarce, with only three power projections across the Alps presenting some sustainability problems. The first, against Toulon in 1707, was supported by the Anglo-Dutch fleet. The second, in 1708, across the Alps to Savoy, saw a major commitment mainly supported by purposely

22 The Italian verb "munire", from which the Italian word "munizioni" and the English word "ammunition" come, means simply "to furnish", "to provide", and hence also "to fortify" or "to protect". When speaking of supplies, at that time it meant "to furnish", and the "munizionieri" were not the people dealing with ordnance or fortifications, but just and only the furnisher of the food. That is why the bread they baked was officially called "Pane di munizione", that is to say ammunition bread. Such a martial sounding couple of words meant simply "the furnished bread", that is to say the bread furnished by the military administration to the soldiers. Being cartridges and balls furnished by the administration, they too were called ammunitions. The difference was marked by an additional word: munizioni da guerra – war ammunitions – meant cartridge and balls, munizioni da bocca – mouth ammunitions – meant food.

23 Provianda is a Latin verbal form meaning "the things to be furnished" or "the things to be provided", so the convoys of the "treno di provianda" were those of "the train of the things to be furnished."

established magazines and mules convoys. The third, toward Lyon, supported in the same way, was small, short, and had no result.

How many animals were needed? Generally speaking, the ratio between men and horses – or horses, oxen and mules – according to French general Puységur,[24] had to be estimated at two horses every three men, thus had Victor Amadeus fielded a 24,000-man army, he needed 16,000 animals to properly support it, cavalry horses included. Although, this 16,000 figure for animals needing hay and fodder rations is completely theoretical and is probably excessive for Piedmont.

Before discussing how and if Puységur's statement can be applied to Piedmont. we must stress some other points. One is that the number of animals was dictated by how much load had to be moved overall, and what portion of that overall load each animal could move.

The load depended on the need, and the need was dictated by the situation. In fact we have to add to the number of the war horses owned by cavalry and dragoons, and of the horses and oxen belonging to artillery, and to the *provianda* trains, also the animals used by the infantry, whose regiments had to get fodder and hay rations for the horses of their officers, ranging from 12 rations for the horses of the colonel commander of the Guards, to the single ration of the ensign.[25] That was still not that much, if one thinks that the colonel commanding His Royal Highness' Dragoons received 20 fodder or hay rations per day. Moreover, even if we want to consider annual budgets, we could not trust the calculations, due to the significant and sudden variations in strength of men and animals. A battle could easily cause a 25 percent reduction of the fighting force and the loss of up to the whole train, as seems to have happened to the French out of Turin in 1706.

A further complication comes from the existing sources, because those related to the Piedmontese logistics during the Spanish succession crisis are not so well known, yet. So, we can get an idea looking at what happened 40 years later to the same army, when it committed the same number of men, and the same assets, in the same war theatres. For instance, when in early 1747 the Piedmontese ermy enhanced the Treno di Provianda for the incoming campaign, the military administration asked for different kinds of mules. Each mule, depending on its size, could carry from 11 to 16 "rubbi", that is to say, being a "rubbio" equal to 9.22 kilogrammes, from 110 up to 147 kilogrammes each. This means that, once the overall payload was stated, the number of committed animals depended on how much load could be carried by each of them. If one had to move, let us say, 150 metric tons, he needed 102 mules if they could carry 147 kilogrammes each, but he needed 136 if

24 Jacques François de Chastenet de Puységur, *L'Art de la Guerre par principes et par règles,* 2 vols (Paris: 1749), vol. 1, p.64. Louis XIV considered Puységur, who served from 1673 until his death in 1743, as his best expert of logistics, thus appointed him "maréchal-général des logis des camps et armées du roi" – general marshal of the lodgements and camps of the King's armies – and regularly consulted him about those issues. During the Spanish Succession crisis Puységur, now a general, commanded mostly in Spain and Flanders. He died in 1743 and his work was published six years later by his son.

25 The ensign was an officer whose rank was just below the second lieutenant. He was the regimental colour bearer.

they could carry only 110 kilogrammes. But 136 mules ate more fodder than 102, roughly 30 percent more, and needed more men to drive them, thus the quantity of daily needed fodder increased, as did the number of carts and animals to carry it.

Now let us see on which ground that payload had to be moved. A mule could carry a half, or also only a third of the load draught by a horse; but the mules suited better to mountains, where wagons could hardly move, or not move at all, whilst the horses could be used at their best on the flat roads of the plain. But the number of the committed animals depended also, if not entirely, on what the army could find. If there were not enough horses, the existing ones had to be left to the cavalry, using mules and oxen for transports, no matter the ground. This could make a big difference in both the movable payload, the timing, and the global fodder consumption, the latter being dictated by the consumption per animal.

Generally speaking, figures tell us that usually the Piedmontese army seems to have relied on the payload of a mule every 10 men. Considering that every column had to bring a four-day supply, that a mule could carry at least 110 kilogrammes, we should assume a 2.5 kilogrammes per day standard supply per man, which is practically the private's daily allowance. Seeing that in 1709 Victor Amadeus led across the Alps a 30,000 men expeditionary force supported by a 3,000-mule convoy, we can conclude the one mule to 10 men ratio to be correct.

But these figures concerned the sole Treno di provianda, and did not include neither the regimental wagons, carts and animals, nor the cavalry's and dragoons' horses, and those belonging to the artillery and infantry. We have an animals/men ratio in infantry differing from cavalry or artillery. The former had two-horse wagons and a horse per officer from the rank of captain up. Both the latter had in fact a horse per man, when considering personal horses, artillery train and wagon train. Now, artillery and cavalry counted for a 10 percent of the overall fighting force, so, unless further evidence arises provided by specific documents, we could conclude that a 24,000 men Piedmontese army needed no less than 6,000 and up to 10,000 animals, all included, and that Puységur's figure probably cannot be applied neither to the Piedmontese army, nor to most of her battlegrounds.

7

1701: Eugene Comes to Italy

I: The Early French Grand Strategy, and the Italian War Theatre

In the Spring 1701, an Imperial army commanded by Prince Eugene of Savoy moved into northern Italy, while a second army formed in Germany.

The army committed to Italy was the strongest organised by Emperor Leopold, for he had no feudal claim on German territories, but had many in Italy, including Milan.

As said, Leopold had merely 42,000 men, and committed no more than 30,000 to Italy, whilst Louis XIV could deploy no less than 75,000 men there. Despite possessing numerical superiority the French maintained a defensive attitude, mostly because at the eve of the war they had to face some logistical problems, and because no French marshal or general could do more than what was explicitly allowed by Versailles, and Versailles wanted no offensive.

Emperor Leopold I in 1701.

In 1701 and 1702 French strategy did not change. French forces in Italy remained on defence, and simply reacted against Eugene's attempts to reach Milan. As we shall see, they were always defeated on a tactical level, but succeeded in preventing the Austrians to reach Milan.

The difference between the current and past wars was France's allies. Two former enemies, Bavaria and Piedmont, allied with France during the War of the Spanish Succession. This meant that it was possible not only to cross the Rhine, but also to rush across the Bavarian Plateau to Vienna thanks to the friendly attitude of Max Emanuel of Bavaria.

The situation in Italy was similar. The French did not like the idea of fighting, for they supposed to have not enough men and assets in Italy to successfully deter the Austrians. Anyway there was an old rule, demonstrated as valid since the early sixteenth century: an allied Piedmont meant a safe passage through the Alps and a safe supply line to the French army in Italy.

II: Pre-war Manoeuvres

In the last days of December 1700 the Prince de Vaudémont gathered the top ranks of the Duchy of Milan to assess what to do with the French troops: had they to be admitted in Milan or not? The general answer was yes. All the generals in Spanish service in Milan but one underlined that the Milanese army was too weak. A French support could be used to strengthen the Duchy, convince the Italian Princes to support the Bourbon side, and deter the expected Austrian invasion. All the military and civil top officers agreed to enhance the army and give Vaudémont the full power to negotiate with Tessé.

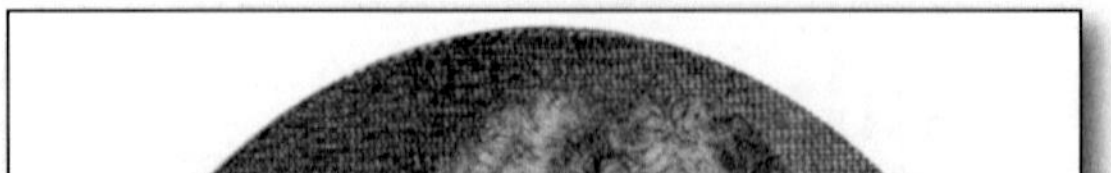
René Froulay, Comte de Tessé.

The result was the entrance of the French army into the Duchy, and the landing of a further 12 French battalions in Finale, whilst the Milanese army prepared the artillery train, a pontoon bridge train, filled the gaps in the existing infantry companies and enrolled seven more companies of foot.

Anyway the French had a problem. The intervention in Italy had been decided so suddenly that their first expeditionary corps, composed of 17 infantry battalions and two cavalry regiments, arrived in Italy without tents; the war minister, Barbezieux, had to tell Tessé to purchase them in Lombardy, for only the subsequent troops – 23 battalions and 56 squadrons – would come with their full equipment.[1] The wagons too, to be used for food and ordnance, had to be asked of Vaudémont, and the French general commissioner committed to Italy was leaving with exchange letters for 100,000 écus, to be followed by further 400–500,000 francs.[2] Incidentally, Vaudémont had told the French that he could give their troopers only bread and straw, thus Barbezieux wrote to Tessé to ask Vaudémont for meat too, half a pound per day per soldier, to be paid later by France. The French expected to pay no more than 10 French liras for a 200-pound sack of wheat, and possibly seven or eight liras only.

According to de Vault, once in Milan Tessé discovered Vaudémont to be the only reliable pro-French official there. The others, as well as the Italian princes, seemed to look to the Empire.

1 The French minister of war Louis-François-Marie Le Tellier, Marquis de Barbezieux, to Marshal Count de Tessé, from Versailles on 25 December 1700, reported in de Vault, op. cit., vol. I, Part II, p.197.

2 The franc no longer existed since, in 1640, Louis XIII ordered the royal mint to produce the new golden coin called a Louis, after his portrait. Nonetheless the word "franc" remained in use, meaning the French lira. After 1697, one needed 12 French liras, or francs, to make a golden Louis, As said before, the golden Louis, or pistole as it was also called, was less than a contemporary English pound, for it equalled – in contemporary English currency – 17 shillings and sixpence. By consequence, a French franc equalled one English shilling, and 5½ pence.

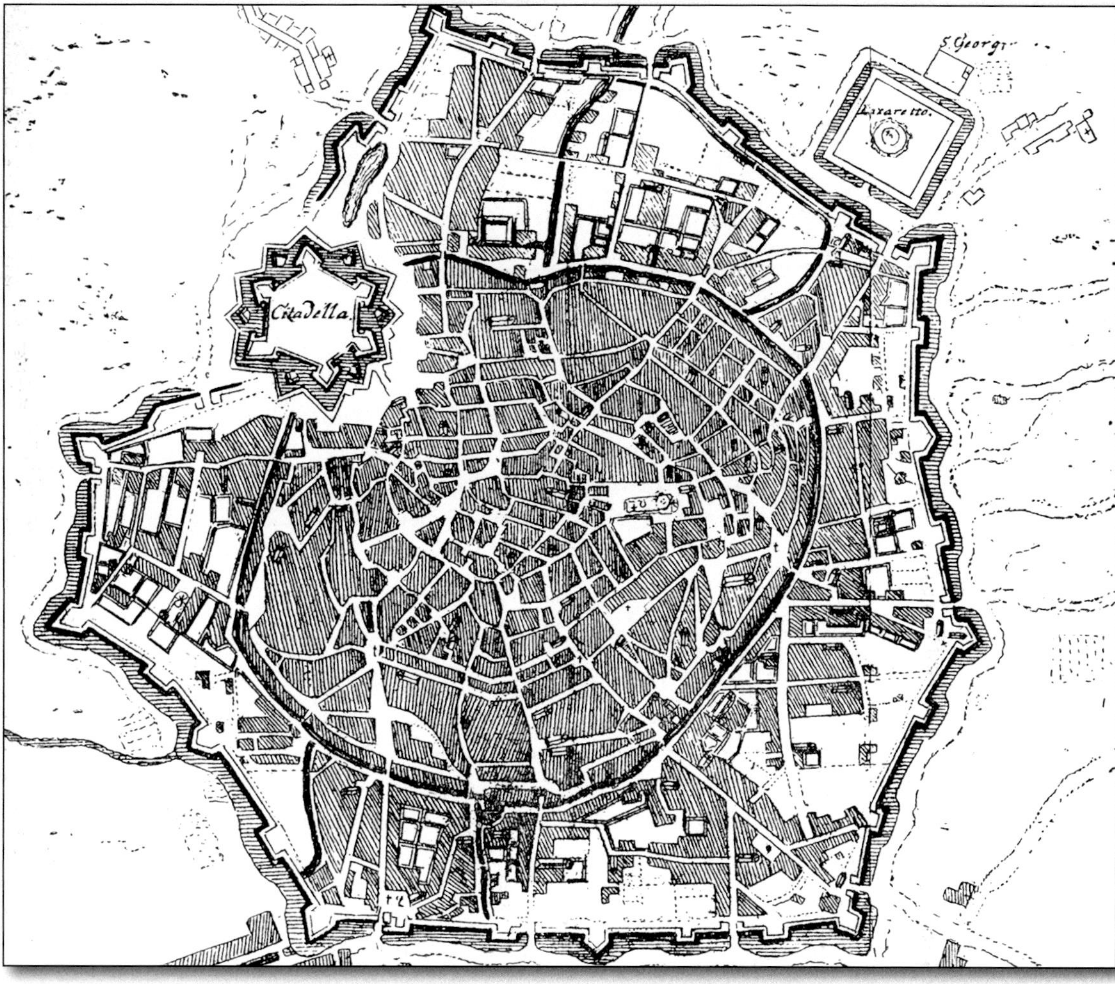

Plan View of Milan.

As I said before, this had to be considered as normal, if one knew Italy, for nobody could expect any Italian prince to declare himself openly for France, and against his feudal lord the Emperor whilst the situation was still unclear, and they were risking their state and their properties. But an assessment such as Tessé's was the typical French attitude at that time and in the following centuries, and apart from it being what the French knew Louis XIV to like – that is to say what Louis wanted to hear – they despised, and suspected any foreigner who was not totally and blindly supportive of France.

The Venetians, for instance, were not supportive. They kept neutrality, but called the militia to arms, and gathered in Friuli two infantry regiments totalling 1,300 men, and two cavalry companies, followed a few months later by a further 1,200 foot paid by the local cities. At the same time in Venetia the cities of Treviso, Verona, Vicenza, Padua, and Rovigo provided money for a further 2,000 foot, to enhance the defensive Venetian line along the Adige river, that is to say facing the French. It was protected by four infantry regiments – Soardo, Sala, Dotto, and Fracanzoni – and 3,500 Cernide, later enhanced by 3,200 Oltremarini – "Overseasers" – as the regular Venetian troops from Dalmatia, and Albania were called. This meant that neither the French nor the Imperial Army could pass through so easily.

Tessé and Vaudémont realised this when they inspected the Milanese eastern border in January 1701. As things were, the enemy could only come down from Trente. Thus there were four different possible routes Eugene could exploit from that side to invade the Duchy of Milan, hence they started to reinforce defences, and create new obstacles. As Tessé reported to Louis XIV, the key point was the fort of La Chiusa. It was small but it was halfway along the Adige Valley and locked it completely. It commanded the road and the stream and the crossing of the Adige river, and could be shelled only by long range fire, which at that time was scarcely accurate.

Of course, there was another possibility: had the Austrians built a pontoon bridge on the Adige near the village of Dolce – actually Dolcé – south of Trento and north-west of Verona, they could easily reach Lake Garda and ship down the Mincio to Mantua. As a consequence, the French – Tessé said – had somehow to pass the Adige west–east in order to prevent the enemy doing the same in the opposite direction, but this could not be done without clashing with the Venetians, so the French had to stay on the opposite side. All this did not stop the Austrians, but they came so slowly that the French had plenty of time to prepare their defence.

In March Tessé and Vaudémont were notified that the first 2,000 Austrians gathered in Bolzano, south of the Alps, and north of Trente. The Venetians had only 400 men in and near La Chiusa, and Tessé feared that they could be overwhelmed by the Austrians, and that Mantua could also be seized in a while.

Thus on 11 March Tessé sent a letter to Louis XIV begging for orders, and on the 16th committed 1,500 foot and 200 cavalry to support the 700 Spaniards in Castiglione, not far from Mantua, the same place where Napoleon would fight at the end of that century. Then Vaudémont and Tessé purchased the right to stay in Mirandola, paying 500 pistoles to Princess Brigida (regent, and aunt of Duke Francesco Maria). Last, they committed six French battalions toward Mantua.

The War Theatre in North-Eastern Italy.

The Duke of Mantua was desperately trying to keep neutrality. He was a prince of the Empire and wanted to act just as the dukes of Parma and of Modena, that is to say raise the Papal flag, declaring himself a subject of the Holy Seat so as to be not involved nor involveable in the forthcoming war. Unfortunately for him, whilst Modena and Parma not only did the same trick faster and sooner than he did, he and his Duchy were on the front line of the forthcoming front, thus no Mantuan neutrality could be accepted by the French.

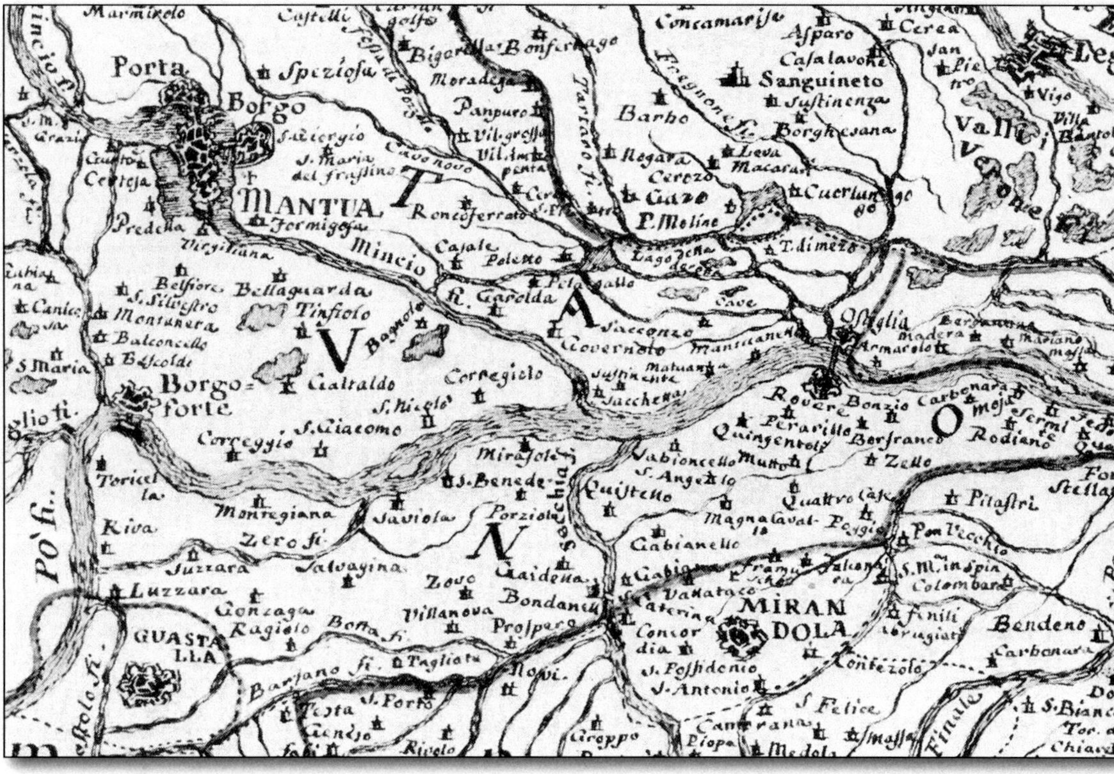

Mantua and the Po.

Then came the answer from Versailles dated 17 March. Louis XIV ordered Tessé to seize the fort of La Chiusa and the Lake Garda area, no matter what the Venetians said or did.

Venice did not prevent the French to do what they could need to stop the Austrians, and Tessé took advantage of it.

Mantua was another issue. When approached, the Duke had not clearly said no, but answered Tessé and Vaudémont that he had made a settlement with the Pope and the Sun King and that he was waiting for His Most Christian Majesty's ratification. Meanwhile the French could enter some villages nearby, and some troops could also be allowed to enter Mantua, but not that many and only after paying a couple of thousand pistoles.

This was not exactly what Tessé liked to hear, but he agreed a comedy be played to save the Duke of Mantua's innocence in front of the Emperor.

On 30 March Vaudémont and Tessé planned to seize the city. During the night of 4 April Tessé blockaded it, or rather surrounded the lake Mantua is built in the middle of. The next morning, 5 April, Tessé gave an ultimatum: the Duke could join the Bourbon side allowing the French troops enter his capital. If he agreed, he would get a lot of money, the rank of general in the Allied army, and Bourbon protection and support. If he refused, the city would be shelled immediately. The Duke played his part well. Mantua opened the gates and Tessé entered the city with seven battalions and six cannons. Now the French and the Spaniards commanded the whole strategic line from Lake Garda to the Po river, that is to say from the Alps to the impassable riverine border with the Papal State. Eugene could come, if he dared.

III: Here Comes Eugene

Eugene dared. He arrived in Rovereto, not far from Trento, on 20 May 1701 and held a council of war. The interim Austrian commander Guido Starhemberg had prepared everything quite well, and Eugene had to move.

Prince Eugene of Savoy.

On the opposite side he had the French and the Spaniards, commanded by his old enemy Nicolas de Catinat de la Fauconnerie. Catinat was an experienced and skilled general, one of the best Louis XIV had. His appointment at the head of the field army had been announced to Tessé by the King's letter of 17 March. The same letter stated the command chain: the Duke of Savoy was the top commander, Catinat was to be his deputy, and Tessé and Vaudémont had to directly obey Catinat. In case the Duke of Savoy was not with the army, it would be up to Vaudémont, due to his noble rank, to formally exercise the superior command, retaining Catinat as his deputy. In other words, no matter who the supreme commander was, Catinat was the chief of staff and in fact the army depended on him.

Catinat had commanded successfully, or as successfully as one could at that time, the French Army in Italy during the War of the League of Augsburg. He won both the field battles the Allies undertook against him, and received the dignity of Marshal of France after the second, at the Marsaglia plateau.

Nicolas Catinat de la Fauconnerie.

During those campaigns Eugene had constantly been on the opposite side. Unfortunately for the Allies he was still too young to be chosen as the commander-in-chief, thus whenever he had to follow other people's orders the result was not as good as hoped, whilst whenever he was free, he obtained remarkable successes. In 1697 in the following war, against the Turks in Hungary, Eugene destroyed the Ottoman Army at Zenta and gained an immortal reputation as an outstandingly skilled commander. As a matter of fact Eugene already was, as Napoleon later stated, one of the seven best commanders that ever existed,[3] and so famous that there was no need to explain to the public who he was.

3 They were Eugene, Gustavus Adolphus of Sweden, Frederick the Great, Turenne, Hannibal, Julius Caesar, and Alexander the Great.

Incidentally, Catinat had a very clear idea of how dangerous Eugene could be: in 1691 the French corps besieging Cuneo in Piedmont had been swiftly attacked and definitively crushed by Eugene, causing a total collapse of the French forces there.

Now Catinat, who arrived in Milan in April, realised well how bad the situation could become. Eugene was a pest, no matter how small his army could be. He was smarter, swifter, and faster than any other general of his time, and there was no way one could leave the initiative to him. On the other hand Catinat had a problem: his cavalry could not survive in a hot Italian summer. There was not enough fodder or grass to feed the horses other than those of the few squadrons of Spanish Cavalry in Milanese service and of the already arrived 12 French squadrons. What to do with the expected and forthcoming 46 squadrons? It was not a good idea to send them into the Venetian Terraferma, for this could push Venice onto the Emperor's side. So one could only ask the Duke of Savoy to host 20 squadrons in Piedmont, and the Duke of Mantua the same in Monferrato, and host the remaining six around Mantua. Apart from this meaning a daily five soldi per horse expenditure, the problem was that keeping the cavalry so distant deprived the Allied army of her mobility. And this was not all. A huge portion of French and Spanish forces were needed to garrison the borders, and 15 French battalions had no tents and no weapons yet; it was so hard to get them from France that Catinat found easier to give those battalions the necessary cash, leaving them free to purchase what they could find on the spot. Straw, too, was lacking, thus the privates had to sleep on the ground.

In the end, after a reconnaissance, Catinat decided not to seize La Chiusa for it was hard to keep and almost impossible to hold. He chose a different defence: trenches and field fortifications. The French and the Spaniards garrisoned the right embankment of the Adige river from near the Lake Garda to the south-east, and then down to south, and at last fortified with trenches and wooden palisades the area between the Adige and the Po. It was amazing, wonderful, and static; just what Eugene needed.

He decided not to come down through the Adige Valley, for it was locked by the French, and chose three different routes from Trento area through the Veronese Pre-Alps. One route went up to 1,206 metres above sea level and then came down to Arsiero. The second reached Schio, near Vicenza, and the last arrived in Verona. All were winding and narrow, very narrow, and they all needed to become three yards wide.

Imperial sappers and soldiers worked hard: an officer and 300 men in Val Fredda, a lieutenant colonel with 1,000 infantrymen and many local workers in Val Leno. Then the workers increased to 3,000 and the miracle occurred: the roads were rendered passable. Eugene ordered similar works to be made towards Lake Garda and took care Catinat was made aware. Last, he made a resounding reconnaissance towards the lake on 23 May, and the trick worked, Catinat's troops gathered nearby.

Meanwhile Eugene gathered 700 mules in Rovereto. Food rations were shared: eight days' allowance on the mules, four days' allowance packed on the shoulders of the infantry, and six more on the cavalry's horseback, total: 18 days.

Verona.

On 25 May the Imperial infantry left Trento and Rovereto and gathered in Ala, south of Trento. Catinat thought it was the first step for an attack on his left side on Lake Garda, and sent additional reinforcements there. But as soon as he did it, and before he could realise what was going on, on 26 May Eugene and the whole Imperial army vanished among the mountains, and on the 28th in the evening reappeared in Breonio, in the plain, 20 kilometres – or 12.5 miles – from Verona.

Catinat was still expecting an attack on the left, had been notified of "some works" made "here and there" on the mountains, and supposed Eugene to be still in Rovereto, whilst the Prince was happily waiting for his heavy artillery and making reconnaissance along the Adige river.

Then on more or less the same day, 31 May, both commanders fully realised the situation. Eugene was on the left side of the Adige and realised the river was impossible to cross. His pontoons were still retained by Austrian bureaucracy very far behind. The French swept away all the boats from the left embankment, and the only way to cross the Adige was on the bridges of Verona, but this meant entering the city, which would mean violating Venetian neutrality and possibly pushing Venice to join the enemy front.

On the opposite side, Catinat was puzzling. Eugene and a river were something quite dangerous. The French troops in Cuneo had felt protected by a river, and Eugene had forded it in a while. The Turks in Zenta had been destroyed whilst crossing the Danube … what could Eugene now do here? Enforce the passage? Move north to Lake Garda? Push on to Venice? March along the Adriatic Sea to conquer the Kingdom of Naples? Or what? Then on 2 June Catinat realised that Eugene wanted to cross the Adige. Eugene needed it, for he needed to have the Adige safe, because all his ordnance and supplies had to come from Trento downstream along that river.

Over the following three weeks the two generals played a sort of chess game, and on the night of 27 June Eugene made 'checkmate'. His troops built a pontoon bridge on the Malopera canal, and at midnight, followed by two infantry regiments, 10 field guns, and 500 cavalry, he crossed the Adige and marched to the Canalbianco. He forded that canal at Castel Guglielmo and at dawn the Imperial troops were on the opposite side and had also crossed the Po.

Catinat was appalled. He was notified only in the morning and immediately realised how bad the situation was. Eugene, with the core of his own forces, was in front of him and threatened the towns of Castagnaro and Carpi di Villa Bartolomea in the area of Verona, Ostiglia in the Duchy of Mantua and the portion of that same Duchy on the other side of the Po. Lastly, they threatened the fortress of Mirandola.

In fact Eugene wanted to secure the Adige, thus he widened his troops in every direction, but started encircling the French right wing, to let them leave Castagnaro and Carpi, for the two towns commanded the Adige.

On the evening on 8 July Imperial troops made a feint from the left side of the Adige against Castagnaro on the right side, a feint which could easily be turned into the main attack if it went well. Meanwhile Eugene took 6,000 foot and 5,000 cavalry and rushed to Trecenta, his actual task. It was night now, and it was raining, The Imperialists build a bridge there and crossed the river, and Eugene led them in two columns on Castagnaro. Whilst marching they found a French post 40 cavalrymen strong, and destroyed it so quickly that no alarm could be given.

By 9:00 a.m. the Austrians were in front of Castagnaro, behind the French who still faced the river. The Imperial guns started firing. The grenadiers supported by the Guido Starhemberg and Bagni Infantry regiments stormed the entrenchment. The French reacted well but had to gather in the church, and started firing through the windows and from the bell tower. The overwhelming Austrians demanded they surrender or, they promised, the church would be burned with them inside. The defenders immediately surrendered.

Eugene left his sappers destroying Castagnaro's fortifications and marched immediately to Carpi: a major battle was in sight.

IV: The Battle of Carpi

The rain ceased, and the southern summer sun made the wet morning very hot and affected by a thick fog. Eugene had the Neuburg cuirassiers in the vanguard, and they were advancing as fast as they could with a few metres' visibility. Suddenly, in the fog, at 6:00 a.m., they crashed into the 1,300 cavalrymen and the grenadier companies commanded by the Sieur de Saint-Frémont, who, alarmed by the rumble of the cannons, was rushing from Carpi to relieve Castagnaro.

Regiment Neuburg was swept away by the French, but the Vaudémont cuirassiers and the Savoy dragoons[4] came and charged the French, whilst the Imperial infantry widened on the wings to surround the enemy.

Saint-Frémont ordered his dragoons to leave their horses and fight on foot, but soon discovered the battlefield to be narrow and the Imperialists overwhelming – perhaps the whole enemy army? – and after a three-hour

4 Charles Henry of Lorraine, Prince of Vaudémont was a first cousin of Louis XIV, and an Imperial subject, for he was a cadet of the House of Lorraine, being the title of Vaudémont normally given to the cadets of that House. In origin Charles Henry was in Imperial service, that is to say Habsburg service, and that is why in 1698 he had been appointed governor of Milan. His only son Charles Thomas, known as "the Young Prince of Vaudémont", born in 1670, was in Imperial service; he too, and was now a general, and a good and close friend of Eugene of Savoy, with whom he fought against the Turks. When the Spanish Succession crisis started, the father, the Old Prince of Vaudémont, chose the French side, whilst the son loyally kept his position in Habsburg service. Both Charles Thomas of Vaudémont and Eugene, when appointed colonel in the past, received a regiment each, which according to tradition had been named after their new owners. That is why there was a Vaudémont cuirassier regiment and a Savoy dragoon regiment (which kept its name until the First World War), whilst the Old Prince of Vaudémont and the Duke of Savoy were soldiering in opposite armies. There was another member of the family of Lorraine, Charles Francis of Lorraine, Prince of Commercy (1661–1702), known as "the Prince of Commercy", or simply "Commercy", who soldiered in the Imperial army and was killed at the battle of Luzzara in 1702. He too was a friend of Eugene, had no sons and his title of Commercy remained with his mother and was later, in 1708, inherited by the Old Prince de Vaudémont.

fight ordered a withdrawal to Carpi. During the retreat, Tessé arrived from San Pietro di Legnago with the vanguard of his 2,000 cavalry and 4,000 foot, which he moved when notified of the fight.

The French reorganised their lines out of Carpi and faced the enemy, but things worsened. The ground they chose was stark and open, but was crossed by so many ditches and filled by so many bushes that they could not see further than 50 yards. This allowed Eugene to fully deploy his infantry, and when the French charged, his foot greeted them deployed in a line, firing by line, with continued and terrible volleys. The French charged no less than six times, and were always rejected. The d'Albret cavalry regiment was destroyed, and the Mauroy and de Ruffey cavalry regiments suffered heavy casualties. On the other side Eugene had two horses killed under him, and two bullets hurt him on the side of the knee.[5] He was immediately cared for and given another horse, continued commanding, and found the opportunity to start a new encircling action. This convinced Tessé to disengage. Carpi was abandoned by the French, and the incoming garrison from San Pietro di Legnago, which had almost arrived at the battlefield, was ordered to withdraw along with the survivors. The French lost 550 dead and 100 prisoners. The Imperialists only 40 dead and 40 wounded, Eugene included: a low price for a resounding strategic success.

V: The Battle of Chiari[6]

The Carpi victory opened the gates of the Padana Plain to Eugene. By now he was still in Venetian Lombardy and had to conquer the Duchy of Milan.

The border was marked by the river Mincio, flowing north–south from Lake Garda to the Po, near Mantua. The Mincio was impossible to ford, and Catinat filled its whole right embankment with garrisons and field fortifications. Meanwhile he waited for reinforcements from France and Piedmont.

Eugene knew it, and knew also that he had to act before their arrival, and organised a new trick. First, some rumours arrived with Catinat about Eugene's intention to move south to Ostiglia, were the Mincio enters the Po. He trusted them and moved troops there, on his extreme right. "Gotcha": Eugene planned to cross the Mincio on the extreme left of the French, thus under Peschiera, just on the shore of Lake Garda. Succeeding meant reaching a Venetian-ruled area, rich, and with plenty of food, crossed by a huge

5 This was reported by Cesare Someri in a letter to Cardinal Astalli, dated from Stienta, on 9 July 1701, "… the Most Serene Prince Eugene [was wounded] in a Leg by two balls, who, having immediately let himself been cared for and the said [balls] having been taken out, and having had his wound embalmed and well bandaged, he anew mounted on a horse again and with more bravery he left toward the Field to continue the undertaken Battle", in Archivio Segreto Vaticano [Vatican Secret Archive] (onward ASVa), *Legazioni*, anno 1701.

6 Seeing how English speaking people normally mismanage the Italian language (as much as the Italians mismanage English), it must be underlined that this town's name must be pronounced "Kyahree".

quantity of ditches, small rivers, and canals, thus quite good for defence, and only 50 miles from Milan.

Imperial squadrons were scattered along all the roads to stalk French communications, and on 24 July Eugene took 4,000 cavalry, and made a long reconnaissancc all along the Mincio from Peschiera southbound to Goito, where Catinat's headquarters were.

Catinat was disoriented: what did Eugene want to do? Catinat extended his troops to Peschiera, blew the bridge at Valeggio and waited.

On that same day Victor Amadeus reached the Allied headquarters in Goito. Seven of his infantry battalions preceded him there,[7] and at camp he found also Prince Eugene's greetings and compliments, as well as a present of six Turkish horses. Victor Amadeus thanked his cousin, kept only one horse, sent him back the remaining five and discovered the Franco-Spanish headquarters to be in the deepest confusion. He looked at what his cousin was doing and more or less realised his intentions. The evidence: when on 28 July in the morning the first reports about Imperial troops near Peschiera arrived, the Duke of Savoy immediately told the other commanders that it was necessary to rush there, with infantry and artillery, taking advantage of the deep river and of the steep embankment to start firing on the crossing enemies, and stop their attempt.

Victor Amadeus II of Savoy.

Tessé and Catinat assessed it to be impossible without further reinforcements, and ordered the local commander, the Count de Bachevilliers, to withdraw to the main camp with all his forces. In fact, had the French followed Victor Amadeus' advice, success was certain. Eugene had faced many troubles: his troops were on the spot by 6:00 a.m., but only one of his pontoons arrived, and at 8:00 a.m. As soon as they started building the bridge at 9:00 a.m., the Imperialists were seen by the French. The work lasted three hours, until noon, thus had the French acted according to Victor Amadeus' suggestion the Austrians would have been repulsed.

Eugene had a good piece of luck, and quite happy with it marched west, whilst Catinat withdrew behind the next unfordable river to the west: the Oglio.

On the 31st the French held a council of war. Vaudémont urged for a battle, because he feared the Milan population would rise up in favour of Austria. Tessé too urged this, but only because he was in competition with Catinat, who supposed Eugene's position to be too strong. Victor Amadeus simply listened.

This was Catinat's last decision as a chief of staff; his political enemies were pushing against him. The French ambassador in Venice, Cardinal

7 The expeditionary corps cavalry included the Guardie del Corpo – the Household – Piemonte Reale, Dragoni di Sua Altezza Reale, Savoia, Dragoni di Piemonte, and Dragoni del Genevese, which is not the current 4th Reggimento "Genova Cavalleria", because it was disbanded after the Carbonari uprising in 1821; whilst, when the whole expeditionary corps was concentrated, the foot were included in battalions from the Guards, Savoia, Monferrato, Aosta, Piemonte, Chiablese, Fucilieri, Saluzzo, and Schulemburg infantry regiments.

d'Estrées, repeatedly wrote to Versailles. Many other French ministers in the Italian duchies did the same, and all the letters complained about the attitude of the French troops.[8]

Louis acted accordingly, and made a terrible error. He committed the Duke de Villeroy, Marshal Villars and General Francesco Albergotti – an Italian in French service – to Italy. Villars, the former French ambassador to Vienna, was the best, but Villeroy was the oldest, and was the King's old and good friend. That is why on 22 August 1701 he took supreme command on the ground, no matter his narrow-mindedness. "His first words were to ask where those rascals of Germans were, for it was necessary to expel them from Italy: words which made whoever heard them shrug."[9] In fact Villeroy was not stupid, as he was depicted later, but he did not know the Italian war theatre and undervalued his enemy, and this was his definitive fault.

Whilst Eugene had troubles because his army lacked money and food, and thus pillaged and looted towns nearby, the French advanced slowly. Eugene made a reconnaissance and realised they were going to attack his camp in Chiari. It was promising: Eugene's camp was in a wonderful defensive position in a cultivated plain, crossed by an incredible number of small ditches and canals needed by the peasants to get water for their fields. It was a bad terrain for fighting, and it had only one open side, and there Eugene was waiting for the Allies. And they came.

Eugene had in theory 34,000 men – 21,000 foot and 13,000 cavalry – but desertion and diseases reduced his forces to 16,000 foot, and a bit more than 7,000 cavalry and 32 guns. The incoming enemy was 36,000 foot[10] and 9,000 cavalry, that is to say a fraction of its forces.

Eugene purposely chose a defensive battle, exploiting his good position. He filled all the houses, mills, and farms nearby with troopers, made an earthwork six feet high along the road near Chiari's outer moat, blew all the small bridges crossing the canals, interrupted the canals, let their water flood the ground on the side of the incoming enemy, and then waited. "Before midday on September 1st some general officers of the Two Crowns advanced to explore the Caesarean posts up close."[11]

---

8 As reported by the Papal Nuncio in Venice to Cardinal Secretary of State from Venice on 10 July, 1701, in ASVa, *Nunziatura di Venezia*, anno 1701.

9 Ludovico Antonio Muratori, *Annali d'Italia*, 13 vols (Naples: 1873), Vol. 12, p.525, year MDCCI (1701).

10 The infantry included 69 battalions: 56 were French, nine Piedmontese and four Spanish; the cavalry had "88 or 90 squadrons" – so Villeroy wrote to the King on 24 August, in his letter fully reported by de Vault, in op. cit., p.304 – and the artillery had 44 field guns. According to Villeroy, each of the first 40 French infantry battalions had from 360 to 400 men, as well as each of the first 65 cavalry squadrons fielding 88 or 90 men. These were the units in Italy since the beginning of the campaign, whilst the recently arrived 25 cavalry squadrons and 16 infantry battalions were stronger. According to Villeroy, the nine Piedmontese battalions were very well equipped, very well drilled, and as much disciplined as needed to be an example to the whole army. The three Spanish battalions were "Naples", and "Lombardy", both composed of Spaniards, and a German battalion. The Spanish units included a cavalry and a dragoon regiment, whilst the Piedmontese cavalry was not mentioned.

11 Anonymous (probably Jacopo Sanvitale), *Vita e Campeggiamenti del Serenissimo Principe Francesco Eugenio di Savoja, supremo comandante degli eserciti cesarei e dell'Imperio* [Life and

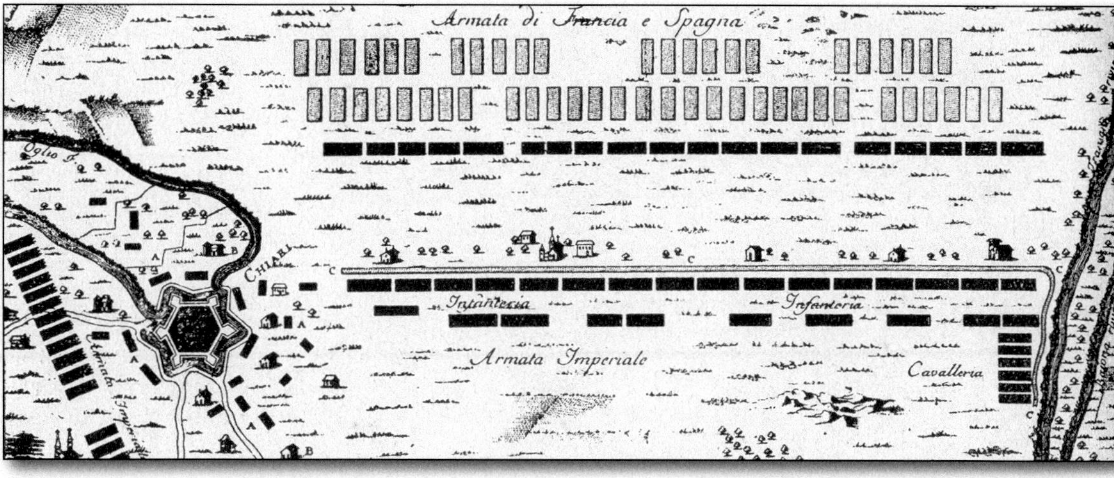

Plan of the Battle of Chiari.

Whilst their troops advanced, the Allied generals held a council of war. Victor Amadeus and Catinat tried to convince Villeroy that the Austrian position was too strong, but he answered that that was not the King's will: they were not there just to look at the enemies through a spyglass, but to eject the Germans.

Around 2:00 p.m. the Allies were almost in the Imperial firing range, and the Allied patrols had not yet been able to discover whether they were in front of the whole Imperial army, as Victor Amadeus and Catinat said, or only its rearguard, as Villeroy claimed. Stubbornly, Villeroy committed only 18 battalions and nine squadrons out of the available 69 and 90 he had. He pushed ahead the French brigades of Normandy, Auvergne, Anjou and Vendôme: 8,000 men. Victor Amadeus commanded the right wing, including his Guards, Aosta and Saluzzo infantry regiments, whilst his cavalry was present but was not involved. Villeroy commanded the left, Catinat the centre.

François de Neufville, Duke de Charost and de Villeroy.

Hardly walking in the muddy ground, the French approached the Imperial line, and were suddenly shot at close range. They charged, and were repulsed. Attacks were made again and again, up to 12 times, feeding the attack with reserves, including the Piedmontese Regiment of Guards, and the Irish Regiment Dillon in French service, but volley by volley they were always repulsed by the Austrians.

campaigns of the Most Serene Prince, Francis Eugene of Savoy, Supreme Commander of the Caesarean and Imperial armies] (Naples: 1754), p.66.

The Battle of Chiari.

After an hour and a half, Villeroy ordered the retreat. He left on the ground 2,000 or 3,000 dead – 10 percent were officers – and lost 120 prisoners and five flags. Eugene lost 36 dead and 81 wounded.[12]

Two days later, Eugene received a 3,000-man reinforcement. It was not that much – even if this was not Vienna's opinion – in comparison to the 80,000 men Louis XIV wanted to keep in Italy, nonetheless it was enough not to lose positions.

The battles of Capri and Chiari are described as extensively as possible in this book to give a clear idea of the clashes in Italy. Their development was heavily dictated by the ground, which seemed flat, but did not suit cavalry. There were plenty of unfordable rivers streaming north–south, thus providing a series of barriers to whatever army moved west or east, and there were four such rivers in the 100 miles between Milan and Verona, that is to say one every 25 miles. Obstacles were further enhanced by a great quantity of creeks and ditches streaming in all directions, and by a huge number of small fortified towns, villages and farms, called cascine.[13] Only a portion of

12 Actual casualties are puzzling, as usually happened at that time. Writing to Louis XIV on 2 September Villeroy admitted 60, or maybe up to 80 officers dead and wounded, and at least 1,000 privates. On 4 September Eugene reported to Leopold that enemy casualties were 2,000 privates and some 200 officers, and 100 more private prisoners, but he added that a drummer of the Bourgogne Regiment told the Austrians the French casualties had been 3,000 privates and 300 officers dead. Last, Tessé, writing to Cardinal Astalli from Lodi, on 13 September, said that the Allies lost 3,500 soldiers and 500 officers, even if such an increase can be explained by the number of wounded who died in the week after the battle.

13 The typical "Cascina" (pronounce "Kahsheenah") in the Padana Plain was – and still is – somehow similar to the Haie Sainte in Waterloo, but was more "fortified" and hard to be seized. It was a square. Three of its sides were – and still are – a high wall composed of houses and stables, up to 20 or 30 feet high, with no interruption in between, and with small windows

them could hold a real siege, but the smallest villages and the farms could at least delay or stop an army for a few hours, or up to a few days, and all them could be exploited as strongpoints to be held, or to support a corps in the field. That is why, as Eugene wrote to the Emperor when preparing the 1701 campaign, in Italy infantry was an "utmost necessary", an opinion later shared by Villeroy, who at the end of August 1701 wrote to Louis XIV that the Italian country was "more cut [by interruptions and obstacles] than Flanders", adding a few days later that it was "a country to be despaired of".

As we have seen, operations in Italy involved far fewer soldiers than in the Rhineland or Low Countries. The casualties too were lower, nonetheless the clashes were as violent as elsewhere and the strategic result was as relevant as in the north. It was a theatre where big results were obtained by relatively few people.

During the two months following the battle of Chiari, the opposing cavalries clashed many times. Generally the Imperialists prevailed, but no fight was really important.

At the end of October Villeroy abandoned the area and moved to winter quarters near and in the city of Cremona, where he remained along with Catinat, whilst Victor Amadeus went back to Turin.

VI: War, and Civilians

Whilst the armies were at camp or in their winter quarters, the civilians were anything but happy. War is never nice. It can be amazing, fascinating, attractive due to the colourful flags, and the brilliant uniforms, the impressive, massive squared ranks, the glory, the trumpets, the drums, whatever; but when one becomes aware of what the war does, of how people are affected by the war, affected by its consequences in terms of pain, fear, violence and suffering, the sight changes.

In a war, people in arms have at least a chance to prevail, and to prevail means to survive, but they who – as civilians – have no weapons, have no chance other than succumb, suffer, and die.

This was particularly true during the War of the Spanish Succession, and we can have a deep insight thanks to the special position it had in the first five years of fighting on the Italian front: the Venetian-owned part of the Po Valley centering on the city of Brescia. Brescia in her history produced very few prominent people, but for one or two exceptions. The first of these few important people started appearing only in the Napoleonic era, thus at least 80 years after the War of the Spanish Succession. Nonetheless, Brescia and its environments were rich with culture-loving people, who loved to

protected by iron grilles. Sometimes there were no windows looking outside of the cascina, at least at ground level. The fourth side of the square was closed by another high wall including a big strong wooden gate. Once the gate closed, as happened every evening, it was impossible to enter the cascina unless passing over the wall using a long ladder. Basically, every cascina was a small fortress, intended to prevent any attempt by thieves or brigands, thus it was a natural military strongpoint.

study and to write, and who often recorded what they knew and saw. Thus a number of diaries and journals were written during the sad days of the Spanish succession crisis and some of them were later retraced, collected and published.[14] They give us an impressive portrait of the situation as it was.

It must be said that no chronicle seems to complain about the French, the Spaniards, and the Piedmontese, whilst all complain, deeply, about the Imperialists. There are good reasons why. On the one hand, since his first instructions, French War minister Barbezieux had clearly ordered Tessé to keep a strong discipline, and to not hesitate to give "examples", that is to say death penalties "to prevent the disorder and the libertinage".[15] On the other hand it must be stressed that the Imperial administration had no money, thus the Imperial army had far less than needed to survive, and had no chance other than finding its food on the spot, at any cost, which, due to their lack of money, meant at no cost. In other words: they stole whatever they could.

Let us examine the French-Spanish-Piedmontese army first, and then the Imperialists.

Carlo Capitanio was a young Venetian subject from the small town of Castelcovati, not far from Brescia, and from Chiari. As all young men who knew nothing of the world but their parish, he was attracted by the military camp the Allies established nearby, and went there many times. He later wrote:

> This camp was all in the fields of Saint Firmo[16] and kept from the castle to Urago d'Oglio, and from the Seriola Castellana[17] to Roccafranca,[18] and they were one hundred thousand soldiers, that no more in my times have I seen such a great quantity of different men during all the time that this camp lasted, and those French gave us a lot to eat and it was a wonder to see the fine order of this camp which looked as a very nice fair due to the wide areas and the wonderful pavilions.

14 Monsignor Paolo Guerrini gathered all the surviving chronicles and journals from all the towns and villages of the province he could find. They were written mostly by members of the clergy and were collected in the fifth volume of his comprehensive work *Cronache bresciane inedite dei secoli XV-XIX trascritte e annotate* [annoted and transcribed Brescian unpublished chronicles of the fifteenth to nineteenth century] vol. V (Brescia: 1933). The list includes Vincenzo Rosa, *Memorie storiche di Palazzolo*; Giuseppe Ruffi, *Relatione della guerra dell'anno 1701 e Rovina di Castel Coati*; Anonymous, *Cronaca di Castelmella, anni 1702–1706*; and G.B. Giacomini, *Cronaca dei fatti accaduti nella riviera di Salò e contorni dopo la morte di Carlo II delle Spagne.* Additional diaries concerning that war theatre are the *Cronaca cremonese* by Carlo Antonio Stefanoni concerning the 1701–1712 period; the *Cronaca di Erbusco* by Giovanni Antonio Girelli, about the years 1701–1707; and the *Istoria dei fatti accaduti nel paese di Palazzolo scritti l'anno 1811 da me Giovanni Pezzoni.* A further two chronicles are mentioned in the following footnotes.

15 The French minister of war Louis-François-Marie Le Tellier, Marquis de Barbezieux, to Marshall Count de Tessé, from Versailles on 25 December 1700, reported in de Vault, op. cit., vol. I, Part II, p.201.

16 The Cascina of San Firmo is more or less a mile west of Castelcovati, and Castelcovati is a mile south of Chiari.

17 A seriola was a creek.

18 Roccafranca is another small village. According to the description, the camp was more or less a square mile wide.

> These French were all of very fine blood, and all rich of money, so that every humblest private was full of fine Spanish doubles. The officers were all well dressed in gold and silver, the general of this camp was Monsù Catinà and the Duke of Savoy. These Lords left to mr. Archpriest Ruffi doubles of Spain 300 to be distributed to the poor of the country [and] to compensate in part its damages.[19]

It is a wonderful vision of health, wellness and good terms with local inhabitants, even if, not so far from there, around Cremona people was so frightened by the war that everybody rushed to the closest city with their property, in such a way that the prince of Vaudémont complained he could not find the wagons and carts needed to carry the French supplies.

The Austrians now, and it will be a completely different story. The place is Chiari, long before the battle. The author, whose name was Girelli, reported:

> In the same hour that the Germans reached Chiari, they started with robberish voracity to rob all the country houses as they were barbarous Tartars in an enemy country, and not Christians in a Catholic and neutral country, thus the poor inhabitants were forced to withdraw into Chiari, leaving abandoned their homes and their laboured properties to save their lives, because those barbarians with weapons in hand threatened with death those who wanted to oppose their robberies, and they were not satisfied with pillaging the homes, because they without mercy stripped the people too, cruelly leaving them dishonestly naked, with no regard to sex and age. It was a matter of great horror to see every morning German soldiers and women flooding like locusts all the fields, picking every fruit, no matter if green, and every plant, no matter if unripe, in such a way that in a very few days we saw one of the most florid parts of Lombardy in the month of August reduced into a desert beach of sandy Libya. Nor there was a place in the Chiari countryside which was still closed, but all had been broken into, without doors, and the windows without fences.[20]

Prince Eugene was usually harsh with thieves, but no matter, and anyway he too sometimes – at least during those years – was not so mild. He asked Archpriest Ruffi in Castelcovati to notify him as soon as the Allies left, to attack them whilst retreating. Ruffi refused, for he did not want to be responsible for a likely massacre. Thus, when on 12 November the Allies left, Eugene was not notified in time. He rushed with men and cannons, but when he reached the Oglio river the enemy was already on the other side, and he could only shell them. Catinat was wounded twice, but the crossing was achieved, no matter the casualties. Nonetheless, the lack of information prevented Eugene from gaining a success, thus he decided to take retaliation on Castelcovati on the spot.

---

19 Carlo Capitanio, *Diario*, rep. in G. Massenza, *Storie di senzastoria. Società, economia e cultura popolare a Castelcovati tra '700 e '800* (Brescia: s.d., but 1980s), p.34.

20 *Cronaca Girelli*, p.15, rep. in A. Redaelli, *Le grandi battaglie della storia bresciana*, p.48 and following.

> [They say] Prince Eugene ordered a universal foraging on us all, which was to our great damage, and this foraging was so barbarous that it lasted all the 12th and until the 13th with so much barbarity that also the Church was completely sacked including the holy pots, except for the Very Holy Sacrament that they could not break into, in spite of how much they tried to open it with irons … and with so much cruelty that, after the things of the houses, they wanted to strip all of us of our clothes, leaving the most part of us naked, as well men as women, my poor Mother and my Father were stripped naked, remaining dressed by only a little piece of rags, to cover the shameful parts … it was so barbarous this foraging, that in my house my aunt Domenica died one hour before the abovesaid foraging, and also dead she was stripped of her clothes, and the body was thrown on the ground among the feathers of the destroyed bed, for they brang away the lining … poor mr Archpriest Ruffi was stripped naked as a baby in presence of his people and remained in that way the whole day long, then an hermit dressed him with a tunic …[21]

There were neither the killings nor the rapes usually made during the pillaging, especially when operated by the French, nonetheless in the next days 525 civilians died due to starvation, fear, cold or misery.

This was what happened in a formally neutral occupied land, where people did not or could not react. Venetian subjects were in quite a bad situation, for no matter how badly or well-trained their militia – the Cernide (the "Selected" men) – could be, it could neither gather nor react for Venice was neutral.

The situation changed in Piedmont when the French started looting there after 1703. The men of the local militia had their own training on the ground in the recently ended Nine Years' War. They were loyal to the Duke and were even more loyal to their families. The French now were no longer friends, and looted the locals. Being unfriendly might not be a problem. Being looted was a matter of survival. What was stolen by the French could not be eaten by the peasants. French looting meant Piedmontese starvation, and death, thus, death for death, it was better to rise up and fight instead of suffer. The latter attitude meant death for sure; the former meant a possibility to survive.

So as soon as it was realised that it was possible to fight or repulse the French threat, the Piedmontese militia fought. Sometimes they were unsuccessful, and suffered terrible retaliations; sometimes succeeded, and saved their properties and families. In some cases the Duke rewarded them as he could, so for instance in 1705 he remitted the community of the town of Govone the taxes due on that year, whilst commoners of Mosso were exempted for the next 10 years. It was not a small gift. Money was the major issue and concern. When the war started, the global value of the circulating money in the States of Savoy was 16.1 million liras. The Duchy paid yearly 7.7 millions for imported goods, and its export provided 8.5 million liras, for a total of 16.2 million, just a bit more than the existing metallic money. This meant every change in the balance between export and import affected

21 *Idem.*

the money circulation in the Duchy, thus was immediately resented, as good or evil, and mostly by the lower classes. Clearly, a war provided plenty of changes and heavily affected money circulation, and by consequence tax collection.

In Piedmont wages for the lower classes, including privates, workers and peasants, never exceeded a few soldi per day. One needed 20 soldi to get a lira, and four liras and six soldi to get a silver scudo, or 15 liras and 15 soldi to get a golden double of Savoy, a coin people from the lower classes could very hardly expect to get, and perhaps to see in their life. The soldi were minted using a silver-copper alloy called "billon". In times before the use of banknotes the value of a coin was supposed to equal that of the metal the same coin was made of. Billon coins could be altered in three ways: keeping the silver/copper ratio, and increasing the formal value; altering the silver/copper ratio but simply enhancing the copper; using a mixture of the previous two systems. This trick had been performed between 1639 and 1675. The State gained very much, but the result was the loss of 50 percent of the purchasing power of the Piedmontese lira. During the War of the League of Augsburg, Victor Amadeus tried to reduce expenses by minting billon coins composed of an altered alloy. The result was not good, and in the following years the ducal mint retired as many small coins as possible,and minted new ones.

If, and when, Victor Amadeus was tempted to widely rely on that system, the Chamber of Accounts always suggested not doing it, and the Duke listened to them. Thus, during the period of the whole Spanish Succession crisis, the Duchy minted alloy coins not exceeding the nominal value of 1.1 million liras, and gained only 104,000 liras, which meant, in military terms, the wage of no more than 1,140 infantry privates during only one year, not that much. Victor Amadeus' States could overall rely on a nine million annual income, which was not that much if one wanted to clash against the Empire or France.

VII: The Austrian Supply (Dis)organisation

In summer 1709 Papal general Ferdinando Marsigli, back from long service in the Austrian army, submitted to the Pope a written memoir about the winter quarters the Holy Seat had to expect to pay the Imperial Army for, after the short war just lost between the two powers.[22] Due to his long experience in Austrian service, Marsigli explained in depth how Imperial supply worked, or rather, how the Imperial supply system relied on occupied lands to let the army survive.

We shall not go too deep into details, but a resume and a partial quotation will be useful, for this seems to be the sole existing eyewitness account from inside about how the Austrian system – if there was one – "worked", or rather how it affected the parts of Europe concerned.

According to the style of the Imperial court, Marsigli wrote, winter quarters were established only in the countries not directly ruled by Vienna,

22 Archivio di Stato di Roma (onward ASR), fondo *Soldatesche e Galere*, "Miscellanea", busta 656, "Invasione dello Stato Ecclesiastico 1708" – *Relazione generale Marsigli*, p.138.

Count Luigi Ferdinando Marsigli.

and lasted always at least from 1 October until 30 April, and sometimes more. This meant transferring the burden of the wages and supplies from the Imperial central administration to the countries hosting the winter quarters, no matter whether allied, occupied, or neutral. This, Marsigli wrote, occurred in 1672 when Leopold supported the Netherlands and his army took winter quarters in Germany, oppressing local neutral princes with heavy demands. As a result, many of them took up arms in 1688 as the Emperor's allies, just to avoid contributions and winter quarters. In 1701 they were much more cautious than in 1688, hence the Emperor found no opportunity for quartering his troops in Germany, and had to rely on money and supplies provided by his own states, no matter how he had already squeezed them during the past wars against the Turks and the Hungarian rebels. The situation was problematic until 1704. The 1704 victory at Höchstadt – Blenheim for the British – was "a great relief from those anguishes"[23] for it allowed the Imperial army to exploit Bavaria. Bavaria provided winter quarters until, after the battle of Turin in 1706, the Emperor could exploit Mantua, and the parts of Lombardy owned by princes other than himself. Milan, now owned by Austria, was not affected, and as soon as Mantua too officially came under direct Habsburg rule, it too ceased to be affected. Seeing that "The states of the Duke of Savoy never gave and never will give a penny to the Germans, and on the contrary they take money from them. The Republic of Venice's Terraferma is left intact due to many reasons", Parma, Modena, perhaps Tuscany, and in 1709 the Pope, had to expect to host the Imperial winter quarters, which were expensive and divided in two parts.

The goods needed to feed a soldier were called "mouth portion", and "horse portion" if it was needed to feed a horse. Portions were daily.

A lieutenant general – the top rank in the Imperial army – received up to 600 portions per day, and such a quantity decreased, according to the rank, down to one and a half for a junior officer, and one for a soldier.

> Hence, when, let God will it not, six thousand heads of men with two or three thousands horses would arrive, it would be worth to compute not nine thousand people, but more than Twenty thousand, due to the quantity of junior and senior officers.

23 ASR, cit, *Idem.*

Mouth portions are computed in 2 pounds of bread, one pound of meat and one wine mug per day. The horses' in 6 pounds of biada[24] and pound[25] of hay."

Those portions concerning real heads [persons] are called by the Caesarean Commissariate *actual*, and the others, which are needed for officers and generals, and to relieve the treasury, are called *vacant*. To evaluate the amount of the vacant portions one comes to the estimation of the values of 2 pounds of bread, one pound of meat, a wine mug, and of the service, which includes salt, pepper, candles, wood and bed. The same is made about the value of the Biada and hay.

This evaluation is usually left to an agreement between the Country and the Troops, without the Commissariate intruding in, but nonetheless sometimes the Commissariate intrudes.

This evaluation is the actual massacre of the countries and there lays the great advantage of the officers, especially when they enter a country, as this year are the Bolognese and Ferrarese, where the dearth is so great.[26]

They immediately demand their portions in nature, that is to say that so much meat, and so much bread, and so much wine will be given to them, and then chickens, and spices, and sweet meats and exquisitenesses, or that an arrangement will be reached about them. Once settled according to the high prices of those foods, the officers find themselves with a considerable saved amount of cash, because they want to get their portion first, and then, thanks to their commanding position, to have their expenses paid.

If in the two States of Bologna and Ferrara they apply this method, which by the way according their system is the most regulated, they will ask the Legates for that many thousands of mouth and horses portions, and to be provided of so much meat, bread, wine, service, biada and hay.

Once entered into the country they will say that, in that sum, they have so many actual portions and that many vacant ones. The officers or the Commissariate will ask for vacant portions to be paid in money, computing their value to the victuals' current price, and, seeing the dearth, they more and more will press for vacant portions and will let the actual portions be where life is cheaper and at lesser price [that is to say: "they will let the troops stay and get the actual portions in the areas where the food is cheaper, in order to get the actual portions where food is less expensive"] …

When the Commissariate will insist on negotiating for portions, in order to allow a further settlement with the colonels of the regiments about the portions' values, which is what is made to put Hungary in ruin and desperation, the commons will have to make a specific treaty with each regiment, finding greater or lesser thieving colonels, it being usual to try the most execrable vexations of troubles during two or three weeks in order to enforce the inhabitants to come to an agreement about a sum higher than the values of the goods, and of a regulated

24 As said in chapter 6, biada is a dry fodder mixture composed of oats, rye, barley, farro, broad beans and vetch, the name for which cannot be properly translated into English.

25 The quantity of pounds of hay is not written in the original of Marsigli's relation, ASR,.cit., p.141.

26 As we shall see, the 1708–1709 winter was exceptionally cold acoss the whole continent and badly affected agriculture everywhere, especially in northern Europe, where prices rose as never before.

> service, but also to demand then the officer's house and stable payment and a present[27] when departing."[28]

Some considerations now. The "mouth portion" was not bad, and it was as big as the Piedmontese private's one, perhaps with less wine. But if – and, as we shall see, it was a great "if" – an Imperial soldier got one daily mouth portion, that could be enough for him, but not to feed his family too, if he had any. Moreover, the Imperial supply system before 1704 worked so badly – and after 1704 just a bit better – that Eugene's soldiers used to eat one day in two, and sometimes in three. For instance, when in early January 1702 Eugene received reinforcements, there was a problem. The new corps included 4,000 Danish foot, who not only dressed in uniforms instead of rags, but, amazingly, expected to be fed daily! And when they realised it would not happen, they started deserting in tenths each time, as Eugene reported to the Emperor. And when in 1704 in Germany Eugene was ordered by the Markgraf of Baden to join Marlborough he got, among the others, the Prussians, who chose to go with him because, as the Markgraf von Baden told the – at that time still young – Old Dessau, had they remained with the main army, they could hardly be fed.

Thus one may easily realise why in Italy and everywhere "every morning German soldiers and women flooding like locusts" destroyed the country around their camps. They had no alternative: to loot, or to starve and die.

VIII: A Neapolitan Plot

During the previous war, Naples served as the major Spanish ordnance and funding facility. The Kingdom was healthy, or at least could provide a remarkable quantity of money and men, and thus it was exploited by the Spanish military system as usual.

As we know, as soon as the quarrels about the Spanish succession started, the news of a forthcoming Austrian invasion made Milan the most threatened land of the Spanish Empire. No matter what its governor Prince de Vaudémont could do, Milan needed men and money, and Naples, as usual, was asked for support. By the end of December 1700, Vaudémont had sent Gaetano Coppola, a Neapolitan nobleman and the lieutenant general of the foreign cavalry in the State of Milan, to Naples, asking for men and

27 This happened. Buste 656, 657, 658, and 659 of the mentioned fondo *Soldatesche e Galere* contains also the list of the damage suffered by the commons of the legations. The papers contain many bills asking the Holy See for reimbursing "presents" to the military on their departure. For example there is a 20 Roman scudi present – a bribe – paid to the officer commanding a detachment of the Prussian infantry Regiment Anhalt, who was going to steal oxen to tow the wagons containing his personal baggage; see ASR, *Soldatesche e Galere*, "Miscellanea", Busta 658: "Danni e spese patite dalle Comunità dello Stato Ecclesiastico a causa delle truppe imperiali – 1709", fascicolo della Comunità di Bondeno, p.1. [Damages and expenses suffered by the Communities of the Ecclesiastic State due to the Imperial Troops – 1709, folder of the Community of Bondeno].

28 ASR, *Soldatesche e Galere*, "Miscellanea", busta 656, "Invasione dello Stato Ecclesiastico 1708", pp.141–143.

money. The viceroy granted 60,000 ducats and 500 recruits, to be shipped north by the galleys of the privately owned galley squadron known as the "Squadra de'particolari o del duca di Tursi" – the private men's or the Duke of Tursi's squadron. On 29 December three of Tursi's galleys came from Gaeta to Naples, and left northbound with 400 Italian foot destined for Milan via Finale.

Neapolitan Galleys in Pozzuoli in 1702.

Further funding needed by Milan, by Spain and by the Kingdom itself for its defence, prepared the ground for a rebellion.

The root of the problem was food and its export, especially olive oil. It may sound odd, but so it was. By the end of 1699 and in 1700 feeding the Kingdom was hard due to taxes. Viceroy Medinaceli – a Spaniard and the former Spanish ambassador in Rome, who had already been in Naples 15 years before as the Kingdom's naval commander – had to find money no matter how. The easiest way had been further taxation on food, notably flour and olive oil.[29] The consequence was a shortage of food. The government reacted, preventing any export. This did not solve the problem, because the prices remained high, but caused a yearly three million damage to the oil producers, including many noble families, and depressed the local economy and the common people's daily life.

The rumours started. The export ban had been issued by the president of the food administration Ulloa, he too a Spaniard, who wanted to stockpile two years of oil consumption in Naples; but, people said, whoever bribed Ulloa could smuggle olive oil from the Kingdom, and that was the actual reason for the ban, and the viceroy did not intervene for he shared the bribes with Ulloa.

Meanwhile in summer 1700 soap too started becoming scarce, the state income lowered by a further 60,000 ducats, and the viceroy was looking for further money to feed the military budget. People were unhappy, and when the news of the Spanish succession crisis came, many noblemen saw it as an opportunity to have a change and started thinking of the Empire as a good alternative.

Things went slowly. It took almost a year after Charles II's death to reach the top of the crisis, and during those long months rumours against the viceroy increased. He asked the nobles for armed men to be used as police support. The nobles committed overall 500 men from their fiefs, but they proved to be half-criminals, if not criminal. Security in Naples was badly affected by them, and the city had up to 90 people killed daily. Moreover, the viceroy presented Philip V with a 200,000 ducat free contribution, and this further affected the budget. At the same time news of Eugene's victories in

29 The Italian lower classes, especially in the south, ate mostly vegetables, bread, or in Naples and other parts of that kingdom, pizza, which is basically flat bread dressed with a bit of olive oil and salt. Olive oil was used also for cooking, as butter is used in other countries, thus taxation on flour and olive oil – a sort of pizza tax – meant a taxation on the most widely eaten foods, which were also the core of the lower classes' nutrition.

northern Italy began arriving. So, no surprise if someone who was against the government started thinking of a possible rebellion.

It is not important here to see how was it prepared and how it developed. It is relevant to say that, in spite of all the rumours and notifications he got, the viceroy undervalued the risk and started worrying only in September. The plot had to occur in early October, but as soon as the plotters realised that Medinaceli was aware, they decided to start in advance.

What was later known as "The Macchia's [or The Prince of Macchia's] Plot" took its name after Gaetano Gambacorta, prince of Macchia,[30] even if he was not the original planner. Actually the chief was Tiberio Carafa, Prince of Chiusano,[31] and no fewer than six members of the most important families of the Kingdom actively took part.

The uprising began on the night of 22 September 1701. Gambacorta and Carafa went to the market square shouting "Hooray for the Emperor!", then ran across the city, freed the prisoners from the city jails, sacked Capuano Castle, and seized the tax bureau and ordered it to lower flour prices by half. Gambacorta then entered San Lorenzo Palace, the city tribunal, put the Imperial coat of arms on it, started enlisting men and took the city gates, except for one towards the sea. Barricades were built everywhere, and prevented a first reconnaissance made by troops commanded by the Prince of Montesarchio.

Meanwhile Medinaceli escaped into Castel Nuovo, gathered as many soldiers as he could, obtained a 30,000-ducat loan on his wife's jewels to get cash for troopers, and the next day the reaction started. Restaino Cantelmo, Duke of Popoli, sallied from the castle and the Prince of Montesarchio swept the rebels away with all the available troops.

By the evening of 24 September the revolution was practically over. One of the main perpetrators, Carlo de Sangro, was kept and executed. Another, Giuseppe Capece, was killed while fleeing. The others survived and reached Vienna, where they continued lobbying and pushing for the Imperial army to invade the Kingdom of Naples. Their activity affected Eugene's operations in Italy, as from 1702 Vienna repeatedly asked or demanded he leave Piedmont aside and march to Naples, no matter how his negative answers were well-grounded in strategic evidence. In 1705 and 1706 Eugene never said no, but always found good reasons to delay, asking for further reinforcements, and demonstrating that no operation could succeed without proper funding, additional troops, and as things were, above all naval support to prevent any French or Spanish reinforcement of the kingdom by sea. Given that the Emperor had no navy, such support could be provided only by England and the Netherlands. But they both had so many engagements and the Empire was so short of money that nothing could be done until 1707, when the French fleet was first locked up in Toulon, and then destroyed by the Anglo-Dutch shelling at the end of the siege conducted by Eugene and Victor Amadeus that summer. Then, and only then, as we shall see, an Imperial expeditionary force was able to enter the kingdom and seize it, even if Sicily remained in Bourbon hands.

30 To be pronounced Mahkkyah.

31 To be pronounced Kewsahno.

Castelnuovo or Maschio Angioino, Naples, on the Eve of the 20th Century.

By now, situation was bad. Medinaceli's reaction caused a panic, which directly caused a financial crisis. All the people cashed in their savings and investments to have cash at hand, and put that cash safe into monasteries, in case the revolution reappeared, or the Austrians came. Three banks stopped payments, one of them offered only a little, its creditors getting only 46 percent of their money back, and this did not improve the situation, nor the Viceroy's popularity.

Medinaceli ordered flour to be sold at a price lower than usual, but vendors refused, for the new price was lower than what they paid in origin, and they did not want to lose money. Confusion arose. Medinaceli asked for reinforcements, and in November got troops from Spain, and from France. Spaniards were more or less welcome, the French were not, because for 200 years they were seen as the traditional enemy. In the end, Medinaceli was relieved. In February 1702 he left Naples to the Viceroy of Sicily, Juan Manuel Fernández Pacheco y Zúñiga, Duke of Escalona and Marquess of Villena, and went back to Spain.

IX: The Great Alliance

Whilst the war was beginning to burn northern Italy and western Germany, William III acted as much as he could to re-establish an anti-French alliance. If anyone could still think of a possible agreement based on Louis XIV's goodwill, and sincerity, every doubt disappeared when the Sun King declared that his grandson, the King of Spain, will keep all his rights to inherit the crown of France. This was a complete infringement of every existing pact, for all the negotiations and settlements France agreed on clearly stated a complete separation between the two crowns of France and Spain.

The night from 5–6 February 1701 provided the last push, if needed. On that night the French troops entered the Spanish Low Countries and seized all its fortresses. French casualties were zero. The strategic result was enormous.

The British reaction was harsh. Since at least when de Ruyter led Dutch ships into the Thames, and destroyed the English fleet at Chatham in 1667, the main task of English policy was to prevent any naval power mastering the waters in front of the Thames Estuary. And now, losing not a single man, France, the most threatening naval power of that time, was just there. Parliament authorised William to enter into negotiation with other European powers, and to conclude the necessary alliances, and so he did. Talks and negotiations were going on, but the more the time passed the more it appeared clear that Louis XIV would never accept a compromise. To leave things as they were meant to present Louis XIV and his family with the rule of the Western world. The Emperor would not accept it, because it was a matter of his family's rights. William could not accept it, because this was exactly what he had fought against his whole life. England could not accept it, for it would mean she was unsafe forever. The United Provinces could never accept it, for acceptance meant the end of their independence, and their death. Thus at last the ambassadors convened and William found it easy to melt their will together. The result was as follows:

> Forasmuch as Charles II, King of Spain, of most glorious memory, having died, without issue, not long since, his Sacred Imperial Majesty has claimed the succession to the Kingdoms and Provinces of the deceased King as legitimately pertaining to his august House, but the most Christian King seeking the same succession for his grandson, the Duke of Anjou, and pretending a right to have accrued to him by a certain will of the deceased King, has seized the possession of the whole inheritance, or Spanish Monarchy, for the aforesaid Duke of Anjou, has forcibly occupied the Provinces of the Spanish Low Countries and the Duchy of Milan, keeps a fleet ready fitted in the port of Cadiz, has sent many ships-of-war to the Spanish West Indies, and by this means and many others, the Kingdoms of France and Spain are so closely united between themselves and cemented that they appear not to be hereafter considered otherwise than as one and the same Kingdom, so that unless it be foreseen, it sufficiently appears, that his Imperial Majesty must abandon all hope ever to be satisfied for his pretension; The Sacred Roman Empire will lose its rights in the Fiefs which are in Italy, and in the Spanish Low Countries;
>
> The British and the United Provinces will entirely lose the free intercourse of navigation and commerce in the Mediterranean sea, in the Indies, and elsewhere; And the United Provinces will be destitute of the security which, from the Provinces of the Spanish Low Countries being interposed between them and the French commonly called a barrier, they enjoyed; And finally, the French and Spaniards being thus united will in a short time become so formidable to all, that they will easily challenge to themselves the whole Empire of Europe. But since, on account of this method of proceeding of the most Christian King, a necessity is imposed on his Imperial Majesty of sending an army into Italy as well for the preserving of his private rights as the Fiefs of the Empire, the King of Great Britain has deemed it necessary to send his auxiliary forces to the United Provinces, whose circumstances are in such a situation as if they were actually invaded, and the Lords the States-General of the United Provinces, whose frontiers lie in a manner exposed on every side, by the breaking and taking away of the fence commonly called the barrier, which screened them from the neighbourhood of the French, are compelled for the safety and defence of their Republic to do all those things which they ought or could have done if they had been engaged in war: and since so doubtful a state of their affairs is more perilous than war itself, and France and Spain take advantage of this state of affairs to unite themselves more and more to oppress the liberty of

Europe, and take away the freedom of commerce, by these reasons induced, his Sacred Imperial Majesty, his Sacred Royal Majesty of Great Britain, and the High and Mighty Lords the States General of the United Provinces of the Netherlands, tending to obviate so great evils as might arise therefrom, and desiring as much as in them lies to provide remedies, have thought a strict union and confederacy between themselves necessary for repelling the magnitude of the common danger, and to this end have given orders and instructions, namely, – His Sacred Imperial Majesty to the most noble, most illustrious and most excellent Lords, the Lord Peter, of the Sacred Roman Empire, Count of Goessen, Lord of Carelsberg, Chamberlain of his Sacred Imperial Majesty,Counsellor of the Imperial Court, and Envoy Extraordinary to the High and Mighty Lords the States-General of the United Provinces, and the Lord John Wenceslaus, of the Sacred Roman Empire, Count Wratislau of Mitrovitz, Lord of Ginetz, and Mallexitz, Chamberlain of his Sacred Royal Majesty of the Romans, and Hungary, Counsellor and Assessor of the Privy Chancery of the Court of Bohemia, and Envoy Extraordinary of his Sacred Imperial Majesty to the Most Serene King of Great Britain, his Ambassadors Extraordinary and Plenipotentiaries: His Sacred Royal Majesty of Great Britain to the most noble, most illustrious, and most excellent Lord, Lord John Earl of Marlborough, Baron Churchill of Sandridge, of the Privy Council of his Sacred Royal Majesty, General of the Foot, and Commander in chief of the army of his aforesaid Sacred Royal Majesty in the Low Countries, his Ambassador Extraordinary, Commissary, Procurator, and Plenipotentiary: And the Lords the States-General to the Lords Dideric Ech de Pantaleon, Lord of Ghent, and Erleh Frederic Baron of Rheede, Lord of Lier, of the District of St. Anthony de Terlee, Commander of Bura, one of the Nobles, and of the order of Knighthood of Holland and West Friesland, Anthony Heinsius, Counsellor and Pensionary of the Lords the States of Holland and West Friesland, Keeper of their Great Seal and President of the Fiefs, William of Nassau, Lord of Odych, Cortgiene, &c., Chief Noble and Representative in the Order of Nobility in the Assembly of the Lords the States of Zealand and of their Deputies; Everhard de Weede, Lord of Weede Dyckvelt, Rateles, &c., Lord of the soil of the city of Oudewater, Dean of the Chapter of St. Mary at Utrecht, on the Rhine, Prime Counsellor and President of the Assembly of the Province of Utrecht, Praefect and Praetor of the Dykes of the river Lech, William Van Harem, Steward of the district of Biltan in Friesland, Chancellor of the University of Franquer, Deputy of the Nobles in the Assembly of the Lords the States of Friesland,-Burchard Just a Welvelde in Buckhorst and Molekate, Lord in Zallick and Wekate, Lord Lieutenant of the county of Ysselmuyd, and Wicher Wichers, Senator of the city of Groningen, Deputies respectively of the Lords the States of Gueldres, Holland and West Friesland, Zealand, Utrecht on the Rhine, Friesland, Overyssel and Groningen and the Omlands to the Assembly of the Lords the States-General of the United Provinces, who by virtue of their mandates have agreed on the following Articles of Alliance:

Article 1.

That between his Sacred Imperial Majesty, his Sacred Royal Majesty of Great Britain, and the Lords. the States General of the United Provinces, there shall be and continue a constant, perpetual and inviolable friendship and correspondence, and that each shall be obliged to promote the advantages of the other, and to avert injuries and inconveniences as much as in him lies.

Article 2.
His Sacred Imperial Majesty, his Sacred Royal Majesty of Great Britain, and the Lords the States-General, as nothing is more pleasing to them than peace, and the general tranquillity of all Europe, so have they judged nothing would be more efficacious for establishing it than procuring a just and reasonable satisfaction to his Imperial Majesty, in consideration of his pretension to the Spanish succession, and that the King of Great Britain and the Lords the States-General should obtain a particular and sufficient security for their Kingdoms, Provinces and Dominions, and for the navigation and commerce of their subjects.

Article 3.
Therefore the Confederates, above all things, shall endeavour to their utmost to obtain, in a peaceable way, and by solid and firm agreement, a just and reasonable satisfaction to his Imperial Majesty in the cause aforesaid, and the security before mentioned to his Royal Majesty of Great Britain, and to the Lords the States-General of the United Provinces, and to this end the Allies will labour diligently and without any intermission for the space of two months, to be counted from the day on which the instruments of ratification shall be exchanged.

Article 4.
But if, contrary to their hope and wishes, within the time limited, the matter cannot be transacted in the way aforesaid, the Allies engage and promise each other, that they will help each other with all their powers, and that according to a specification to be determined in a peculiar convention, that so they may acquire the satisfaction and security before rehearsed.

Article 5.
The Allies, to procure the satisfaction and security afore said, amongst other things, shall exert all their powers to recover the Provinces of the Spanish Low Countries, that they may be a fence and rampart, commonly called a barrier, removing and separating France from the United Provinces for the security of the Lords the States-General, as they have served at all times, until lately the most Christian King occupied them with his soldiery, as also to recover the Duchy of Milan, with its dependencies, as a Fief of the Empire, and serving to the security of the hereditary Provinces of his Imperial Majesty, together with the kingdoms of Naples and Sicily, and the lands and islands on the coasts of Tuscany, in the Mediterranean sea, that belong to the Spanish dominions, and may be of the same use, and also will be of advantage to the navigation and commerce of the subjects of the King of Great Britain, and of the United Provinces.

Article 6.
That it be lawful for his Royal Majesty of Great Britain, and for the Lords the States-General, by common consent, for the use and advantage of the navigation and commerce of their subjects to occupy with their arms whatsoever lands and cities of the Spanish possessions in the Indies they shall be able, and whatever they may so occupy shall remain in their possession.

Article 7.
Should necessity require, that the Allies, for obtaining the aforesaid satisfaction to his Imperial Majesty, the security of the King of Great Britain, and of the Lords the States-General, be compelled to engage in war, they shall faithfully communicate to each other their designs, both for warlike operations and for all things relating to the common cause.

Article 8.
That it shall not be lawful to either of the parties having once taken up arms to treat of peace with the enemy, but jointly and having communicated their designs with the other parties, that peace be not made unless there first be obtained for his Imperial Majesty a just and reasonable satisfaction, and for his Royal Majesty of Great Britain and the Lords the States-General a particular guarantee of their kingdoms, provinces, dominions, navigation and commerce, and unless it be provided beforehand by fitting securities that the kingdoms of France and Spain never come under the same government and be united, and that one and the same person shall never be King of both kingdoms, and especially that the French never come to the possession of the Spanish Indies, and that navigation thither for the sake of traffic be never permitted them directly or indirectly, under any pretext whatsoever, and lastly, unless full liberty be granted to the subjects of the King of Great Britain and the States-General to use and enjoy all those privileges, rights, immunities and liberties by sea and land, in Spain, in the Mediterranean sea, and in all the lands and places which the late deceased King of Spain possessed at the time of his death, as well in Europe as elsewhere, which they used and enjoyed, or which the subjects of both or either of them, by right, acquired before the death of the said King of Spain, by treaties, by agreements, by customs, or by any other means might have used and enjoyed.

Article 9.
At the time when the said agreement or peace shall be made the allies shall agree between themselves as to all those matters which shall be necessary to the strengthening of the navigation and commerce of the subjects of the King of Great Britain, and of the Lords the States-General in the lands and dominions which they may acquire, and which were possessed by the late deceased King of Spain, as also of the manner whereby the Lords the States-General shall be secured by the aforesaid fence commonly called the barrier.

Article 10.
And because certain controversies in religion may arise in places to be forcibly occupied by the allies, as they hope, they will also agree amongst themselves concerning the exercise thereof at the same time as is aforesaid.

Article 11.
The allies are bound to assist and aid one another respectively with all their powers against the aggressor, if the Most Christian King, or any other should attempt to invade any one of the allies on account of this Treaty.

Article 12.
But if either now an agreement can be made concerning the often-mentioned satisfaction and security, or after the necessary commencement of war, peace shall again be made, after such either agreement or concluded peace, there shall always be and remain between the contracting parties a defensive alliance for guarantee of the same agreement or peace.

Article 13.
All Kings, Princes, and States who shall desire, and to whom a general peace is dear, shall be admitted to the participation of this Alliance, and because it is of great interest to the Sacred Roman Empire, that the public peace should be preserved and here, amongst other things, the recovery of the Fiefs of the Empire is discussed, the said Empire shall be specially invited to the participation of this Alliance: moreover, it shall be lawful to the Allies conjointly, or separately apart, to require the accession to this Alliance of those whom they shall think fit to require.

Article 14.
This Treaty shall be ratified by all the Allies in six weeks, or sooner if it can be done.

In confirmation whereof, we, the aforesaid Plenipotentiaries, have secured the present Treaty with our hands and seals.

At The Hague, the 7th day of September, in the year 1701.

It was signed in the several instruments separately, as follows:

On the part of his Imperial Majesty.
Petrus Comes a Goessen. Johannes Wenceslaus Comes. Wratislau ä Mitrovitz.

On the part of his Royal Majesty of Great Britain,
Marlborough

On the part of the Lords the States-General of the United Provinces,
D. W. ECK.
W. PANTON.
HEER W. GENT.
F. B. V. RHEEDE.
HEINSIUS.
V. De NASSAU.
E. DE WEEDE.
W. WAN HAREN.
B. J. V. WELVEDE.
W. WICHERS.

With seals affixed to the names of each.[32]

32 The original text was in Latin, started saying *Quandoquidem morto sine liberis…* and can be seen as *Trattato della Grande Alleanza contro la Francia, fatto all'Aja il 7 settembre 1701*, in Solaro della

As stated in Article 13, whoever wanted to join the Allies was welcome, and this was a covert invitation to Portugal and Savoy first; then, just in case, to Sweden and the Italian States.

Actually, it being the task of the treaty to get all of Spanish-ruled Italy, the Low Countries, and Spanish-held America, which at that time included not only Southern and Central America, but also one fourth of what later became the United States of America,[33] nobody could expect neither Philip V nor Louis XIV to accept an arrangement.

There were two more issues. The first was caused by Louis XIV. Nine days after the signature of the treaty James II Stuart died. Louis immediately recognised Prince James Stuart as James III King of England, Scotland and Ireland, and such intrusive and aggressive behaviour pushed England into the clash. William immediately ordered the English ambassador to leave Paris, and this could be seen as a first step toward war.

The second question, more subtle but by no mean less important, was resumed by William himself when, addressing the Parliament on 31 December 1701, said the war to be necessary: "In respect to our Trade, which will soon become precarious in all the valuable Branches of it."[34] In fact he mentioned also "our Peace and Safety at Home", and "the part England ought to take in the Preservation of the Liberty of Europe", but trade was mentioned by the first, and not by chance. This happened when the treaty was already on.

Antonie Heinsius, Grand Pensioner of the Republic of the United Provinces.

Basically as said in Article 3, and considering the six weeks needed for ratification, the treaty left time for negotiation until 19 December, that is to say in fact the whole last trimester of 1701.

In case negotiations did not succeed, as everybody expected, war had to be made. In fact, the last trimester being the first period of winter quarters, when no operation was possible, the three Allies simply prevented any fighting occurring in the Low Countries and the Rhineland before the eve of the next 1702 campaign, in the spring.

This is a summary, of course. Things were not this so easy, and did not go that smoothly, or fast. Talks, and discussions took a lot of time. The English,

---

Margarita, op. cit, II, pp.220–229. Here is used the English translation reported in W. Blackly, *The diplomatic correspondence of the Right Hon. Richard Hill,* cit., part II, Translations, pp.930–936.

33 Spain held at that time what later became the American states of California, Nevada, Utah, Arizona, New Mexico, Texas, Florida, and half of what was later the State of Colorado, that is to say more or less a fourth of what now comprises the United States.

34 *Journal of the House of the Lords*, XVII, p.6, 31 December 1701, reported by John B. Hattendorf in his *England in the War of the Spanish Succession* (Newport, RI: 1978), p.62.

Queen Anne.

the Dutch, and the Imperial visions differed, and the Imperial vision was not necessarily the same as the Habsburg vision, for some German princes preferred to stay neutral, or to lean towards France. Moreover the armies were not ready, and it was not that easy to have them paid. The Dutch wanted no active commitment: merely border protection and stop. The English needed time to muster and above all to drill their troopers. The Emperor wanted the whole Spanish inheritance, which London would prefer to give him only partially, especially in Italy, to avoid likely support for France by the Italian Princes. King William's death in March did not improve the situation, but at least Queen Anne made it clear that no change in English policy was in sight. By early May 1702 the declaration of war was signed, and what composed "the Allied armies" slowly started moving. They were late. Things in Italy were already moving since January.

8

1702: "French acknowledge Bellona, your luck has no equal: for you kept Cremona, and you lost your general"

I: Winter Pause

In late autumn 1701 the armies in Italy went to their winter quarters, and Victor Amadeus issued some new rules[1] about wages and supplies to be provided to each man of his army, rank by rank.[2]

---

1 See the *Regolamento delle piazze di Quartiere d'inverno, di quali gioiscono gli Uffiziali di fanteria regolati a ss 10 caduna ed a R 1 di fieno caduna il giorno, come anche del contante che godono li Bass'Uffiziali e soldati come infra,* in vigore dal 12 dicembre 1701, manuscript 129, handwritten copy in AUSSME, L 3, *Stati Preunitari*, 6 Piemonte

2 The resulting list of ranks, from the top, according to their daily wage, was: infantry or cavalry general, 15 liras per day; lieutenant general or artillery general, 11 liras per day; lieutenant marshal, 7 liras and 10 soldi per day; infantry major general, 6 liras per day; general lodging marshal of the cavalry, 4 liras per day; aide de camp, 2 per day; battle general or brigadier, 6 per day; general quartermaster, 4 liras per day; general adjutant, 6 liras per day; train director 2 liras per day; colonel 6 liras in the Guard, 4 in the infantry per day; lieutenant colonel, 4 in the Guards or 3 in the infantry per day; major, 3 liras and 10 soldi in the Guards and 2 and 10 soldi in the infantry per day, adjutant major, 2 liras per day in the Guards, 1.10 in the infantry; captain, in the Guards 2 liras and 10 soldi per day, in the infantry 2 liras; lieutenant, 1.10 in the Guards and 1 lira per day in the infantry (the same wage was paid to the ensign of the colonnella company in the infantry); ensign, 1 lira in the Guards, 0.20 in the infantry; sergeant, 0.20 in all the corps, corporal, 0.01 – 1 soldo – and 6 denari, private and drummer 0.01 per day, no matter whether in the Guard or in the national infantry. No roll was found for the cavalry, but usually they enjoyed the same wage of the Regiment of the Guards. The regimental staff included under the major received: quartermaster, 1.10 liras in the Guards, 1 in the infantry; "Auditore" (regimental military judge), 1.10 in the Guards, 1 in the infantry; grand provost (only in the Guards) 0.60; provost (in each infantry regiment but the Guards) 0.20; colour bearer, 0.20; hautbois major (only in the Guards) 0.20, and drummer major 0.20 in all the regiments; chaplain, 0.10 in both the Guards and infantry; surgeon major, 0.10; archers and carpenters, 0.10. Wages were improved by two fringe benefits: places and hay. A place equalled 10 soldi, that is to say half a lira of Piedmont, for one needed 20 soldi for a lira. The hay share was 1 rubbo, that is to say 9.22 kilogrammes. Usually there were as many places as hay shares. Not to make this footnote too long: the infantry and the cavalry generals received 30 places (1½ lira of Piedmont)

Piedmontese financial situation was not at its best. In 1702 the State debt was 26 million liras, and the income did not exceed nine million. The military budget absorbed that year 5,330,000 liras,[3] that is to say a bit less than 60 percent of the State income. It was right that Louis XIV promised a yearly 600,000 French écus support to Piedmont, but this was not enough.

On their side, the Spaniards too had problems, and needed money. They reinforced Lombardy and gathered troops in Naples: 400 dragoons arrived, some more troops were shipped from Spain by the French naval squadron commanded by the count d'Estrées, and 10 new cavalry companies were organised, to have a 15,000-strong army in the Kingdom of Naples. In February additional troops arrived in Naples: 300 men from the Spinola Regiment were followed by three cavalry regiments, and the Trinchera infantry tercio from Spain. but that was not enough.

In the same period the Pope too started worrying about the situation on his borders, and on 11 February 1702 committed two inspectors to check the Papal fortresses on the Adriatic coast near the war theatre, and report on their conditions.[4]

Winter 1701–02 saw no actual stop in operations. On 2 January 1702 Eugene had in theory 25,800 men, but only 21,344 were present, and in fact there were just 15,031 really fit for duty.

On the opposite side the Two Crowns had 60,255 foot, and 15,480 cavalry, that is to say 75,735, well-equipped, properly dressed, and regularly paid and fed men.

Eugene was waiting for 4,000 Danes – who, as already said, when on the spot amazingly demanded to be fed daily – plus Ebergeny hussars and the 1,000-man Prince von Liechtenstein's Regiment. Moreover Eugene had a mere 61,400 kilogrammes of gunpowder stock left, and was asking for 200,000 more kilogrammes, a further 7,000-man reinforcement, the wages in – deep – arrears, and new horses.

Eugene began operations in winter, in early January, which was absolutely unusual. Commercy was committed towards the Mincio with 2,000 cuirassiers to meet the arriving Danes, then he had to threaten Mantua, seize Ostiglia, and expel the enemy from the Lower Po area. There he had to join Eugene, who was moving towards Mantua too. The next step, according to Eugene's plan, was to enter Modena, and Parma.

After Commercy's departure Eugene marched along a semicircle, with Mantua inside and the enemy outside. He seized Ostiano, then besieged Canneto sull'Oglio – which surrendered to his discretion – and went on, seizing Marcaria, and Redoldesco.

---

and 30 hay shares; the colonel of the Guards – and presumably a cavalry colonel too – received 12 places and 12 shares; a captain 5 and 5 in the Guards, and 4 and 4 in the infantry; an ensign 2 soldi and 2 shares in the Guards and 1 and 1 in the infantry. The grand provost, the provosts, sergeants, corporals, archers, carpenters and troopers received none.

3 Prato, op. cit., p.260.

4 ASR, *Soldatesche e Galere*, busta 657, "Relazione del Signor Abramo Paris e del Capitano Stefano Bladi sulle ispezioni fatte alle fortezze di Ascoli, Ancona, Senigallia, Pesaro e Rimini nel 1702". [Report by Mr. Abramo Paris and Captain Stefano Bladi about the inspection made to the fortresses of Ascoli, Ancona, Senigallia, Pesaro and Rimini in 1702].

Left: Mantua.
Right: The Castle of Mirandola.

Villeroy immediately left his winter quarters, gathered his troops, and moved to hold his last two bridgeheads, But Eugene seized the first, thus Villeroy abandoned the second, Gazzuolo, having destroyed its fortifications.

As soon as he reached the confluence of the Oglio and the Po Eugene turned, left Villeroy at his back, and marched toward Borgoforte and Governolo, having Pálffy, Vaubonne, and Mercy in the vanguard. His task was Mantua. Tessé was there, and realised the risk of being encircled, hence he came out with a flying column composed of 800 grenadiers and cavalry. By chance they captured Mercy, who had left his men, and was making a reconnaissance. Mercy was so shortsighted that he did not realise the group of cavalry he was approaching was composed of enemies, and that was it. Moreover, once taken he spoke – a lot – thus Tessé realised that Eugene was coming with the bulk of the Imperial army and rushed back to Mantua, where he had 5,000 foot and 1,000 cavalry.

Meanwhile Eugene seized both Borgoforte and Governolo, committed Starhemberg to seize Guastalla before Villeroy could reach it, and found an agreement to get Mirandola with Princess Pico, who remembered to be a feudal subject of the Emperor. The local Spanish–French garrison, 400 strong, was suddenly attacked by the militia and the ducal carabineers of Mirandola, and overwhelmed. The Imperialists had free entrance.

Mirandola, on the right side of the Po a few miles from the river, was the bridgehead Eugene needed to lock up Mantua. Once he had seized Mirandola he established his headquarters in the abbey of San Benedetto Po and started thinking of the future, asking the Duke of Modena to allow a German garrison into the fortress of Brescello. Rinaldo d'Este also remembered to be a Prince of the Empire, and wisely said yes. That was a further bridgehead, and moreover on the confluence of the Enza and the Po, just on the border of Parma, whose entrance it commanded. This had further consequences, which indirectly caused the next war, but this is another story.

Eugene also asked Parma for entrance, but the Duke claimed to be a Papal subject, answered that the Papal flag was on his fortresses, thus no way. Insisting meant to complicate things and Eugene focused on other tasks, the best being Cremona, the French headquarters.

II: The Surprise of Cremona

It is not known exactly when Eugene first contacted Don Antonio Cozzoli, the rector of Santa Maria Nuova parish in Cremona, to gather information for a surprise attack, but probably it must have been in 1701. Whilst the contact proceeded, Eugene formed a plan. He summoned his generals in Luzzara on 28 January, and gave instructions: Starhemberg had to gather in Ostiano 2,500 foot, and 1,000 cavalry, approach Cremona, and enter it through a sewer with two tasked groups, each composed of four teams. Once in the city, he had to rush to the Ognissanti Gate, open it, and fire three signalling rockets.[5] Then Young Vaudémont with 2,000 foot and 2,400 cavalry had to rush in.

The first team of the first group, commanded by Major Hoffman, was three companies strong. The second, led by Major Nazzari, had a grenadier company and 100 fusileers. The third, as strong as the second, was commanded by Lieutenant Colonel Kufstein. The fourth, headed by Lieutenant Colonel Scherzer included a grenadier company and 300 fusileers. A 25-grenadier platoon had to get into the moat first as vanguard, an artillery officer and team of gunners had to come as rearguard. Scherzer had to stay on the external side of the moat. Hoffman had to go down into the moat, and, following a guide provided by Don Antonio, had to prepare a passage, enter the sewer, and stay there until the arrival of the two remaining teams. Then they had to enter Don Antonio's cellar, go upstairs, and get outside. Whilst in the street, Hoffman had to rush to the Ognissanti Gate, open it, and fire the rockets. Nazzari had to storm the main guard, seize the city hall, and hold it. Kufstein had to reach Cinquinella street, find and seize the deputy-governor's palace, and hold it. Scherzer, as soon as he spotted the three rockets, had to rush in, along with 1,300 hussars, and cuirassiers commanded by Mercy, who had recently been ransomed. Then Scherzer had to watch the bridge and the gate, whilst Mercy had to enter, and cross the city to the opposite side, find and open the Po Gate, and allow Young Vaudémont to enter with his men. Then a decision would be made over what to do next.

Don Antonio had prepared everything. In January he asked for official permission to clean the sewer. Both the city administration and the French headquarters allowed him: there was no danger, Eugene was far away, and the sewer was 46 centimetres – 18 inches – wide, and as high as a normal man, that is to say no more than five feet and four inches; thus now the sewer was dry, and passable.

Don Antonio kept Eugene aware about the poorly watched walls, and about how much the French were enjoying carnival, but his best piece of news came at the end of January. He let Eugene know that he was going

5 Many historians have written that the Imperialists entered through Santa Margherita Gate, but I rely on Carlo Antonio Stefanoni's *Cronaca cremonese*. This *Cronaca* was partially published in the *Cronaca di Pontevico*, by Berenzi (pp. 457 and 458), but the original manuscript by Stefanoni, an in-folio volume 767 pages long, is lost since long ago. The last owner, on the eve of the twentieth century, was Monsignor Gaetano Bazzi, who preceeded Angelo Roncalli (later pope John XXIII) as the secretary of Monsignor Bonomelli, Bishop of Cremona. Stefanoni was quite precise, that is why I trust him in full and prefer follow his accounts.

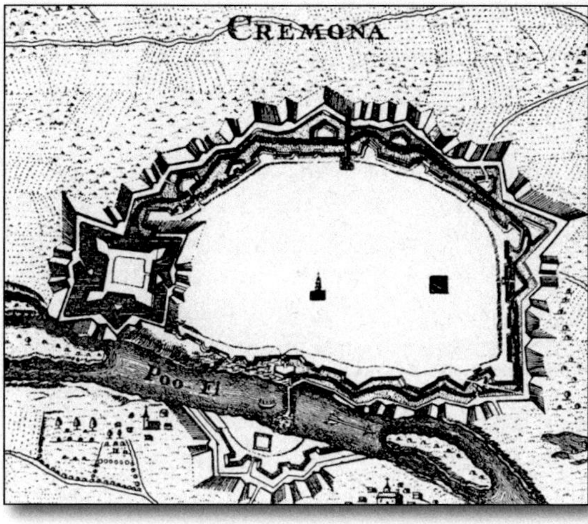

Left: The Fortifications of Cremona.
Right: Map Showing the Location of Cremona.

to send him a man; then he called a commoner, and rewarded him with a pair of new shoes if he went to Pontevico, looking for a certain man about a certain small business.

Once in Pontevico the commoner was suddenly arrested, and transferred to the Prince. Eugene asked him some questions, realised he was the man he was waiting for, and said in Italian: "throw those shoes away", and, in Latin added "noli timere" – do not worry, and then, again in Italian "do not have doubts", that is to say: "trust me". His shoe sole was cut, and divided. Between it, and the inner part of the shoe, there was a letter: on 1 February a big French detachment was to leave Cremona.[6]

Eugene ordered the commoner to be fed, and not allowed to leave without his order, and on the night of 1–2 February Eugene crossed the Oglio with his troops. Gathering so many troops in Ustiano and moving was not something easily kept secret. In fact the French were notified – we shall see later by whom – and Villeroy quickly went back to Cremona with his men. The garrison was now 9,000 strong anew. Eugene knew it, but decided to go on.

On 2 February at dawn, the Imperial troops were on the spot, and the first team entered the moat, followed by the others. It was a complete success. They entered in the sewer, and then passed into the city, reached the Ognissanti Gate, killed the sentries, and opened it. Mercy rushed in, and the clash in the streets started. Later Eugene reported that his troops "found Marshall Villeroy, who wanted to gather his people near the square and from there withdraw into the Castle, and kept him prisoner."[7]

It was a nice account, but it was not factual. Stefanoni reported that a portion of the Imperial troop:

> ran to Lord Count Carlo Ofredi's palace, where there was so much blood that the grand stair was all filled by it, and ran to the bed, and kept prisoner H.E. the

6 Carlo Antonio Stefanoni, *Cronaca cremonese*, cit. p.225.

7 Eugene, to Emperor Leopold I, report from the Camp in Ostiano, on 3 February 1702, rep. in *Campagne del Principe Eugenio di Savoia*, (hereafter "Campagne", 21 vols, (Turin : 1889–1892), vol. IV, supplement, p. 29.

> Generalissimo. But he Monsù Vilaroè, ashamed of being made prisoner in the bed, promised, and made an agreement with those German officers, to whom he promised with oath not to escape from their hands, but that they let him get out of house on horseback, and that later it had to be said that he had been arrested in the City. Thus so it was accorded to him, and so was done, and made.[8]

Meanwhile the Imperial situation was not turning out well. The Irish Regiment in French service watching the Po Gate held well. The French scattered in the city grouped occasionally at strongpoints, and started reacting. Moreover the Imperialists were still outnumbered 3 to 1, and, as another chronicler of that time, Giacomini, pointed out a few days later,[9] they were short of ammunition, did not know where the enemy ordnance was stored, were severely hungry, thus as soon as they could they started looting, just to find something to eat. That is why they could not hold the city, and Eugene had to leave. Disorganised Austrian supply prevailed once more, nonetheless the result was remarkable.

The French and the Spaniards immediately evacuated the whole area between the Oglio and Po rivers, except for the town of Sabbioneta, and abandoned a huge quantity of materials.[10] In Cremona the French lost 2,000 dead, 480 prisoners, five standards, three flags, two pairs of kettledrums, and 550 horses. Moreover they were disoriented because, lacking Villeory, they did not know who was now their supreme commander, and the post was provisionally held by the Old Vaudémont.

When the news arrived in Paris, it was considered as a great victory – did Eugene withdraw or not? Yes, hence.... In Milan Vaudémont ordered a Te Deum to be chanted, but French public opinion did not share that view. According to them, the only really good achievement was the loss of Villeroy. Voltaire wrote later:

> Marshall de Villeroy, extremely unlucky on this occasion, was condemned in Versailles by the courtesans, with all the rigour, and the adversion inspired by the favour he enjoyed, and by his character … The king … irritated that so high a choice of his was criticised, let slip out from his mouth: "They attack him because he is a favourite of mine": words he never used about anyone else, but this sole time in his life.[11]

Though protected by the King, Villeroy remained unprotected against satire. The most famous piece, "sung at the Court, in Paris, at the Army" said: "French let acknowledge Bellona, your luck has no equal: for you kept Cremona, and you lost your general."[12]

8 Stefanoni, op. cit., p.226.

9 G.B. Giacomini, op. cit., rep. in P. Guerrini, op. cit., p.176.

10 The Imperial Comissariate listed bridge materials, ammunitions, gunpowder, 294 big sacks of flour, 192 sacks of corn, 50 of rice, 6,000 of oats, and 32 wagons of hay. Probably it was enough to feed Eugene's army for a week.

11 Voltaire, *Le siècle de Louis XIV* (Paris, 1792), vol. I, p.326.

12 Rep. in Voltaire, *idem*.

Villeroy was released almost immediately. Leopold did not ask for a ransom, and when Eugene received the 50,000 thalers Villeroy sent him from Milan, he graciously refused them, for the Emperor had refused the ransom first.

Louis greeted Villeroy in Versailles, and then appointed him to a command in the Rhineland, where in 1706 he was defeated once more in Ramillies. So no wonder that one morning a drum was found suspended on his palace's main gate in Paris, with a paper saying: "they beat me on both sides." Voltaire added:

> the Duke de Vendôme was immediately appointed to command in Italy. He was not known as one who prepared his plans as deeply as Prince Eugene, and who mastered the art of supplying the Armies as much as he [Eugene] did. He neglected the details too much; let military discipline perish; the mess and drinking stole from him too much time, as much as they did to his brother. Such a weariness put him more than one time in danger, but one day of action repaired all, thanks to a brightness and to a cleverness that the danger rendered more active; and he always looked for those days of action; he was less good – according to what was said – at defensive warfare then Prince Eugene, and as much good [as prince Eugene] in offensive warfare.[13]

Louis de Bourbon-Vendôme,
Duke de Vendôme.

Louis de Bourbon-Vendôme, Duke de Vendôme was a "natural" member of the Royal House of France. His, and Victor Amadeus of Savoy's mutual great-grandfather was Henry IV of France. Vendôme's mother was the sister of Prince Eugene's mother – they were two of the Cardinal Mazarin's three nieces – and Vendôme's father was a cousin of Louis XIV, although their grandmothers had been respectively Henry's mistress Gabrielle d'Estrées, and Queen Maria de'Medici.[14]

Voltaire's assessment about him as a general is correct. Even if his arrogance often rendered him impossible to deal with, Vendôme was probably the smartest, and most skilled French general of his time. Villars could be considered maybe as good as he was, but not better. Anyway, two of the best generals of their time were now going to clash, the 1702 Italian campaign was about to begin.

---

13 Voltaire, op. cit., p.327.

14 Just to close the ring: Eugene's grandfather Tommaso di Savoia had been the younger brother of Victor Amadeus II's grandfather, Duke Victor Amadeus I, whilst Max Emanuel of Bavaria's mother was a sister of Victor Amadeus II's father, Duke Charles Emmanuel II of Savoy. So, Eugene was a close cousin of Vendôme, who was a distant cousin of Victor Amadeus II, as Eugene was, whilst Max Emanuel was a close cousin to Victor Amadeus, but had not real relation to Eugene of Savoy. Anyway they all called each other "cousin", as Louis XIV did to Vendôme, and to Victor Amadeus, even if they were younger than he was, and belonged to his son's generation.

9

The 1702 Italian Campaign

I: An Intrusive King, and an Opposing Council

Vendôme reached Milan on 18 February 1702. His task was simple: hold Milan, and relieve Mantua. Vaudémont explained the situation to him, and then Vendôme submitted a plan to Louis XIV. He wanted to commit 2,000 foot, 6,000 cavalry and 12 cannons against the smaller part of the Imperial forces, under Young Vaudémont's orders, on the right side of the Po. He wanted to expel the Imperialists from the Duchy of Parma, and to raid the Lower Oglio area.

Vendôme's actual problem was the impossibility of getting orders in time, and their occasional lack of clarity once they arrived.

A point must be underlined here, known by the experts, but not that much by the normal reader. Louis XIV's generals had as much autonomy as Hitler's generals in World War II, or less, that is to say from zero to less than zero. The King was more than intrusive. He wanted to direct all, and gave detailed instructions to be fully followed, and nobody could try not to act accordingly, or the result would be quite bad.

Such an intrusive attitude heavily affected operations. Whatever one wanted to do, whatever unexpected opportunity he may have, he had to ask Versailles first, and then wait for the answer, no matter if meanwhile the opportunity vanished.

Louis XIV Writing.

Only in a very few cases, a general could act after his own initiative: if the King explicitly allowed him in advance, or if the opportunity occurred on the spot, and was a matter of life or death. In all the other cases, one had to ask Versailles first.

Clearly, this needed time. A letter had to be written, and the couriers had to go, and to come back with the answer. It was a matter of days, sometimes a matter of weeks. The closer to Versailles the front, the less the damage, thus in Flanders things went reasonably well, but in Italy, and in Germany it was not so. A courier may need up to seven days to reach Versailles from Northern Italy, and seven more days to return. Hence the King took a decision based on information at least a week old, and when his instructions arrived at the destination, they were based on a no longer existing situation, perhaps so different that by no means was it possible to act according to Louis' instructions.

For instance, we shall see that on 25 May 1704 Vendôme received a letter from the King ordering him to move against Vercelli,[1] but according to the French official relation, that letter was issued on 18 May, and if we look at its date, we realise it to be 16 May, so Vendôme received instructions seven to nine days old, because that was the time the couriers had needed to ride from Versailles to central Piedmont. He was lucky, for the situation meanwhile did not change that much. Within two years the Duke of Orléans would not be as lucky as him.

This point is included because of a tendency I realised to exist many years ago among some historians,[2] or so they called themselves, who stated that the failures of the French military system were a symptom of a more general decadence during the last years of the Sun King.

It was definitely not so. Had at least the telegraph existed at that time, the results would have been much better, and such a centralised system would have worked well. Louis was simply trying to do from home what he did in the past when young at the front, that is to say what William III, or Victor Amadeus II were successfully doing: melting together policy and warfare, exploiting the latter to improve the former.

So, Vendôme had to deal with the King's orders, no matter how deeply he disagreed with them, and no matter how longer his operations lasted, and could be delayed. This problem always affecting French operations in Italy seems to have appeared here for the first time, and it was ultimately the reason why the French lost the war in Italy, or, at least it was the reason why they lost it earlier than elsewhere.

Now Vendôme begged the King: could His Majesty let him know his will, telling him whether had he to act offensively or not? Louis said yes, if Vendôme remembered his main task to be the relief of Mantua.

That did not work. The action against the Young Vaudémont had been planned to supply Cremona, short of food and fodder, and that action was the indispensable premise to the next march to Mantua. But the King implicitly denied the permission to act against Cremona, and underlined the priority of the attack toward Mantua, which, as things were, was impossible. Anyway, the King spoke, and the attack had to be made.

On 21 March the council of war held by Vendôme in Binasco formed a complicated plan to relieve Mantua. The Army of the Two Crowns had to gather south-west of Milan, and act on both the sides of the Po at the same time. Old Vaudémont had to cross the Oglio between Pontevico and Soncino, eastbound with 34 battalions, and 39 squadrons; Vendôme with 38 battalions, and 54 squadrons had to take care of the right embankment.

1 Fully reported in de Vault, op. cit., vol IV, 1704, pp.220–223.

2 As I had to argue during question time after a panel during SMH 2003 annual conference at University of Tennessee in Knoxville, on 1–4 May.

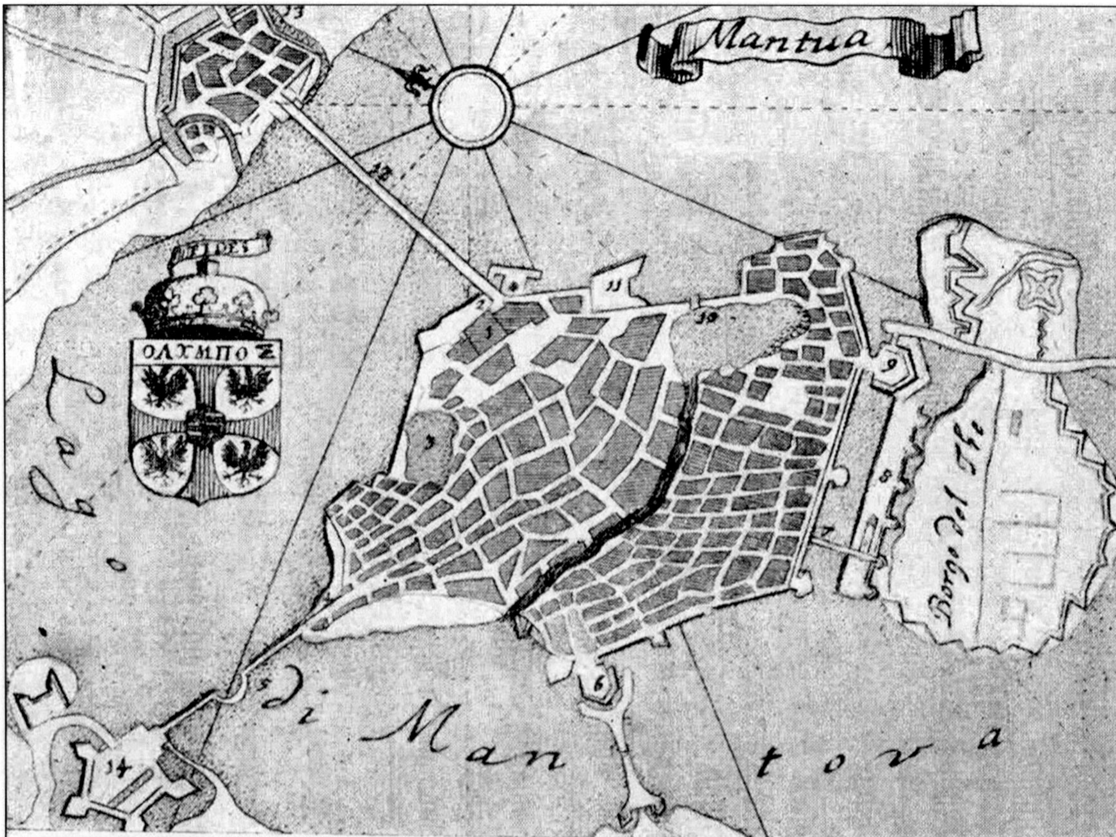

Plan of the Fortifications and Street Layout of Mantua.

Food and fodder were concentrated in Soncino, wagons and charts in Lodi, and the operation was planned to start on 26 March by concentrating the troops in Stradella.

On 27 March the Army of the Two Crowns moved along the Tidone river, in fact a creek. Eugene was immediately notified. As he bitterly reported to Vienna, the best he could do was to slowly withdraw, for he was too short in men and assets. He could, in case, make a bridge at Brescello to speed the passage of his troops to the left side of the Po, but that was all.

On 29 March the French and the Spaniards were on the Trebbia river, and on the 30 they reached the Nure, and put their headquarters in Ponte di Nure, but the enemy had already left.

There is one thing to be said now: Vendôme's arrogance had no limits. He basically respected the King, but there he stopped. Thus he spoke with no respect for, or to, anybody. Now, in those days of Spring 1702 the target of his arrogance was the Emperor. This lack of respect, also when targeting an enemy sovereign, was one of the things no monarch accepted, and sometimes did not pardon: a "brother", as the monarchs addressed each other, could never and by no means be mentioned with less than due respect, no matter whether an enemy or not.

Eugene was notified of his cousin's talks and reported to the Emperor:

> I have often been notified that as well he, the Duke, as his brother and the whole Nobility talk evilly, and with mockery of Your Imperial Majesty, and of Your Arms, thus I was compelled to let the Duke know that I was informed of such scandalous "discourse" of his nobility, and to ask him to make them stop, in order not to see me compelled to take other "measures"; I anyway did not go as far as saying that I knew how he in person, and especially his brother, and Marquess Boscoli had part in it.[3]

Emperor Leopold I.

This may appear a negligible issue, but it was not so. Something similar in 1706 would cause Vendôme's displacement to Flanders, as we shall see, and it would cause real damage to the French arms in Italy.

Back to operations. Eugene was sure the French march on the right side of the Po to be a feint. Anyway his worst enemy was not in front of him, it was behind him, far behind, in Vienna: it was the Aulic War Council. The Aulic War Council was one of the worst bureaucratic organisations Austria ever had: it was slow, ineffective, corrupted, badly organised, and it was only thanks to the so-called "proverbial luck" of the House of Austria that the Aulic War Council never achieved the total defeat of the Empire. Eugene had to clash with the Aulic War Council several times, as more or less unsuccessfull, his predecessors did too. But now, in Spring 1702, the situation was reaching its worst.

Eugene asked for reinforcements, and received nothing but a letter – an "Imperial rescript" – dated 8 April, basically instructing him how to hold on until the arrival of the reinforcements. He answered with a long, and detailed report. The suggested operations were impossible, he wrote, for the ratio was more than two enemies to one Imperialist in "infantry, which in this country is properly the backbone of the army". The promised, and never committed weak reinforcements could not balance the situation, because the enemy would have 15,000 men more. It was impossible to build – as suggested – a third bridge between Ostiglia and Revere, because "It is known to Y.I.M. how I, at my entrance in Italy, had not a boat, and no other bridge material, and neither a specialised man, but the Chief inspector of the bridges."[4] Nonetheless there were now two bridges on the Po, and three on the Oglio.

Regarding the money needed to build fortifications, Eugene had been told to take it from the treasury; but, he answered, "I really would not know which treasury it can be",[5] and anyway there was still a remarkable quantity of debt. Last – surprisingly, one would say – there were problems regarding – guess what – feeding the army. Imperial supplies were embarked in Trieste, and shipped through the Upper Adriatic to Goro, in the Po Delta, a matter of 79 nautical miles. From Goro the supplies had to proceed upstream along the Po to Mesola, near Ferrara, where they were downloaded into the closest

3 Eugene to Emperor Leopold I, from the camp at Luzzara, 24 April 1702, rep. in "Campagne", vol. IV, supplement, p. 98.

4 *Idem.*

5 *Idem.*

Imperial magazines. In the best case it was a matter of two days, because the standard wind speed in the western and central Mediterranean did not exceed 2.5 knots.

Eugene complained that the ships were not escorted, and asked for an escort by small armed men-of-war. He complained also because the promised 200,000 florins funding to sustain the transport "recently assigned to that task, somewhere had not yet been fully put in order",[6] a nice way to say: I've received nothing yet.

Well, what happened? Nothing, which in a war is the worst thing. The Imperial administration waited a bit more, and that was enough. A week later the French established on the Po a riverine fleet two galliots strong. That was the beginning. Then the Empire continued doing nothing. The French increased their Adriatic fleet to four vessels, and eight galleys and galliots commanded by Forbin, one of their two best admirals at that time. As a consequence, on 1 September 1702 Eugene sadly wrote: "about the supplies, there is nothing more to expect from the Adriatic."

II: The French Fleet in the Adriatic

In 1701 the Most Serene Republic of Venice accepted the presence of both Imperial and French troops on its land, if outside the cities, but prepared to react with four big men-of-war in case of naval intrusion in the Adriatic Sea, or the Gulf of Venice, as it was known at that time.

When Cardinal d'Estrées, the French extraordinay ambassador in Venice, demanded the Republic prevent the Imperial troops' shuttle or it would be up to the French navy to act, the Senate reacted quite badly, and voted: there were 160 ballots in favour of active reaction against any intrusion, and only 33 against it.

Claude Forbin.

Nonetheless, in March 1702 a small French naval squadron under s Spanish flag entered the Adriatic. Count Claude Forbin, one of two the best French naval commandes of that period, led it.

According to the French official histories, he had been notified that Venice was not respecting neutrality. Actually it was not so. Venice was keeping a strict neutrality, and Forbin had been ordered not to disturb it, thus he received restrictive orders: he had to cut the Imperial traffic from Trieste and Fiume, but by no means was his small squadron allowed to cruise in front of the mouth of the Adige river, the main port attracting Imperial traffic.

Thanks to Turkish support – a further indication of how clearly Venice assessed the international situation when choosing neutrality – Forbin could exploit the southern Dalmatia harbour of Durazzo as his naval home

6 *Idem.*

base. Then, Louis XIV obtained Papal permission to use Ancona too.

Forbin had two small frigates, one carrying 10 guns, and the other carrying eight. He started searching for all the ships entering Venice or Venice lagoon shipping Imperial assets and men. According to French stories, he stopped 80 small and big ships shuttling between Trieste and the Po area, and wanted to burn them, but it is unclear how many fishermens' boats were included in that number.

Map of the Coastline of the Upper Adriatic.

Actually, when looking at Venetian sources the reality appears a bit different. Forbin seized a commercial frigate in Parenzo, in Dalmatia, then entered Chioggia harbour, in the southern extremity of the Lagoon of Venice, and burnt two more commercial frigates, suspected to be shipping Imperial supplies.

The Senate summoned d'Estrées, and it was not a nice interview. Louis XIV calmed the waters, promised that Forbin would no more harass Venetian ships, and asked for an interruption of Imperial traffic. Forbin had just burnt a Venetian merchant ship sailing to Fiume when received his new orders. Thus he focused on the *Bonadventure*, an English 36-cannon vessel, armed by the Austrians as a privateer. Forbin now put his flag on the *Perle*, a 50-cannon man-of-war, and found the *Bonadventure* in Malamocco harbour, in the Lagoon. His ships remained at a distance but committed five boats, which reached and burnt the *Bonadventure*. Then Forbin went to the Senate to justify his action as tasked against an enemy, even if in a neutral harbour. It must be said that the legal terms of neutrality were still not that clear, thus they were quite flexible, and that the Venetians were not too unhappy: a possible intrusive Imperial presence in their Gulf had been destroyed by the French, who by the end of the war would leave, whilst the Austrians would stay. Some weeks after Malamocco, the Venetian vessels started acting as a fleet in being. The "public ships", as the Venetian military ships were called, *San Domenico* and *San Andrea*, found that off Caorle Forbin was pursuing some small ships, which joined the Venetian squadron. As soon as he realised, Forbin stopped, saluted, and formally excused himself.

Venetian Vessels.

Abram Duquesne.

Then the Senate recalled from Levant the *Aquila Valiera* and the *San Vittorio*. Both watched Pola, and in October and November 1702 reported that, whenever spotted by the French, the French ships immediately sailed away.

Just in case, the Senate reorganised the galley squadron of the Capitano della Guardia dell'Isole del Quarnaro e delle Rive dell'Istria – Captain of the Watch of the Quarnaro Islands and of the Shores of Istria – which had ceased to exist around 1618. Anyway nothing more occurred to the Venetians, even if Forbin returned to Trieste, and bombed it. Then he was committed to Tunis, and at last went back to Toulon.

From 1703 to 1705 Forbin successfully protected French merchant traffic in the Mediterranean, then he passed to the North Sea, whilst the other best French naval commander of that time, admiral Duquesne, succeeded him in the Adriatic. Duquesne focused on the Imperial privateers, based in Fiume and Segna. Once more the Venetians did not dislike it, as well as not minding too much when notified about the French raid against the Imperial harbour of Aquileja.

In 1704 the French and Neapolitan ships, commanded by Bouquier, tried to blockade Segna, but a north wind prevented them succeeding, and pushed them away. Then Bouquier was called into the Tyrrhenian Sea, due to the arrival of the Anglo-Dutch fleet, and the French ships never came back.

III: Spring Walks Around Mantua

By mid April 1702 Vendôme sent Louis XIV the plan for the final advance against Mantua, to be carried out by 69 battalions, and 112 squadrons. The chosen gathering area was very much ahead – between Castelponzone, and Scandolara Ravara – in order to attract Eugene. Vendôme thought that Eugene would advance from the Oglio; and this would have allowed the Franco-Spaniards to pass the same river halfway, and fall on the Imperial rear lines.

Eugene suspected something like this, and ordered the army to concentrate. Then he told his subordinates to expect the enemy action on Mantua to start on 2nd or 3rd of May. He noted that the enemy army was more than twice as big as his.

On 4 May Vendôme began his passage from the right to the left of the Po. Eugene got out all the troops he could, and what was "in a position to serve with this misery that afflicts the Army and I myself think of leaving tomorrow with the escort of God to do what is humanly possible."[7] What was humanly

7 Eugene to Leopold I, from the Camp of Luzzara, 6 May 1702, rep. in "Campagne", vol. IV, supplement, p.118.

possible consisted in leaving the blockade around Mantua, concentrating on the Lower Oglio all the troops from all the small garrisons on the river, and making cavalry raids against the enemy to disturb them, while he waited to discover which tasks Vendôme had in mind.

Carefully, gathering all the available troops and artillery, and feint by feint, Vendôme crossed the Oglio, and bypassed the right wing of Eugene who was approaching Ostiano. That was a surprise; Eugene did not expect it. According to the rules, he had now to withdraw to the north-east to keep communications with Trentino, but this meant leaving the Po and the Padana Plain, and to waste and cancel all the work done in the last 12 months.

Eugene was Eugene, and did not follow the rules, or at least not always. This time he did something unexpected: on 15 May he moved with all his 27,000 foot and 13,000 cavalry into the so-called Mantuan Serail, put his headquarters in Borgoforte on 18 May in order to master the crossing on the Po, and stayed there. The Mantuan Serail was a wide and healthy area south of Mantua, between the Lower Mincio and the Po. Eugene found there plenty of food, water and fodder, and was well protected by the rivers and canals bordering the Serail.

Prince Eugene of Savoy.

Vendôme was disoriented by his cousin's initiative. What did Eugene want to achieve? By now, Vendôme had made propaganda and announced that he gained a victory because he forced Eugene to withdraw without a combat, and in fact that is what it seemed. Actually it was not so. Eugene disengaged his army and kept intact his operational manoeuvring mass. He was now in an easy to defend area, with plenty of food, and could endanger the enemy whenever, and wherever he liked. For example: Vendôme committed a 4,000-man reinforcement to Mantua, and shouted about what a success he gained when the column entered the city. What he did not shout, and kept hidden, was that the column had been attacked by Eugene's forces, lost 1,000 men – that is to say a quarter of the original force – and all the supplies, thus as a chronicler of that time remarked, once in Mantua they were an additional burden instead of a help, especially because Mantua did not need additional troopers but did need food.

Eugene had now a considerable problem to solve. He realised very well that the French manoeuvre brought the situation close to the decisive moment – surely a field battle. He realised also that, his overall strength being inferior, he had to avoid a coordinated action by Vendôme and Tessé's units from Mantua, who acting together could crush him. But what to do?

The War Theatre in Lombardy, 1701–1705.

First he bombed and demolished the enemy defences outside Mantua, in front of the Cerese Gate. Then he established there a bridgehead facing the city, to at least prevent any of Tessé's forces exiting from that side. This made safe the Imperial rear. Then, to secure communications with Commercy, Eugene built two bridges across the Mincio near the Virgiliana. Last, on the 22nd, when he noticed Vendôme's main corps approach, and that it seized Castelgoffredo, he scattered cavalry patrols in the countryside to observe and stalk the enemy, and on 23 May withdrew behind the Fossa Maestra, the Main Canal.

Cautious, Vendôme secured his rear lines. He seized Castiglione delle Stiviere on 1 June and placed a strong garrison there.

Meanwhile Eugene had urgently sent general Pálffy to Vienna, hoping to shake the Court's immobility. There was nothing else to do.

Pálffy pushed very much to get an audience with the Emperor. He easily succeeded in speaking to the Crown Prince, Joseph, the King of the Romans, to Emperess Heleonor, and obtained ample and sincere promises of support, but when on 8 June he could finally meet Leopold he saw all his hopes vanishing. Yes, the situation in Italy was highly regrettable, the Emperor said, and certainly he would do everything to send the money for the wages in Italy as soon as possible, as well as the 8,000 promised Saxons. And what about the

Leopold I in Vienna.

necessary recruits? Well, here, for those, one had to see... it took longer then expected, there were questions ... And what about the ships to protect the traffic in the Adriatic? Additional hesitations.

The fact was that the reports by the Aulic Council of War accompanying Eugene's reports from Italy tended to let the events appear always distorted, and most unfavourable to the Prince. If he wrote that he achieved a success, that meant that there was no need for reinforcements. If, on the other hand, he suffered failures, this meant that he was evidently incapable of executing what he had been ordered and instructed to do by Vienna, and hence, but this was not clearly stated, in case he had to be replaced.

Leopold, Pálffy noticed, was obviously annoyed by the Aulic War Council's intrusiveness, but he did not seem able to do anything to avoid it.

The last visit Pálffy paid – and it had been postponed three times – was to the president of the Aulic War Council. Mansfeld, extremely ill, so much that it was impossible to recognise him, muttered that everyone was up against him, and that he was hurted by the moral pain caused by so many slanders scattered about him in the Court and in the city.

What could the army of Italy expect? Pálffy asked. There were additional murmurs, from which Pálffy deduced that the army had to be kept on the defensive until September, because there was no way to send it reinforcements before then. Pálffy objected that Eugene would not like that. "For now, he must deal with it, and can do nothing else" was the answer, with a shrug.

Pálffy left. He was now convinced that there were no great hopes. Every fact was wrong or purposely distorted, or misinterpreted. The tables did not include the figures about sick, wounded, detached, unassembled, and unavailable men, and, last, "They exercised me not that badly on the maps of the country – some of these Ministers – each of whom led the army with his finger up, and down around Mantua; however, since these maps, without exception, are full of errors, so too are those who think about it."[8] To top it all off, Eugene was seriously ill, and Vendôme prepared for the final blow.

By the beginning of June, the Imperial army had 55 infantry battalions, and 97 cavalry squadrons. They all were well below their theoretical strength, thus they in fact were 22,255 foot, and 13,058 cavalry – and 1,371 of them had poor, or no horse – with 124 cannons, and four mortars, 1,281 wagons, 216 draft horses, and 1,000 oxen. However, when considering also the 11 detachments scattered along the river, it was possible to list another 4,200 foot, and 160 cavalry, who increased the total to the impressive figure of

8 Pálffy, letter to Prince Eugene, Vienna, 14 June 1702, rep. in "Campagne" vol. IV, supplement, p. 137.

Philip V, King of Spain.

about 26,500 infantry, and 13,200 cavalry. One thousand of them were ill, and another thousand or more prisoners, but still listed in their roles; total theoretical figure: 38,000.

Vendôme had 103 battalions, and 132 squadrons, equal to 60,315 infantry, and 15,780 cavalry including French, Spanish, Milanese and Piedmontese[9] troops – with excellent transport, well-stocked warehouses, and powerful artillery.

Eugene, as we have seen, locked himself into the Serail. His southern limit was the Po, his eastern one the Mincio, his western limits were the Fossa Maestra – a large moat with marshy shores – and the Cavo of Curtatone, then a dam 3m 60 cm – or 12 feet – high on the side of Buscoldo; in the remaining part there were protections, and artillery places to Borgoforte, with a strong garrison in Curtatone castle. Vendôme decided to blockade Eugene into the Serail, and prepared the crossing of a portion of his troops to the right bank of the Po. But each movement was postponed until the arrival of Philip V.

The King of Spain had asked Louis XIV for the permission to go to Italy visiting the headquarters of the Army of the Two Crowns. Torcy had pleaded his case, and Louis gave permission.

Philip arrived in Naples in April. He stopped there some months, as we shall see later, and then left by sea, and sailed north. After a stop in Leghorn, where he met the Grand Duke of Tuscany, he landed at Finale and travelled to the army. He was greeted by his father-in-law Victor Amadeus of Savoy – and the meeting went so badly that it was the final push to Victor Amadeus to leave the alliance – and in fact greeted everywhere: in Modena; in Milan;

The Medicean Fortress at Leghorn (Livorno).

9 The Piedmontese corps included now only three battalions, and a regiment of dragoons: some 4,000 men.

in Cremona, where the Duke of Parma went to pay his respects to him, and now Philip was coming to Mantua.

Everything was moving, there. The Imperialists had just attempted a surprise against the headquarters of Vendôme to take him prisoner – the plan failed by a whisker. Vendôme reacted by sending 12 heavy cannons to shell Eugene's headquarters in Curtatone, in whose walls they opened so many holes that Eugene had to rush away.

On 13 July Vendôme met Philip V and promised him a very happy and glorious campaign. Philip inspected 4,000 cavalry and 12,000 infantrymen leaving for Casalmaggiore, and started the operational cycle tasked to unblock Mantua.

Eugene ordered the building of entrenchments in Borgoforte, and committed Visconti to guard Santa Vittoria with the Darmstadt, Commercy, and Visconti regiments of cuirassiers – 1,800 men in all – at the confluence of two small rivers, the Crostolo and Tassone. That was a rather strong and naturally defended place, due to its banks and how deep both the rivers were there. That is why the cuirassiers encamped casually, not caring about their lack of infantry, and why they did not put out advanced sentries.

Vendôme knew it, and on 26 July he advanced against them with more than 2,000 cavalry, and 24 grenadier companies. This mass of men attacked the Austrians, and caught them whilst their horses were free, and scattered in the grass. The French charged, and the Austrians suffered heavy casualties: 300 dead on the spot, and 300 prisoners. The French seized also 14 standards, two pairs of kettledrums, a few hundred horses, and most of the firearms, and armour – and all this triumphally occurred under Philip V's pleased eyes.

Impression of the Layout of the Streets and Fortifications of Modena.

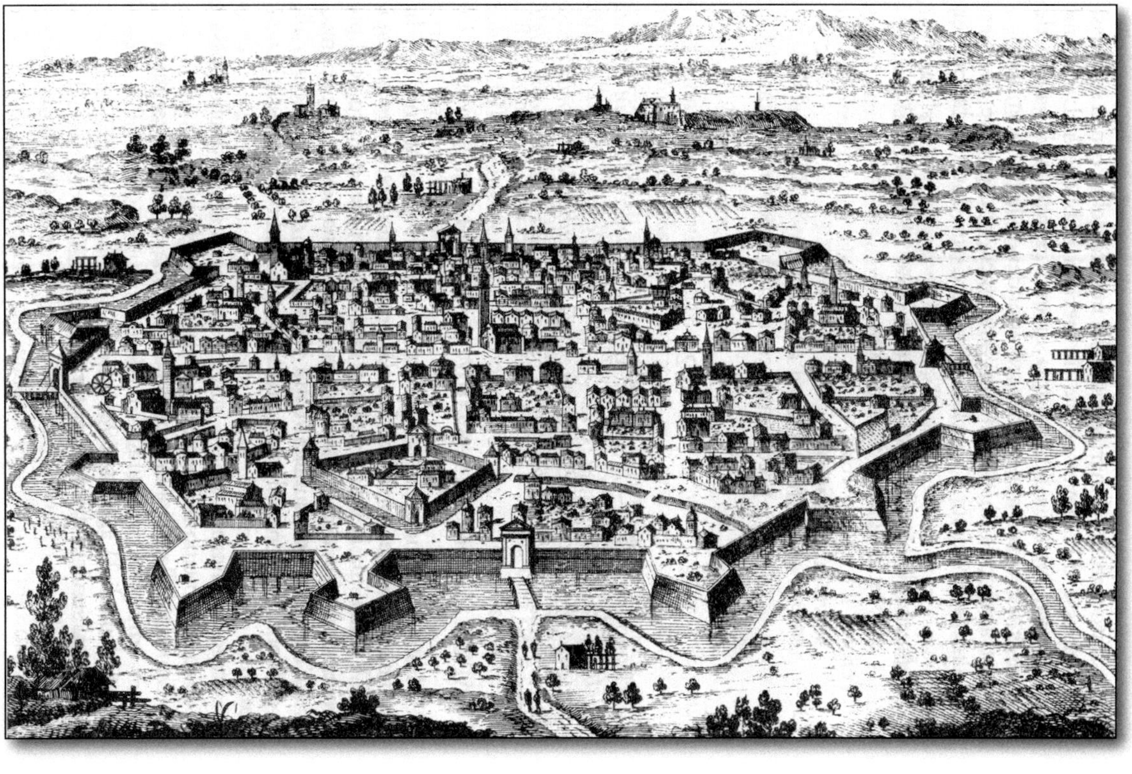

The survivors were saved by the arrival of the Erbeville and Count Montecuccoli Regiments, who protected their escape; but given the loss of horses and materials, Eugene was forced to use the survivors as additional infantry throughout the campaign.

On 28 July the French–Spaniards sacked the Modenese area. The Duke of Modena sent the Bishop of Reggio to Vendôme to avoid the worst, but got nothing, and was forced to flee with his whole court to Bologna, under the protection of the Papal Legate, whilst the French entered Modena, and settled in Reggio, Correggio, and Carpi.

Vendôme received a further 8,000-man reinforcement, and after a two-week pause started moving again, whilst Eugene, after Visconti's defeat at Santa Vittoria, on the 31st ordered the concentration of all his men on the Po, and the definitive complete entrenchment in the Serail. This meant the end of the Mantua blockade; and at that point the Army of the Two Crowns had only to organise its entrance into the Serail to destroy the Imperial army.

The Old Prince de Vaudémont arrived as far as Borgoforte, where Eugene had packed 5,000 infantry, and 100 cavalry in strong trenches. Then Albergotti came from the Modena area with another corps, followed by further reinforcements. Last, the Imperial headquarters was notified about the existence of the French riverine flotilla, consisting of two 10-gun galliots supported by five ordnance barges. The flotilla, accompanied by other boats carrying the material needed to build two bridges, had to go downstream to ensure communications between the French–Spanish units operating on the two banks of the Po. The French could now move.

IV: Luzzara

What was now King Philip's army silently decamped the night before 15 August. Its vanguard was preceded by the Duke of Vendôme with 24 grenadier companies, 600 dragoons, and 400 heavy cavalrymen. The army arrived in Luzzara before 8:00 a.m.; the Catholic King followed Vendôme and led the right column of the army, and the Count of Tessé the left.

His Majesty arrived near Luzzara between 9:00 and 10:00 a.m. He hoped to find accommodation there, and supposed he would find only a few Germans. They were immediately demanded to surrender, and it was expected they would do it on the spot. It was not so.

Eugene was waiting for the enemy. Since it was clear that the French were going to leave for Guastalla or Luzzara, he ordered General Solari to leave Brescello at night with 2,000 men, and enter Guastalla. From Guastalla Solari had to commit 400 men to the castle of Luzzara, which they had to keep at any cost.

> It is called Castello, or Torre di Luzzara, that small part of the Land westbound towards Guastalla, where the Parish Church is, and a few houses. But at that time it was not surrounded by strongly built walls, as by chance existed in ancient times, and then were demolished. There it remained a small ditch with water, and,

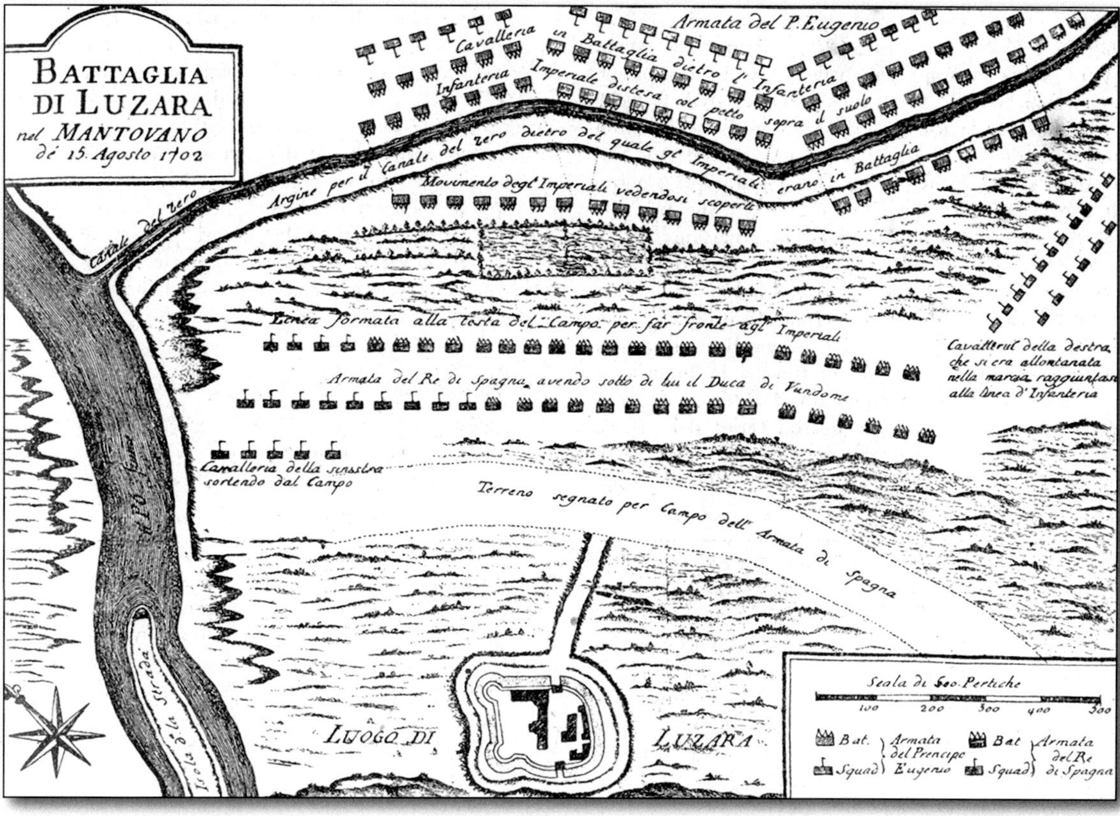

Dispositions at the Battle of Luzzara.

behind it, a few mounds of earth, and a large robustly structured tower, which commanded the main Luzzara road, and the fields around it.[10]

Vendôme boldly demanded the garrison surrender. Baron von Hitendorf refused. Vendôme prepared to attack the castle with grenadier companies, and ordered the bulk of the army to encamp a little further on, letting the army take up on the ground a shape similar to a Z, oriented north to south.

The Po had two constructed banks there at that time. One was used to retain smaller floods, the other, about 800 metres – or half a mile – further, had to retain the largest ones. The road to Borgoforte ran along the top of this second embankment.

Map showing locations of Guastalla, Luzzara and Suzzara.

French infantry from the left wing and from the centre encamped between the two embankments – the first part of the Z – along with several dragoon companies, and extended the camp a mile more, until under Luzzara itself, where the camp ended in a wide brush. The infantry of the right wing, and the rest of the dragoons, surrounded Luzzara – the last part of the Z – and cavalry was distributed here and there, as a possible support to the infantry in case of need.

10 *Vita e Campeggiamenti*, cit., p.105.

Since no enemies were seen around, Vendôme gave the troops permission to rest and to leave the ranks to look for food.

All the Allied generals felt so safe due their numerical superiority, that they were reasonably sure that Eugene would never dare to support the garrison of Luzzara. Their 53 battalions and 101 squadrons – 28,900 men – were not negligible. Eugene too thought them to be a lot of soldiers, but had no alternative: to act or to be destroyed, maybe not immediately, but soon. Thus:

> trusting in the skill of his people he marched to Luzzara after midday, to fight. He left the old guards, and the Visconti Regiment, and all the Hussars as watch. He led the first line on the banks of the Po. The Prince of Comercì the second along the Tabellano. The Lord Vaubon with a detachment went ahead, to make prisoners, and to investigate the situation of the French camp.[11]

Eugene had 34 battalions and 75 squadrons, as usual weaker than they had to be. Therefore he was leading only 19,643 fighters, escorted by a few cavalry.

Around 2:00 p.m. he found the enemy's extreme left wing encamped in the brush. The position was hard to attack, and he would have done it on the spot had his left column not been a hour late. So Albergotti had time to spot him, arrange the defences in the brush by cutting as many trees as he could, placing the artillery, and, finally, giving the alarm to the bulk of the army.

Nonetheless, it was a big surprise. Vendôme ran to deploy the Piedmont, Vessel, and Ile de France infantry brigades from the river to the main embankment, and supported them with the dragoons of the Senetterre Regiment and of the State of Milan. He set additional artillery on the embankment, and protected them with infantry backed by cavalry. Lastly he called 900 dragons, 400 carabineers, and 1,000 gendarmes led by Philip V in person, as a support behind the infantry of the right wing.

Since the surprise did not succeed as he had hoped:

> Prince Eugene set his right between the Po, and the great bank facing the Boschetto. He fixed the centre in front of the bank, under the command of the Prince of Comercì, and turned his left to Luzzara under the direction of General Count of Staremberg, and the Young Prince of Vaudémont. The Infantry, and the dragoons attacked by the first. The cavalry entered the fight, where it found it to be possible. General Varner put on the lower bank several Artilleries, which rendered a good service.[12]

The delay of the Imperial second line increased to 90 minutes, and it was decisive: Eugene would not prevail:

> If the second group had not remained far behind me that much, and had I not to wait for it an hour and a half, the enemy would have been beaten totaliter, and for many years one would not have heard of a victori so great, since all the prisoners

11 *Idem.*, p.105.

12 *Idem.*, pp.106–107.

> and deserters confess that everything was already in complete confusion between them …[13]

Finally at half-past four in the afternoon the Imperial artillery started firing. After an hour long preparation, the Imperial infantry advanced to cross the main bank, and attack the enemy camp. Commercy went ahead with the first line to lead the assault: "He was one of the first, and perhaps the first of all who was killed by the second of the two arquebus shots, which threw him from the embankment; and that shot him between his neck, and his chest, immediately smashing him on the ground."[14]

The Germans lost a good commander; Eugene a very dear friend he fought together with during years. When they brought back his body, the Prince burst into tears; but immediately recovered, and gave orders for a new attack. In fact, having seen Commercy falling, the Imperialists stopped, and some corps begun to withdraw, and were immediately assaulted by some enemy squadrons. Guttenstein and Bagni came in with their troopers. The attack re-started, and the height of the main embankment was seized, and crossed. Eugene fed the action by a reinforcement of infantry and dragoons, pouring them into the furious fight occurring between the two banks.

> finally the Lord of Boineburg with the Danes in Cesar's pay, General Bagni with other Regiments obtained, with a great mortality, to defeat the French brigades of Sault, of Grancei, of Perché, and some Irish Corps … and forcing other brigades to withdraw with notable loss a few hundred steps towards Luzzara. They did not advance further, because they feared a second line behind the first, that actually there was not.[15]

Even so, the Imperialists had in any case greatly damaged the enemy, separating its left wing from the centre, and arresting and putting in disorder Count d'Ormessons' cavalry, which was trying to fill the breach.

Further, the Prince of Liechtenstein was fully engaging three more French brigades, which thanks only to the example of the Sieur de Langallerie, the only surviving brigade commander, held until sunset.

In the centre the Two Crowns line was in a complete chaos, and held only thanks to Vendôme's cold blood. As for the right wing, after a first and very costly success against the Imperial infantry it had been half disbanded by the Imperial infantry counter-attack, made along with the cavalry charge led by the Young Prince de Vaudémont, and by General Visconti, who retook ground, damaged the enemy cavalry, and threateningly advanced.

The sun set shortly after 7:00 p.m.[16] on a confused and fierce hand-to-hand fight. It was still possible to recognise the two armies on the wings,

---

13 Eugene to Joseph of Habsburg, King of the Romans, from the Camp of Luzzara, 21 August 1702 rep. in "Campagne", vol. IV, supplement, p. 205.

14 *Vita e Campeggiamenti*, cit., p. 107.

15 *Idem*, p.108.

16 It may seem a late sunset, but in Italy on 15 August the sun appeared at five o'clock in the morning, and remained in the sky more than 13 hours and 50 minutes in 24 hours; no formal legal time existed then, it was introduced during World War I.

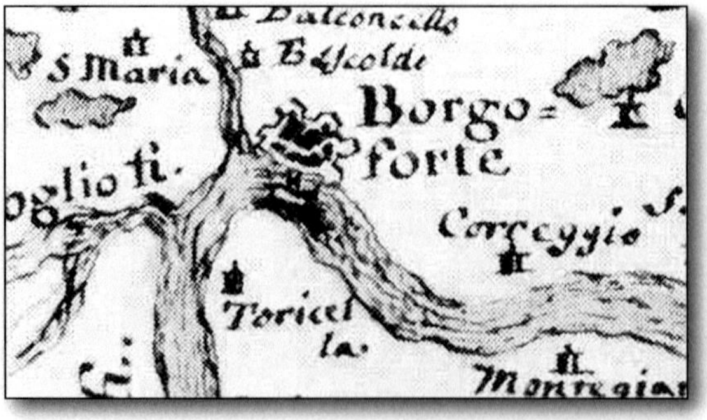

Borgoforte.

but in the centre they were so melted, that the Sieurs de Pracontal, and de Tessé risked being taken prisoners, because they throw themselves "among the Germans, believing them to be from their cavalry."[17]

One hour after sunset the fight was stopped. Eugene sent a messenger to Borgoforte calling in an additional 1,000 soldiers to reinforce his left wing.

Vendôme examined the ground and realised that, between the river and the village, the main embankment made an arc which was made impassable by bushes. Thus at 10:00 p.m. at night Vendôme ordered the commanders of the left wing to retreat silently to that new position. Once that movement achieved, he let the right wing withdraw to the small embankment east of Luzzara, under the church of the Augustinians. Then he filled that line with strongpoints, by inserting grenadier teams in all the houses, ditches and hedges he found.

Lastly, Vendôme took care of the centre, which ran from the main embankment to the church of the Augustinians. Vendôme garrisoned it using the most of his infantry, and there too he set strongpoints in every existing building. At the end, his front looked as a crescent, which his sappers were fortifying as fast as they could.

Whilst the work was going on, Philip V was sleeping in the Gonzaga Palace nearby, the Duke of Mantua on some straw on the floor of the Church of the Augustinians, and Eugene was issuing his last orders concerning the next day. He was absolutely willing to restart the battle at dawn, and once he had checked the distribution of the ammunition "he enveloped himself into his cape, and laid down behind a bush to get a short rest."[18]

At dawn Eugene was on horseback, observing the battlefield. He looked at the enemy camp: there were tents, wagons, ammunition, equipment, wounded, but no enemy. Puzzled, he then ordered his men to advance to where the enemy was now set, and carefully looked at their new positions. He wanted to discover whether was it possible to attack them, or it would be better to send a relief column towards the Castle of Luzzara to allow that garrison to leave. Nothing: he went to opposite extreme wing, toward the Augustinians, to see if any opportunity appeared: nothing even there. Vendôme had done a good job.

Given the situation, Eugene decided to fortify the area where he was, and stay and see. Thus his men made entrenchments of earth and faggots, just out of the maximum range of the enemy rifles, between the Po and the main embankment, and between the latter and the village. He filled the line with cannons, started an artillery duel with the enemy, and sent out cavalry and hussars to forage, and to damage enemy convoys.

It was the morning of 16 August, and whilst Philip V inspected the embankment under heavy rifle fire, Vendôme decided to seize the castle of

17 *Vita e Campeggiamenti*, cit., p.108.
18 *Idem*, p.111.

Luzzara. He did the job so well, that around noon on the 17th he took it, along with 500 prisoners and a wheat store.

The arrival of the Old Prince de Vaudémont with his troops, the fall of Luzzara, and the incoming riverine flotilla, allowed the Two Crowns to build some bridges and settle comfortably in the area.

Eugene reported to Vienna that he had won, losing 791 dead, and 1,905 wounded – half of the enemy's casualties – and let a Te Deum to be sung.

Cousin Vendôme simply sent a message to Louis XIV, and did not feel victorious enough to have a Te Deum sung, which instead was readily performed both in Milan and in Paris as soon as the couriers arrived.

From a military point of view it is easy to assess who was right. Usually the winner is the one who reaches the strategic goal, or at least the tactical goal he had in mind in origin. Vendôme planned to take Luzzara – and he succeeded – but wanted it as a first step to seize Guastalla, and later destroy the Imperial presence in the Po area. This did not happen either in that moment or later, for after the battle he stood fearing to be defeated and fully destroyed, due to his position with his back to the river.

On the other hand, Eugene stopped the enemy manoeuver, even if he could not prevent Luzzara's fall. He held the control of the ground because Vendôme left it, then he had fewer casualties, and held his positions. If these were his initial goals, he could be defined as the winner. Had he intended to destroy his adversary, he was not the winner either. But, since examination of his correspondance clearly shows that all he wanted was to stop the enemy and avoid annihilation by a pre-emptive attack, and since he succeeded in that, we can safely conclude that he was right when he wrote to the Emperor that he gained a remarkable victory.

V: Ending the Campaign

At the end of August Vendôme ordered Guastalla to be taken. It was easy: Solari held it. He had around 2,000 men who were short of ammunition and had no artillery but four cannons, which he moved continuously from one ruined bastion to another.

After nine days of open trenches Solari had to capitulate honourably, and was allowed to come out with the whole garrison – 1,900 men, including 300 sick – on 9 September. He had to cede the cavalry horses and stop fighting until April 1703, but was allowed to take away 24 shots per soldier. He went away to Trentino.

Guastalla was handed over to the Duke of Mantua, and the Army of the Two Crowns made no further move until the beginning of November.

Both armies remained in the same positions for more than two and a half months. They made many artillery duels, and minor clashes between their cavalries, the kind of operations in which the Marquess Davia, from Bologna in Imperial service, distinguished himself very much. His best performance was a long raid he made together with Paul Dèak's Hungarian hussars. They rode through the Piacenza countryside, the Pavia area, and crossed Milan – where the Imperial cavalrymen calmly passed screaming "Long live the

Emperor!" They then came back to Ostiglia, and returned to the friendly lines with a lot of cash and no damage.

On 2 October Philip V left the camp, preparing to return to Spain, followed by an escort of 1,000 cavalry and 800 grenadiers. Eugene did not move. Disease spread among his horses and left him with thousands of cavalrymen on foot. Fodder was lacking, and there was no way to provide it, because the surrounding area had been stripped of everything. Eugene decided to leave Borgoforte go to winter quarters around Mirandola.

The Borgoforte garrison slowly diminished, leaving about 300 men behind. Eugene sped up his movement only on 5 November, when Vendôme blew up the tower of Luzzara and left the area, he too moving towards Mirandola across the Secchia. Borgoforte was attacked by land, and river by the French, and was seized by the Sieur de Langallerie, after some resistance.

Then Vendôme decided to take Governolo, and opened a trench in front of it on 18 December. Eugene rushed to the other side of the Mincio with a strong column, allowed the garrison to disengage, covered them with intensive fire, and settled in Ostiglia. There he passed command to Starhemberg, and on 27 December left for Vienna. He had to start the winter campaign against his most dangerous enemy: the Aulic Council, and he would remain in Vienna and in Germany during the next two years.

VI: Two Dukes and an Abbot: Alberoni's Dawn

In those first two years of war, Bourbon preponderance seemed such that all the Italian Princes could feel safe. When Eugene widened the area he occupied, troubles started appearing.

As we have seen, in winter 1701–1702 the Imperialists marched west to have their winter quarters in the Duchies of Mantua, Modena, and Parma. Soon they reached the confluence of the small River Enza with the Po, an area commanding the eastern access to the Duchy of Parma. So Eugene committed Colonel Locatelli to Parma, asking for permission of sending an Imperial garrison into Piacenza, but as we know, Duke Francis Farnese answered he could not allow it, for he was a subject of the Holy See.

On the other hand Francis was keeping a secret link with the French, and the connection was provided by a relatively young abbot, whose name was Giulio Alberoni.

The story of how Alberoni was committed to the French headquarters is complicated by the longstanding, bad and insulting propaganda affecting his memory. That propaganda, based on the completely fake and misleading accounts written after his fall in 1720, in order to let him appear a totally unreliable sneaking plebeian rascal, and justify both the King of Spain and the Duke of Parma, was enhanced especially by Saint Simon, who provided a bleak account of facts he was not an eyewitness of, and whose source he did not mention.[19]

19 Saint-Simon, Louis de Rouvroy, Duke de, *Mémoires de M le Duc de Saint Simon*, edited by Boislisle, 20 vols (Paris–Geneva: 1976), vol. VII; on Vendôme see pp.283–285; on the meeting between Vendôme, the Bishop, and later Alberoni see pp.286–287.

Plan of the Fortifications and Street Layout of Parma.

An entire dedicated biography is needed to successfully challenge this version. I published it,[20] but there is no room here to get into details, only to tell briefly how Alberoni's affairs went before 1702, and what he actually did at the French headquarters.

Giulio Alberoni was born into a plebeian family. They were neither poor nor really healthy, but they were healthy enough to let him study in the best college of the city of Plaisance, the one held by the Jesuits. He proved quite well, and realised that the only career he could undertake was within the Roman Catholic Church, for no other organisation at that time allowed – at least in theory – a plebeian to go far.

In 1700 the 36-year-old Alberoni was a doctor in civil and canonic law, an Apostolic protonotar, and the secretary of the Bishop of Borgo San Donnino, Monsignor Alessandro Roncovieri. Alberoni's family had been protected by Count Roncovieri in the past. Monsignor Alessandro's brother, Count Guglielmo, had been the tutor of Giulio Alberoni after his father's death, and Giulio Alberoni had been introduced to Monsignor Alessandro, at that time the Apostolic Legate in Rimini, when spending some months in that town in 1685–86, thus they knew each other long ago. Hence no surprise if

20 Ciro Paoletti, *Il cardinale i duchi la strega: vita di Giulio Alberoni* (Rome: 2021).

Roncovieri, as soon as he was consecrated and appointed Bishop of Borgo San Donnino in Spring 1700, chose Alberoni as his secretary.

Just before becoming the Bishop of Borgo San Donnino, Roncovieri, between December 1697, and March 1700, accompanied the Duke of Parma's youngest brother, Prince Antonio, in a tour of Europe. During the tour they stopped in Versailles, thus Roncovieri, who may have met Catinat, was introduced to Louis XIV along with Prince Antonio, and surely met Villeroy too.

So as soon as the operations due to the Spanish succession crisis began, and the French Army came to Italy, the Duke of Parma did not hesitate, and committed Bishop Roncovieri as his representative to the French headquarters. And Roncovieri was followed by his own secretary Alberoni.

When the Imperial troops came too close, and Villeroy was kept in Cremona, things changed. Actually the story told by Saint Simon and widely spread later about how badly Roncovieri reacted to the first meeting he had with Vendôme is absolutely unreliable. It is unclear whether Roncovieri already met or not Vendôme in Versailles when there, but it is more than likely, and Vendôme's way of acting was always the same. His arrogant bad manners were widely known. Thus Roncovieri knew perfectly what could he expect, and how to deal with it. No, he did not leave the French headquarters for he felt offended by Vendôme raising half naked from the potty, and cleaning his own arse in front of him; the reason was quite different. Given the threatening Imperial advance into the Padana Plain, the Duke of Parma probably decided to downgrade his representative at the French headquarters, so as not to have troubles with Vienna.

Roncovieri said to be not well,[21] thus Francis Farnese – officially – took the opportunity, and agreed to the Bishop's request to resign due to illness. Alberoni remained, held the position, and often shuttled between Plaisance and the French headquarters.

That could sound fine: instead of a noble bishop whose brother was a count, the Duke's agent was now a poorly known abbot from a plebeian family. Nobody in Vienna could protest about it. The problem was that Alberoni since at least 1690 was serving the Duke in reserved affairs, so reserved that the archives only mention some of the payments he received, but do not say a word about why did he deserve that money, other that it was due to "the Duke's service".

As the facts show, Alberoni was the connection between Parma's intelligence and the French headquarters, and funnelled to Vendôme all the information about Imperial movements the Duke's intelligence gathered in the whole war theatre. It is unclear how soon he started, and whether he acted on Roncovieri's orders or not, probably not, although Roncovieri surely was aware of what was going on.

21 At that time he was 60, but died in 1711 when 69 years old.

We deduce it from information provided by Alberoni's first Italian biographer, Don Bellardi, whose work is still handwritten, and who got first-hand accounts directly from Alberoni in person in the 1740s.[22]

The first issue was about Cremona. Alberoni notified Villeroy in advance, telling him that:

> Prince Eugene with 4 thousand men and 4 pieces of cannon marches toward Parma; to seize such a City, few are the Troops and the Artillery; to occupy Monticelli they are too many, thus, Lord Marshal, all the necessity is to watch well your Bridge, which you have on the Po in front of Cremona.[23]

This was the first of a series of relevant information Alberoni provided. Some will be mentioned later, but one thing must be stressed now. Information was so complete, and came from such different and distant places, that it could be collected only by a wide intelligence net, so wide that no abbot could have enough money to feed it. But if an abbot, as Alberoni was, could not, who could pay that much money? There is only an answer: Francis Duke of Parma, Alberoni's master.

Why? We know why. We have seen why the Italian Princes were so reluctant to the Austrians, and so pro-French. Focusing on this specific case, during the previous war Parma had to host – and thus pay – the Imperial winter quarters. In 1696 Francis Farnese had to pay 36,000 doubles to the Imperial treasury. Then he was in such a bad financial condition that he had to start a hard spending review. Things were so bad that he preferred to marry the wife of his late brother, Sophia von Neuburg, not only to keep his links with the Empire, but mostly because by that marriage he could avoid giving her back her dowry.

The Imperial threat to Parma's independence, and money, was the root of some Imperial bad results, of Alberoni's flamboyant career, and dramatic fall, and also of many other things, such as the accession of Elisabeth Farnese to the Spanish throne, the next War of the Quadruple Alliance in 1718, and the arrival of a Bourbon dynasty in Naples in 1734. But by now, in February 1702, nobody knew it, and what was going on was later realised to have been Alberoni's dawn.

22 Filippo Diego Bellardi, *Sbozzo della Vita del Cardinale Alberoni*, manuscript in Biblioteca Ambrosiana, Milan.

23 Bellardi, *Sbozzo*, cit., chapter I, rep. in Giovanni Felice Rossi, "L'Alberoni al servizio di Francesco Farnese duca di Parma e Piacenza", in Giovanni Felice Rossi, *Cento studi sul Cardinale Alberoni*, 4 vols (Piacenza: 1978), vol. 1, p.157.

10

1703: Back to the Great Alliance

I: Strategy and Negotiations: A New Strategy, and New Plans

If in early 1701 Louis XIV could still hope to somehow deter the Austrians in Italy, the battles fought in that year let him lose this hope. The following year situation worsened, and in late 1702 the general situation necessitated a quick victory within a short term. When it became absolutely clear that Austria did not intend to accept a Bourbon on the Spanish throne ruling all the Spanish-owned territories in Italy, and insisted attacking, Louis decided to switch to the offensive. Consequently, in 1703 he started pursuing an aggressive strategy.

Louis XIV.

It was a turning point, for the strategic scheme inaugurated in that year was regularly repeated in all the French wars of the eighteenth century, and the Napoleonic Era, and was more or less re-used after 1915 in First World War. The plan envisioned the coordination of French armies in Germany and Italy. In specific, a French army would pass the Rhine moving through the Bavarian Plateau to Austria. The second, having crossed the Alps, had to march through the Po Valley to the Trentino, and across the Brenner Pass, where it would join the other French army in Austria. Thereafter the two joint armies could advance upon Vienna. It is interesting to note that these strategic routes continued to serve as military objectives during the Cold War, but in reverse. Soviet plans foresaw an invasion west through the Bavarian Plateau, and in the north through the plain of Lüneburg, whilst in the south a Hungarian corps, backed by the Soviets, would later invade Italy. In the Cold War that was considered a secondary route due to the obstacle of the eastern and western Alps, during the Spanish succession crisis it was not: it was as important as the other one.

Louis notified Vendôme about that great strategic plan by a letter dated on 24 May 1703 from his Sunday residence in Marly.[1] Villars and Max Emanuel of Bavaria had formed a plan, that he was forwarding to Vendôme. The French–Bavarian army had to go down the Danube, and seize Passau to secure Bavaria. The next step was invading Austria, or Bohemia, depending on circumstances. The Austrians were weak. They had a few men under Count Schlick in Bavaria, who could not hold out unless reinforcements came from their armies in Germany or Italy.

Maximilian Emanuel von Wittelsbach, Prince Elector of Bavaria.

Louis XIV supposed that, seeing the situation in Germany, the Emperor would withdraw his troops from Italy, thus, he said, Vendôme had to move. He had to reach the Tyrol, cutting any possible contacts between the Imperial corps in Italy and in Bavaria. Had he succeeded, the Imperial army in Italy would collapse due to lack of reinforcements and supplies; that in Bavaria would collapse too, due to the overwhelming force facing it from the south – Vendôme – and from the west. This would finish the war because, as Louis concluded, such an operation was "the surest means of ruining the Emperor's army in Italy, to finish this war – the most embarrassing which I could do – and to bring it to Vienna"[2] for at that point, once Vendôme was in the Austrian Tyrol, nothing could prevent Villars and the Elector to move ahead, in whatever direction they liked.

Why in 1703 did Louis alter his strategy? Sustainability is the answer. He was fully aware that France could not afford a long war. It was too costly in money and men, especially after the long Nine Years' War. Victory, therefore, had to be obtained quickly. An additional reason for such a change was the opportunity to support, and exploit the Rákóczi rebellion in Hungary. French agents were active in Poland and Hungary since 1701, and money was sent to the Hungarians from France. It is not a mere coincidence that the 1703 parallel offensive by the two French armies on Vienna occurred at the same moment the Habsburgs faced revolt in Hungary.

The 1703 French campaign in Germany went well, and in that summer the French and their Bavarian allies deployed forces on the Austrian frontier. More or less the same occurred in Italy. Eugene was now in Vienna and his main task was to rebuild the whole Habsburg military organisation, starting from logistics, whilst other people took care of economy and finance.

Deprived of its genial commander, the Imperial army in Italy found itself pressed by the Franco-Spanish army. In September 1703, as we will see, a

1 King Louis XIV to the Duke of Vendôme, Marly, 24 May 1703, rep. in de Vault, op. cit., Vol III, 1703, p.186 and following.

2 Louis XIV to Vendôme, cit., p.187.

French army advanced from Lombardy upon Trente, south of the Brenner Pass. The threat to Austria relented when the inhabitants of Tyrol rose up against the French, but in fact abated only when the Duke of Savoy changed sides. This cut supply to Italy and communications to France, and the French army immediately withdrew to Piedmont to re-establish and secure her communications. Then in 1704 the French northern route through Germany failed when the Allied commanders Marlborough and Eugene destroyed the Franco-Bavarian army at Höchstadt/Blenheim.

The French still had a possibility to succeed from the south, but the Piedmontese defection completely changed the situation. The French had to re-establish their communications through Piedmont – first – and only later could they try to go back to Trentino and to the Brenner Pass to enter Austria.

In 1704 and 1705 Piedmontese stubborn and bloody resistance, fortress by fortress, delayed the main French effort longer than expected. When in 1706 the French tried a final attack and besieged Turin, it was too late. They were engaged under the walls of the city after a three-month siege and were so severely defeated that they had to completely abandon Italy and Louis XIV's strategic plan. If after Blenheim the French could still act offensively in Germany and the Low Countries, and if after Ramillies they were able to retake the initiative in a very short time, Louis XIV did no more attempt to invade Italy after his 1706 defeat at Turin. At Turin his offensive strategy definitely failed, and his armies stood on the defensive on the Italian frontier first, and after the following year, in the Rhineland and the Low Countries too.

II: A Wedding, Some Hopes, and a Full Delusion

To discover what did happen in 1703 in Turin, and why it happened that way, and in that moment, we must go back a couple of years to 1701, to the complicated negotiations before the French–Piedmontese alliance.

We have seen how Victor Amadeus tried to widen his lands in Italy, not to be locked between the two branches of the House of Bourbon. He wanted to keep his independence. Had he not succeeded, his future would be that of the House of Lorraine, whose princes almost all lived in Versailles as Louis XIV's clients and subjects.

Victor Amadeus knew quite well this project to have been in France's mind long ago. France invaded Piedmont and Savoy in the early sixteenth century, and retained it until the 1560s. During the following century Richelieu and Mazzarino did their best to subdue Piedmont, which was reduced to a client state, and only Victor Amadeus' smart policy, and a stubborn fight in the last decade of the seventeenth century, during the Nine Years' War, gave back to the Savoyard States their political autonomy.

Now, in 1700–1701, the military side seemed to be the core of French pressure on Turin, but it was not. The core was politics, once more. It was a further French attempt to subdue Piedmont, a further attempt by France to attain a stable position across, and on the other side of, the Alps, once for ever, and ever.

As things were, by early 1701 Victor Amadeus had done all he could to escape such a fate, unsuccessfully. The Emperor had been as slow as demanding. England, and the Netherlands too had been quite slow. The Italian Princes had preferred neutrality, thus Savoy found no support, realised how impossible was to try to hold against France and Spain, and accepted many agreements.

As said, the military alliance was the most apparent part of the problem, but it was not the core of it. Tessé later wrote in his memoirs that Victor Amadeus offered his younger daughter as Philip V's wife, after a suggestion by Victor's eldest daughter, now the Duchess of Bourgogne, that is to say the wife of Louis XIV's eldest grandchild, the presumed future king of France. True or not, what is sure is that no trace of such an idea by Victor Amadeus seems to exist in Turin, or other Piedmontese archives. Anyway, according to the French, Louis XIV desired this wedding as an acknowledgement of the goodwill shown by Piedmont in joining the alliance, or so was said. But there were a couple of covert tasks. On one hand Louis avoided any possible engagement between Philip and a daughter of Emperor Leopold, as Charles II of Spain had suggested when still alive. On the other hand, as soon as they started talking about the French–Savoyard wedding, the French ceased to speak of any further compensation linked to the alliance. Victor Amadeus asked for the three million of his grand-grandmother Catherine's dowry Spain promised long ago to give the House of Savoy, to be paid from the State of Milan's incomes. From Versailles they answered him now that Spain would pay, but they did not say when. He mentioned the right his House had over Flanders, just to suggest taking Monferrato instead of them. The French answered it to be the matter of a future settlement, and anyway a problem, for Philip's inheritance could not be deprived of a sole square inch of ground. At the end Victor hoped the wedding between his daughter Maria Luisa and Philip V to be a possibility, or an opportunity. To be the King of Spain's father-in-law "could" give him more strength in negotiations, for future Spanish support for him was likely. Anyway, there was not that much to do other than accept, so he did.

The Bourbon Philip IV, King of Spain.

In late spring 1701 the Spanish special ambassador, Marquess de Castelrodrigo, reached Turin. On 4 July 1701 the wedding contract was signed, and Maria Luisa left the city bound for Spain.

Victor left too, bound to the allied headquarters in Goito, and reached it, as we know, on 24 July. When there, he realised the situation to be far worst then one could suppose. If the French ambassador in Turin, Phélipeaux wrote to Versailles that Victor Amadeus was surely in touch with the Maritime Powers, the

Goito headquarters was a real nest of snakes. Quarrels among the generals poisoned the atmosphere. Tessé wanted Catinat's post. Vaudémont supported Tessé, and wanted Victor Amadeus' post, due to the princely heritage of his own Lorraine. Letters flooded Versailles reporting rumours and gossip and telling lies. Whatever Catinat did, was badly done. Vaudémont had to be regarded with suspicion for he was a Prince of the Empire, and his son was serving in the Imperial army; Victor Amadeus was said to be in secret touch with the Emperor – which was true – through Prince Eugene, which was fake and proved the gossip not to be based on evidence, and to be right only by chance.

When Eugene crossed the Oglio, the French – as de Vault later reported – protested it to have happened because Victor Amadeus notified his cousin in advance, whilst as we have seen, Victor told the French to rush to the river and fight. Chiari too was considered lost due to Victor Amadeus, no matter how bravely he fought in the first line.

After the 1701 campaign, Phélipeux started changing his mind about Piedmont. He began suggesting to Versailles that it could be better to give Victor Amadeus some payback. One could not expect Piedmont to fight for free, nor the Duke to accept to pay on his own to support France's interest without payback. Nobody in Versailles cared. The best Phélipeaux received was the King's consent to a reduction of the Piedmontese Expeditionary Force in Lombardy for the next campaign. When receiving the letter, Victor Amadeus claimed to be honoured and grateful, but in fact he was furious. It was further evidence of how France did not care about him.

In winter the Duke knew that his son-in-law, the King of Spain, was coming to Italy. That could be an opportunity. In fact it proved to be the gravestone of the few hopes he could still have about the results, if any, of the French alliance.

The first issue was what to do about the next campaign: to go or not to go to the front? Victor was in doubt. Had he gone, he was sure that the French would secretly write to the Sun King he to be there just to spy, and to damage operations. On the other hand, to reach in person the Bourbon army once more could be a bad signal to the Maritime Powers. One more reason not to go was his incoming son-in-law. As soon as Philip V was with the army, as a king he would naturally get the supreme command, and Victor would lose it, no matter what the alliance treaty said. So, what about staying home?

The last knock came through his intelligence. At last Victor officially decided to rely on Louis XIV's statement. Whatever the King said, he would act accordingly, as he told Phélipeaux. Louis answered through Phélipeaux that Victor was free to act as he liked. But Savoyard intelligence, directly headed and managed by the Duke himself, received a different and true version. It corrupted a secretary of the French embassy who held copies of the secret correspondence. Thus Victor Amadeus got many letters, including that of the King's which secretly warned Phélipeaux that he wanted the Duke to not go to the army. That was not all. Louis went on to write that the ambassador had to speak and act covertly in order to get that result. That was enough to retain Victor Amadeus in Turin, but politeness and respect engaged him to go at least to greet Philip V. It was an additional and definitive disaster.

Philip left his wife in Spain as regent, and sailed to southern Italy. After his coronation, this was the sole travel he made in his whole life out of Spain. He landed in Naples, and was quite well greeted. Then he re-embarked, and sailed north. His ships stopped in Leghorn, where he was greeted by the Grand Duke of Tuscany, Cosimo III de'Medici. Cosimo asked for a favour: would, please, the King not pay to the Duke of Savoy a greater respect than that he was paying now to the Grand Duke of Tuscany? Philip promised.

Cosimo III de'Medici, Grand Duke of Tuscany.

It can seem nothing, but it was not so. Savoy and Tuscany competed for a political supremacy among the Italian Princes. According to tradition, the Pope was above them all. Venice came second, but it was a Republic, hence something strange. Who ranked third, which in fact ranked as the second crown in Italy just after the Pope? The contest was on for decades. After the previous war, in 1697, Victor Amadeus received the so-called Royal Treatment, that is to say that he was considered as a king by other European powers, and addressed as "Your Royal Highness", and his ambassadors were considered royal ambassadors, whilst nothing of that happened to Cosimo III, and to his diplomats. It can appear a pure formality, but formalities dictated the diplomatic rules.

Well, the consequence of this promise was quite bad for Victor Amadeus in the short term, but proved quite the worse in the mid and long term to Philip, and his grandfather Louis.

Philip landed at Finale and met the Duke of Savoy in Acqui whilst en route to Milan, and Victor Amadeus was considered no more important than any other duke, no matter that he be the father of both Philip's wife, and his sister-in-law.

Plan of the Fortifications of Finale.

In summary, Philip did not want to stay with him in the same coach bound for Alessandria. In Alessandria, where the whole court of Savoy was waiting to greet the King of Spain, Victor was notified that he would not have a chair as fine as the King's at the mess. Quarrels started. Victor let Philip remember that he deserved the Royal Treatment: no way. That was the last straw, thus the Duke declared that he had a cold, did not attend the meal, and on the next day left for Turin.

When Philip moved east, bound for the army, Victor moved west, bound for home, and to the Great Alliance. It would be an uneasy trip, but if the Bourbons did not care for him, if they mistreated him now, what would they do in the future once the war was won? It would be his, and his state's, political death. He had to leave the Bourbons in order to survive, thus he had to help the Allies make Louis XIV lose the war. He did, and he succeeded, and as we shall see it is at least doubtful that without his help to the Allies the war could end as it ended.

III: Negotiating with Former Friends

Once he had decided what to do, Victor Amadeus had to realise how to do it. As we know, and as Montesquieu wrote 25 years later, "as soon as Vendôme arrived, they wrote to him from the court to remain in Turin."[3] Short, and clear.

Meanwhile, however, Victor Amadeus started negotiations with the Austrian and English courts for a change of alliance. At the same time he had further reduced the corps to be committed to the French–Spanish army by 1703 down to some 3,000 men, commanded by Field Marshal Count Amedeo di Castellamonte.

In May 1703, Leopold I appointed Count Auersperg his plenipotentiary in Turin to deal with the Duke about the alliance.

French spies were everywhere; and the news slowly filtered to Versailles. According to Savoyard informants, Cardinal Grimani in Rome seems to have been the first to have talked about it. The news would have come to the ears of Cardinal de Janson, who would have forwarded it to Louis XIV and Vendôme, stating that according to the current rumours the treaty would be made public in seven to eight months, in January 1704. But Victor Amadeus, despite being worried by these rumours, did not lose the opportunity to take advantage. He realised that Leopold I did not like the idea of rewarding him also with the Vigevano area, thus in the secret text of the treaty, in article two, he inserted the condition that:

> having in the Court of Vienna, and in others made public, not in the due time, and against the concert of this negotiation [the content of the Treaty], this provided H.R.H. with the greatest risk ... so H.R.H. believes to be able to look for some sort of indemnity by the fairness of H.M. about so much prejudice that precipitated the commitments, disrupted the measures, and decreased the forces of H.R.H. Therefore having H.R.H. asked H.Ces.an M. the Vigevinasco to this effect ... it was therefore agreed to remit the determination of this point to H.M., who, in case he had any regret at to the cession of Vigevinasco, will be able to payback, and indemnify H.R.H. with a proportionate equivalent in the State of Milan.

Meanwhile Victor Amadeus received the first signals that the French were aware. It seems that the first official warning was an encrypted letter by General di Castellamonte to the Duke on 21 August 1703:

3 Charles Louis de Secondat Baron de Montesquieu, *Viaggio in Italia* (Bari, 1971), p.44.

> Having been on the 18th of this month with the marquess of Saint-Frémont, lieutenant general, and speaking with him about the situation of the affairs of Italy, he told me that it was necessary to put at the head of Your Army Your Royal Highness and let this business end; after a few words on this subject he made to me the following speech: You know that the public voice ensures that H.R.H. makes a treaty with the Emperor, that He enters the Great Alliance, and that the count of Auersperg is in Turin incognito tasked for that? I replied: "They are gross rumours that the enemies use to render H.R.H. unreliable to the Two Crowns." He replied: "What I told you is something I said just to talk, because I do not trust it, but it can be read in the gazette." I wanted to know if anybody really talked about it. The Count of None, who read the Berne Gazette in the Prince's of Vaudémont Room on the morning of the same day, assured me that indeed in the article from Vienna it is said that Y.R.H. enters the Great Alliance.[4]

Victor Amadeus promptly ordered a denial of everything; but meanwhile a great number of couriers had started coming from Versailles to the French camp. They arrived every day "with encrypted messages, which kept the Duke of Vendôme's secretaries busy during 10 or 12 hours",[5] whilst "it is said that 22 officers have been detached from this army and have been scattered in various directions on the roads to Piedmont, and along the Po to observe our movements."[6]

Victor Amadeus II in 1702.

Victor' Amadeus' defection was not well received in Versailles. The news, bad by itself, became even worse given the general situation.

During the two previous campaigns the results for the French had not been excellent. They had begun to move into the Netherlands, where Boufflers' 90,000 men faced Marlborough's Anglo-Dutch army. But Marlborough turned to Germany, and occupied Venlo and Liège whilst going to Cologne.

In Germany the situation was simple: France, Bavaria and the Electorate of Cologne seized Ulm, but after the battle of Friedlingen on 14 October 1702, situation was balanced.

In such conditions a minimal change could let the scale lean, causing the collapse of one of the two parts concerned; and what was happening in Turin was not a minimal change. The Savoyard change of alliance would interrupt communications between France and the Army of the Two Crowns in Lombardy, preventing it from getting reinforcements, and in the worst

4 Count Amedeo di Castellamonte to Duke Victor Amadeus II, San Benedetto Po, 21 August 1703, rep. in Carlo Trabucco, *La volpe savoiarda* (Turin, 1978), p.24.

5 The Count of None to Duke Victor Amadeus II, San Benedetto Po, 16 September 1703, rep. in Trabucco, op. cit., p.25.

6 Report by Intendant Count Lamberti to General Amedeo Count of Castellamonte, forwarded to Duke Victor Amadeus II, San Benedetto Po, 15 August 1703, rep. in Trabucco, op. cit., p.25.

case surrounding it and condemning it to complete destruction, making the wider strategic plan fail.

On the other hand, the Allies were exulting, because for the second time in a war they had attracted the Duke of Savoy, and could turn the strategic situation to their advantage. It was no longer just a question of conquering the Duchy of Milan. Great opportunities were glimpsed. It was necessary to help Victor Amadeus because his states could once again become, as in the Nine Years' War, the starting point for a deadly attack on southern France. There was an opportunity to eliminate the Bourbon influence in Italy, creating an empty area the Maritime Powers expected to fill commercially, whilst Austria wanted to replace France as the commanding regional power.

Lastly, in May 1703 Portugal, too, threatened in its maritime interests by the suggested Bourbon blockade, passed among Louis XIV's enemies, providing them with an excellent strategic base in the Iberian Peninsula, directly threatening Spain, and easing the Anglo-Dutch fleet's route to the Mediterranenan.

IV: The English Fleet Enters the Mediterranean

England already committed her men of war into Italian waters, and more generally the Mediterranean in the seventeenth century, thus the related problems were well known.

During the Spanish Succession crisis the Cabinet and the Admiralty had begun thinking of such an expedition since at least autumn 1701, but as Sir Charles Hedges remarked, it was impossible at that moment: the season was too far advanced and there were no ports to rely on.

In spring 1702 Count Wratislaw z Mitrovich, the Imperial ambassador, proposed to send the English fleet to Naples, but the answer was no. Sustainability was still the main problem, and as the official answer to Wratislaw's proposal said, the fleet could not "go so far as Naples not having any Port in the way without being exposed to the utmost dangers of the sea."[7]

Had Cadiz been seized, Sir George Rooke already had discretional orders to send a squadron into the Mediterranean to secure and assist Imperial transports across the Adriatic, but Cadiz was not seized and the fleet remained outside the Strait of Gibraltar.

In 1703 the plan foresaw an Anglo-Dutch fleet entering the Mediterranean. London thought the fleet could let the Berber – North African – pirates attack French traffic, encourage the French Protestants living into the Cevennes, in southern France, to rise up, as the Sicilians were also hoped to do at least in Palermo. Then the fleet could assist the Emperor to transport his troops across the Adriatic:

> but above all to induce the Duke of Savoy to declare for the House of Austria by giving such diversions ... to the French in Italy... A fleet in the Mediterranean was

7 Official answer to Count Wratislaw's Proposal, issued on 8 April 1702, rep. in Hattendorf, op. cit., p.98.

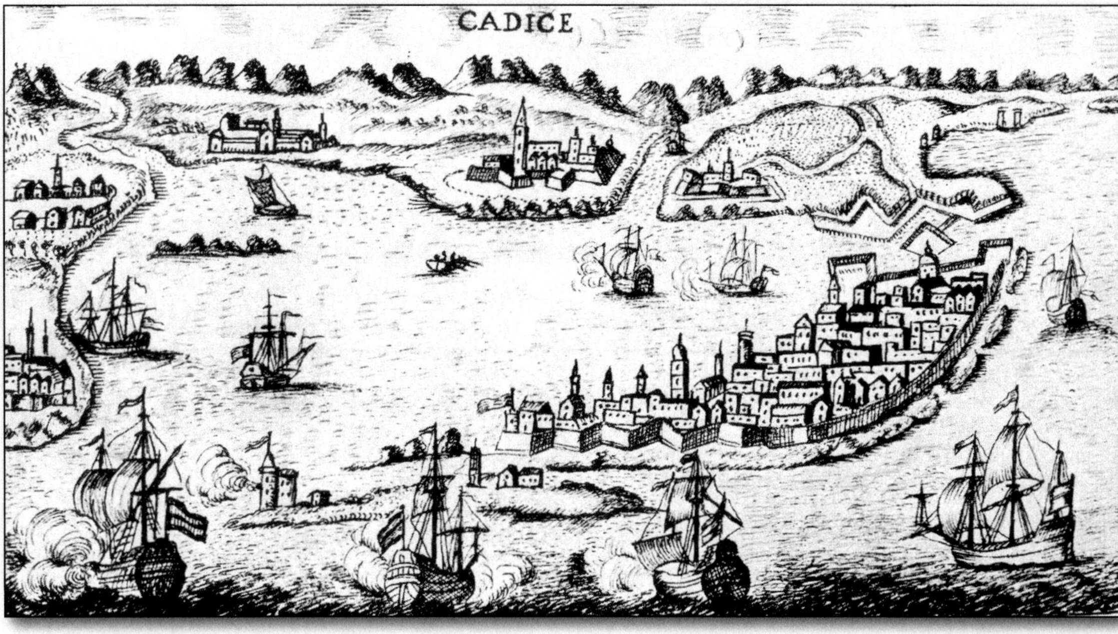

Drawing of the Bay of Cadiz.

> necessary to encourage the Duke of Savoy by letting him see how zealous we are to support the House of Austria everywhere.[8]

At the end of June Admiral Sir Cloudesley Shovell received his orders, and left. He had to fight against the French fleet, and prevent the French Mediterranean squadron joining the French Atlantic one. This was an additional reason why Louis XIV was worried, and decided to destroy Piedmont.

V: Victor Comes Back to the Old Allies, and Causes the Failure of the French Grand Strategy

On 1 June 1703, six days after receiving Louis XIV's letter describing the plan to finish the war, and the mission he had to accomplish in Innsbruck and Austria, Vendôme started organising the march of his men toward Trent, Bolzano, the Brenner, and the Austrian Tyrol. He first moved east, to secure the Padana Plain as much as possible. As he wrote to the King, he had just over 22,000 men, Vaudémont had as many as he had, thus the Army of the Two Crowns had 45,000 men, plus a very few thousand around Brescello, on the right side of the Po. The Austrians had 30,000. Had he in these conditions to nonetheless march north with 20,000 men as the King stated?

Vaudémont too was worried. He formally had the supreme command, and his forces included 38 battalions and 51 squadrons, including Spaniards, French, and Piedmontese.[9]

8 Lord Nottingham to Great Pensioner Heinsius, 24 May 1703, in British Library, Additional Manuscripts, 29, 595, fo. 230, rep. in Hattendorf, op. cit., p.101.

9 The Piedmontese Expeditionary force had six battalions and nine squadrons only.

Tyrolean guerrillas fighting against the French-Bavarians.

By mid June the situation was under his full control, and Vendôme notified the King that he was ready to move north.

Villars and Max Emanuel of Bavaria were following their plans, but they did make some changes. Max Emanuel left aside Passau, and by mid June was marching into Tyrol towards Innsbruck, asking Vendôme for support.

Tyrol is separated from Italy by the Alps and can be reached through the Brenner Pass. South of the pass there was a relatively small quantity of Imperial troops, commanded by General Vaubonne, whilst in the extreme east of Padana Plain, Starhemberg somehow still held on.

Vendôme was going to engage the Imperialists on the Secchia river, and thought such a battle to be decisive, thus he let Max Emanuel know it, adding that as soon as that battle was won, he in person would come, and that meanwhile he ordered preparation of 200,000 rations of biscuit.

Then, on 24 June, Vendôme received a King's letter dated the 17th. It was politely threatening. It started by saying "Dear Cousin" as usual, and went on to say that Vendôme had free choice, of course, but the King preferred him – that is to say in fact wanted him – not to make offensives in Italy, as he was doing, because offensives could push the Venetians towards the Austrian alliance. Vendôme had to keep a defensive attitude, protecting Lombardy, Parma, Modena, and Mantua, and sent a detachment to Tyrol.[10]

10 The King to Vendôme, Trianon, 17 June 1703, rep. in de Vault, op. cit., vol III, p.214, and following.

Vendôme decided to go on preparing the sought action on the Secchia, but on 30 June he put all aside. On that day he discovered that the Elector of Bavaria had already seized Kufstein and Rattenberg, and was going to reach Innsbruck, which he expected to enter that same day. Thus Max Emanuel asked Vendôme for help in occupying Tyrol, cutting the enemy's communications to Germany, and invading Austria and Bohemia.

Vendôme was now ready to leave on the spot, along with 32 battalions, and 29 squadrons, leaving the other troops to Vaudémont, and informed the King on 1 July. With his utmost surprise, on that same day he received a letter from the King dated 25 June: Louis wrote that he had been informed about the forthcoming Victor Amadeus change of side. Rumours said that the Duke of Savoy intended to receive the Anglo-Dutch fleet in his Villafranca harbour, near Nice. From Villafranca the Allies were to march toward Alessandria together with the Piedmontese troops, and once Alessandria and Novara seized they intended to enter deep into the Duchy of Milan, and attack Vendôme's army. Thus, the King wrote, Vendôme had to notify Vaudémont with the deepest secrecy, and prepare their countermeasures, that is to say that they had to prepare to neutralise, and capture the Piedmontese.[11] This news affected the whole French strategy in Italy, as we shall see, and in Europe.

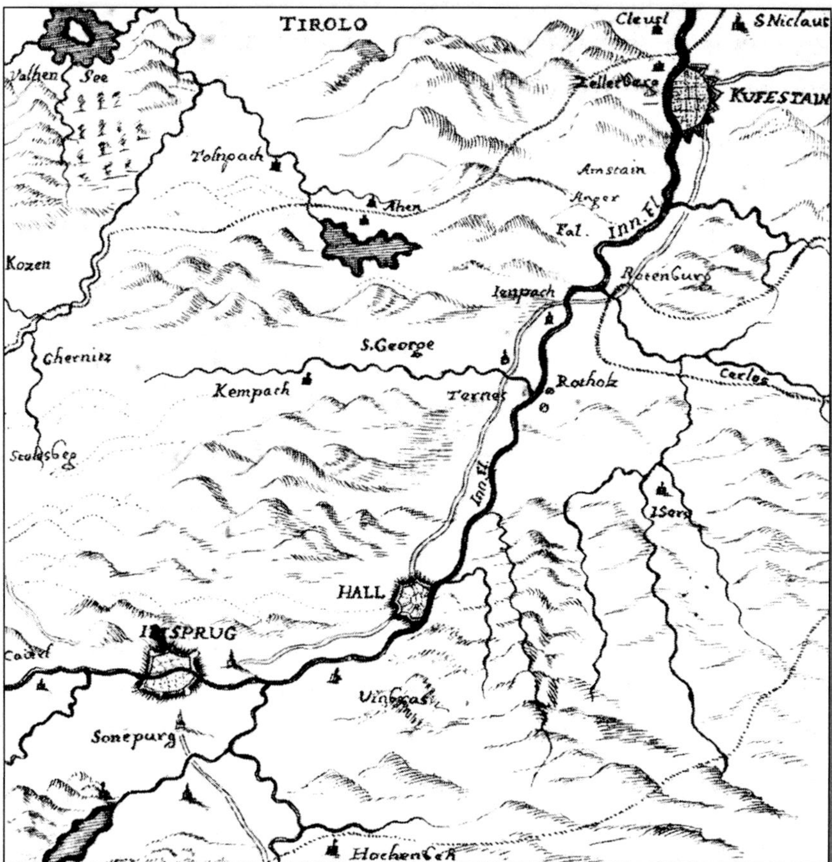

Map of the Tyrol.

11 The King to Vendôme, Trianon, 25 June 1703, rep. in de Vault, op. cit., pp.223–225.

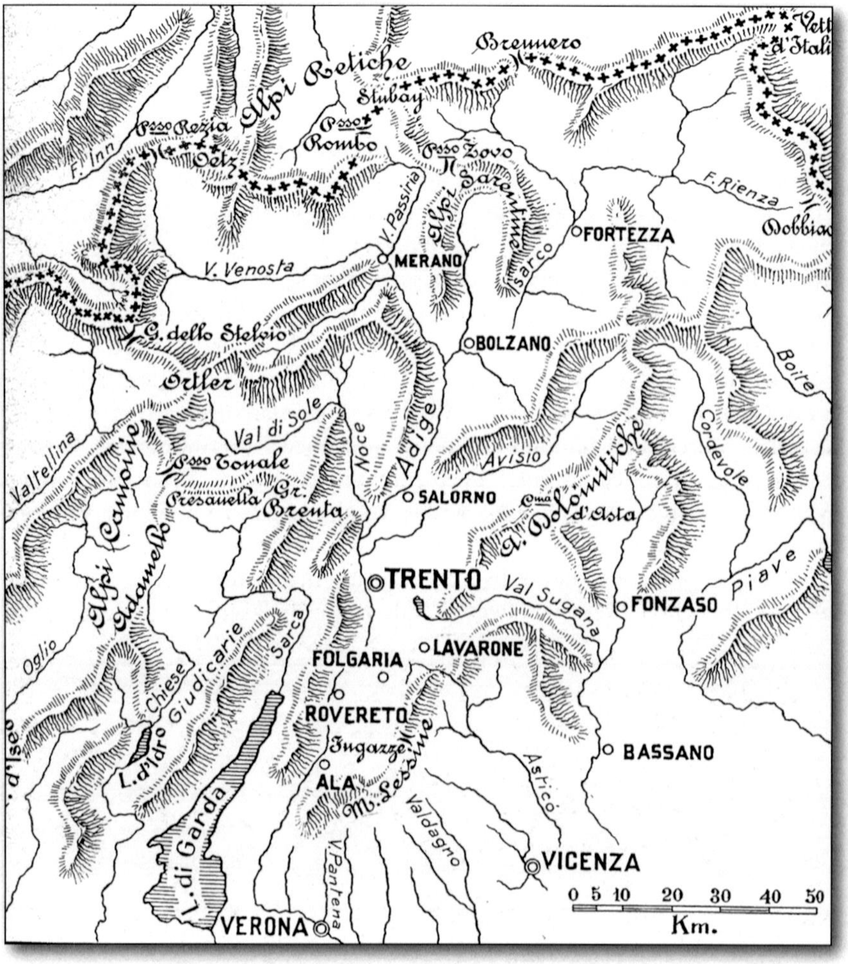

Trentino and Upper Adige.

Vendôme answered on 2 July, and waited for further orders. He received them on 15 July by two letters dated on 6 and 8 July containing his marching order to Trentino: he had to commit Besons, or could go in person if he liked, with 20 battalions, 25 squadrons, 10 field cannons, and two 24-calibre guns. Vendôme decided to leave heading 32 battalions, 32 squadrons, 21 cannons, and two big mortars, and left 36 battalions, 80 squadrons, and 44 guns to Vaudémont. Then he received a letter from the Elector: Max Emanuel, on 9 July, wrote that he seized Innsbruck, and that he was ready to march south through the Brenner to Bressanone to join Vendôme.

So, Vendôme left northbound on 24 July, passed Monte Baldo, and on the 28th his vanguard entered Trentino from Brentonico. On 31 July his men blockaded Nago. The garrison of the castle – 90 regulars, and 40 Trentine militiamen – refused to surrender. Vendôme was puzzled: the castle lay on a rock that his sappers and miners could not pierce, and artillery could poorly damage its walls, nonetheless he started the siege as usual, and on 4 August the garrison surrendered. Vendôme now stopped. He no longer had news from the Elector, did not know whether to proceed to Bolzano or not, and begged the King for orders.

Plate 1
Duke Victor Amadeus II of Savoy, Turin, 7 September 1706.
(Illustration by Bruno Mugnai © Helion & Company)
See Colour Plate Commentaries for further information

Plate 2
Savoy-Piedmont: Dragoon Regiment *Genevois*, Private 1706;
Cavalry Regiment *Piemonte-Reale*, trooper 1704-09.
(Illustration by Bruno Mugnai © Helion & Company)
See Colour Plate Commentaries for further information

Plate 3

Savoy-Piedmont: Infantry Regiment *Aosta*, NCO 1701–1705;
Infantry Regiment *Monferrato*, grenadier, 1704.

(Illustration by Bruno Mugnai © Helion & Company)

See Colour Plate Commentaries for further information

Plate 4
Savoy-Piedmont: Artilleryman, 1706–11; Senior Commander, 1709–14.
(Illustration by Bruno Mugnai © Helion & Company)
See Colour Plate Commentaries for further information

Plate 5

Savoy-Piedmont: Infantry Regiment *Guardie*, grenadier 1709;
Infantry Regiment *Savoye*, fusilier, 1712–15.

(Illustration by Bruno Mugnai © Helion & Company)

See Colour Plate Commentaries for further information

Plate 6

Savoy-Piedmont: Infantry Regiment *Hackbrett* (Valais), fusilier 1712–14; Infantry Regiment *Reding* (Valais), officer 1704.

(Illustration by Bruno Mugnai © Helion & Company)

See Colour Plate Commentaries for further information

Plate 7
Papal States: Infantry Regiment *Ruspoli*, fusilier 1708;
Infantry Regiment *Serlupi*, ensign 1708.
(Illustration by Bruno Mugnai © Helion & Company)
See Colour Plate Commentaries for further information

Plate 8
Duchy of Parma and Piacenza: Infantry Company *Guardia Irlandese*, fusilier 1704–12; Grand Duchy of Tuscany, fusilier 1708–14.
(Illustration by Bruno Mugnai © Helion & Company)
See Colour Plate Commentaries for further information

Savoy-Piedmont: Infantry Regiments Uniforms 1704-1712

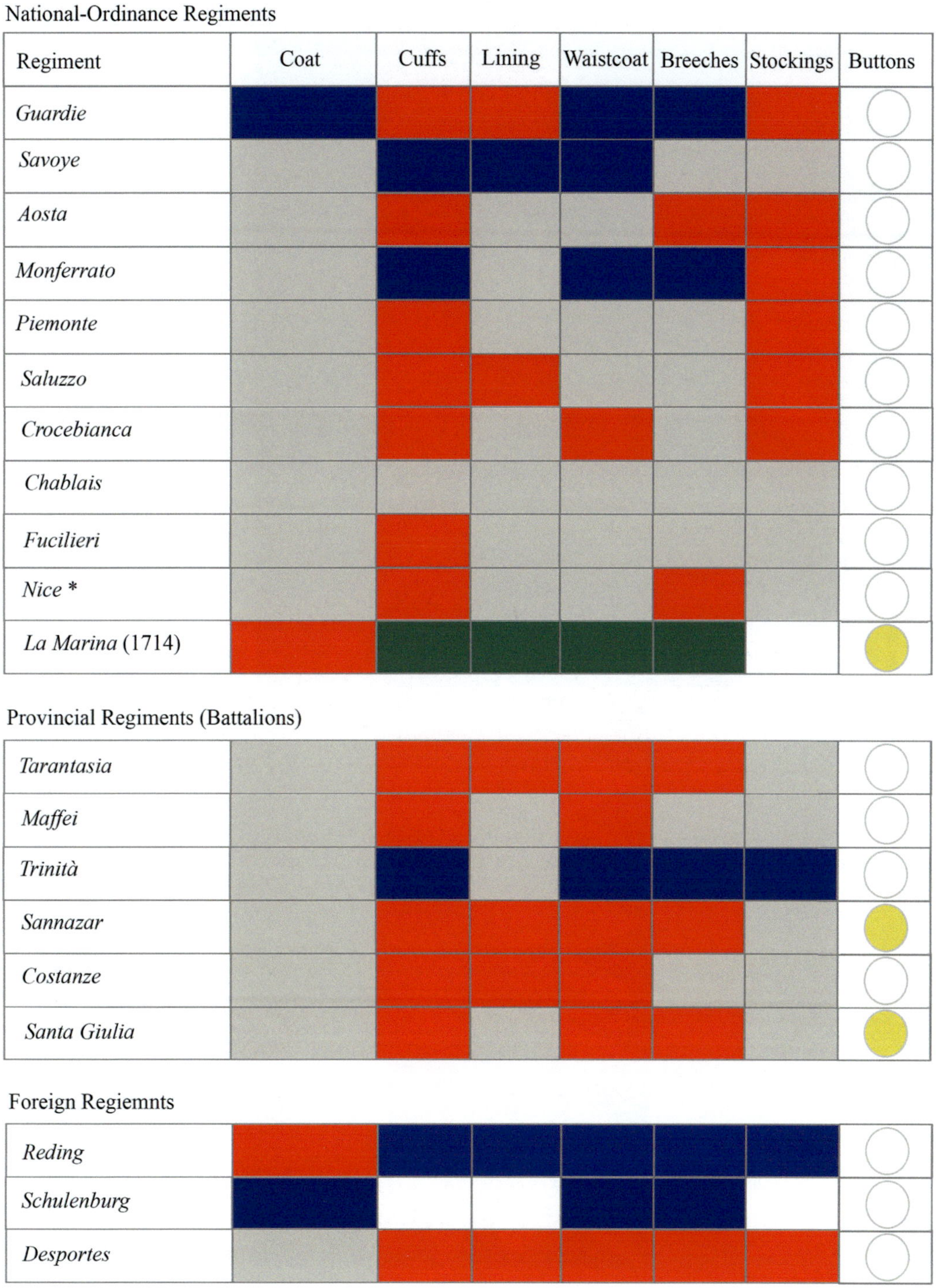

* *Nice* becomes *La Marina* in 1714

Plate 9
Uniforms of the Savoy-Piedmont Infantry.

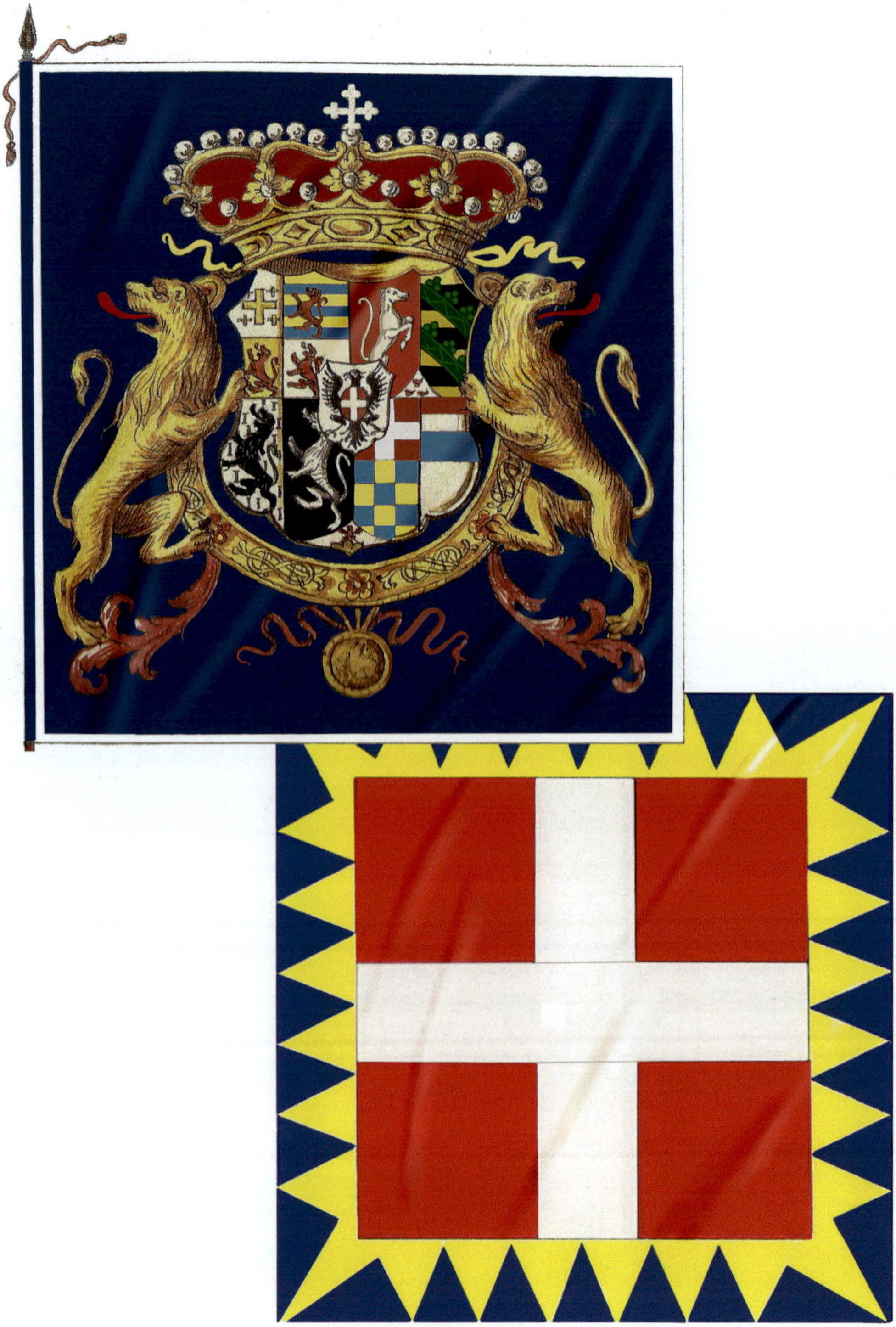

Plate 10

Savoy-Piedmont: above, *Reggimento delle Guardie* colonel's colour; below, *Reggimento delle Guardie*.

(Illustrations by Bruno Mugnai © Helion & Company)

See Colour Plate Commentaries for further information

Plate 11
Savoy-Piedmont: above, possibly Infantry Regiment *Nice*; below, Infantry Regiment *Fucilieri*.
(Illustrations by Bruno Mugnai © Helion & Company)
See Colour Plate Commentaries for further information

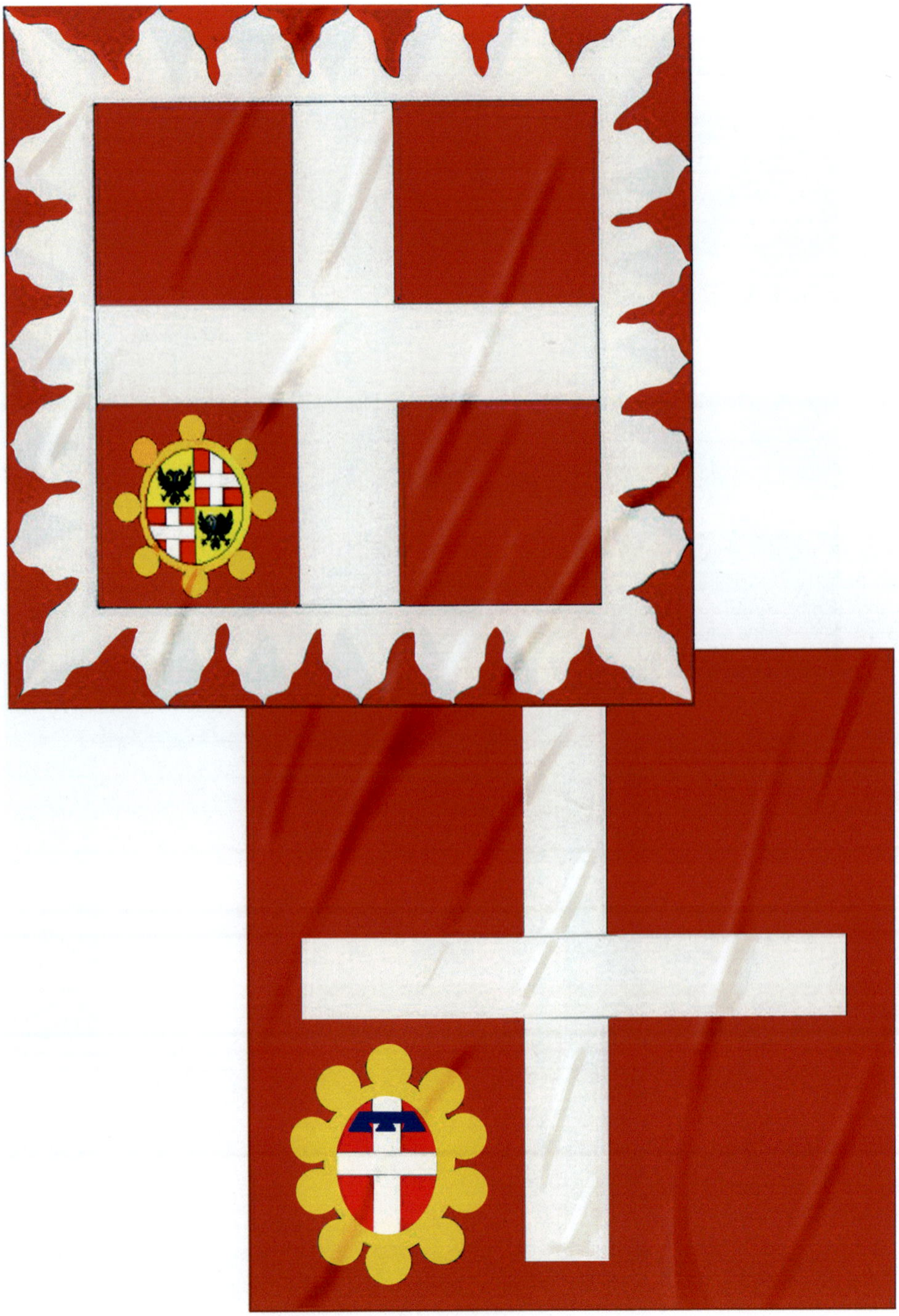

Plate 12
Savoy-Piedmont: above, Infantry Regiment *Savoye*, below, Infantry Regiment *Piemonte*.
(Illustrations by Bruno Mugnai © Helion & Company)
See Colour Plate Commentaries for further information

Plate 13
Savoy-Piedmont: above, Valais Infantry Regiment *Reding*, below, possibly Swiss Infantry Regiment *Alt*.
(Illustrations by Bruno Mugnai © Helion & Company)
See Colour Plate Commentaries for further information

Plate 14
Savoy-Piedmont: Three ordinance colours.
(Illustrations by Bruno Mugnai © Helion & Company)
See Colour Plate Commentaries for further information

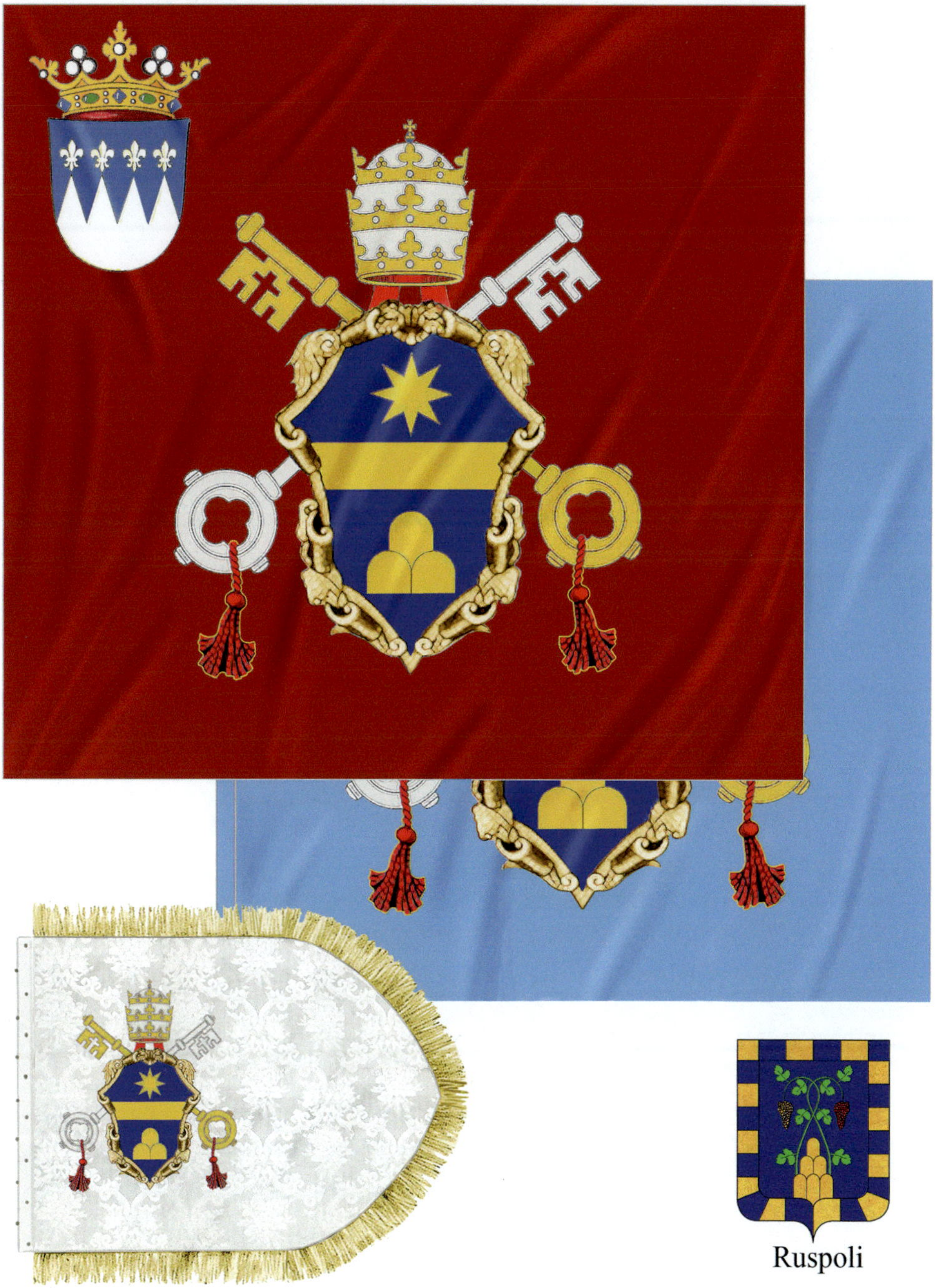

Plate 15

Papal States: above, Infantry Regiment *Serlupi*, company colours over Infantry Regiment *Ruspoli*, company colours; below, Dragoon Regiment *Fasanini*, colonel's cornet.

(Illustrations by Bruno Mugnai © Helion & Company

See Colour Plate Commentaries for further information

Plate 16

Review of the Infantry Regiment *Ruspoli* in Rome, in 1708.

See Colour Plate Commentaries for further information

Louis XIV felt now sure that Victor Amadeus had engaged with the Allies. The situation, he explained to Vendôme, was dangerous, and Milan could be lost.

Waiting for further news, Vendôme went ahead to Arco, not far from Trento, and on 6 August besieged it. The trench was opened on the night of 8–9 August, and on the 9th in the morning the French artillery started firing. The town was seized on the 10th, and the castle surrendered on the 17th, with his garrisons composed of 500 regulars, supported by 21 cannons.

Two days later a letter came: the Elector was chasing the Tyrolese insurgents between Innsbruck and Bavaria, and hoped Vendôme would go up to Bressanone to join him.

Vendôme moved ahead, and on the 29th his vanguard recognised Buso di Vela, four kilometres from Trento, but in those days he got so many rumours about a forthcoming defection by Victor Amadeus that he started having doubts about what to do: go ahead, or stop, or withdraw to the Padana Plain? Then he was notified that the Elector had abandoned Innsbruck, went back to Bavaria, and held only Kufstein, hence he decided to go back to the Po, leaving on 12 September, no matter if he had free way to Bolzano, 45 miles away. Just one day before leaving, on 11 September, he received an urgent letter from the King: he had to go back immediately, for Victor Amadeus' betrayal was certain. The operation to Austria had to be stopped. It was never resumed.

VI: The Trap

Vendôme gave orders to leave, then left the army and rushed ahead as fast as he could, and arrived at Vaudémont's headquarters in San Benedetto Po on 15 September. There he received the latest orders, dated 10 September. Louis wrote that Victor Amadeus' defection could cause terrible damages in Dauphiné and in the Duchy of Milan. He could attract huge French forces from different fronts, thus Piedmontese forces in Lombardy had to be neutralised, and their horses had to be given to the French cavalry. Once this was achieved, Vendôme had to invade Piedmont with 25 battalions, and 25 to 30 squadrons, to neutralise the Duke. Louis wrote that he did not want to deprive Victor Amadeus of his own states: he wanted him only to reduce his troops to 6,000 men, and to give two of his fortresses to the French army.[12]

Spanish and French troops were gathered, and put in close contact with the Piedmontese. Not only did the Piedmontese soldiers not suspect what could happen, but their commander too, the Count di Castellamonte, was totally unaware of his master's plan. This was probably due to Victor Amadeus' schedule. Initially, at least according to some authors, Victor Amadeus wanted to wait until his triennial alliance with France and Spain ended at the end of 1703, even if the Treaty did not mention any expiration term. Then he intended to reorganise his army during winter, and sign

12 The King to Vendôme, Marly, 10 September, 1703, rep. in de Vault, op. cit. vol III, pp.271–3.

an official pact with the Great Alliance, so September was too early to let Castellamonte know anything, it was safer to notify him when back in Turin, in winter quarters. But there was no time.

On 1 October 1703, Count Landriani, the Savoyard resident in Milan, sent a message to the Duke of the utmost urgency:

> These my few lines have to come just to let Y.R.H. know as in this moment comes from the San Benedetto camp an extraordinary [courier] who passes to France, who said that Y.R.H.'s troops in the aforesaid camp of San Benedetto, last Friday, on the day 28th last, have been disarmed and arrested as war prisoners with all the officers.[13]

What happened exactly? All the troops composing the Army of the Two Crowns had been gathered into San Benedetto Po camp, where on the 28th they were joined by those coming back from Trentino.

Louis de Bourbon-Vendôme, Duke de Vendôme.

Vendôme on that day announced a general review to be held on the next day, 29 September, to inspect the army before marching against the enemy. The review had to be made after a council of war. Count di Castellamonte attended the council of war with his officers, and to his total surprise he heard Vendôme announcing to the attendees that the Duke of Savoy was betraying the alliance, thus Castellamonte, and all his officers were prisoners of war. The other attendees were so many that there was nothing he could do, and the Piedmontese were arrested.

Outside, it was the same. The French official relation says that the Piedmontese ceded their weapons with no resistance, but does not say why: they had been called to a review, thus came with their weapons unloaded, while the French were ready to fire, hence why apart from the surprise, no resistance was possible. The French seized 2,004 prisoners, plus 1,000 who lay sick in the hospitals, and 700 horses.[14]

When on 3 October the news of the men seized at San Benedetto Po arrived in Turin, no matter what Louis XIV could have had in mind, Victor Amadeus' reaction was completely different, and harsh. He immediately let the ambassadors, and the subjects of France and Spain, be arrested, confiscating their goods and assets. Then he called the Waldensians to arms, ordered the enrolment of six regiments within the Duchy, and a selection of the men belonging to the militia Battalion of Piedmont to refill the regiments who provided the Corps in Lombardy, as well as to organise new units. He could also re-employ a good number of his

13 Count Landriani to Duke Victor Amadeus II, Milan, 1 October 1703, rep. in Trabucco, op. cit., p.21.

14 The French seized nine squadrons belonging to the Savoia Cavalleria, Piemonte Dragoons, and Genevese Dragoons, one battalion of the Guards, and of the Aosta, Piemonte, Croce Bianca, Chiablese, Fucilieri, and Savoia infantry regiments. Keeping the prisoners was not that easy. Those who did not succeed in escaping were sent to France and forced to enrol into the French regiments committed to Tallard's army in Bavaria. We shall see later what did they did in 1704.

captured soldiers, who escaped and came back to Piedmont thanks to poor watches by the Spaniards. In a few months Victor Amadeus could field a good army anew.

VII: The Alliance with Austria

As said, on 3 October 1703 Victor immediately summoned the Imperial ambassador too. On the 4th he wrote to Guido Starhemberg:

> You will already be informed about the violence the French practised last Saturday against my troops who were within their army, they have disarmed and seized prisoners of war all the soldiers, and officers; and this equals to a declaration of rupture. The consolation that I receive in all this is the means that it gives me to put myself openly on the side and on the interests of the Emperor as soon as possible.[15]

Then he committed Tarino as his representative in Vienna, adding Priero too, later. On 7 November Tarino reported from Vienna:

> Immediately after my arrival I went to Prince Eugene, in whom I recognised a very lively zeal to serve Y.R.H., and later I was with the Counts of Kaunitz, Mansfeld, Harac, and the Duke of Moles, with whom I performed in the form prescribed to me by Y.R.H. presenting them Your letters respectively, and they all expressed to me their obsequious senses about all that concerns Y.R.H.'s service.[16]

Whilst Tarino was en route, Count Auersperg had officially entered Turin on 26 October 1703, no matter if he actually arrived on 12 July.

Secret negotiations had required him to be hidden in the Marquess di Priero's palace, to avoid any disaster. Now propaganda needed to show the alliance with Austria to be a consequence of the French betrayal and attack. The most important parts of the negotiation had been settled by 26 July, but, having the ambassador arrived "officially" on 26 October, nobody could decently expect such an important alliance to be suggested, discussed, and signed within 24 or 48 hours, thus the treaty between Savoy and the Emperor was "officially" dated on 8 November, 1703, the day ducal ambassador count Tarino was already in Vienna. Officially on that day Savoy and the Emperor concluded the following treaty:

> After his Sacred Imperial Majesty was compelled to undertake the present war against the House of Bourbon for most weighty causes sufficiently known to the whole world, and had invited the Most Serene Prince Lord Victor Amadeus, Duke of Savoy, to join arms with him for effectual causes, and particularly with the

15 Victor Amadeus II to count Guido Wald Rudiger Starhemberg, Turin, 4 October 1703, rep. in Trabucco, op. cit., p.29.

16 Count Tarino Imperiale to Duke Victor Amadeus II, Vienna, 7 November, 1703, rep. in Trabucco, op. cit., p.33.

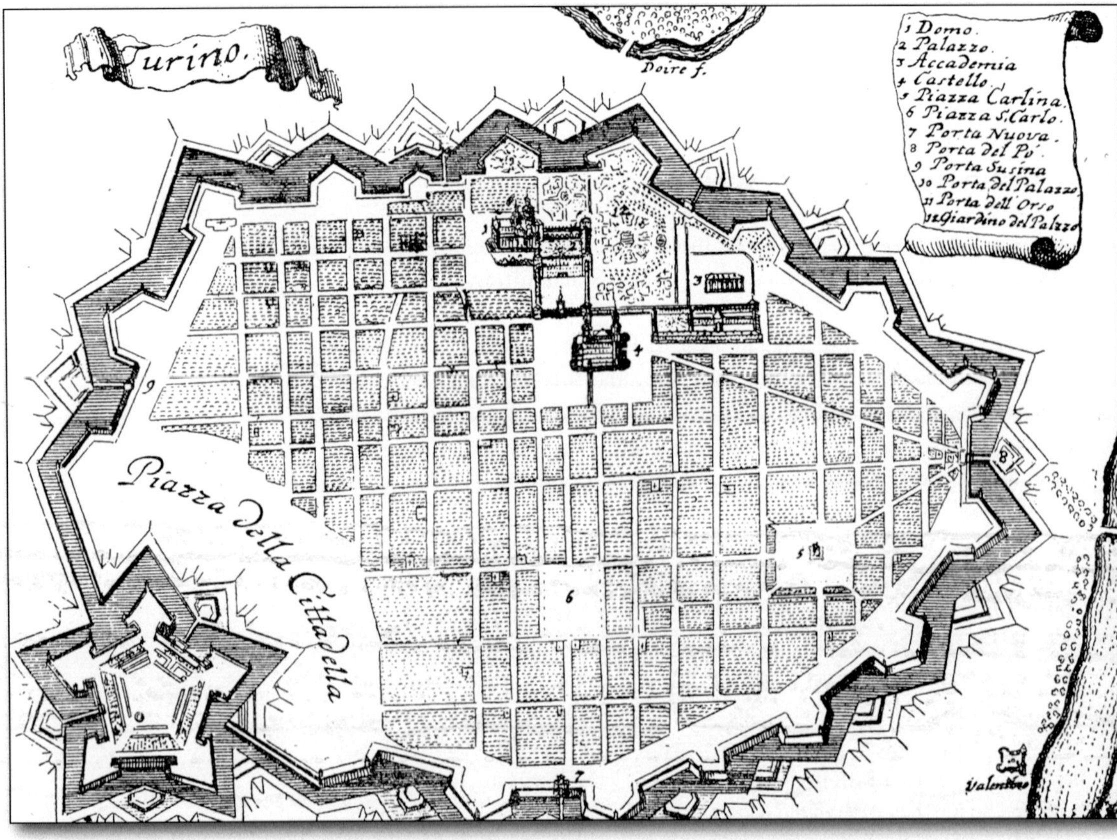

Plan View of Turin.

view of vindicating his own proper right of succession to the Spanish Monarchy, clearly established by the will of Philip IV, King of Spain, of glorious memory; His Royal Highness, considering both the alliance which exists between him and the House of Bourbon, and the situation of his dominions far removed from all communication with the Empire, has hitherto indeed remained undecided in doubtful deliberation; at length however he has determined not only to accept without longer delay that invitation, and the conditions offered him by his Sacred Imperial Majesty, but also earnestly to desire his most powerful protection against the unexpected and unheard of violence of the King of France, who, against the laws of nations and good faith, commanded his troops of France and Spain, warring in Italy, to be disarmed and detained captives; and further commanded a great and the best part of his Italian army to advance towards Piedmont in order to invade the Provinces of his Royal Highness, and entirely enslave the same; therefore his Royal Highness, being moved by this evident danger, and perilous state of affairs, and relying on the assistance most generously offered to him by his Sacred Imperial Majesty, in his own and in the name of his Allies, has signified his readiness to enter into the League with his Sacred Imperial Majesty, and his Allies, to the Count d'Auersperg who had been commissioned by his Sacred Imperial Majesty to certify his Royal Highness of his Sacred Imperial Majesty's very friendly mind towards his same Royal Highness. And since he, as well for complying with the generous intention of his Sacred Imperial Majesty, and quelling the first efforts of both the powers which conspire for the damage of his Royal Highness, as on account of the proper and clear reasons of his Sacred Imperial Majesty, whom it concerns especially to preserve from imminent oppression, a Prince who in the last war, to the great benefit of the common cause, bravely opposed himself as the firm barrier of all Italy to the attacks of the enemy, and who is no less able at the present time to promote the public benefit, and is able to afford advantages of great weight for the establishment of the august House of Austria in Italy, has repaired without delay into Piedmont, at length it has been brought to pass that his Sacred Imperial Majesty and his Royal Highness by their Plenipotentiaries, viz., in the name of his Sacred Imperial Majesty by the aforesaid most illustrious and most excellent Lord Count d'Auersperg, Counsellor of State, and Chamberlain to his Sacred Imperial Majesty, and on the part of his Royal Highness by the most illustrious and most excellent Lords, the Marquis de Prié, Knight of the Order of the Annunciation of the blessed Virgin Mary, and Minister of State to his Royal Highness, and the Marquis de St. Thomas, Minister and Principal Secretary of State to his said Royal Highness – the diplomas of their full powers being reciprocally exhibited,— agreed on the following articles.

Article 1.
There shall be between his Sacred Imperial Majesty on the one part, and his Royal Highness on the other, a strict treaty and firm and sincere union; And his Sacred Imperial Majesty will take care to have included, yea and, as much as in him lies, will henceforth in his own and in the name of the Empire include his Royal Highness in the treaty which exists between him with England and the Lords the States-General of the United Provinces and other Princes; And the principal scope of this Treaty shall be the defence or preservation of public justice, security and tranquillity, like that of the peace of Ryswick, and the preceding treaties, especially that of the Pyrenees, to which purpose his Royal Highness joining in council with his Sacred Imperial Majesty and his allies shall unite with all his forces in the present war against the House of Bourbon and its adherents as shall be explained below.

Article 2.
Whereas it is necessary to that end, and for the defence of his Royal Highness, that in addition to the army in Lombardy, where the war will be prosecuted with all vigour by his Imperial Majesty, another should be assembled in Piedmont, his Sacred Imperial Majesty will send without delay into Piedmont, to remain during the present war, so many companies of his choice and veteran soldiers as shall amount to the number of 20,000 men, whereof 14,000 to be infantry, and the remaining 6,000 cavalry, who all may be united to the regiments of his Royal Highness, and that his Sacred Imperial Majesty shall furnish his own forces at his own cost, and shall supply them with cannon, and other necessary munition. But if the artillery may not be able to be transported thither on account of the roads and other difficulties, his Royal Highness shall in the mean time supply others with this limitation, that his Sacred Imperial Majesty shall undertake at his own expense their carriage and necessary attendants: And where his Royal Highness has judged it possible that the Imperial forces may winter in his dominions, his Royal Highness shall be bound to give them nothing else than shelter or lodgings; but rations and pay shall be supplied from the Imperial Commissariat;

for the more ease whereof, his Royal Highness will take care that the aforesaid Commissariat may procure corn and provision at the current price. On the other hand his Royal Highness promises that he also will keep in pay forces of soldiers to the number of 15,000 men, whereof he will draw out into the field that part which the service of the common cause shall require, and the security of his fortresses suffer: Wherefore it shall be lawful to his Royal Highness to recruit soldiers publicly in the Empire, and to conduct them through the territories of the Empire according to the customs and laws there received.

Article 3.
His Royal Highness shall have the supreme command in both armies, as well that which is in Piedmont, as that which is employed in Lombardy, and shall direct their movements and operations under the auspices of his Sacred Imperial Majesty, as the common service and necessity shall require it; likewise for promoting the better service of his Imperial Majesty and the common cause, the Commissariat of war of his Sacred Imperial Majesty shall depend in all things and in all matters on the direction of his Royal Highness.

Article 4.
His Royal Highness shall receive from the most Serene Queen of Great Britain, and from the Lords the States of the United Provinces jointly, a subsidy of 80,000 crowns, or ducats de banco as they are called, per month, which shall begin to be current from the third day of October, as from the day on which his Royal Highness published his breach with France at Turin. His Royal Highness shall have likewise from the aforesaid Powers the sum of 100,000 crowns, or ducats de banco, once for all, towards the first expenses and appointments of the war, and that to be paid down without diminution of the monthly subsidy, which subsidy shall be imprested to him every two months; and for the sum of the aforesaid 100,000 crowns, as also for that of the first two months, bank-bills shall be transmitted without delay, either to Turin, or to other neighbouring places, whence the said sums may be conveniently drawn, that his Royal Highness may be able to lay them out for his occasions as soon as possible.

Article 5.
His Sacred Imperial Majesty, as a compensation worthy of the great zeal with which his Royal Highness has exposed his States, and his own proper person, for the interests of his most august House, and of the common cause, so useful and so necessary a sacrifice, and in consideration as well of this public advantage and service, as also of the renunciations of his Royal Highness made below, as to the dower and dotal pensions of the late Infanta Catharine Duchess of Savoy to his said Royal Highness pertaining, of his absolute and full Imperial power, and with due respect to the strong pretensions of the House of Savoy, cedes and transfers to his Royal Highness, his heirs, and successors, that part of the Duchy of Montferrat with which the Dukes of Mantua were invested, and all and every the towns, castles, villages, lands, and places thereunto pertaining, with all property, dominion, jurisdiction, royalties, rents, and all rights and interests whatsoever thereto pertaining, or there on depending, without any exception; to be held and possessed

for ever under the Emperors and Sacred Roman Empire, as the Dukes of Mantua formerly held and possessed them, or should have held and possessed them; and his Sacred Imperial Majesty takes upon himself the burden of indemnifying all who may now or hereafter make any pretension to the same Duchy of Montferrat, so that his Royal Highness, and his heirs, and successors may always remain in peaceable possession of the said Duchy, and that they be not hereafter ever molested on any pretence whatever.

Article 6.
Furthermore, his Imperial Majesty, to render his remuneration the more adequate to the service redounding to his most august House, and the common cause, by the said sacrifice of his Royal Highness, and also for other causes and motives aforementioned, cedes and transfers to his Royal Highness, his heirs, and successors, together with all property, dominion, and jurisdiction, the Provinces of Alexandria and Valenza with all the lands lying within the Po and the Tanaro, also the Province which is called Lumelline, and the Valley of Sesia, with all the towns, castles, villages, lands, places, royalties, rents, and generally all rights and interests whatsoever pertaining thereto or dependent thereon, nothing excepted; so likewise to be held and possessed under the Emperors and Sacred Roman Empire, as the late Kings of Spain held and possessed the same, or should have held and possessed them; to which end his Sacred Imperial Majesty separates for ever the aforesaid territories and places from the State of Milan, and derogates, as much as is for this required, from all that which may in any manner be or be thought contrary to the aforesaid cession and separation, still saving throughout the direct dominion of the Empire as above; and where amongst the aforesaid regions ceded as above, some villages or places may be found intermixed with them, or boundaries including the whole, but not depending on them, so as they be not above four, they shall be comprehended under this cession; but if the number exceed four villages or places, a reasonable exchange shall be made for those which exceed by a just arbitration of Commissioners for that purpose by both parties.

Article 7.
And whereas his Sacred Imperial Majesty had already determined with himself the transfer to his Royal Highness of the aforesaid Provinces or members of the State of Milan, and to that end had given instruction and authority to the Count d'Auersperg, by virtue of his full powers, to cede those aforesaid provinces to his Royal Highness; He now further promises that he will procure, within the space of 3 months next ensuing, from his Most Serene son the Archduke Charles, already proclaimed King of Spain, the ratification of this treaty, and in particular of the abovementioned cession of the aforesaid portions of the State of Milan, as to a thing at this conjuncture of the times very profitable to the King and his general interests.

Article 8.
The towns of Alexandria and Valenza are to be ceded, together with the fortifications, in the state in which they now are, but the fortifications immediately on the conclusion of peace shall be razed to the ground at the expense of his Royal

Highness, leaving only a simple wall, and shall never be rebuilt; as regards Casal, it is thought advisable that it shall always remain and be kept in that state to which it was reduced at the time of its surrender in the year 1695; however it shall be permitted to his Royal Highness to entrench the aforesaid city with a simple wall, but it shall not be permitted to his said Royal Highness, or his successors, to erect other fortresses in the aforesaid ceded places. For the rest all the towns, places, and forts above ceded shall be given up to his Royal Highness with all the cannon, victual, corn, arms, and other military stores belonging to those places, and with their official records and archives.

Article 9.
A free passage shall be open through Montferrat, as often as need shall be, for conducting military forces from the State of Milan to Finale, and towards the dominion of Genoa, and by turns from the dominion of Genoa and Finale to Milan, and that by the shortest way possible, to define which Commissioners shall be deputed from each party, who shall together specially determine on the regulation of such passage, namely, to what forces and whither tending it shall be granted, how long time shall intervene between two passages, and how the notification is to be forwarded. Such forces shall pay as they pass for their food and entertainment the current price, and whatever belongs to them shall be conveyed by that way.

There shall also remain a free passage for conveying salt from the dominion of Genoa to the State of Milan, and for ever free from all custom due to his Royal Highness; so however that it shall be lawful to his said Royal Highness by all means to prevent such salt being expended in his States.

Article 10.
The aforesaid cessions shall take their full effect whatever time and manner the present war be finished after the signing of this Treaty, so that whatsoever peace or composition follow, his Sacred Imperial Majesty shall defend those cessions, and the aforesaid lands shall remain for ever ceded to his Royal Highness and his successors.

Article 11.
His Sacred Imperial Majesty shall be bound to give to his Royal Highness actual and full possession and the entire property of the states above ceded, as they shall successively be occupied, for obtaining which with all expedition no forces shall be spared, always having regard to the common good and mutual necessity according to the disposition of the third article.

Article 12.
His Imperial Majesty willeth also that the diploma which he granted to his Royal Highness, the 8th of February in the above year 1690, for the acquisition of certain fiefs therein set forth, shall remain throughout in its entire force, and take its full effect, so that no prejudice be ever done to the tenor thereof on any account; wherefore he expressly confirms it in the present article, and by virtue hereof likewise transfers to his Royal Highness all right or exercise of right in those fiefs which may fall to the State of Milan by any prescription or title whatsoever, and

at the same time fully releases his Royal Highness from all debt which he may by any means still owe to him for the concession of the said diploma. as likewise his Royal Highness on his part renounces all debts which may remain due to him from the Imperial Commissariat.

Article 13.
His Sacred Imperial Majesty engages for himself, and his successors, that he will preserve the right of his Royal Highness to the succession of the Spanish Monarchy, according to the testamentary declaration of the late Philip IV, King of Spain, of glorious memory, competent, entire, and untouched, and that he will not consent, in war or in treaty of future peace or composition, that any prejudice be offered thereto, nor will ever permit that before his Royal Highness any third claimant be introduced to the aforesaid Monarchy, or any part thereof. But for the greater security of the said rights, and for the security and preservation of the natural position of the House of Savoy and its dominions, and as it is of the greatest importance that the communication between them and his most August House and the Roman Empire should never be severed, his Sacred Imperial Majesty promises that in the letters of Investiture of the above ceded States he will recognise the same right of his Royal Highness to succeed to the Spanish Monarchy, as immediate after his most August House, with addition of a clause, that his Royal Highness and his successors be now, so far as is needful for such event, considered and remain as invested therewith.

Article 14.
His Royal Highness renounces for himself, his heirs, and successors all rights and actions which accrue or may accrue to him and them by reason of the dowry and residuary revenues of the deceased Infanta Catharine, daughter of the late Catholic King Philip II, Duchess of Savoy; and his Royal Highness declares for himself, and his heirs, that dowry, and residuary pensions to be fully compensated and paid by the abovementioned cessions; so that under this head neither he nor his successors at any time whatsoever may or ought to demand anything from the crown of Spain.

Article 15.
When, by the blessing of Divine Providence, Spanish Lombardy shall have been recovered by the arms of the Empire and Savoy, all the forces shall be employed, not only in recovering the other Kingdoms and Provinces of the Spanish Dominion in Italy (reserving however continually, for the safeguard of Piedmont and of the State of Milan, that army of 20,000 Imperialists, whereof above in the second Article,) but also in acquiring that district which is situated on this side Mount Genevro, whereby the common security may be the more confirmed, and every place for the subsistence of the French army on this side of the Alps taken away, but the acquisition of that district between Piedmont and Mount Genevro shall belong to his Royal Highness only, and his successors; and his Sacred Imperial Majesty, as well in his own name as in that of his allies, promises to use all diligence in future treaties of peace that this acquisition may remain entire and unshaken to the most Serene Duke.

Article 16.
His Imperial Majesty shall ratify the present Treaty in his own and in the name of the Empire, and shall concede to his Royal Highness, on his request, the investitures of the States and dominions ceded, according to the tenor of the Investitures granted by Charles V to Philip II, and his successors, and the Dukes of Mantua respectively, with the sole restriction to the male line, as well of the Most Serene Duke as of the Princes of this House; in like manner his Sacred Imperial Majesty shall be bound to invest his Royal Highness, according to the form and tenor of investiture already granted by Ferdinand II, in the year 1632, with that part of Montferrat also which was before possessed by his Royal Highness, and was acquired by virtue of the peace of Westphalia confirmatory of the Treaty of Cherasco.

Article 17.
Furthermore, his Sacred Imperial Majesty shall be bound to obtain the approbation of this treaty from the Most Serene Queen of Great Britain, the States-General of the United Provinces, and the other allied Princes, so that they may take the aforesaid cessions into their care and protection, and defend them so as they may come to full effect, by whatever means peace or agreement shall follow; and for the greater security of this article, the said cessions shall be included in the preliminary conditions, without which no treaty of peace shall be entered upon; Likewise the said Powers shall engage themselves in the same manner and form as his Imperial Majesty has engaged himself in the 15th Article concerning the acquisition and maintenance of the lands situated on this side Mount Genevro in favour of his Royal Highness; and further, they shall oblige themselves specially as to their proper deed to preserve the immediate right to the Spanish Monarchy inviolate to his Royal Highness after the august House of Austria, and never to condescend unto or enter upon any treaty, whereby this right shall be in any manner prejudiced, or any third Prince introduced before the House of Savoy into any of the aforesaid states of the Spanish Monarchy.

Article 18.
His Sacred Imperial Majesty and his allies will enter into no peace, conventions, or truces, except his Royal Highness be restored to all places and dominions which haply may be occupied by the enemy, so that this restitution shall be inserted likewise in the preliminary conditions, without which they shall not be able to proceed to the said treaties.

Article 19.
Whereas his Sacred Imperial Majesty and the allied power shall be quite unable to enter into any peace, agreement, or anything else, without including his Royal Highness in the manner aforesaid; so, on the other hand, his Royal Highness shall be bound to adhere inseparably, and to remain united to his Sacred Imperial Majesty and the common alliance, and to aid their cause with his arms, until the conclusion of peace; nor shall it be lawful for him, on any account, to separate himself from them. And this is one of the principal conditions, and as it is called a *sine qua non* of the aforesaid cessions, which shall receive their ultimate and full force and effect only from the entire and accurate accomplishment of this condition.

We, the Plenipotentiaries aforesaid, by virtue of our respective instructions, have concluded and confirmed the present treaty, and thereto have affixed the seals of our arms; promising that we will procure the ratifications of our respective masters authorising us; that of his Sacred Imperial Majesty within 3 weeks, and that of his most Serene Royal Highness within 8 days. Dated at Turin the 8th day of November in the year 1703.

Il Conte d'Auersperg	Il M.e di Prié.	de St. Thomas.
L. S.	L. S.	L. S.[17]

Resuming: the Duke promised to field a 15,000-man army. The Emperor promised to send him a 20,000-man one, and to appoint the Duke the supreme Imperial commander in Italy. Then the Emperor engaged himself to convince the Maritime Powers to make a treaty and to subsidise the Duke, and promised to give him the Monferrato, Alessandria, Valenza, the Lomellina, the Sesia Valley, five towns near Novara, the city of Vigevano and its territory, the few but strategically important still French-owned lands on the Italian side of the Alps, and to share Lombardy with Savoy. Territorial gains had to be reassessed later, and the Emperor refused to ratify the clause about the town of Vigevano and its territory.

As things officially were, no matter the existing negotiations, and contacts in London and The Hague, Victor Amadeus, as a Prince of the Empire, had to wait for the Imperial ratification before concluding a treaty with the Maritime Powers.

The Duke was all but naïve. He knew which kind of people sat in Vienna, and how to manage them. The first evidence came on 21 November when Tarino reported the Treaty to have been published, and that there was a rising opposition to the cession of Monferrato.[18]

On 12 December Victor answered by an encrypted letter, Tarino had to tell the three well-known ministers – Harrach, Kaunitz and Mansfeld – that the Duke was terribly short of money, and hoped they would pardon the delay, but they could be sure that, as soon as the Treaty was ratified, he would be in a better situation, thus he would be able to reward them with 50,000 florins each. In other words: stop creating obstacles, push the Emperor to let him ratify the treaty, and, once ratified, I'll get the money, and from that money you'll get the bribe, the generous bribe you are looking for.[19] That was the way to get things done in Vienna.

17 *Secret Treaty and articles of alliance between H.R.H. Victor Amadeus Duke of Savoy and Emperor Leopold to continue the war against the crown of France*, text in Latin starting saying "*Postquam Sacra Cesarea Majestas praesens bellum…*", rep. in Solara della Margarita. cit, II,, pp.203–219. English translations reported in "Hill – *Letters*" (London: 1845), part II, Translations, pp.936–945.

18 Count Tarino Imperiale to Duke Victor Amadeus II, Vienna, 7 November 1703, rep. in Trabucco, op. cit., pp.33–34.

19 Victor Amadeus II to Tarino, Turin, 12 December 1703, rep. in Trabucco, op. cit., pp.35–36.

Part II

THE WAR AGAINST THE FRENCH

11

The 1703 Campaign Against the French

I: A Bad Situation

The "San Benedetto Po capture" had remarkable consequences on both the French, and the Piedmontese. The former had to stop their march to Austria, and would never be able to try it again in the future, thus they lost a – if not "the" – major opportunity to win the war. The latter had an enormous strategic problem to solve. The Duke lost at San Benedetto Po a huge share of his best professional troops. Although scarce in number, they were the core of his professional army. He now had to enrol as many people as he could, but had also to spend time to drill them properly, and money to pay them.

Money was the second problem. In 1703 military expenditure had a minimal improvement to 5,450,000 liras.[1] Actually it would not have been different from the previous year had the Duke not suffered from his change of alliance. The last trimester provoked a real earthquake also in financial affairs, and Victor Amadeus so suddenly needed money that he pawned the crown jewels in Genoa.

However both England and the United Provinces were expected to start paying subsidies: two thirds would be up to England and one to the Dutch, but a formal treaty was needed first, and it took a long time, far more than one would expect, for it was signed only in summer 1704.

On the other hand the French military reaction occurred far sooner than expected. They had time to enter Piedmont and Savoy before the winter pause. How could the Duke stop them?

As we know, long ago the case had been foreseen by Duke Emmanuel Philibert when he built the ring of fortresses, having that of Turin as its centre. The problem was that the system was planned to hold against the French from across the Alps until reinforcements arrived from Milan, or against the Spaniards from Milan until reinforcements arrived from France. Vice versa, now Victor Amadeus had the French crossing the Alps, and coming

1 Prato, op. cit., p.260

from Milan. The reinforcements, if any, had to come from east, but how long did Victor need to hold? The Piedmontese fortified system, no matter how improved it had been in the last century and a half, had been built with a two- or three-month long resistance in mind, perhaps an entire campaign in the worst case; but now? At the end of the story, the system planned for holding a campaign against an enemy coming from one side proved much more successful than expected, for with some help it held against an enemy coming from both sides during the last couple of operational months in 1703, and the three entire following campaigns: a result nobody could expect. But by now, in October 1703, Victor Amadeus had no idea what the future would bring.

II: The French Need to Secure Supply Lines

The Piedmontese change of sides caused a real problem to the French: it cut their supply lines. The first orders issued by Victor Amadeus as soon as he was notified of what happened in San Benedetto Po caused the loss of three French cavalry companies in Piedmont, and of all the French convoys.

Lombardy could not feed the French Army, as we know, especially where it concerned fodder, and it was too late to organise an invasion of Piedmont from across the Alps, because October meant snow. Thus Louis XIV could rely only on Vendôme's army in Lombardy, but this was not easy. Those troops – 28,000 foot and some 4,000 cavalry – were mostly back from Tyrol and Trentino. They were fatigued, and needed to rest and be supplied. Operations against Piedmont meant a probable loss of men and horses, a lot of time, and the risk of an Imperial action on the back of the operating army. There were 14,000 Imperial troopers on the back of the French, and an unknown quantity of Piedmontese troopers, who might or might not be up to 10,000, in front of them.

Thus, whilst Vendôme moved 30,000 men from San Benedetto Po on 30 September, marched slowly to Pavia, and encamped on the border along the Sesia river on 16 October, the King sent him new instructions. On 18 October Vendôme offered Victor Amadeus a peaceful solution: had the Duke given the French the fortresses of Verrua, and Cuneo, and reduced the army to peacetime strength, all would be settled. Cuneo was the terminal of the roads from Provence to Piedmont across the Alps. Verrua commanded the Po valley in Piedmont. Had Victor accepted, Louis would secure free and safe passage to his supplies. Victor refused on the 19th. On the 20th Vendôme crossed the Po near Casale and marched to Asti. On 24 September the Duke declared war on France.

III: Visconti's Ride, and Alberoni's Spies

War propaganda and successive literature celebrated the glories of Piedmont, and of the House of Savoy, depicting heroic defences everywhere. This was close to the actual situation, but was not exactly it.

The Piedmontese fortified system was the main obstacle for the French. Forts and castles commanded the entire road and river network. They were so many, and so close each other, that it was foolish not to care. Each of them could be the base for a raid or a big attack. Each of them could prevent the French from using the roads nearby, thus each of them, or most of them, had to be seized.

There was a question: how strong were those fortresses? Quite strong, according to official contemporary sources, but it was not so. According to studies made during the third centenary of the war, the fortified system in the second half of the seventeenth century could be considered good in the Alps, but not that good in the east, in the Po valley.[2] Except for Verrua and the related fortified system in Crescentino, the eastern fortresses were old-fashioned, and not as strong as needed to hold against the enemy. The fortified ring protecting Turin, and the core of the Duchy seemed impressive. In fact it was far less impressive and threatening than one could expect, nonetheless somehow it held, and delayed French progress less perhaps then hoped, but much more than expected.

Victor Amadeus' problem was the lack of men, and the lack of time. Had all gone as planned, his troopers had to come back to Piedmont for winter quarters. During winter he could enrol and drill as many men as needed. Better negotiations could be made, leaving time to define all the details, and at the end, on the eve of 1704, he could switch sides and declare war on France, having all his assets ready.

As things were, he had been taken by surprise from three up to six months earlier than expected, thus almost nothing was ready. He could gather men by calling the militia to arms, but needed time to organise and drill them properly, so he asked the Austrians for reinforcements. On 4 October Victor Amadeus wrote a letter to Starhemberg, asking immediately for the help of 3,000 men. Starhemberg did not care for any authorisation from Vienna, and immediately committed general Annibale Visconti to Piedmont with 1,220 cavalrymen.

Visconti had to leave from Quistello, a small town near Mantua, on the left side of the Po. Parma intelligence was notified, and the Duke passed the information to Alberoni, who passed it to the French. They did not believe him. Information provided by General Colmenero, in Spanish service, said that Visconti planned to pass through the Valle dei Ratti. Alberoni insisted: Visconti planned to pass through San Sebastiano Curone, not far from Alessandria, in south-eastern Piedmont. That was a wise idea, because San Sebastiano was on the widely used, and well-kept "via del sale", the salt road, used to ship salt from Genoa to Plaisance and Milan. On 18 October Visconti was on the right embankment of the Po, and moved west.

2 See for instance the survey by Micaela Viglino Davico, in her "Le difese verso levante del Ducato sabaudo", in Guido Amoretii, Patrizia Petitti, *La scala di Pietro Micca 1958–1998* (Turin: 2000). Other good surveys are provided by Roberto Sconfienza, "Fortezze e piazzeforti quadrilatere in Piemonte: modelli ed esempi tra XVI e XVII secolo" in, Guido Amoretti, Patrizia Petitti, cit., and by Dario Gariglio, *Le sentinelle di pietra – fortezze e cittadelle del Piemonte sabaudo* (Cuneo: 1997).

Guidobald von Stahremberg.

In Casale Alberoni insisted more and more. On the 20th Vendôme received additional information confirming Alberoni's, thus he made an arrangement with a big gang of brigands, headed by Carlo Castellini. They had to attack, and possibly stop Visconti in San Sebastiano, whilst the French cavalry gathered and rushed on him. The brigands tried, but at night on the 25th Visconti destroyed them, and went forward.

the French cavalry arrived late, and engaged the Imperial rearguard, commanded by Marquess Davia in the pass from San Sebastiano to the next village of Dernice. After a five-hour fight, Davia disengaged with heavy casualties and joined Visconti 40 miles south, at Voltaggio. The next morning Visconti was notified that the two possible routes to Piedmont were closed by the French, and by the Monferrato militia depending on the Duke of Mantua, so, he tried to cross Genoese territory to enter Piedmont from south. But on the 27th the Genoese troops prevented him passing, even if they allowed him to move east within the territory of the Republic. Visconti stopped near Genoa, and on 2 November made a further attempt. Once more the Genoese stopped him. Then Visconti sent Davia to ask the English minister in Florence, Blackwell, for ships to ship him and his men and horses to a Sabaudian port. Blackwell got the advice of the Dutch minister, and the answer was "no": there was still no formal treaty between Maritime Powers, and Savoy, thus nothing could be done.

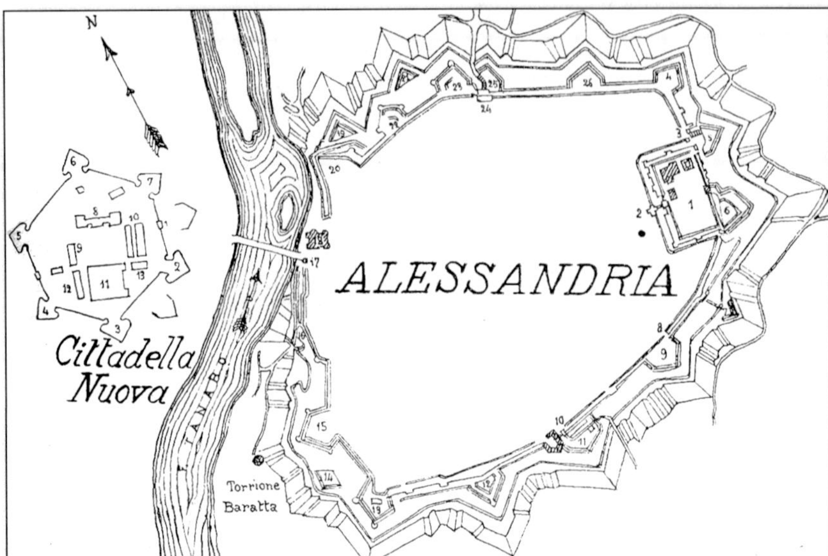

Plan view of the Fortifications of Alessandria.

Vendôme stated the enemy mission to have failed, and moved his troops into Piedmont. He started by besieging Asti on 7 November, and took it immediately.

Meanwhile, Victor Amadeus was flooding Imperial headquarters with letters asking for support. Six letters to Starhemberg, and one to Eugene achieved a result. Starhemberg sent Count von Daun to Turin to define a march schedule and held two councils of war, on 16 November, and 4 December. At the same time he confirmed to Eugene, who had been in Vienna for almost a year, that it was a matter of "aut vincer, aut mori" – win or die – for, had they not relieved the Duke, Piedmont was lost.

Victor Amadeus was trying to gather all he could, including Visconti. That is why the Piedmontese Baron de Saint-Rémy sent Visconti two ships from Oneglia, the small Savoy-owned principality on the sea. All those among Visconti's men who lost their horses were shipped west, whilst Visconti rode with the remaining 560 men along the narrow and winding paths of the Ligurian Apennine. He carefully avoided Genoa, exploited possibilities offered by the local small Imperial fiefs, entered southern Piedmont, and at last, on 20 November, met the Count of Santena with the Piedmontese militia of Mondovì and Ceva. Mission accomplished, even if Visconti lost 632 horses and 212 men.

At the same time in Vienna Eugene was pushing on the Emperor. At the end Leopold said yes. Orders were sent, and on 24 December 1703 Starhemberg left the Young Prince de Vaudémont and General Leiningen near Mantua, on the Secchia river, and marched west with 14,000 foot, a little over 3,400 horses, and 20 cannons.

Parma's intelligence knew those orders as in advance as it needed to pass them to Alberoni on time. Alberoni notified Vendôme. Vendôme summoned a council of war on 23 December, that is to say the day before Starhemberg's departure, and asked for opinions. Almost all the generals agreed: there was nothing to do, they were too weak to pursue, and stop Starhemberg. Alberoni softly put a problem flat on the table: if the French did not stop them, once the Austrians were in Parma his Duke would be forced to pass on the Imperial side.

This resolved the question. Vendôme moved with 16,000 of his men and 40 cannons, but it was too late. On 29 December Starhemberg entered the Duchy of Parma, passed through Borgo San Donnino and Pontenure, and approached the Trebbia river.

IV: The Autumn Campaign in Savoy

In October the French invaded Savoy. It was a matter of control of enemy territory, but it was also a way to secure supply lines from Lyon and the Rhône valley to Milan and the war theatre in the Po valley.

Tessé, appointed on 17 October, was in charge. What may appear strange is that, no matter how much stronger they were, the French were really worried by the Piedmontese. The day after his arrival at his headquarters in Grenoble, Tessé sent Chamillart a detailed report.[3] He wrote that he was

3 Tessé to Chamillart, letter from Grenoble on 23 October 1703, reported in de Vault, op. cit. vol. IV, 1704, p.80, and following.

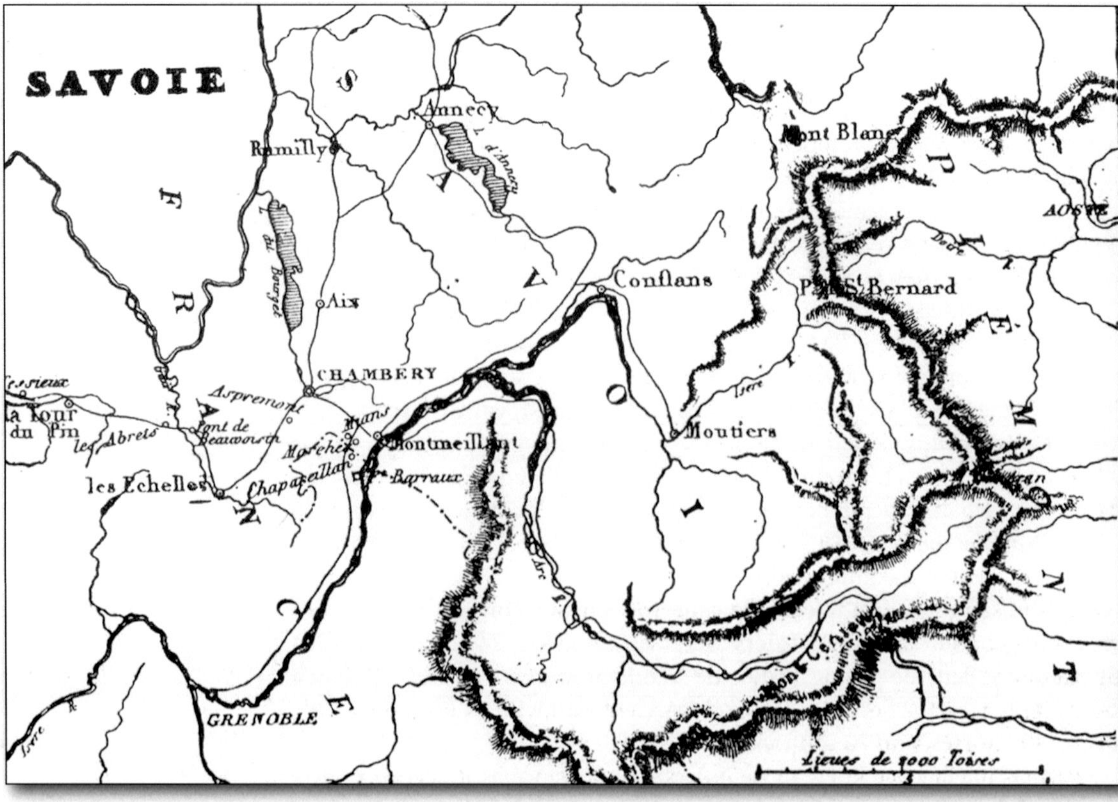

Map of the Savoy Region.

sending a battalion and a cavalry company to Fenestrelle to control Pragelato Valley – one of the passages across the Alps – because he felt unsure. The local people around Grenoble were composed of 40,000 former Protestants, who had only recently been forced to convert to Catholicism. Tessé knew how close they felt to the Piedmontese Waldensians, successfully employed by the Duke as mountain light infantry and raiders since the previous war, and who were now tasked with protecting the valleys of Perosa and Pragelato. Adding 800 more militiamen from Dauphiné, Tessé hoped to keep the Valleys of Exilles, Oulx, and Bardonecchia. At the same time he committed Lieutenant Colonel Planque, of the Roergue Regiment, to Briançon. Four more companies from Dauphiné moved to Queiras castle.

Eight battalions remained, but as Tessé remarked, one of them had fewer than 300 men. Anyway he committed one, commanded by La Fare, to Fenestrelle, and gathered the other seven at the head of the Isère river near Fort Barraux. Meanwhile he ordered the organising of three more Dauphiné militia regiments of 1,000 men each.

Tessé was worried by what Victor Amadeus on one side of the Alps, and the Count de Sales on the other side of the Alps were doing. The former raised two cavalry regiments, and was raising 12 militia infantry regiments, commanded by his best and most prestigious and loyal noblemen. The latter was gathering six battalions in Savoy, was fortifying Chambéry, and threatening to raid the French border. Lastly the Duke of Savoy – Mr. de Savoie – let his men distribute a declaration of war on France! And he had weapons he was distributing, and gave "prostituted" money to his recruits, paying up to 10 soldi per man – which, as we know, was the normal wage of a Piedmontese private – and 1,000 scudi to each colonel!

Reading Tessé, one could only wonder how did Victor Amadeus dare to defend himself and his States against the French? And he was gathering troops and paying them! What a shame!

Shame or not, actually Victor Amadeus was in real trouble, and was doing what he could. He purchased 1,500 horses in Switzerland for his cavalry, and if he had 6,000 men in the Aosta Valley, it was more urgent to use them against Vendôme in Piedmont than in Savoy.

The first French troops arrived in Grenoble from Languedoc on 31 October. They were followed by the rest, and by artillery. Then on 15 November Tessé left two battalions and many dragoons at Fort Barraux to cover his back, and led into the Duchy a small army corps – in fact a task force – composed of five infantry battalions, two dragoon companies, and six cannons.

No matter how small his task force might be, the Ducal forces commanded by the Count de Sales were smaller: no more than 2,000 foot and 1,100 horse, thus roughly a half of the French manoeuvring mass, and

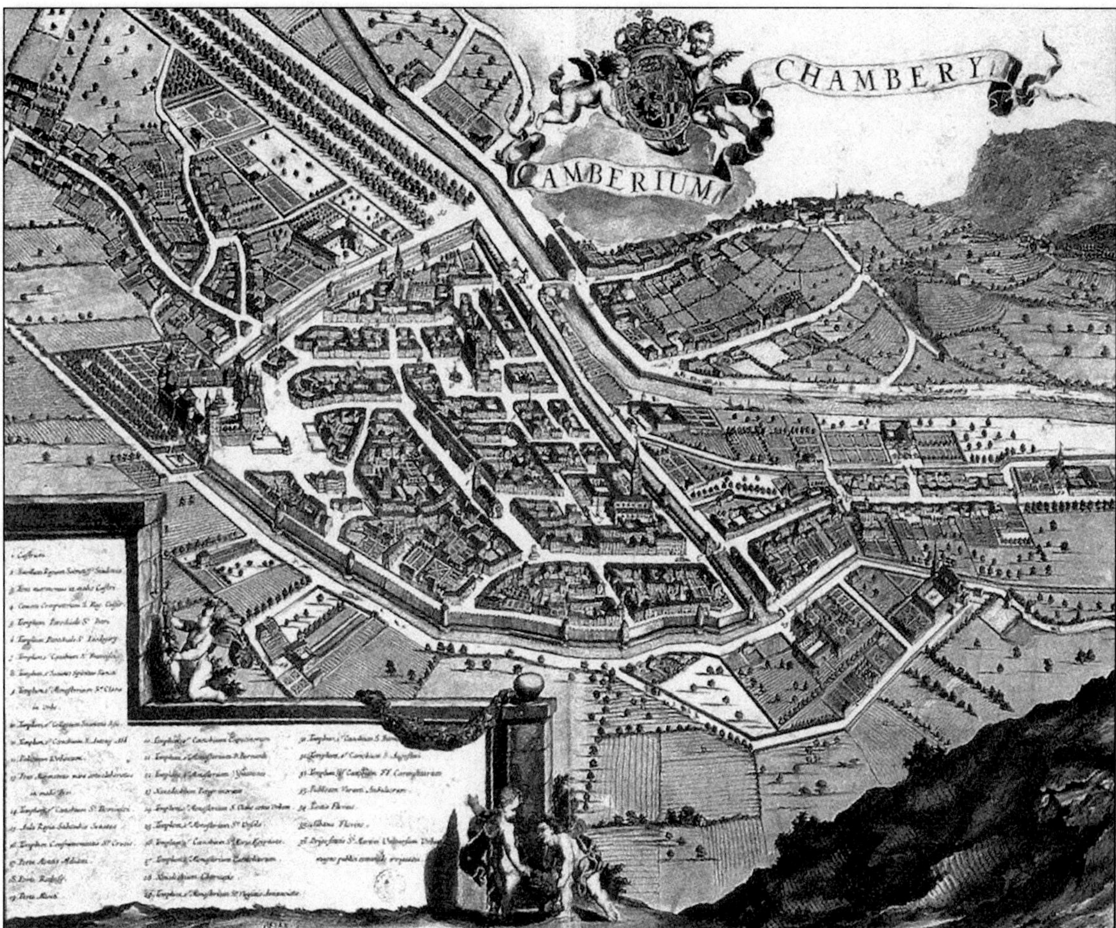

Plan of the City of Chambéry.

The Fortress of Montmélian.

could do nothing, or less, to stop it. Moreover morphology favoured the French. Italy geologically is part of Africa crashing into Europe; the Alps are the result of this collision. On the Italian side, the side of the crash, they are very steep, but on the French side they are not, and the ground climbs more or less smoothly toward the heights. Savoy is on the French side of Alps, thus its small garrison could not rely on the ground to stop a French offensive.

De Sales appeared on the river marking the border between Savoy and Dauphiné, realised the French were stronger and withdrew to Fesson, at the entrance to Tarantasia. Later he moved back a little and encamped near Montmélian first, but then left garrisons in some castles, and moved to the Aosta Valley, in order to prevent the French passage across the Alps.

The garrison of Savoy was not big – due to the detachment sent to Lombardy – and no position supported by the local forts could be successfully held. The strongest fortress of the Duchy, Montmélian, had been destroyed after a long siege in the previous war, and the few years of peace had not been enough to rebuild it, for there was no way to restore it. The remaining strongpoints – Miolans, la Roche d'Allery, and Annécy – were strong, but not as strong, and as big to hold as much as needed, that is to say until an Imperial or Allied relief could come.

Chambéry was the first to be besieged. Actually it capitulated in a while, as soon as Tessé offered very good conditions of surrender. Then he seized Annécy, Rumilly and "all the cantons of Savoy which were not occupied by the troops of the Duke,"[4] that is to say he succeeded where no opposition was found.

A French battalion and a dragoon company were sent to Moriana, as soon as Tessé knew that de Sales left it, whilst another battalion was committed to Thonon, and a third to Evian, to protect Annécy and cut communications between the French Protestants and the Duke of Savoy. But both the battalions were called back to Fort Barraux as soon as Tessé knew that Victor Amadeus had sent 400 cavalry – who were all French Protestants – to join de Sales, who had been ordered to re-enter Savoy. Nonetheless, nothing happened. Tessé did not move, nor did the Piedmontese. The snow prevented big movements across the mountains, and Victor Amadeus preferred to keep his forces. De Sales, reinforced by a certain quantity of militia and Protestants, left the bulk of his force in the Aosta Valley and dispatched a detachment to Aiguebelle. From Aiguebelle he had the possibility to go back to relieve Montmélian. Anyway neither he nor Tessé felt strong enough to take the initiative, and both stood.

On 10 December Tessé left the command to the Duke de la Feuillade. La Feuillade was 30-year-old; later literature depicted him as an odd and inexperienced commander, but it fact he proved not bad, and was successful until the defeat at Turin three years later. Now, in January 1704, La Feuillade besieged Montmélian.

4 *Idem*, p.85.

12

1704: Castle by Castle

I: First Operations in Piedmont

Victor Amadeus was gathering men and organising regiments, but he needed further forces, and above all money. He borrowed 460,000 liras from bankers Lullino and Nicolas to purchase horses in Switzerland, and summoned the militia to arms.

According to his 1703 budget the Duke had 15,908 men-at-arms. He lost a few more than 4,800 in San Benedetto Po, thus he still had 11,000, that is to say 8,500 foot (4,800 Italian foot in five regiments,[1] 1,651 Swiss foot, and 2,063 Germans) and 1,610 horses (dragoons, and cavalry), plus 480 artillery, and 330 household. By the end of December his troops increased to 18,600 foot and 2,630 horses. New professional recruits, 4,500 conscripts, and 600 Piedmontese veterans who had escaped from Spanish prisons in Lombardy were poured into the army, and merged with the men of the militia.

New militia provisional regiments were established. At the beginning they had their commanders' names, but some of them were later confirmed as standing corps.[2] Then the Duke signed the contracts for foreign professionals,

---

1 Guardie, Savoia, Nizza, Saluzzo, and Monferrato.

2 The militia from Cuneo was organised into the Maffei Regiment, but later it became the Cuneo Regiment of the Sardinian army, and then the Cuneo Brigade, and with that name remained in the Italian Army, survived the two World Wars, decreased to a battalion and as "7th Cuneo Infantry battalion" existed until the end of the Cold War, then was turned into a regiment with the same number, disappearing in 2001. The militias of Alba and Fossano became the Count della Trinità's Regiment, but did not survive the Spanish Succession crisis. The militia of Asti was commanded by the Marquess of Cortanze. Later it became Asti Infantry Regiment, but did not survive the Napoleonic era. The same happened to the Nizza Regiment, commanded by the Count of Duvillar. The militias of Pinerolo and Saluzzo composed the San Nazar Regiment, which later divided in two regiments named after the two cities, and as Saluzzo Infantry Regiment and Pinerolo Infantry Regiment, remained in the Royal Sardinian Army. Saluzzo did not survive the Napoleonic era; Pinerolo did, was increased to a brigade, and remained in the Royal Italian Army until after the Second World War, when in the 1980s it changed its name to "Valbella", after a First World War fight it had won. Lastly the militia of Turin, commanded by the Marquess de Trivié, disappeared at the end of the eighteenth century due to Napoleon, but was reorganised as Turin Infantry Brigade in the 1870s, survived the two World Wars, was reduced to the 82nd "Turin" infantry battalion, and existed until the end of the Cold War. The militia of Ivrea composed the Count of San Damiano's Regiment, but disappeared with that war, and

expected to be in Anglo-Dutch pay once the Alliance Treaties achieved, and ratified. They were 11,000 Protestant soldiers from Germany and Switzerland, who had to compose six regiments, organised into 12 battalions of 900 men each, plus a free company composed of 200 Grisons.[3]

Carlo Emilio San Martino, Marquess of Parella.

Lastly, on 5 October 1703, the Duke issued a manifesto to raise French Protestants against the Sun King. It had worked in the previous war, and worked in this one: 3,300 refugees volunteered. Three thousand composed some "Religioners" infantry regiments. Two, De Merolles (sometimes mentioned as Dumeyrol) and D'Albenar included French deserters and Huguenot refugees; one, Desportes, commanded by colonel Lodovic Des Portes, included French protestant, Irish refugees, and German and Dutch professional. The last regiment was composed of Protestant refugees from the Cevennes area, and was commanded by their leader Jean Cavalier. The remaining 300 recruits composed three free dragoon companies.

These troops were still gathering and drilling when the Marquess of Parella with the Duke's household as cavalry, and the foot of the Regiment of Guards, and of the German infantry regiment Schulemburg in Sabaudian service moved toward the villages of Montà and Pralormo. His intention was to force the enemy to leave their line on the Bormida and Tanaro rivers. He succeeded.

On 3 January Starhemberg seized the Castle of Stradella, surrendered by its 300 Spanish foot garrison commanded by the Milanese Count Arborio di Gattinara. On the 4th the Austrians were in Voghera, 20 miles away – as evidence of how the marching schedules in Italy did not respect Perjés' supposed rules – and two days later he crossed the Scrivia river and reached Castelnuovo Scrivia. After Bosco Marengo he moved toward Castellazzo. When approaching it on 9 January he was engaged by the French troops commanded by Philippe de Vendôme, the younger brother of the marshal, known as "the Grand Prior", for he was a grand prior of the Order of Malta. So when on the morning of 9 January the French coming

reappeared as Ivrea Infantry Brigade (161st and 162nd) only during the First World War. The Count d'Este commanded the regiment composed of the militians from the cities of Biella and Vercelli, which did not survive beyond the eighteenth century.

3 The Prussian-recruited regiment Aygoin, German-recruited regiment Fridt; Swiss Regiment Tscharner from Bern, called "La Reyne", in honor of Queen Anne; Swiss Regiment Halt, from Freiburg; Swiss mixed Regiments Lombach and Schmidt. It is interesting to underline that the La Reyne Regiment passed into the Sabaudian army as a regular standing one, and fought in all further eighteenth-century wars. It was reorganised after the Napoleonic era, always holding the name La Regina – the Queen – even if the public did not remember after which queen it was originally named. It bravely fought all the Risorgimento campaigns as La Regina Brigade, composed of the 9th and 10th La Regina Infantry Regiments. It took part in the First World War and Second World War. Later it changed its name, but kept its number, and its traditional white badges, and still exists as the "9th Bari Infantry Regiment."

from Alessandria appeared suddenly on the other side of the Bormida, Starhemberg let the Grand Prior think that he wanted to cross the river at Castelnuovo, but ordered construction of a bridge south, at Cassine; when it was ready, he started crossing. Unfortunately the bridge was not as strong as required, and collapsed under the passing troops. This, and repairing it, delayed the crossing until Vendôme arrived in person with his men. The Imperial rearguard was engaged. Two Imperial generals were killed, and Starhemberg lost also 400 wagons and six flags, but crossed over. He was lucky, because on the other side the Grand Prior did not move: fearing the Piedmontese on his back, and unaware of the arrival of his brother's troops, he went back to Alessandria.

On 10 January Victor Amadeus in person with 10,000 men moved to meet Starhemberg, who on the 13th moved north along the right side of the Bormida, reached Terzo, and found there the Marquess of Parella. On the next day they joined the Duke and the Piedmontese main corps in Canelli, then the Imperialists went to their winter quarters around Trino Vercellese. Sabaudian troopers were scattered among the fortresses of Vercelli, Crescentino, Verrua, Chieri, Moncalieri, Turin, Alba, Cuneo, Aosta, and Nizza to prepare for the enemy attacks expected during the coming spring.

Meanwhile Victor Amadeus gave the militia free rein, sometimes supported by regular troops. The castle of Mornanengo was stormed seizing 200 French carabineers. Then groups of peasants attacked, and destroyed all the French detachments, and teams sent out foraging, or in reconnaissance. In March the biggest fight occurred near the town of Cocconato, when the peasants, supported by some companies of the Savoia Infantry Regiment, ambushed 1,000 French cavalry, and killed 100.

II: Raiding the French in Savoy

We left the Duke de la Feuillade besieging Montmélian. He could not go as fast as he wanted, because he had troubles caused by French Protestant insurgents in the Cevennes.

Whilst the French were engaged in the Cevennes, Victor Amadeus tried to relieve Savoy. He planned to commit two light columns through the Little San Bernardo, and Mount Cenisio passes. The latter was watched by a French garrison in Chiomonte 600 strong. The Duke committed 300 men of his Waldensian militia, particularly skilled in mountain warfare. On 4 February 1704 they sneaked into the town of Chiomonte, but were spotted and repulsed by the enemy, losing four dead and four wounded.

The Great and Little Saint Bernard Passes.

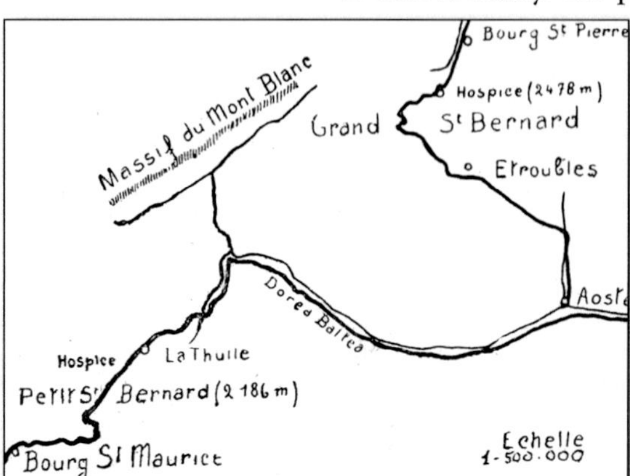

In the second half of March Tessé sent eight foot battalions and one dragoon regiment to Chiomonte. Piedmontese Colonel Renato de Blagnac attacked them there on 28 March with

View of Montmélian.

600 grenadiers and fusileers. The surprise failed, but the Piedmontese forced the gate, entered the village, and seized it. They lost 13 dead and 55 wounded, the French 100.

This was the first step, just to open the route. That same afternoon Blagnac crossed Mount Cenisio with 350 men, and on 29 and 30 March seized the bridges of Lanslebourg and Thermignon in Savoy. Meanwhile, the German general Schulemburg entered Moriana with two foreign infantry regiments in Sabaudian service. The local garrison, 5,000 strong, feared to be encircled and withdrew step by step to Barreaux, whilst de Blagnac got reinforcements, joined Schulemburg, and went down along the Arc river valley. In a few days de Blagnac reached Montmélian: no more French in sight. He went ahead, and on 15 April appeared in front of Chambéry with seven battalions, 600 dragoons, and two mountain cannons.

The French garrison refused to surrender: 400 Piedmontese grenadiers attacked, protected by the big barrels they made rolling ahead, but lost 50 dead and were repulsed. Then de Blagnac was notified that La Feuillade was coming from Pont Charra with reinforcements, thus he left towards Montmélian. En route his troops raided the Grande Chartreuse of Grenoble, the garrison of Les Echelles, and the town of Chapareillan. Then on 23 April de Blagnac moved back towards Italy, and on the 28th crossed the Little San Bernardo and re-entered Aosta.

III: Preparing for the War in Piedmont

Vendôme's army received reinforcements and supplies during the winter, from Naples and Marseille via Genoa and Finale. In spring, on the eve of the campaign, he had 30,000 men under his direct orders, plus a further 10,000 in the Mantua area, preventing any Imperial attempt. Now Vendôme had clear ideas, and clear plans: seize Turin first, and this would end the war.

He submitted a project to the King, but the King rejected it. Vendôme insisted, and on 7 February received a letter. Louis XIV told him that he had deeply and carefully considered all Vendôme's suggestions, but as things were, the siege of Turin was unlikely to succeed. The city could not be blockaded if one did not master the neighbouring Cappuccini Hill, which was quite hard to seize.[4] The conjunction between the Piedmontese and the Austrians, Louis said, meant Victor Amadeus was more than 30,000 men strong with a huge cavalry, so there was not that much to hope. But, the King added, the most important point was to cut all the possible routes the Allies could exploit to relieve the Duke of Savoy. That meant not only to seize Nice, Oneglia, and the Alpine passes, but also the roads in the plain; thus, as Louis XIV openly and clearly stated, Vendôme had to seize Vercelli, Ivrea, and Verrua, in this order. This, the King concluded, was the general plan, and it had to be kept completely secret; Vendôme could tell only those who had to fulfil a portion of the plan, and they too had to be notified of only just as much as was needed to accomplish their tasks. Vercelli had to be seized to protect Milan, and Lomellina from enemy raids. Ivrea had to be seized to stop the stream of supplies and of Swiss and German soldiers from Switzerland, and from the San Bernardo pass to the Allied army.

Louis de Bourbon-Vendôme, Duke de Vendôme.

This message let a real dance of letters start. It would be complicated and boring to describe letter by letter what happened. Basically, the Piedmontese raid in Savoy that March deeply affected the French plans, and altered Louis XIV's mind. At the end of the story Louis, who had practically left free hand to Vendôme about all but a siege of Turin, changed his mind once more. Whilst Vendôme was preparing to besiege Verrua first, on 25 May he received a letter from King: Louis wanted him to besiege Vercelli, Ivrea, and Verrua, in this order. After a flood of letters during the last three months, and 18 days the situation was back to the original plan.

IV: The Fall of Susa

The plans made in Versailles were clear. The army of Italy must be supplied properly, and speedily. The experience of the previous war demonstrated the necessity of a safe Alpine crossing, thus the passes, or at least some of them,

4 This is something that must be explained to a non-Catholic reader. The Franciscan monks strictly following St. Francis of Assisi's rules are grouped in the Franciscan branch known as the "Cappuccini" (literally "small cowls" – whose robe colour later gave the name to the coffee drink mixed with a little milk, thus called Cappuccino) and according to their rules did not live in a city, no matter how small or big. Thus their monasteries were always outside the walls, usually on a hill nearby. That is why so often the "Cappuccini Hill" is mentioned in war accounts in many different places in Italy: wherever there was a siege, there was always near the besieged city a hill with a Cappucini monastery, and usually that hill commanded the city, or at least was as high as the city itself.

had to be secured. The valleys having Cuneo and Pinerolo as terminals would have been the best choice, but if reinforcements came from Northern France, the passage through the Aosta Valley or the Moncenisio, whose traditional terminal was Susa, were the best opportunities. Vendôme had to secure the plain, La Feuillade the mountains, thus the latter was ordered to leave aside Nice, and seize Susa.

Once Susa and the whole plain was taken, Turin would be the next step, and the war with Piedmont would be over. Once Piedmont fallen, all the troops could be moved to other fronts, perhaps resurrecting the southern branch of the great strategic operation against Austria.

La Feuillade blockaded Montmélian, and left Briançon on 26 May. He had 20 infantry battalions, four dragoon regiments, 20 cannons, and six mortars. On the 29th he was in Chiomonte, and on the 31st he was across the Alps on the Dora river, not far from Susa. The siege of Susa was considered so important and demanding that the King assigned its planning to Louis de Fieux, Count de Lapara, his second-best engineer after Vauban, and a pupil of Vauban himself. Lapara was 53, and in his outstanding career he successfully undertook 20 sieges. Susa was one of his last, for he was killed in action in Spain in 1706.

Drawing of the Street Plan of Susa.

Following his plans and orders, on 1 June the city surrendered after a few shells. Count de Blagnac withdrew with 1,000 foot and 300 cavalry to the neighbouring Brunetta entrenchment. La Feuillade started the task against it. On 3 June his men opened the first parallel. On the 4th his batteries started shelling the Brunetta from the Giaglione heights. On the 5th, at dawn, the French grenadiers attacked La Brunetta, suffered heavy casualties, and asked for a two-hour[5] truce to pick up dead and wounded. Then the fight restarted violently, and at sundown the defenders withdrew toward Avigliana, where they met a relief column composed of three battalions led by the Count di Castellamonte.

Once he had secured the Brunetta, La Feuillade focused on the fort of Susa. For only a month it had been commanded by Giuseppe Tommaso Bernardi, who had 510 men. Le Feuillade had still more than 10,000, and there was not that much to do. On 7 June the outer stronghold was lost. On the 8th the French attacked, and were repulsed. On the 11th they set a battery of 11 cannons and

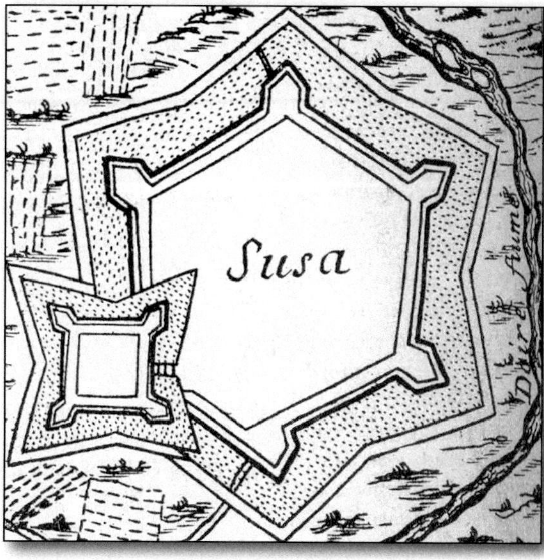

The Citadel of Susa.

5 Two hours according to the letter by La Feuillade to Chamillart, reported in de Vault, op. cit., vol. IV, 1704, p.131. According to Italian sources, the truce lasted four hours.

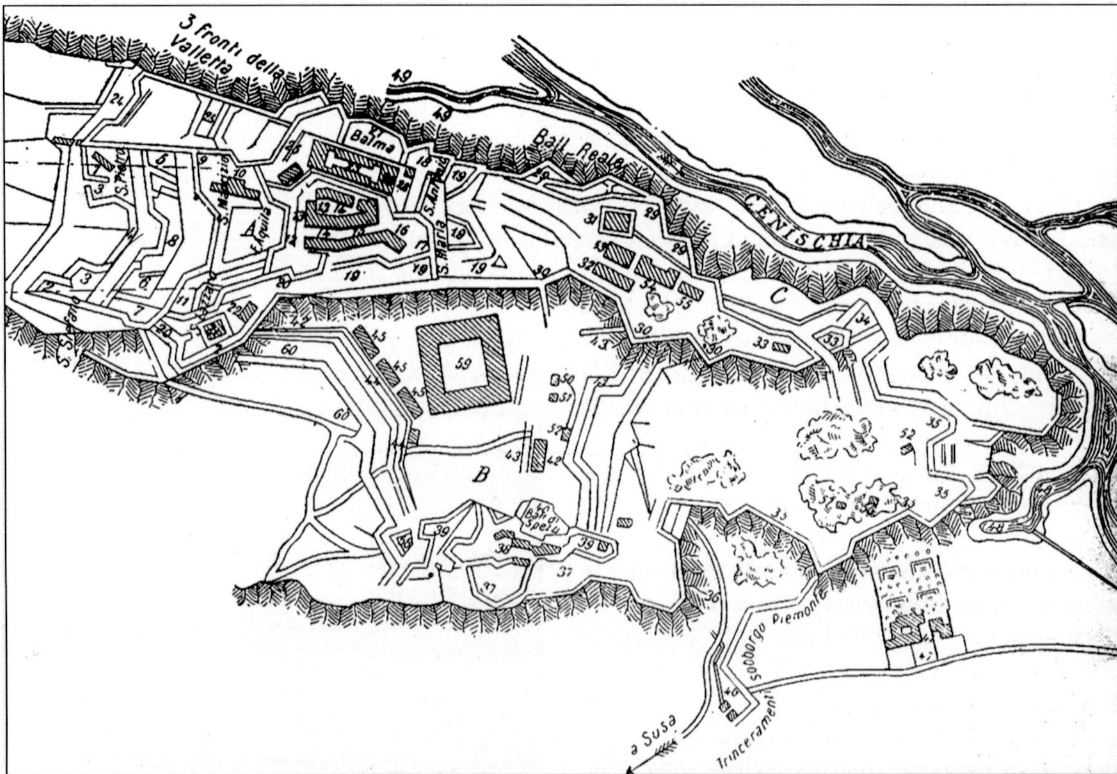

Plan View of the Fort of Brunetta.

two mortars. Bernardi summoned the council of war. He had only 200 men left, and agreed to surrender. On the 12th La Feuillade allowed his exit, with the honour of arms, and free passage to Turin.

V: The Intrusive King, and the Siege of Vercelli

On 26 April Victor Amadeus had left Turin, inspected Crescentino – part of the Verrua fortified system – and Trino, and reached his army not far from Casale. Meanwhile Vendôme lazily made his preparations.

On 6 May, at dawn, the French army had crossed the Po at Casale. Vendôme had 42 battalions and 66 squadrons. Spanish general Las Torres had six battalions, and 15 squadrons. Albergotti had to stay in Monferrato with a further six French battalions and seven squadrons, whilst six more French battalions garrisoned Casale, Asti, and Acqui.

Victor Amadeus was not far away, near the Sesia river, and preferred a withdrawal to Trino. The French pursued him with their cavalry, and entered the camp the Austro-Piedmontese had just left. There they held a council of war. The plan was to go to the Crescentino-Verrua fortified system, prepare for its siege, and wait to see if any enemy attack occurred. Then the siege of Verrua could be undertaken, and Vendôme was sure that, once Verrua was seized, and then Ivrea, Vercelli would surrender. He preferred this solution because Vercelli had 14 bastions, and its garrison was supposed to be 5,000 men strong.

Then on 25 May the King's last letter came. So, on the 30th, the French army left Verrua, and marched north-east to Vercelli. General Albergotti remained in Monferrato with 15 battalions, and 31 squadrons – more or less 10,000 men.

Following the King's order, on 5 June 1704 Vendôme's French and Las Torres' Spaniards – including Neapolitans, Belgians, and Milanese – blockaded Vercelli. They were 39 battalions and 58 squadrons. Communications between Vendôme and Albergotti were assured by a further 25 cavalry squadrons: nine in an entrenched camp in Trino, six in another entrenched camp in Tricero, and nine in Desana.

Louis d'Aubusson, Marquess and then Duke de la Feuillade.

Vercelli's garrison, according to the French, had 12 Piedmontese and Austrian battalions, and 800 or 900 cavalrymen, that is to say no more than 7,000 men. Unfortunately for the garrison, Victor Amadeus had to care about what was going on in Susa, for at that time La Feuillade was attacking it, thus the outnumbered Piedmontese had to share their attention and their troops in two opposite directions.

After some small clashes in the fields outside the walls, the French opened the trench under Vercelli on 10 June,[6] and on the 11th set a siege battery 48 guns strong. That same day La Feuillade was doing the same against the fort of Susa.

Vendôme inspected the front, and was not that happy. The city was at least as strong as he had been notified, and the garrison could be by one battalion stronger in infantry, although by a squadron or two weaker in cavalry, which meant much more trouble. Then he decided to follow a scheme which would be repeated in the next three sieges at Verrua, Ivrea, and Turin; a costly one. Having not enough men to lock up the city, he opened the first parallel only along one side, thus left the city watched, but essentially not locked up along as much as half of its walls. Then he planned two different attack approaches: a fake one on the Spanish front, towards the abbey of Saint Benedict, to attract the garrison's attention, and the real one, between the citadel on the left and the Gate of Milan on the right. Siege artillery was increased, and by 19 June the front of the real attack was supported by 40 cannons and 16 mortars.

As things were now, Vendôme had no doubt about the result, even if, as had happened since 1702, he had to deal with the King's intrusive letters.

Whilst in front of Vercelli, Vendôme tried to get indirect support from both his brother the Grand Prior, and La Feuillade. The Grand Prior was

6 *Breve e succinto giornale del memorabile assedio di Vercelli* (1704) [Short and concise journal of the memorable siege of Vercelli] handwritten, typewritten copy in AUSSME, L 3 Stati Preunitari, folder 6 "Piemonte", file 6. The author, who probably was a civilian, wrote that the trench near the walls was opened on the night on 14–15 June.

the commander in Eastern Lombardy. He had been tasked by his brother, who executed more general orders by the King, to stay there and prevent any Imperial attempt to penetrate into Piedmont. La Feuillade, after the fall of Susa, was asked by Vendôme to move towards Vercelli. But La Feuillade preferred to employ his men in securing the Alpine area: he moved south along the Alpine chain, entered the Waldensian Valleys, and went down eastward to Pinerolo. No matter what Vendôme thought, La Feuillade did what Louis XIV wanted (though had not explicitly stated), because, as we know, the King's original plan had been to seize Nice, and to secure the Alpine area in order to cut Piedmont's communications, secure the French supply lines across the mountains, and destroy the Protestant upaising in the Cevennes, which were supported from Piedmont nearby through the Alps. So Vendôme had to deal with the King's orders, no matter how deeply he disagreed with them, and no matter how long his operations lasted.

Back to Vercelli now. Inside the city, things did not look that good. Victor Amadeus appointed General Baron des Hayes to command the defence, relying on a garrison 600 dragoons and 7,000 foot.[7] On 31 May, realising how close the beginning of the siege was, the Duke had rushed into Vercelli two battalions of the Guards, transported on horseback by tasked cavalrymen.

The French official relation implicitly suggests that the siege went well, and smoothly; that the French behaved in a gentlemanlike manner, and describes how simply the garrison surrendered. But three diaries written by people from the city tell a different story, and we will follow them too.

Vercelli started shelling the French on 7 June and did not stop in the following days, harassing French preparation as much as possible. Des Hayes organised many sallies, and small clashes occurred outside the city. A huge number of allied soldiers, mostly Swiss and Irish, deserted to the French, whilst a huge number of French and Spanish soldiers deserted to the city.

Then the Sesia river flooded on the 17th, damaging the French earthworks and forcing the Spaniards to move their camp. The water subsided only two days later, but the French realised that the garrison had flooded the moat using the water from the Sesia, so they had to dig an exit for the waters. Then they decided to flood the outer defensive trenches. Thus they gathered as many peasants as they could, and enforced them to dig a ditch from the river to the trenches. What the French did not say was reported by Count Avogadro di Casanova, a Piedmontese officer, who sadly admitted: "we had to fire on our very unlucky peasants, enforced by enemy violence to work

7 There were 400 men of the dragoons of Genevois Regiment – the Green Dragoons – commanded by Colonel Doria di Prelà, and 200 Imperial dragoons, the 2nd (including many Irish soldiers) and 3rd Battalions of the Guards Regiment, two battalions of the Savoia Infantry Regiment, three Imperial battalions of the Harrach Infantry Regiment, Regiment Desportes composed of French protestants, Irish refugees and German professionals, and six Swiss battalions, (some were from Tscharner Regiment), plus the local militia. This is according to the official records, but the situation was not so rigid. According to the list of dead, there were also men from other corps, and especially from the Frydt, Croce Bianca, the Marquess d'Este, San Damiano and the Nizza infantry regiments, as well as an occasional corps composed of the city clergy. The Bernese troopers were considered the sloppiest and most cowardly.

on our damage, and killed plenty, twice miserable victims, for they lost their lives by their brothers' hand."[8]

On 18 June, no matter how big the garrison's ordnance was, the commander of the city ordered removal of the lead covering the dome of the Beate Amadeus church, to cast bullets. When on the next day the French started shelling using their new batteries, the first ball fell on Saint Mark's Convent, crossed the refectory where the monks were having their meal, and fell into the cellar. As one of the diarists, an unknown monk, remarked: given its target, it had to be a hungry ball.

Three people were put on the bell tower. They had to ring the bells whenever they saw a light at the mouth of one of the mortars or cannons, to let the people find shelter, but in a few hours this proved to be useless: 3,000 bombs were calculated to drop on the city on the first day. On the 24th the French made their first attack. It was repulsed. They went on shelling, and by the eighth day the city had been hit by 9,000 bombs and balls, and most of the houses were burned or smashed.

Meanwhile the French came closer. On the 28th they were at the foot of the walls. On the 30th they set a new 15-gun battery to open a breach, and smashed both the Milan Gate and its bridge. The garrison prepared a wood and earth barricade inside, and laid mines underground. The French attacked, stormed the barricade and, whilst hooraying, the mines blew under their feet. Then 500 armoured cavalry sallied out and pursued the survivors away, whilet the position was reconquered.

However the garrison situation was bad, and worsened every day. An epidemic started during the first days of the siege, and on 11 June there were already 300 sick in the city hospitals. The diarists spoke of pestilence but probably, according to the descriptions, it was typhus. Baron des Hayes got it, and command passed to General Count Doria di Prelà, who faced a dramatic situation. A great part of the city was destroyed and burnt. Intensive French shelling kept the rate at 1,000 shots per day, at its height on the 18th and again on the 21st June when, according to the defenders, the city was targeted by 3,000 cannon shots. The epidemic did not decrease. Casualties among the citizens and the garrison were huge, deserters too. Thus not only the defence, but also internal security was in danger, with gangs of thieves, sometimes including soldiers, murdering and robbing here and there.

Meanwhile all the neighbouring villages and towns had been raided by the besiegers. The peasants had no protection, for all the weapons and the militia had been gathered into Vercelli. Whoever nonetheless tried to react was killed, as happened to eight unknown peasants, who were shot by the French on 1 August.

On 14 July another battery was set by the French. It had 22 cannons, and proved dramatically effective. Within 24 hours there were three new breaches in the facing bastion. On the 16th the Milanese troops in Spanish service seized the main bastion, and held it against the garrison counter-

8 Avogadro di Casanova, *Journal du siège de Verceil fait par les Français l'an 1704* (first edition Vercelli, 1845), rep. in Faldella, op. cit., p.73.

attack.[9] On the 20th, after a council of war, Doria di Prelà made the drums roll the call, offering to capitulate. Vendôme refused: prisoners of war, or nothing. If they refused, the city had to be stormed and the whole garrison, sick and wounded included, had to be killed by the sword. As things were, Prelà had 5,600 foot and 500 dragoons still alive, but 2,000 of them where in the hospitals, hence he could rely on more or less 4,000 men, instead of the original 7,600. The city had been hit by 75,000 shots. One third of its citizens were dead.[10] Its walls had wide breaches, and there was no way to get relief, or hold against a massive attack, so on 20 he agreed to surrender.

On 21 July the French got the Turin Gate and demanded 20,000 scudi, and all "the bells, the tin, the bronze, the brass, and the lead from the churches as well as from the inhabitants". The city council negotiated, and getting 3,000 golden Louis cash, Vendôme agreed to put aside the demand for metals, and not to loot the city. He received 1,000 Louis on the spot, and the remaining money later. The defenders are supposed to have killed a little under 4,000 French and Spaniards. Vendôme admitted to have lost only 200 dead and 830 wounded, and reported to the King that he had seized 26 flags, 72 cannons, 70,000 cannonballs, and a huge quantity of gunpowder. The King, happy, ordered the razing of Vercelli's walls.

Victor Amadeus was quite upset. He considered both des Hayes and Prelà to have not held as long as they could, and found them to have had a considerable lack of initiative, and energy. Imperial colonel Saint Saphorin wrote more or less the same to Prince Eugene, to whom Victor Amadeus also complained about how badly the Piedmontese officers were performing. In fact it is really hard to know now whether that defence was really weaker than it could have been or not. What is certain is that, when surrendering, they had lost roughly 50 percent of their forces, even if their ordnance was still huge. The Duke had tried at least to disturb the besieging army, but he was too weak. His troops were outnumbered one to two, and when he moved his cavalry, French cavalry reaction was overwhelming, and he in person barely escaped it.

He was doing what he could, but was short of men, and no further Imperial reinforcement could come because the Grand Prior succeeded so well in stopping them in Eastern Lombardy, that they were expected by the French to go back, up to Trento. La Feuillade was storming the Waldensian Valleys with thousands of troopers, where the local Protestant militia did not exceed 1,800 men, and the Duke had to take care of his defensive system: he had to hold the longer he could, until reinforcements, and above all money could arrive from his Allies. But what about his Allies? What were they doing almost one year after he joined them?

---

9 Las Torres had Belgians belonging to the Count de Aquilar's Brabant Regiment, and both Milanese and Neapolitan troopers. About the former, there is a funny note: Ponchinella soldiered among them, or rather, there was Martino Polincinella, obviously a Neapolitan, serving as a sergeant in Fra Tommaso Caracciolo's Regiment of Foot; cfr. the list of dead reported by Faldella, in op. cit., pp.82–84.

10 Alberoni wrote to the Duke of Parma that there was no house which had not been damaged, and that when the epidemic widened in the countryside, every day 70 wagons or chariots carried the sick people to Novara and Casale.

VI: The Treaty with England

As we know, the treaty between Savoy and the Emperor was officially dated on 8 November 1703.

In October 1703, soon after the declaration of war, Count Annibale Maffei reopened the Sabaudian embassy in London. But more than two months earlier, on 26 July 1703 Old Style, Queen Anne had graciously appointed the Hon. Richard Hill as her "envoy extraordinary" to the Duke of Savoy. The States General did the same, and appointed Mr. Van der Meer.

A deacon – and later, when ordained after the war, a Fellow of Eton College – Hill had been employed by William III during the Nine Years' War as deputy paymaster of the army in Flanders. The King greatly appreciated him as a minister of the greatest "vigilance, capacity and virtue". Then in 1699 he appointed Hill as the English ambassador in The Hague, and sent him to Max Emanuel of Bavaria too. In 1700 Hill became Lord of the Treasury, and left that post when in 1702 was appointed Commissioner of the Admiralty, and counsellor to the Queen's husband, the Prince of Denmark. Hill, who already met the Duke of Savoy in 1699, received his instructions dated 26 July 1703.

Negotiations with Savoy went smoothly, but the Treaty could not be concluded without the previous ratification of that between Savoy and the Emperor. And the Emperor, as we know, went slowly due to the exceptions made, and the doubts supposed, because of the bribes sought in Vienna. Once that Treaty was ratified, it was also thanks to Hill if, at the end, on 4 August 1704 the Treaty with England was achieved.

> First Article.
> Her Britannic Majesty receives and includes His Royal Highness in the Treaty of the Grand Alliance concluded at The Hague, the 7th of September, 1701, between his Imperial Majesty, the late King of England, and the Lords the States-General, engaging with his said Royal Highness to the entire and inviolable observation of the said Treaty, as if he had been one of the first parties thereto. His Royal Highness on his part enters, without any reserve or exception, into all the obligations and all engagements, into which the Powers have entered who have concluded it, borne by the same Treaty, the tenor whereof follows:[11]

Then the Treaty of the Great Alliance made in 1701 was included word by word, and was followed by the

> Second Article.
> As His Royal Highness enters as above into all the engagements stipulated in the aforesaid Treaty of the Grand Alliance, her Britannic Majesty promises reciprocally to ratify and guarantee in all and each of its points the Treaty concluded at Turin between His Imperial Majesty and His said Royal Highness, the 8th of November, 1703; Her said Britannic Majesty engaging herself generally, as she does specially

11 English translations reported in "Hill – *Letters*", part II, Translations, p.944.

> hereafter, to all the obligations and guarantees borne by the same Treaty, the tenor of which follows:[12]

Once more a treaty – the one of Savoy with Austria now – was inserted word by word, thus England recognised, accepted and accessed its terms. Then it went on saying:

> Third Article.
> The knowledge which her Britannic Majesty has of the important services which his Royal Highness has rendered, and may render, to the common cause, induces her to desire the extension of his dominions and of his forces, that he may have further means of being useful thereto, and wishing to give him a more particular proof of the great interest she takes therein, obliges herself and promises expressly to guarantee and maintain all the cessions made by the Emperor in favour of his Royal Highness, and his successors, by virtue of the a foresaid Treaty of the 8th of November 1703, viz., of the part of the Duchy of Montferrat with which the Dukes of Mantua were formerly invested, of the Provinces of Alexandria and Valenza with all the lands which lie between the Po and the Tanaro, of the Province of Lumelline, of the Valley of Sesia, and of the lands which shall be included within the aforesaid ceded countries, in all and throughout as it is set forth and explained by the 5th and 6th articles of the abovementioned treaty, so that the said cessions shall always take their full effect, whatever be the treaty of peace or agreement concluded, declaring that they shall be included in the preliminaries as one of the conditions, without which a negotiation for peace shall never be entertained.
>
> Fourth Article.
> Furthermore, her Britannic Majesty promises never to have a hand in or conclude any treaty of peace, agreement, or truce, unless his Royal Highness be entirely re-established in all the States which the enemy may occupy, which restitution of states so occupied shall also be comprised in the preliminaries as is set forth in the preceding article.
>
> Fifth Article.
> Moreover, her Britannic Majesty, having all that concerns the public interest much at heart, and particularly desiring by all means to contribute to the security of the States of his Royal Highness, by depriving France of the footing which she has on the hither side of the Alps, and making Mount Genevro a barrier against that crown, engages herself to use all her endeavours in the treaty of general peace for the acquisition of the district which is on the hither side of Mount Genevro to the advantage of his Royal Highness, so that he and his successors may enjoy the whole sovereignty thereof for ever.
>
> Sixth Article.
> Her Britannic Majesty, aware of the known and incontestable right which belongs to his Royal Highness, and which was declared by the will of Philip IV,

12 Reported, as we know, in "Hill – *Letters*", part II, Translations, pp.936–938.

King of Spain, of glorious memory, to the succession of the Spanish Monarchy, immediately after the House of Austria, engages herself specially, as to her proper deed, to maintain it inviolate, promising that she will never consent to any treaty of peace or agreement, and will never sign any, whereby any prejudice shall be done to the said right, and that she will never permit that any third Prince be introduced before his Royal Highness and established in any of the dominions of the said Spanish Monarchy.

Seventh Article.
Her Britannic Majesty, to give his Royal Highness some real proof of her friendship, and of the interest which she takes for his protection, and to furnish him the means of better contributing to the good of the common cause, obliges herself to give him a subsidy of 66,666 crowns and two-thirds at once, solely for the first expenses of this war, and further, she settles on him a monthly subsidy of 53,333 crowns and one third; which she promises always to pay punctually two months in advance in this present city of Turin, computing the crown at the rate of 82 sols current money of Piedmont, and that to commence from the 3rd of October last 1703, the day of the declaration of his Royal Highness against France, and to continue during the course of the present war, and two months after.

Eighth Article.
In consideration of the subsidy specified in the preceding article, and of that of 26,663 crowns, to which their High Mightinesses, the Lords the States-General of the United Provinces of the Low Countries, shall oblige themselves by the Treaty which his Royal Highness shall also conclude with them, making in all the sum of 80,000 crowns per month, his said Royal Highness obliges himself always to keep on foot a body of his own troops of 15,000 men, viz. 12,000 foot and 3,000 horse, and more if he shall be able, during the course of the present war; of which body of 15,000 men, he shall employ yearly in the field the greatest number which the interest of the common cause shall require, having regard to the security of his fortresses. His said Royal Highness further undertakes to cause arms, victual, and ammunition to be furnished to all the refugees who shall come to serve in the Valleys, also, during the course of the present war, so that they may be usefully employed to the service of the common Cause.

Ninth Article.
As a greater mark of the zeal which his Royal Highness has to cement more firmly by every means this strict union and correspondence with her Britannic Majesty, his said Royal Highness, desiring that it may pass also among the subjects of both parties, by the introduction of commerce, which her said Majesty has likewise indicated that she wished for the reciprocal advantage of both nations, promises to give every protection for the good success of the said commerce.

He will to that end command the regulation of the tariff of the customs on merchandise of England and Ireland which shall come into his States, observing the same proportion with respect to them as for those wares which come from France and other foreign countries, in consideration of their quality and their price; and in respect of transit goods, he will reduce the transit impost to a third less than is set forth by the tariff.

We, the Plenipotentiaries aforesaid, by virtue of our respective full powers, have concluded, agreed, and signed the present treaty; and have set thereto the seal of our arms, promising respectively the entire and inviolable observation thereof, and undertaking to supply the ratifications thereof, in good and due form, viz., that of her Britannic Majesty in six weeks, and that of his Royal Highness in eight days.

Done at Turin, the 4th day of the month of August, in the year of Grace 1704.

Rich.d Hill. C. E.L D. Vernon.
L. S. *L. S.*[13]

As things were going, this diplomatic result meant that had the Duke held a bit more, the money and the men would be obtained. The problem was, how long could he hold?

VII: The Loss of Ivrea, and Bard

During the siege of Vercelli Vendôme received many letters from the King, who told him to feel free to chose between Ivrea and Verrua as the next to be besieged. Vendôme was not stupid; he knew what the King had in mind. Had Verrua been next, and that siege had failed, the result would be really bad for him. Thus he answered saying that Ivrea will be next. The King was very pleased.

The distance between Vercelli and Ivrea did not exceed 25 miles, but there were so many marshes, ditches, canals, and ponds, that it was not that easy to move the entire army properly. Moreover the French, and the Spaniards were short of supplies. The Old Vaudémont shipped food and ordnance from Milan faster than expected, thus Vendôme split his army in three parts, each forming a convoy, and moved them one by one to Ivrea. The first French brigades, led by Vendôme in person, encamped in front of Ivrea on 29 August and the whole army gathered within the next two days.

The Castle at Ivrea.

Ivrea was weak. Its walls were old-fashioned. Its garrison, commanded by Count Perrone, and Imperial general Kriechbaum, included 3,200 foot,[14] whilst some cavalry was near the city.

13 *Treaty, secret articles and separated article about the league between H.R.H. the Duke of Savoy Victor Amadeus II and the Queen Anne of England against France*, original in French starting *Comme son Altesse Royale de Savoie à toujours*, rep. in Solaro della Margarita (ed.), *Traités*, cit., II, pp.220–229. English translation reported in "Hill – *Letters*" (London: 1845), part II, Translations, pp.944–947.

14 There were four Piedmontese battalions from the Fusileers, Maffei, Trinità, and Duvillard regiments, mostly militia, two Swiss battalions, two battalions belonging to the Schulemburg Infantry Regiment, and one belonging to the Aygoin Regiment, paid by England, and they all were in Sabaudian service, plus two Hungarian haiduk battalions.

Vendôme had plenty of troops: 34 battalions, 79 squadrons, 64 cannons, and 12 mortars, but once more he felt too weak to properly besiege the city. Diseases badly affected his forces. The epidemic that started during the siege of Vercelli played the main role, but the season too was responsible for how bad things were going. At that time the poorly fed soldiers ate whatever they could, no matter how rotten or green, that is to say not yet ripe, it could be. The French knew quite well how bad things normally were since the end of August and until early October in wine-producing areas such as Piedmont, and Italy more in general, due to the great quantity of unripe grapefruit the soldiers ate; whose effects, when it is still green, are harsh. As a result dysentery spread all across the armies, but probably, especially in wet areas filled by stagnant waters in ponds, and ditches, malaria played an additional major role.[15]

Now, this is precisely what happened to the French under Ivrea. The official relation written by General de Vault clearly says, by the first time during that campaign, if not during that war, that "there was actually among the infantry such a great number of sick that, during the siege of Ivrea, one could not make the service by battalions, but only by detachments",[16] and if such an admission was made, the situation must have been really hard.

Thus Vendôme reduced the attacks to only one side of the city. As a first step he let his troops sweep away all the enemy outposts on the hills and around Ivrea. Then he seized the Cappuccini Hill, from which his artillery could shell the city. On 4 September the artillery firing started. By 10 September the besieging lines were achieved and communications, between Ivrea, and Turin, if any were left, were completely stopped.

But whilst he was performing so well, the bad news of the French disaster at Höchstadt/Blenheim arrived.[17] Vendôme immediately realised how

15 It can be useful to underline that in the whole Mediterranean area people are often affected by the so-called beta thalassaemia, called Mediterranean anaemia. This kind of hereditary disease has, or may have, many bad consequences, although in spite of what one may think, normally – as I know by personal experience – it is not fatal, and often does not cause any inconvenience. It has also a positive effect: whoever has Mediterranean anemia cannot have malaria, because the red cells are too small to let the plasmodium, the unicellular protozoan parasite causing malaria, develop within the blood. Thus whilst the French troopers, whose majority were not from the Mediterranean wet areas, could be affected by malaria, a certain number of the Piedmontese peasants, that is to say both militiamen and soldiers, probably were not because they came from malaria areas, and were probably affected by the Mediterranean anemia. Thus, one may also wonder of how much Mediterranean anemia may have preserved the Piedmontese army's combat readiness, whilst malaria put the French army out of order.

16 De Vault, op. cit, vol. IV, 1704, p.266.

17 There is a story about Blenheim, which deserves to be told, and this is probably the very first time it is told in English. When, in the afternoon, the Duke of Marlborough was prevailing between Blindheim and Oberglau, Tallard let his first cavalry line charge. As is well known, they were repulsed, and the Anglo-Dutch troops restarted advancing, gained ground, and climbed. The Allied cavalry and infantry had time to reorganise behind their advancing line and then moved on, and pushed Tallard's French back. Thus Tallard called in his Infantry brigades, and then their nemesis came, as the unknown biographer of Prince Eugene wrote in the early eighteenth century (in *Vita e Campeggiamenti*, cit., p.135): "there were among those foot many Piedmonteses taken prisoner in Italy, and passed under the Most Christian King's flags more due to necessity than to will. Thus, assailed by the Count of Noyelles with the Guards of Hesse, and the Battalions of Luneburg, they easily ceded, and, in disorder, they withdrew on other

heavily such a defeat could affect French operations in Germany, and not that much later, in Italy too. The Sun King realised it too, thus Vendôme received orders to send 10 battalions and 10 squadrons east, to help his brother to stop whatever Imperial attempt was made in Italy. In exchange for the departing troops, he had to get reinforcements from La Feuillade.

Anyway Vendôme was short of infantry. So he immediately sent 13 squadrons, but no foot at all, for he intended to keep as many foot as he could for the next siege of Verrua. At the same time he realised the local situation was better than supposed, thus he extended the siege ring and completely locked up the city. Meanwhile shells and bombs hit Ivrea so much that on 16 September the garrison rolled the call. Vendôme refused any capitulation of the city unless it included the citadel and the castle. He received a negative answer, and the shelling restarted.

On 18 September the garrison withdrew into the castle, the citadel, and the fortified outer suburb between the city and the citadel, and blew the bridge. It was on that day that Vendôme discovered the garrison to be composed of 11 battalions, instead of seven as the deserters told him before.

During the night of 19–20 September the French opened the trench against the suburb. On the 20th they started bombing it, and by the 25th they had opened a breach in its wall. On the 26th in the morning eight grenadier companies, followed by 600 men, stormed the suburb. The defenders fled into the citadel but the attack went on, and thus a white flag was raised. Vendôme wanted them to surrender as prisoners of war, and they did – they were 140 officers and 1,400 men, included the sick and wounded – but the castle was not included in the capitulation. There were at least 700, perhaps 800 men in it, and they held. Vendôme restarted artillery fire. The castle held two days more. On the 28th Vendôme demanded the commander surrender, otherwise, he said, once he seized the covered road there would be neither capitulation nor quarter to expect. Talks went ahead whilst the artillery continued firing. On 29 September in the morning the garrison surrendered, reduced to 32 officers and 600 men. The French entered the citadel the next day.

The Siege of Ivrea, 1704.

Vendôme underlined to the King that by losing Vercelli and Ivrea Victor Amadeus lost also 24 infantry battalions, which – Vendôme said – were the core of Piedmontese army, and that was the best result.

Then Vendôme moved to Bard. The Fort of Bard locked – and still locks – the entrance to the Aosta Valley from Piedmont. Vendôme had hoped La Feuillade would seize it, but La Feuillade had

Battalions and put them in confusion". The Anglo-Dutch cavalry commanders realised it, and charged the French cavalry on the right wing, cutting it in pieces. One could state it to have been the revenge for San Benedetto Po.

The Fortress of Bard.

moved south-west along the mountains to Pinerolo, thus it was up to Vendôme to seize Bard too.

On 5 October he made a reconnaissance. The fort was so strong that it was considered impossible to seize, thus the people from the villages and towns nearby had placed their money and valuables there. Bard was held by Swiss colonel Reding commanding a small garrison, mostly composed of Swiss soldiers, with some militiamen. Meanwhile, La Feuillade arrived too.

On the 6th the French seized the suburb, placed some cannons, and prepared their attack. On the 7th Vendôme demanded Reding choose between surrender or being hanged. Reding answered by asking for military honours, and an eight-day delay. Vendôme refused. Reding asked for a face-to-face talk. Vendôme agreed. The French official relation says simply: "and the result of that meeting was that he surrendered as a prisoner of war."[18] Fake: the result of the meeting was that the honest and reliable Swiss professional delivered to the French the Piedmontese fortress he promised to hold, kept the assets the trustful people gave him in custody, and was appointed field marshal in the French Army.

Mr. Hill resumed on 1 October:

> The enemies are now masters of Ivrea, of the Cite d'Aoust, and of all the valley d'Aoust, and of all the passages which can give them a communication between Savoy and the Milanese through the Val de Sesia : they are, at the same time, in possession of all the passes which have yet been known between Piedmont and Switzerland. They have, by this means, opened a passage for their troops, for their recruits, and for their equipage of war, between France and Lombardy; and, at the same time, they hinder us from sending so much as a letter to any part of the world, except by the way of Genoa, which is also very precarious. I am not now surprised at what the Duke de Vendôme has done. I wonder that he did not do it sooner.
>
> What he has to do next is to join all his forces, and to attack us at Crescentin, or to endeavour to take Verrue, or to come and take post at Chivas, to look very near upon us at Turin, or to come and settle his army in quarters in the rich plains of Piedmont. His Royal Highness does not abandon himself, though he is abandoned. He is marched over the Po, to see if he can beat up Albergotti's quarters; but, now we have nothing left at Ivrea, his Royal Highness cannot go far from us.[19]

Now the shortest route across the Alps was open to the French, and not that much remained to Victor Amadeus but Turin, Cuneo, and Verrua. Would he

18 De Vault, op. cit, vol. IV, 1704, p.277. A footnote adds that Reding surrendered because, as Vendome reported to Louis XIV, he had sought for a long tine to serve the King of France.

19 Hill to Sir Charles Hedges, Turin, 1 October 1704, in "Hill – *Letters*", vol. I, p.433.

still be able to hold? And by which assets, and means? Well, there was at least some good news: the money was next to come. Payments by the Maritime Powers started just that month.

VIII: The Money from the North

In 1704 the disaster of the French capture of Piedmontese troops in September 1703, the cost of new recruits, horses, and materials nearly doubled the military budget, pushing it up to 9,877,230 liras.[20] The trimester from October to December 1703 had seen a huge expenditure. No less than 600,000 scudi were spent to find new troopers and to restore the fortresses. At the same time incomes lowered because the taxes, and revenues were severely affected, probably by 50 percent, that is to say by a couple of million liras per year, due to the French conquest of Savoy and Nice, as well as by the French presence in Piedmont.

In autumn 1704 Maritime Powers started supporting Victor Amadeus, as they did in the Nine Years' War. At that time they provided 15.7 million liras. This time they were going to give roughly thrice that sum: 43 million, even if, in theory, the overall amount would have to be 49 million liras. England allocated to the war in Italy one tenth of her yearly expenditure during the war. Why that much? As it was summed up by John Hattendorf: "the key point in English strategy was the maintenance of active armies in several theatres which would force France to disperse her troops. It seemed hardly possible to the English government that victory could be achieved on the Continent by one army alone."[21] and "In the English view, it was the balance amongst the different theatres which would defeat France."[22]

Hence, to keep war alive in Italy or in south-east France, was as vital as to keep it alive on the Rhine, and in Spain.

The Piedmontese Treaty with England, as we have seen, foresaw:

> [a] subsidy of 66,666 crowns and two-thirds (63,565 scudi) at once, solely for the first expenses of this war, and further, … a monthly subsidy of 53,333 crowns and one third; 82 sols current money of Piedmont, and that to commence from the 3rd of October last 1703, the day of the declaration of his Royal Highness.[23]

For England provided two thirds of the funding and the remaining third was paid by the Dutch, Amsterdam had to pay half of what London paid, meanwhile Turin received 100,000 "crowns" to start, and was ensured a further monthly 80,000 crowns instalments until the end of the war.

Now we must clarify: the English translation quoted here speaks of crowns, but the original text of the Treaty is in French and speaks of écus –

20 Prato, op. cit., p.260

21 Hattendorf, op. cit., p.89.

22 Hattendorf, op. cit., pp.89–90.

23 *Treaty, secret articles and separated article about the league between H.R.H. the Duke of Savoy Victor Amadeus II and the Queen Anne of England against France*, cit., Article VII.

scudi. Thus the Treaty did not speak of the silver English crown equal to five shillings, or quarter pound, normally minted at that time,[24] it was speaking of Piedmontese scudi. But if the Piedmontese scudo equalled 86 soldi, not 82, so what? The difference between the values of the Piedmontese scudo in Piedmont and in the Treaty is four soldi, that is to say 4.65 percent. Why such a difference?

Did the Piedmontese scudo suffer inflation and lose that much? The answer is negative. The scudo was a valuable silver coin and, as the golden double of Savoy, was rarely seen by the lower classes, including soldiers and peasants, whose wages were in liras, soldi and denari. Now it is right that during the war the Duke altered the alloy of small coins, and minted coins whose formal value was higher than that of the alloy they were made of, but this simply meant that in fact – in terms of value of the metal – a scudo equalled far more altered coins than in the past. In other words, even if in 1700 one needed the weight of the metallic alloy needed to mint 86 soldi to equal the silver of a scudo, in 1704, after the State intrusion on alloys, one needed more than 86 soldi to equal the value of the silver of a scudo, not less. And if the Treaty spoke of 82 soldi per crown/scudo, this meant an increase of the value of the soldo to the scudo, for one needed fewer soldi to get a scudo, thus it was a deflation and not an inflation.

What is interesting is that the final result did not change. If the English Treasury paid in London 53,333.33 scudi, each composed of 82 soldi, the Piedmontese Treasury had to receive in Turin 50,852,71 scudi composed of 86 soldi each. In terms of figure it seemed less; in terms of manpower wage, such a monthly instalment, no matter whether of 53,333.33 scudi of 82 soldi each, or of 50,852 scudi of 86 soldi each, equalled – in both cases – the monthly wage of 29,155 infantry privates, which, when adding the Dutch funding, rose to 43,732: a remarkable support for an army promised to field 12,000 infantry and 3,000 cavalry, and which never fielded more than 25,000 men throughout the war.

So, back to the original question, why such a 4.65 percent difference? The only answer is that it reflected the fee expected to be paid for the letters of exchange.[25] Their price during the previous war had not be considered in origin, and in fact badly affected the English and Dutch funding, because a remarkable portion of it was lost in transactions, and never arrived in Piedmont. Thus it is clear that now, due to the lesson learned in the Nine

24 I am very grateful to Professor (PhD) Jeremy Black, and to Dr (PhD) Nigel Ramsay for the valuable help kindly given about English crowns.

25 A letter of change was a document issued by banker who received a payment from a customer, and ordered another banker, acting in another city, to pay a certain sum to a certain beneficiary. It relied on the credit the issuing banker could have there, that is to say on how trusted he was in the place where the payment had to be made. Thus, the letter of change worked only among bankers, or merchants, with a mutual business relationship. That is why, due to the scanty foreign trade of Piedmont towards non-Italian countries other than France, British or Dutch letters of change could be paid in Italian mercantile cities as Genoa, Venice or Leghorn, but scarcely in Turin, because of its lack of direct commercial links to the Maritime Powers. The letters of change paid in an Italian city out of Piedmont had to be converted into a further letter of change issued to be paid in Turin, thus there were at least two stages before Victor Amadeus got the subsidy, and each was charged fees.

Years' War, the Maritime Powers and Piedmont agreed a fictional charge, which actually kept the stated purchase power in spite of the shipping fees, the latter being in fact included in the funding. This seems to be the only possible explanation. Not by chance the Lullino and Nicolas bank in Turin, when asked to remit the subsidy to the Duke, replied they could not accept paying more than four liras per scudo, which meant a 4.44 percent fee.

Anyway, if the Treaty was signed on 4 August 1704, it had to be ratified by Queen Anne within six weeks – in fact it was ratified on the first day of the sixth and last week, on 9 September 1704 – and the money could come only later. Meanwhile, Victor Amadeus needed money, thus he borrowed it from Lullino and Nicolas, who granted the loan thanks to the forthcoming English subsidy.

The French situation was not better. Richard Hill wrote in January 1705:

> I cannot yet find that the Duke of Vendôme does want money to carry on his works at Verrue; but I am assured, that the French garrisons at Suze, and Ivrea, are very ill paid, and that money does grow very scarce in France. I am well persuaded that Mons. de Chamillard does give 12 percent for all the money which he sends to Italy, for which he gives assignments to the bankers of Lyons, Genoa, Milan, or Geneva, up on which assignments he allows one percent interest per month until they are paid. Besides this, the King loses 20 percent upon all his expenses made in Italy, because he pays the louis d'or there on the foot of 12 livres, which goes in France for 15.[26]

So, fees badly affected whatever monetary transaction, no matter the army; and the bankers seemed to be the real, if not the only, winners in that war. Both London and The Hague remembered quite well how much money destined to Savoy had been wasted in fees paid to the bankers in London, Amsterdam, Genoa, Leghorn, Geneva, Venice, and Turin, as well as they perfectly remembered how effective a different system could be. Thus, as we have seen, at least a portion, a huge portion, of the Anglo-Dutch support was allocated to the more or less direct funding of Protestant Regiments, contracted to serve in Piedmont, under the Duke's orders, but in fact in British, and Dutch pay. Of, course, that money was supposed to come later, but nonetheless Victor Amadeus in autumn 1703 had been able to sign the contracts to raise the abovementioned 11,000 Protestant soldiers from Germany, and Switzerland, who, when the Treaty was ratified, were already serving, and, in many cases, were already dead.

Anyway, when the money began arriving, it was just in time: the French were starting the siege of Verrua, the bloodiest, longest, and most demanding of the whole war.

26 Hill to Sir Charles Hedges, Turin on 3/14 January, 1704/5, reported in "Hill – *Letters*", part II, Translations, pp.480–843.

IX: The Terrible Siege of Verrua

After Vercelli and Ivrea, and not considering Bard, according to the schedule stated by the King, now it was the time of Verrua. In spring Chamillart more or less openly pressed Vendôme to let him leave aside Verrua, and undertake the siege of Turin.

It is unclear how aware of Louis XIV's secret order to Vendôme Chamillart may have been, in other words it is unclear whether he was sincerely trying to get Verrua first, or if he was attempting to put Vendôme in trouble with the King. It is a possibility, for Chamillart was close to the Lobby of the Ministers, that in Versailles opposed the so-called Lobby of Meudon, which Vendôme belonged to. Although Chamillart did not dare too much to push directly, for Vendôme had Royal blood, and thus was more than welcome to the King, who never refused a favour to him. In case of a clash, whatever reason Chamillart had, he would lose against Vendôme. So regarding Verrua, he turned around the obstacle and exploited his son-in-law La Feuillade. La Feuillade many times asked Vendôme to besiege Turin, but Vendôme always refused, and by the end of July 1704 explained why:

> About the siege of Turin, I'll tell you that it is impossible to do it without having seized Verrua, and being the master of the Po. Since the moment when the rains start, wagons no longer move in this country here, nor in Monferrato, and this so many things are needed for such a great siege, that it is indispensable to have a river for shipping all that is necessary. It would be too dangerous to engage themselves in such a great enterprise without having mastered in advance the navigation on the Po from Casale to Turin. The enemies, with all the Allies' mightiness, and no matter what happened during the summer, would have never been able to take Namur without the commodity of the Meuse.[27]

As Vendôme likely supposed, La Feuillade on 6 August forwarded this letter to Chamillart, and not a word more was spent about besieging Turin before Verrua.

After the fall of Ivrea Vendôme immediately started planning the approach to Verrua. Bard delayed that siege a little, but not that much. On 7 October, whilst Vendôme was still in front of Bard, the bulk of the French army started leaving Ivrea bound for Verrua, a matter of 45 kilometres, or 28 miles.

The fortress of Verrua was – it no longer exists, other than ruins – on the top of a relatively low hill, not that easy to climb, and only by one side. It commanded the wide flat plain crossed by the Po, and was halfway between Turin, west, and Casale, east, on the right side of the Po. Mentioned since the tenth century, the fortress was practically the only one besides Turin, in a good situation. In the plain and less than 20 miles from the capital, it provided a relevant threat to the rear to whoever wanted to besiege Turin itself.

27 The Marshal Duke de Vendôme to the Duke de La Feuillade, Vercelli, 29 July 29 1704, in de Vault, op. cit. vol. IV, p.165.

Victor Amadeus organised a complicated defensive system in Verrua. It relied on a wide underground network of mines, and was enhanced by the fortified block of Crescentino on the other side of the Po, which in that area at that time formed an island. Crescentino was linked to Verrua by a covered road, quite well protected and fortified. From Crescentino the road crossed the Po on two bridges – one to the island, and one from the island to Verrua – and reached the foot of the hill. There it had a terminal, a fortification called Forte da Basso – Downstairs Fort – and that was the beginning. Then, if one wanted to enter the castle of Verrua, he had to climb three big steps, three different levels, protected by one bastion each, thus by three lines of bastions. In origin this was all, and was demanding, but now there was more. Starhemberg had just built three additional field fortifications with bastions. The first, the Wallis Redoubt, was in the plain between the Forte da Basso and the river. The second, the Ridotta Ognissanti – All Saints Redoubt – was on the island. The last, simply called Testa di Ponte – Bridgehead – was on the left of the Po, and was linked to Crescentino fortress by a double trench. Last, and additionally, there was another fortification on the Heights of Carbignano, 1,000 yards from Verrua: the Forte Reale[28] – the Royal Fort – reinforced by two smaller earthworks east and west called Opera a corno and Ridotto staccato. It was linked to Verrua by a wide and strong entrenchment.

As things were, the first step had to be the conquest of the Forte Reale. Vendôme's troops arrived around Verrua on 14 October split in two columns, the first led by Vendôme in person and the second by Albergotti and Las Torres. They totalled more than 30,000 men, divided into 46 infantry battalions and 47 cavalry squadrons, supported by a large quantity of artillery.

Victor Amadeus in person was facing them. He had gathered in and around Verrua the last battalion of the Guards, and his infantry regiments Saluzzo, la Reyne, Halt,[29] Aosta, Tarantasia,[30] and Cortanze, whilst his cavalry included the Guardie del Corpo, Savoia Cavalleria, Piemonte Reale, His Royal Highness' Dragoons, the dragoons of Piedmont, and those of Genevois. The Piedmontese artillery comprised 70 different cannons and five mortars, enhanced by 27 spingards. The Imperial infantry included Guido Starhemberg, Maximilian Starhemberg, Daun, Kriechbaum, Wallis, and Regal infantry regiments.

The Duke concentrated 15 battalions at Carbignano – including 11 Imperial battalions – and as soon as the French siege artillery arrived on 17 October, the siege began.

28 Normally in eighteenth-century military Italy the adjective "reale" – royal – was given to the main military asset in a group, to underline its importance. Thus the most important ship of a fleet was "la Reale", and hence here Forte Reale did not mean the King's Fort, but simply the main fort.

29 It was a Swiss infantry regiment from Freiburg, composed of Catholics.

30 Tarantasia was a newly organised Ordinanza Regiment. It included the pre-existing six companies of the Militia of Savoy, five companies composed of Savoyards from the Piemonte Infantry Regiment, and all the privates of the Savoia Infantry Regiment who escaped from enemy captivity.

Vendôme concentrated his troops against the Forte Reale. The trench was opened on the 22nd, and on the 26th 30 cannons started shelling the fort. On the 30th the defenders sallied, but in the afternoon the French made their first general attack. Volleys and mines first stopped, and then repulsed them.

On the next day a further general attack succeeded in seizing the Ridotto staccato, but as soon as the French took it, the Piedmontese let the mines blow: nothing remained.

Vendôme insisted focusing on the Forte Reale: no success. On 6 November he tried a feint and sent 20 battalions and 20 squadrons toward Crescentino. They could not cross the Po, widened by the last heavy rains, nonetheless the feint succeeded. Victor Amadeus had been notified in advance by some French deserters, thus he concentrated his men back in Crescentino, who destroyed Carbignano before leaving it. Vendôme considered it a good piece of luck, and his men occupied the empty height of Carbignano. Meanwhile, both the armies had sent their cavalries away. The season was bad, there was no possibility of cavalry actions. Thus on 11 November Vendôme sent his cavalry apart from 200 hussars to Monferrato, and on the same day Victor Amadeus kept 600 cavalry, and sent the others to Chivasso, where they were joined by the Imperial cavalry on 14 November.

On 7 November the French started besieging the castle of Verrua. It was commanded by Savoyard general Pierre de Lucas, Count de la Roche d'Allery. A skilled veteran, he had fought in the French army in 1672, then joined the Imperial army and brilliantly defended a gate of Vienna in 1683 against the Turks. Later in that same war he served for a long time in the Venetian army in Greece, before going back home to fight against the French during the Nine Years' War.

Given the relatively small size of Verrua, la Roche d'Allery did not need more than a couple of regiments to hold it. Thus he had an Imperial regiment and a Ducal one. Both were occasional regiments, composed of men from the other units stationed in and near Crescentino. The soldiers spent a period in Verrua, and then came back to Crescentino to rest. Colonels Regal and de Blagnac respectively commanded the Imperial and the Ducal occasional regiments in the fortress.

Once more Vendôme applied his restrained scheme, and attacked only one side of the fortress. He was later reproached, but, given the ground, there was not that much he could do differently, and if the scheme succeeded the three previous times, there was no reason for it not to work now. It did work, but with terrible casualties.

On 9 November French artillery started bombing, using 42 guns. La Roche d'Allery held well, and reacted with artillery and sallies. His sallies on the 21st and 22nd were particularly effective, also because Vendôme had such a huge ratio of sick among his men, that he reduced those serving daily into the trenches to no more than 36 men per battalion, supported by 400 grenadiers.

On 5 December the French reached the fortifications. On the 7th, and again on the 9th, they tried to seize the covered road along the walls, but failed. Heavy rains rendered the siegework hard, thus operations went slowly, or, at least not as fast as Vendôme hoped. On 16 December, after a long stop caused by the rain, the French artillery started targeting the San Carlo and Santa Maria bastions, that is to say the first and the second steps. La Roche d'Allery reacted using mines and artillery,but by Christmas both the bastions were ruins. On St. Stephen's day – 26 December – the garrison sallied. One thousand grenadiers came out from the "Fort Downstairs", turned, climbed to Carbignano, and attacked the left wing of the besiegers, whilst Regal sallied from Verrua, destroyed whatever he found, and seized the third, and the second parallel. The French reacted. After a terrible hand-to-hand fight they reconquered their second parallel, but by midnight Regal was holding the third parallel, and the covered road. Vendôme had now in front of Verrua only two cannons on duty, and had to do all anew.

And here is how the situation looked on the eve of the new year to the English envoy. Richard Hill had been in Verrua since 17 November, and after two months reported to Sir Charles Hedges from Turin on an Anglican 3 January 1704, which in a Popish – although astronomically, more advanced – land it was 14 January 1705:

> Sir,
>
> … I have been since then [17 November] at Crescentin to see the wonderful effects of courage, constancy, and resolution. It is this day three months that the Duke of Vendôme is tormenting himself, and us, before Verrue. It is more than five weeks that he is lodged upon the counterscarp of the castle, which had no outworks; in which five weeks, he has not got one inch from us, above ground. We reckon he has fired above 100,000 cannon-shot upon the place, and thrown 20,000 bombs, besides infinite quantities of stones upon us. He has had time to wear out one set of artillery, and to consume all his powder, and to have recruits of cannon, mortars, and ammunition from France. We have had the good fortune to kill him five of his General-officers, his chief engineer, and the commander of his artillery. We have stifled a great many of his miners, and have reduced five companies of his cannoneers, which were of 45 each to 46 in all. Five of these cannoneers deserted yesterday, and came to us at Crescentin, and gave for the reason of their desertion, that their officers grew peevish, and impatient, and charged them à coups de baton, because the cannon did not make more impression upon our breaches. We have, indeed, two large breaches upon two of the bastions; but the care, which we take every night to clear away the rubbish which falls into the ditch, leaves an escarpe of six or eight feet high, which hinders them from attempting to lodge themselves upon these bastions, until they can throw them quite into the ditch by their mines, which they had carried almost under them. We have had the good fortune to spring one of those mines, and to blow up their gallery; and we are very hard at work to meet with the other. This long laborious defence is very expensive, as you will believe, in all respects, to his Royal Highness; but the immortal honour which he gets by it; the hindering a superior enemy from taking winter-quarters in Piedmont; the wearing out an insolent enemy; and, above all, the gaining time for a slow ally to come to our assistance, are the great advantages which are due to his Royal Highness's virtue, and patience. Mons, Belcastel, who served our late

> King, [who] is a pensioner of her Majesty's, and a Major-General in Holland, is with us at Verrue as a volunteer, and is of great use to his Royal Highness, by his experience, his zeal, and his mettle.[31]

The year ended, and the end of the siege was not yet in sight. What could the garrison expect?

31 Hill to Sir Charles Hedges. Turin on 3/14 January, 1704/5, reported in "Hill – *Letters*", part II, Translations, pp.481–482.

13

The 1705 Campaign

I: Winter Planning

In January 1705 the French situation appeared still good, but grey clouds were gathering, and he who was wise could easily expect the future to have some possible bad surprises.

Firstly, even if it seemed not that important, last July Sir George Rooke had seized Gibraltar. This was meant to open the way to the Mediterranean for the Anglo-Dutch fleet. Allied navies already entered the Mediterranean, but now they could do it in an easier and safer way, moreover creating real obstacles for the enemy fleet.

Secondly: after the French–Bavarian disaster at Höchstadt/Blenheim, Marlborough was managing the war in Rhineland and Flanders, but Eugene was coming back south, and that was very bad news.

Thirdly: the French situation in Spain was not bad, and not good, as well as it was not bad and not good in Italy too.

Victor Amadeus was still holding out, because Verrua held, and Turin could not be besieged before the fall of Verrua. Now, Eugene being southbound meant that the situation in Italy had to be expected to turn quite bad, unless he could be stopped, and Verrua, and possibly Turin could be taken before the end of the campaign. Stopping Eugene was not a joke. No matter how ragged, starving, and penniless his men could be, he knew how to exploit them to get the best from them. Thus it was vital to deprive him of his target, that is to say it was vital to defeat Savoy, once and forever.

Was it possible? Perhaps yes, may be not, because now Victor Amadeus was getting money, and money meant men, and weapons, and the possibility of holding out. Victor Amadeus' 1705 military budget

Dispositions at the Battle of Höchstadt/Blenheim.

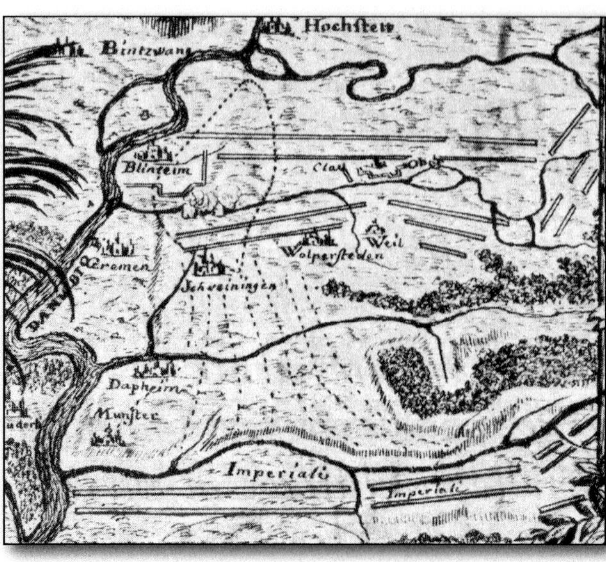

The Conquest of Gibraltar.

absorbed 4,917,002 liras.[1] The situation was so bad in invaded Piedmont that it was almost impossible to collect taxes and revenues and so to gather them in Turin. They could be used on the spot to pay local garrisons and local suppliers, but that was all. Thus no surprise if in early May Van der Meer reported to The Hague that minister Gropello told him the subsidies were the only revenues the Duke could count on.

In summer 1705 Lullino and Nicolas defaulted and Count di Borgone, the finance general, asked the Colomba bank to care of the transactions from London and Amsterdam.

II: The Fall of Verrua

Vendôme promised Louis XIV Verrua would be seized by 15 January 1705, but that day came, and passed, and Verrua still held. Attacks, mines, and sallies played a major role, with no remarkable result, but a slow advance toward the walls, and a major wound to la Roche d'Allery, who on 9 January passed command to the Count of Frinco, and was evacuated to Crescentino.

Vendôme then listened to Lapara's advice. Verrua held because it was supplied from Crescentino. Had communications been cut, the fortress would fail. The core of the problem was the supply line, and the core of the supply line was the Ognissanti Redoubt, on the island. Hence the French attacked it by surprise two hours after midnight on 2 March 1705 using eight infantry battalions and 24 grenadier companies, split into three columns, and heavily supported by artillery. The Aosta and Tarantasia infantry regiments were

1 Prato, op. cit., p.260.

suddenly overwhelmed more than 10 to 1, and were destroyed. Starhemberg tried to retake Ognissanti, but failed.

Once communications between Verrua and Crescentino were interrupted, there was nothing more to do. Victor Amadeus assessed the situation. He knew Eugene was gathering an army in Trentino, thus it was vital to hold on as long as possible. Verrua was basically lost, for there was no way to reopen the contact between it and Crescentino, thus it was better to think of the next French step, which he expected to be Chivasso. Hence on 14 March the Duke abandoned Crescentino and moved most of his forces north to Chivasso, which he ordered strengthened by earthworks made on Castagneto hill.

The day after, the new Verrua commander, Austrian Baron Christian von Fresen, who promised to hold until his last drop of blood, rejected a first offer to surrender. On the 16th he rejected a further offer.

Communications were continued by putting letters into empty bombs, to be shelled from Verrua into the Piedmontese camp, and vice versa. Food was lacking. By 20 March soldiers started getting only 16 ounces – 416 grams – of bread per day.

Fresen originally intended to hold out until 8 April, but he soon realised he would be too short on food, and above all, ordnance. The weather was quite bad. Heavy rains prevented both sides from using their artillery, thus allowed the resistance to last a bit longer than expected. By 1 April Verrua was practically out of artillery ammunition. On 3 April at night Fresen repeatedly fired many series of three rockets each: it was the signal asking the Duke for the permission to surrender. Victor Amadeus allowed it in a similar way.

On 6 April Fresen sent a drummer to Vendôme offering to have a meeting. Vendôme met the Austro-Piedmontese officers, and as usual told them that he was very sorry, but they had to surrender without condition, or they would get no quarter at all – which in that case meant to be killed – once the fortress was stormed. The answer was that they were not yet in a condition to fear those threats. Firing restarted, and the first shell from the fortress landed on an ordnance warehouse. The warehouse exploded and many enemies were killed. Artillery fired throughout the next day. On 8 April Fresen, now out of food, gathered the garrison and entered the donjon of the fortress, leaving the wounded outside and blowing the walls.

On 9 April the French entered, passing through the ruins. Firing restarted from the donjon; the French answered, then Fresen let the drums roll the call. Vendôme once more refused any capitulation: prisoners, as in Ivrea, or death. Fresen accepted. He had held as long as planned: mission accomplished.

During the siege the fortress had been targeted by 200,000 balls and 50,000 mortar bombs, and answered with 120,000 cannonballs and 30,000 mortar bombs.

The butcher's bill was terrible: Piedmontese and Austrian dead, missing in action, deserters, wounded, prisoners, and sick were 7,000; Vendôme's casualties were higher at 12,000, including six generals, 547 officers, and 30 military engineers. It was a bloody costly success, which badly affected French operational effectiveness.

Chivasso next.

III: Chivasso

The Duke had been reinforcing Chivasso for a long time. On 4 January 1705 (1704 Old Style), Richard Hill had said: "We are hard at work to fortify Chivas, a little place 10 miles hence, which is to be our frontier when Verrue does fall."[2] Chivasso commanded the confluence of the Dora into the Po, and relied now on a fortified and entrenched system connecting it to Castagneto hill. Victor Amadeus had 26 battalions and 19 cavalry squadrons, and commanded the defence there.

Vendôme came along with his men, slowly. The casualties at Verrua had heavily affected his army, and his men needed time to recover, thus he arrived only on 16 June. Having learned Verrua's lesson, this time Vendôme listened to Lapara, and followed his advice, thus he targeted immediately the centre of the defensive system, the Castle of Contrabue, and the so-called "Trucchetto", on the right bank of the Po, where the entrenchments of the plain linked to those of the hill.

On 18 June at night a surprise attack failed, particularly because the two incoming French columns met each other, and both supposed the other to be the enemy, and thus fought and lost 80 men before realising the misunderstanding.

So, on the next day, the French had to undertake a regular siege. On 25 June their guns started firing against the Trucchetto, defended by the Savoia Infantry Regiment. On the 29th the French attacked using seven fusileer battalions and 600 grenadiers, but were repulsed. They counter-attacked, and were repulsed again, and lost 140 men.

Mr. Hill announced:

> We shall hold Chivas as long as we can hold these cottages, which his Royal Highness defends with his presence; and if he can hold them a week longer, it will equal in merit, though not in glory, the defence of Verrue.[3]

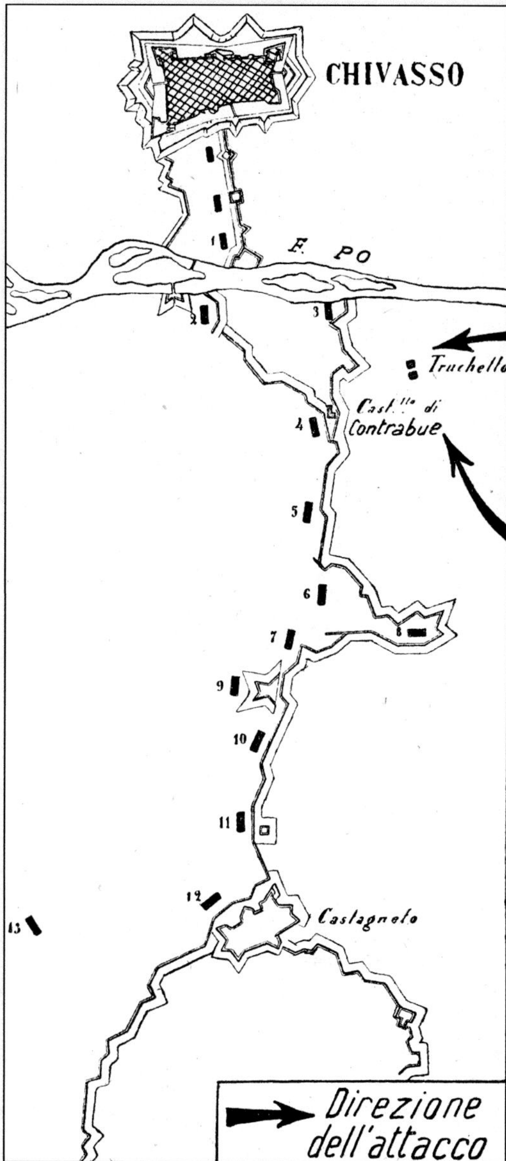

The Siege of Chivasso.

During these same days Prince Eugene's men's actions were causing so much damage to the Spanish and French forces in Eastern Padana Plain that as soon as the news arrived, Vendôme had to call in La Feuillade and then leave.

La Feuillade arrived on 10 July with 10 battalions and three squadrons. The next morning Vendôme left for Lombardy with 10 battalions and nine squadrons, leaving to La Feuillade 73 cannons and 22 mortars.

2 Mr Hill to the Duke of Marlborough, Turin, 4 January 1704/5, in "Hill – *Letters*", vol. I, p.478.

3 Hill to Sir Charles Hedges, Turin, 8 July 1705, in "Hill – *Letters*", vol. II, p.565.

On 18 July La Feuillade's cavalry crossed the Orco creek and attacked and defeated the Austro-Piedmontese cavalry commanded by Imperial General Fels. This cut Chivasso's communication to Turin, so La Feuillade planned a general attack for 30 July. The night before, Victor Amadeus left with as many troops and as much artillery and ordnance as he could, and on the 31 re-entered Turin.

La Feuillade seized the empty Chivasso, and then moved to Turin along with 20,000 men. He made a long tour, and on 8 August was at Venaria Reale, in front of Victor Amadeus' last fortress. He wanted to besiege it, but he was too weak, and it was too late.

IV: The French Conquest of Nice, the Surrender of Montmélian, the Surprise of Asti

On 16 March 1705 the French arrived in front of Nice by land and by sea. Louis XIV was worried: the English Mediterranean fleet was proving more and more threatening, thus it was necessary to secure all the coastal areas the Duke of Savoy could still exploit to receive a sea-shipped support. On 1 April Nice's military harbour, Villafranca, surrendered after a long shelling. Five days later the Forts of the Saint Hospice, and of Montalbano capitulated too.

The garrison of Nice had left the city before the enemy started shelling and withdrawn into the citadel, which was simply blockaded by General d'Usson. Then, as soon as they could, the garrison sallied and swept away the French. Louis XIV's army could not come back that soon, thus the Savoyard flag remained above the city of Nice until October.

The Duke of Berwick, the natural son of late King James Stuart, and Arabella Churchill, the Duke of Marlborough's sister, commanded the operations against Nice. On 25 October 1705 he started the siege with 17 battalions and two regiments of dragoons, supported by 50 24-pound cannons and 12 mortars. By sea, four men-of-war plus many smaller ships supported land operations. On 9 November Berwick succeeded in compelling the garrison to withdraw into the citadel anew. Then he set 80 cannons and 13 mortars on Montalbano's commanding heights, and dug a parallel to the beach.

After a week the French opened a breach in a bastion, and on 5 January 1706 the 800 survivors of the garrison had to surrender. They were allowed an open passage to Turin.

At the same time, on 17 December 1705, after a two-year blockade, the starving garrison of Montmélian had to surrender. Its commander, Carlo Ottavio Benso, Count of Santena, obtained military honours and free passage to Turin, keeping two cannons and all the weapons. At the same time the French suddenly and mistakenly left Asti, which was immediately reoccupied by the Piedmontese.

Now Victor Amadeus could still rely on southern Piedmont, on Turin, and Asti. He had 18,000 men – 13,000 foot, and 5,000 cavalry – left. Casualties in 1704 had been severe: Bard, Ivrea, and above all Vercelli had meant a loss of 12,000 men, but 1705 had not been a joke. If he still had an army it was only because he could use the funding from the Maritime Powers to pay and feed his recruits. In fact Victor Amadeus issued a further decree on 7 July 1705: 8,000 men were called to arms to create anew 20 battalions, each 400 men strong. In London Colonel Thomas Fairfax, Lord Fairfax of Cameron, gathered 1,000 French Protestant refugees from the Cevennes into a regiment and sent it through Holland to Piedmont under the command of the Marquess of Miremont. Lastly: the Count of Santena came back across the Alps from Montmélian, and a further 800 men came from Nice. These were small drops, but when one is thirsty a drop is a treasure, even if it can only delay death. The only way to survive was to get reinforcements. Cousin Eugene had to lead them, but where was he?

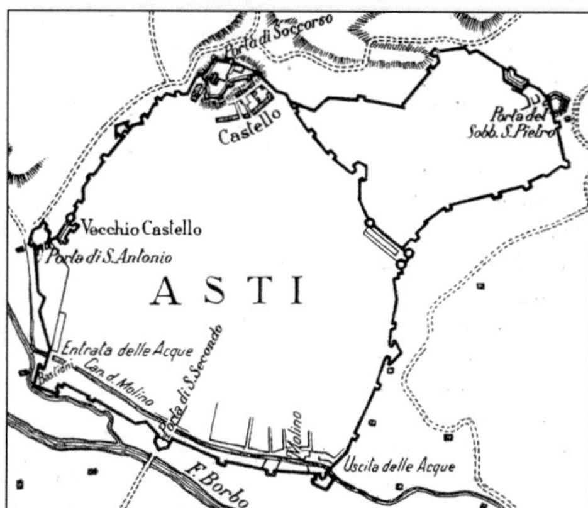

Top: Nice, 1705.
Middle: James FitzJames, Duke of Berwick.
Bottom: Plan View of Asti's Fortifications.

V: Eugene and Vendôme at Cassano

The 1705 campaign did not start well for Eugene. He had only 20,603 infantry and 7,973 cavalry, with only 6,397 horses. His strategic task, as he anticipated in Vienna, was to open the road to Piedmont. The Two Crowns began the campaign by besieging Mirandola, whose garrison was greatly weakened by disease and desertions. When Eugene arrived at the army it was already too late. On 11 May, after days and days spent under the fire of 24 cannons and seven mortars, the commander of Mirandola, Count Königseck surrendered with the 500 surviving men.

Meanwhile Eugene was supervising his troops' movement, divided into two columns. The first was under General Bibra toward Gavardo and Salò in the Brescia area. The other was directly under Eugene's orders, and marched on the Veronese. On 11 May, while Mirandola surrendered, Eugene appeared in front of Peschiera to cross the Mincio. This time the French reacted. Vendôme issued very clear orders, and after an exchange of gunshots and cannonballs over several hours, Eugene retreated and took the road to Lazise and Bardolino on the eastern shore of Lake Garda. He then succeeded in sneaking along the southern coast of the lake to the western side.

Vendôme moved his troops against the Imperial positions at Gavardo and Salò, on the western shore. He set up camp, placed his cannons on the facing hills, and opened fire on Gavardo; then, since he had more urgent things to do in the west, he left the command to his brother the Grand Prior, and moved to Piedmont to personally direct the operations against Victor Amadeus.

Eugene had the Grand Prior in front, the lake on the left, and steep mountains on the right. He succeeded crossing the mountains, bypassed the Grand Prior, and reached the plain around Brescia stopping in a village called Roncadelle. The Grand Prior realised this late, and at least to prevent the entrance of the Imperialists into the Cremonese and Mantuan areas, he went south-west and stood in Manerbio.

Eugene decided not to attack him in such a strong position, protected by too many canals and swamps. So, he moved west to the Oglio river where he smashed the 4,000 Spanish soldiers commanded by General Toralba, who were watching the river at Calcio, and entered the Cremonese, threatening the main French warehouses.

The Grand Prior was now far away and with a river between him and Eugene.

The Spaniards abandoned the warehouses and depots at Pontoglio and Palazzolo, destroying everything. They left weak strongpoints here and there and turned north-west, toward Bergamo, to settle on the Adda river. The Imperial cavalry, commanded by Visconti, pursued them and just outside Bergamo engaged their rearguard, later destroyed by the incoming Imperial infantry.

Meanwhile, the Grand Prior moved west too in order to reach Eugene, and sent urgent messages asking his brother to leave Piedmont and rush to help him in Lombardy. By mid July Vendôme arrived in Ombriano with 9,000 men, crossed the small river Serio, and surprised and destroyed the Imperial garrison of Zenivolta, a place commanding the area between the Serio and the Oglio rivers.

Eugene wanted to reach the Po, but Vendôme in Zenivolta disturbed him, thus he decided to go to Ostiano and Canneto, toward Mantua, to cross the Po there, but his cousin the Grand Prior arrived with 6,000 men and this possibility also vanished.

It was a nasty situation. Eugene could cross the Adda, the last big river before Milan, but if so he would be too far from the garrisons he left in Brescia, and would risk having his communications cut with Lake Garda, and with Trentino across it. Now, it is unclear if he made a first unsuccessful attempt to cross the Adda, or chose a feint. I think he chose a feint, but other authors are not sure. Anyway he marched to the Bergamo area, as he wanted to cross the Adda. Had his eldest cousin, the Marshal, followed him, Eugene would turn, and attack.

So on 10 August the Prince started moving north, and purposely marched slowly, keeping an eye on Vendôme. He left the Cremasco, passed the Gera d'Adda and Brembate, and began to calmly lay a bridge over the Adda, far upstream from Cassano.

Vendôme was disoriented. What did Eugene want to do? Did he go to the Adda? Good: he ordered his brother to come, stop and stay at the newly built redoubt in Cassano. Meanwhile Vendôme took 1,500 dragoons and tried to discover what Eugene was doing. Eugene started building his bridge; Vendôme arrived; Eugene covered the work in progress by shelling Vendôme's

Cassano d'Adda.

side of the river with his artillery; Vendôme reacted. The area where Eugene was preparing his bridge was commanded by steep embankments, a sort of canyon where the river streamed in a relatively narrow valley. It is still practically as it was in 1705, and it was perfect to fire cannons each against the other, but was not that suitable as a place for crossing the river. And actually this was not what Eugene had in mind, nonetheless Vendôme did not know it, and called in 15 more battalions from Cassano.

Eugene completed the bridge, and on 15 August his first patrols crossed it. The French reacted. Skirmishes occurred everywhere, whilst artillery rumbled. At sundown the clashes stopped. Eugene had realised where and how his cousins were placed with their men, thus he silently dismantled the bridge during the night and swiftly marched downstream to Cassano, where he actually wanted to cross the Adda. When close to the town, he deployed his infantry ahead, the cavalry behind, and advanced.

Cassano is a natural crossing of the Adda river, so no surprise if a lot of people fought there. Before Eugene many medieval clashes had occurred – the biggest in 1259 – and after Eugene, again in the Napoleonic era. The town is on a rock on the right side of the Adda, whose left side is flat there. Just in front of the rock, on whose top Cassano Castle commands the crossing, the Adda splits and creates a triangle-shaped island, with its longest side along the Adda's main stream. The other sides are in fact canals called the Ritorto and the Piccolo Ritorto, both crossed by bridges. The island is some kilometres long, and quite wide. Downstream the canals and the river waters merged, creating several marshes, and rendered the ground difficult, if not impossible, to pass.

Basically, to enter Cassano, Eugene had to seize a stone farmhouse protecting a first bridge, cross the Ritorto through that bridge, seize the island, seize a wooden fort protecting a pontoon bridge, cross it under the fire from the castle, cross another small island, seize a last bridge and at last climb to Cassano: a joke. Nonetheless, he tried.

Far upstream, when in the morning Vendôme spotted Eugene's bridge dismantled and no trace of the Imperial troops, he immediately realised what a dirty trick his cousin was undertaking, and rushed with the cavalry to rescue his brother in Cassano.

When in Cassano he did not find his brother – who was quietly sleeping and nobody seemed to know were he was – but found a careless, enormous confusion: the baggage stacked in the meadows, the bridge over the Adda

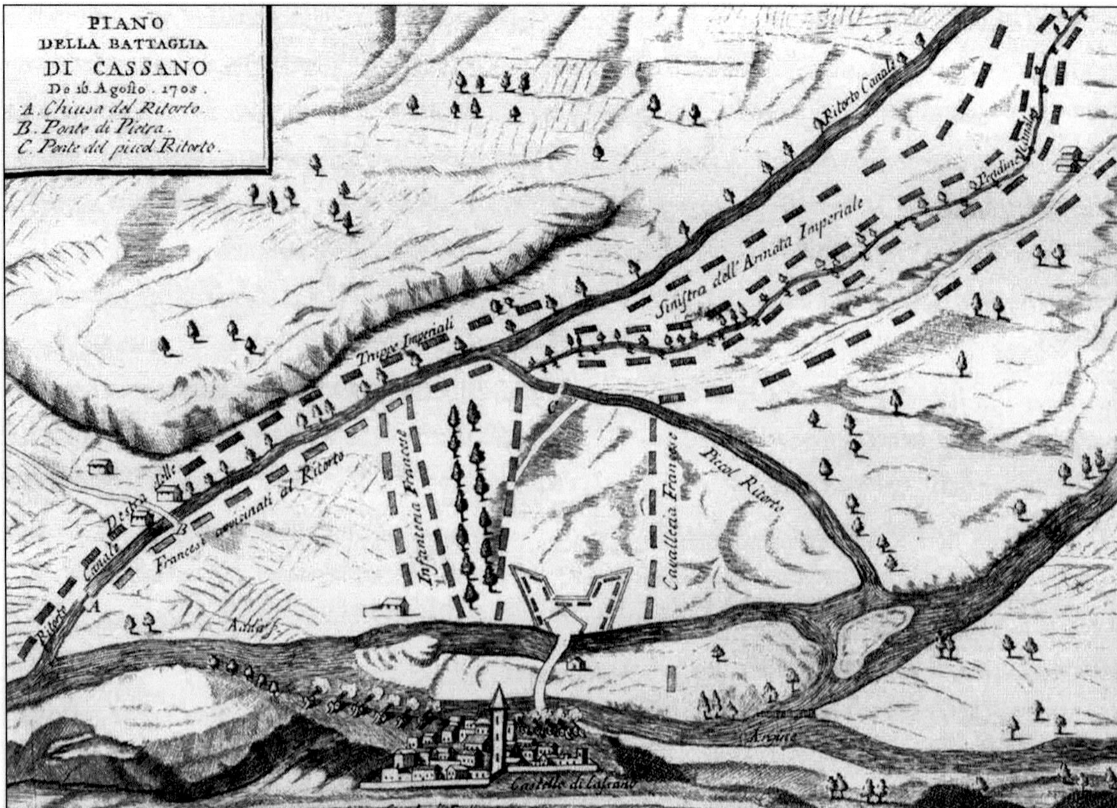

Map of the Battlefield of Cassano.

crossed by wagons of every kind preventing the movement of the infantry, no shelter on the shore ... he shouted orders at full blast, and began distributing the troops on the banks of the Ritorto as soon as they arrived. Just in time. At a half past noon Eugene attacked, stormed the farmhouse, and massacred the French grenadiers who were trying to flee.

As soon as he took the farm, Eugene set up a battery which commanded at least the enemy camp on the island. Imperial guns started firing, whilst Eugene's men seized and closed the 12 wooden gates commanding the stream into the canal. The water dropped, and within two hours, whilst the Imperial cannons bombed the enemy, the canal was fordable.

Vendôme tried to keep his units in order, but it became hard when Eugene began attacking the bridge. Three times Vendôme lost it, and three times he reconquered it, but the fourth time his men collapsed; the Imperialists crossed the Ritorto, and Eugene reached the island. He immediately deployed his men in line and they started firing. The Imperialists advanced, and then entered the French artillery range, whose cannons started targeting them from the castle.

Eugene committed his 4,000 Prussians to the marshes to cross downstream, and turn the French. The Prince of Dessau, later known as the Old Dessau – as we shall call him from now on, even if at Cassano he was only 29 – led them, but unluckily the water made their gunpowder wet, thus prevented them firing. Albergotti saw both their dangerous movement, and their troubles; took advantage, and stopped them into the marshes under a rain of volleys.

Three hours before sundown the two opposing infantries stopped for a tacit truce. The fight had been furious. Over four hours Vendôme had his horse killed under him, had been wounded in the leg, and survived only because a captain was killed whilst protecting him from an enemy grenadier. On the other side Eugene took two bullets: one in the neck, the other below the knee. He could no longer stay on horseback, and suffered enough to need evacuating. While he was being cared for, he realised that new French battalions were coming down from Cassano to support the fort, thus he ordered his officers to withdraw around and into a farm not so far away from the fort. With this movement the action stopped.

The French could not advance, and continued to shell the island from Cassano. The Imperialists were too tired to seize the fort, and both the opposing generals were badly injured. Eugene controlled the battlefield, but not the opposite bank, and also Old Dessau's bridgehead downstream was useless, being locked by Albergotti, who killed 600 Prussians. So, troops were tired, enemies were increasing, and it was useless to continue.

The surprise did not succeed, and cost Eugene 2,000 dead and 2,500 wounded and prisoners. Thus during the night he ordered a withdrawal. Vendôme on his side was not that happy. He lost 3,000 dead, and suffered 4,000 wounded, but at least prevented the crossing. Eugene continued to look for a way to reach the Po, but Vendôme kept an eye on him. No other battle occurred, but all the further Imperial attempts to sneak to the Po failed, until Eugene moved to winter quarters around Brescia, while Vendôme garrisoned the entire bank of the Serio.

Meanwhile, Victor Amadeus II had been reduced to the minimum.

In the autumn, no danger seemed possible to the French from Lombardy, where the two brothers de Vendôme were on watch. La Feuillade decided to begin the siege of Turin.

VI: The French Approach to Turin

La Feuillade could have an independent command as long as he operated alone. Whenever he joined Vendôme, he had to obey him. Thus when they had joined under Chivasso, he had received orders. Whilst leaving for Lombardy, Vendôme told him to besiege Turin, no matter how weak he felt, and no matter the rules.

Basically this "no matter the rules" meant also applying to Turin the scheme successfully used against Vercelli, Susa, Ivrea, Verrua, and Chivasso: the strongest first, thus, here, the citadel first. It was a scheme dictated by the lack of men, and resources, which worked by luck, and due to the inferiority of the enemy. But Turin, as we shall see, was all but an easy task. Vendôme could not have realised it, but La Feuillade soon did.

His men were fatigued, and few. They crossed the Dora river on 28 September, and stopped in front of the citadel, having their right at the Crocetta, and their left on the Dora river. On 30 September they opened the trench, and on that same day La Feuillade received a letter: the King ordered him to commit reinforcements to Lombardy, and to come back to winter quarters in France.

14

Preparing the Siege of Turin

I: Planning in France, and Desperation in Piedmont

The 1706–07 Savoyard financial exercise saw military expenditure rising to 7,896,546 liras.[1] It was a remarkable improvement in comparison to 1705, but more than two million less than it had been in 1704, and a bit less than what it would be in 1708/09. The Duke looked for money everywhere, and once more pawned the crown jewels in Genoa. Queen Anne provided a 50,000 pounds gift[2] – 203,488.35 scudi of Piedmont – and the Dutch gave 30,000 scudi, even if a portion of their subsidy was used on the spot, in Amsterdam, to purchase military supplies for Piedmont.

The troops' situation was not good. In winter 1705–1706 a further 8,000 militiamen were called to war duty, thus the budgeted force was now 15,919 foot, 547 artillery, and 3,760 cavalry. The problem was, in this case, how effective they could be. Artillerymen were all professional and well trained, cavalrymen and dragoons too, but what about infantry? More than half of them were recruits, how well could they perform? Apart from the overall situation, and the long since planned defensive strategy centred on resisting inside the castles, this could have been an additional reason to confirm in the Duke the idea of a passive resistance. He could, as he did, rely on well-trained and relatively effective cavalry as a mobile force, whilst keeping the infantry protected within the walls, spending time drilling. Now, at the eve of 1706, the main and almost only fortress he still had was Turin, and it was going to be besieged. Could his mostly non-professional infantry hold it?

1 Prato, op. cit., p.260.

2 A normal Piedmontese Scudo was a half a double of Savoy. The double of Savoy was a golden coin minted since 1638; its weight was 6.69105 grams and contained 6.06376 grams of fine gold, title 906.25. The scudo, the white scudo mentioned in chapter 3, was a silver coin, minted since 1658. Its weight was 27.32178 grams, and contained 25.04496 grams of 916.67/1000 silver; cfr. Giuseppe Felloni, *Il mercato monetario in Piemonte nel Secolo XVIII* (Milan: 1968), p.28, tables 3 and 4. A double of Savoy was 15 liras and 15 soldi and equalled roughly 18 shillings, and one needed 20 soldi to get a lira of Piedmont, and 4 liras and six soldi of Piedmont, or 86 soldi, to get a white scudo, thus 50,000 pounds equalled 55,555.55 doubles of Savoy. Now, 55,555.55 doubles of Savoy equalled 874,999.91 liras, that is to say 17,499,998.9 soldi, which meant 203,488.35 scudi.

II: Approaching Turin

Top: The Mastio of Turin. The only surviving part of the citadel on the ground. Above: Sebastien de la Prestre de Vauban.

The focus of military attention throughout northern Italy in summer of 1706 was Turin. At that time it had 46,000 inhabitants, and was protected by walls and by a five-bastion citadel, built in 1565 by Francesco Paciotti after an order by Duke Emanuel Philibert I. The citadel no longer exists, like the whole battlefield, which is now completely covered by buildings. The citadel was in what is now the urban area close to the city centre, but in 1706 it was peripheral, in the south-western part of the fortification. It was quite strong. Its underground mine network was considered probably the best, and the most dangerous in Europe. But no information on it was updated. Victor Amadeus progressively enhanced the network. Works went on in the deepest secret for years and years, and in 1706 nobody imagined how dangerous the system was, and how far it extended.

The city walls were a ring 12 kilometres long, protected by 21 bastions, including two bastions of the citadel, facing towards the city. The artillery comprised 226 cannons and 28 mortars. The stocks amounted to 370 metric tons of gunpowder, and five months of food.

The problem of a possible siege of Turin had been studied during the previous summer, in France, by the best expert of the time, that is to say Vauban. He stated that the siege would need 55,000 men and no less than three months spent in long and complicated operations. The city had to be attacked on all sides before being seized. His opinion was not considered. "Whatever the Sieur de Vauban may say, I do not see the importance of a place being well or badly invested." Vendôme wrote to the King. La Feuillade initially wrote: "I hope to seize Turin in Cohorn's way",[3] and later added boldly: "May Your Majesty cut off my head if I do not take Turin against the rules."[4]

The idea was to start from the strongest side, the citadel, attacking its three bastions looking outside the walls. Once the citadel seized, the city had to fall. This was quite optimistic. A first reason why the city could further hold, was that the citadel in fact did not really command the city, for it was not high enough. A second reason was provided by history: the last time

3 Rep. in Voltaire, op. cit., p.363.

4 François de La Feuillade Marquis d'Aubusson to Louis XIV, rep. in Clemente Assum, *Eugenio di Savoia* (Turin, 1936), p.126.

The Citadel of Turin Besieged.

Turin was besieged, in 1640, the enterprise went in one of the oddest or most amazing ways ever seen. A pro-French Piedmontese garrison obeying the orders of Victor Amadeus' grandmother, Christine of France, Duchess of Savoy, held the citadel against a pro-Spanish army commanded by her brother-in-law, and Eugene's grandfather, Prince Thomas of Savoy. Whilst Thomas besieged the citadel from all the sides, a French army committed by Richelieu to relieve the Duchess arrived and besieged the whole city held by Thomas' troops. Then a Spanish army came from Milan to help Thomas, and besieged the French relieving army which, outside the city. was besieging Prince Thomas' pro-Spanish Piedmontese army, who, inside the city, was besieging the Duchess' pro-French Piedmontese garrison in the citadel. Last, a further French corps commanded by Turenne arrived, and nine months later neither the citadel nor the city had been seized.

No matter the precedent, in spring 1706 45,000 French–Spanish soldiers appeared under Turin, with about 250 guns.[5] As said, La Feuillade wanted to use them only against the citadel, focusing on the military gate of the Soccorso (the Relief Gate), located between the San Maurizio and Beato Amedeo bastions. Basically he wanted to repeat the Verrua scheme. He dismissed Vauban's statement that "the city will supply the citadel with everything it needs; therefore the defence will not suffer either shortcomings or inconveniences", as well as not considering that Verrua, seized "against the rules", cost the French army a frightening price.

In the apocryphal Prince Eugene's memoirs, written by the Prince de Ligne when speaking about the siege of Turin, it is said: "Luckily, thanks to Louis XIV's discernment, La Feuillade was commissioned. The place was very poorly invested."[6]

But the problem was much harder, and La Feuillade far less stupid than it might have appeared to Prince de Ligne more than 50 years later. The

5 As usual, figures vary according to the accounts, but it is certain that the French had no more then 250 guns according to Brunet, and no fewer than than 231 according to Blondel, no matter their type, and calibres.

6 Rep. in Assum, op. cit., p.130.

fortifications of the citadel of Turin were incredibly low,[7] and it was very difficult to hit them, as one may still realise. Actually, even though the citadel was razed in the second half of the nineteenth century, its underground mine network still exists. It can be visited, and the visit normally ends through a small exit, out to a sort of very small square underground, lit by the daylight passing through deep glass set into the walkway of the street above. Turning, the visitor finds themselves at the exit of the most contested fortification of the whole siege, the Soccorso half-moon – or crescent – and it is amazing to realise how low it is: a matter of roughly seven feet. Thus a cannon shot from a distance could hardly be grazing enough, hence the most of the long range shots fell on the backside of the citadel, into the city. Cannons were effective only when placed at a single point, and we shall see what happened when they were set there. Moreover La Feuillade could not increase the 45,000 men he had – 10,000 fewer than Vauban stated – who were not enough to complete the ring around the city, because the additional 48,000 men the Two Crowns had in Italy were needed to protect the Duchy of Milan, and to stop Eugene.

That is why La Feuillade was convinced that he had to act against the rules. Had he applied the rules, he simply could not even start the siege. He amassed substantial supplies in Susa and Chivasso, and still had no doubts when he advanced on 12 May 1706. He had 64 battalions and 80 squadrons, and on that day they crossed the Stura and encamped in the Venaria.

The Savoyard cavalry, overwhelmed by the enemy, did what it could, then cut the bridges on the Dora and withdrew. The situation looked bad, and the Piedmontese tried to find some hope in omens:

> This day was remarkable for an extraordinary Eclipse, which took place between nine and ten in the morning: for there had never been such dark shadows on the earth, having the solar disk remained more than an hour hidden to our eyes. Those who assess the events of this world by the examination of the Stars, drew a bad omen for France.[8]

The interpretation was based on the fact that the sun, personal symbol of Sun King Louis XIV, had been obscured and thus it rendered visible the constellation of Taurus, the Bull, Turin's coat of arms.

> On the next day, May 13th, around nine o'clock in the morning, were seen in battle order on the plains of the Madonna di Campagna the enemies, who camped

7 Each of the defensive external redoubts and walls of the citadel was not higher than two Piedmontese feet above its outer defensive work. Being the Piedmontese "piede liprando" 51.3766 centimetres long, two feet and half equalled less than 1 metre and 3 centimetres (1 metre, 2 centimetres and 7 millimetres and a half, that is to say 40.43 inches).

8 Giuseppe Maria Solaro della Margarita (edited by C. Paoletti), *Journal historique du siège de la Ville de Turin l'année 1706*, in *Manoscritto Preziosissimo del Conte Giuseppe Maria Solaro della Margarita Maggior Generale d'Artiglieria che contiene l'Originale del suo Journal Historique du siège de la Ville de Turin l'année 1706* (Turin, 2006), p.19.

around midday beyond the range of our cannon, leaning their right hand on the Castle of Lucento, and their left to the Castle of the Old Park on the Po.[9]

III: Approaching the Walls, and Setting Up the Batteries

The operation to surround the city proceeded slowly. On 14 May the French began preparing intercommunicating earthworks all along their front. Victor Amadeus reacted immediately, committing 300 men and four cannons to raid along the river, on the side of San Mauro. It was a success. The enemies quickly withdrew, leaving horses and materials in huge quantities. Meanwhile the Piedmontese worked hard to strengthen and supply the citadel with everything they could need, before having communications with the countryside completely cut. They destroyed all the country houses the enemies could exploit as shelters or strongpoints, or which could obstruct the Piedmontese artillery firing range, whilst the French began building a bridge across the Dora at Pianezza.

On 19 May clashes occurred around the castle of Lucento, and the French lost the food warehouse they had established there. An additional Piedmontese raid took place on the same day in Alpignano. On the 20th the French bridge was completed. From 26–29 May many convoys arrived, and the French continued to work as hard as they could. The garrison was still uncertain about which part of the walls was their real target. On 3 June the French raised their flags on the parallels, a signal that they were ready.

The Duke had the city guard strengthened, and attended the celebration and procession of the Blessed Sacrament with great pomp. At the same time the Piedmontese artillery started firing to disturb the siegeworks, whilst the inhabitants neighbouring the citadel were ordered to leave their homes. The disturbing fire continued. On the 5th Victor Amadeus realised there was little time left, and decided to leave within a couple of weeks, along with his cavalry. On 21 May he had appointed Count de la Roche d'Allery – the former commander of Verrua – governor of the Citadel of Turin, and now, on 5 June, he appointed Angelo Isnardi de Castello, Marquess of Caraglio governor of the city. Caraglio had proved quite competent when commanding the defence of the Castle of Nice, and now disposed observers, an alarm service, and a fire alarm, then organised security against French spies in the city.

Last, Count Daun was appointed to command the defence. The garrisons within the city and the citadel had over 8,000 Piedmontese, 1,500 Austrians, eight battalions of city militia, and a regiment of suburban militia, plus artillerymen, and some cavalry.[10]

Then it was heard from deserters that the enemy could start firing on the 10th from their battery. So:

---

9 *Idem.*

10 *Daun relation* – better known as *Hackbrett relation* – says: "total de la garn. Au commenc du siège 9.996" [total of the garrison at the beginning of the siege 9,996]. The Piedmontese were 7,981 according to the "Assedio giornale", by an anonymous author.

> Nine pieces were placed on each side of the attacked bastions of Beato Amedeo and San Maurizio; fifteen pieces on each side of the two counterguards, four others on the half-moons, not to mention those that were on the facade of the San Lazzaro guard and on the sides of the Wall towards the same attack: so that there were all together seventy-five pieces of Cannon opposed to their Battery, placed in parallel in front of their entrenchments.
>
> There were also in very good order fifty-five Cannons against the approaches to the City on the new city walls. In addition to this: fourteen mortars in the Citadel, ten in the City, of which five were before the esplanade, among which two, which had fourteen inches in diameter at their mouth, were forward in the covered road, to shoot the stones further on the Workers.
>
> Nobody ever saw, as far as I believe, in any other Place a more beautiful Cannon front, since it was superior to that of the besiegers.
>
> There were good leaders with brave officers to command this artillery; and more than a thousand Gunners and Soldiers were destined to serve her. It was a double joy to see at nightfall more than one hundred and thirty cannons and twenty-four mortars put in a state of firing, and to learn at the same time the news that Milord Duke of Malborough had defeated our enemies in Flanders.[11]

Lorenz Wierich, Count von Daun.

Giuseppe Maria Solaro, Count della Margarita.

Such remarkable artillery proved to be probably the main defensive asset, not because of its number, but because of how it was used. As already briefly mentioned when discussing tactics and logistics, due to the relatively small quantity of gunpowder available, the commander of Ducal artillery, Giuseppe Maria Solaro, Count della Margarita, preferred to leave aside the normal general firing system, and for the first time anywhere in the world he concentrated the fire from all the pieces on a specific target, and only at the due time. He discovered, or invented, what would later be known as the fire concentration principle.

11 Solaro della Margarita, *Journal,* cit, pp.34–35.

Applying this principle to a careful cooperation with the infantry, Marquis of Caraglio, Count Daun, and Solaro della Margarita inflicted on the French appalling casualties in men and, above all, in materials. Describing a normal firing day, Solaro coldly noted "Our bombs go to place fire, as usual, in one of their gunpowder stores." He added that the shooting rate during artillery duels was so high, and this so much filled the sky with balls and bombs, that often balls fired by the opposing artilleries could be seen colliding in the air. This was no surprise: from the beginning to the end of the siege, that is to say in 54 days, the Piedmontese artillery fired 150,072 projectiles, a 2,780 daily average, while the French answered so intensively that they fired up to 8,300 shots in one day.

The first French cannonballs were fired on 15 June. On the 16th the Court and the Ducal Family left. On the 17th the Duke too left. He rode to Carmagnola with about 4,000 cavalry and dragoons, as a mobile manoeuvring mass to harass enemy logistics and to join Eugene, when and if he came.

La Feuillade immediately left the siege and began pursuing Victor Amadeus, regardless of the initial clashes occurring in the following days. Again, historians later criticised and stigmatised La Feuillade's lack of cleverness, but they were wrong. Actually, as Montesquieu later explained: "The Duke de la Feuillade wanted to take the city of Turin by the means of the citadel, and the citadel by means of the Duke",[12] that is to say La Feuillade thought that, once the Duke was captured, he would solve the matter by forcing Victor Amadeus to surrender the city, and sign peace with France. That is why La Feuillade took 10,000 men and 42 cannons, and immediately departed to try to engage the Duke.

Whilst the chase was going on, approach operations under the walls were further hampered by the besieged garrison's sallies.

IV: The Elimination of Vendôme

Whilst the situation was so bad, Victor Amadeus exploited a typical aspect of his time and got an immense result: Vendôme was ordered to leave Italy to take a command in Flanders. According to current historiography, it happened because Louis XIV, worried by the defeat at Ramillies, decided to commit his best general against Marlborough, and Vendôme left Italy in July, a month and a half after the battle. Seeing how fast Louis XIV normally took his own decisions, one can only wonder why did not he commit Vendôme sooner. Twenty years later Montesquieu found an answer, if not the answer. He had talked about it with General Bonneval and the French consul in Venice, and the latter claimed that:

> the loss of Italy had to be considered as due to the Duke of Savoy's cunning, who, having seen that all his places had been dismantled, realised that Vendôme would do the same in Turin; and so he thought of getting him fired. Therefore he

12 Montesquieu, *Viaggio in Italia*, cit., p.291.

> started speaking well of Vendôme in public, while in private, to some prisoner French officers, he said plague and horns about him, so that they might repeat all to him, as it happened. Vendôme was caught by such an anger that he said to an emissary of the Duke of Savoy: "Tell your master that he is a coward, etc.; that I, by commanding the armies of the King, consider myself greater than all the dukes of Savoy have ever been." The Duke of Savoy complained in writing and Vendôme was reprimanded. Bonneval told me he saw the letter. Vendôme was sent to Flanders.[13]

This very same thing occurred years before, when Eugene notified the Emperor about his intervention to halt the lack of due respect in Vendôme's speech. The difference was that at that time the question was settled among the two cousins; this time Victor Amadeus exploited it for his own military purposes.

As said, nobody could disrespect a sovereign, and Louis XIV acted accordingly. He moved Vendôme to Flanders, and thus made a big favour to the Allies in Italy: they no longer had to face the best French general, no more competition between the opposite two best commanders. Only one remained, was no more contested, and prevailed: Eugene.

Eugene accompanied his cousin's departure with an advice to the Duke of Marlborough, a message giving him important information:

> Y.H. will by no doubt be aware of the change of generals. The Duke of Orléans and Lord de Villars are expected here at any moment. Lord de Vendôme must go to Flanders as soon as they arrive, making these gentlemen no difficulty in receiving the army in the situation in which he left it to them, after the assurances he had given to the King and to all. What I can say about him to Y.H. is that this is a man loved by soldiers; when he has taken a resolution he follows it, without anything to distract him; (he is a) great trench-maker, but if for a short while his plans are unravelled, he has great difficulty remedying it, especially during the action, leaving up to the case to remedy. Daring in the sieges, he is capable of teasing an army, but not of attacking it if he finds that army willing to wait for him, unless there is a great superiority.[14]

And Marlborough would soon remember these details, and exploit them.

13 Montesquieu, op. cit., p.291. It is remarkable that de Vault, who normally went as deep as he could, providing documental evidence and reporting letters in full, did not spend a word about why Louis XIV acted this way. He simply says that the King announced Vendôme's move to Flanders, but does not say on which day he announced it or why.

14 Eugene to Marlborough, from the Camp of Castelbaldo, 10 July 1706, rep. in Piero Pieri (ed.), *Principe Eugenio di Savoia. La Campagna d'Italia del 1706* (hereafter *La Campagna d'Italia*; Rome, 1936), p.146.

15

Preparing the Imperial Campaign

Things were moving also on the opposite side of the Po valley. Eugene had left the army of Italy by mid January 1706 to go to Vienna, where he arrived on the 23rd. He hoped to find a situation better than previous year but it was not really so.

Leopold died on 5 May 1705 after a 47-year reign. Many years later Eugene would write that Leopold had been a father to him, Joseph a friend, and Charles a "gracious Lord". So, the father was dead and now the friend, Joseph I marked the beginning of the sought for administrative and financial reformation of the Empire.

Several people left their posts in the Aulic War Council and in the Conference, and were replaced by others who were more active, honest, and competent. But the change at the top could not suddenly turn a bad situation into a good one. Time was needed, but time was exactly what was lacking, or rather, money was lacking and there was no time to find enough.

Emperor Joseph I.

We will not go deep into details about the Hungarian, German, and Italian situations that the Imperial military and civil administration had to deal with. Here it is enough to say that, once more, both the Maritime Powers had to provide money.

England knew it. The failures of the Empire in Italy had been determined by the pre-agonic state of its troops, due to the comatose state of the Imperial finances. The situation more or less held until Eugene was in command. When in early 1703 he had been called to Vienna by the Emperor to chair and reorganise the Aulic War Council, and when in 1704 he had been moved to the German war theatre where he joined Marlborough to defeat Tallard at Höchstadt/Blenheim, the situation in Italy became close to collapse. Now both Eugene and Marlborough were convinced of the strategic value of Northern Italy, and of the Piedmontese alliance. William III had that opinion at the time of the Great Alliance; and the situation was essentially still the same.

Moreover Eugene could rely on the Queen of England's interest, indeed, on her personal involvement. Queen Anne cared a lot about the family; she did not forget to be a Stuart, and Victor Amadeus' wife, the Duchess Anne, was a Stuart on her mother's side, thus had to be helped. So, thanks to the Duke of Marlborough, and to the kinship between the House of Savoy and Queen Anne, England and Holland gave Austria money. Marlborough himself had to come to save the southern front, not as a general but as a financier. Arriving in Vienna in November 1705, he agreed to a special 300,000 thalers loan, provided by the Maritime Powers with the precise and binding purpose of paying German troops for the Imperial Army in Italy. Last, Marlborough negotiated a further 250,000 English pounds loan. It had to be underwritten by individuals, starting with him, and like the other loans it was payable in Venice but exclusively to Prince Eugene.

Meanwhile, Victor Amadeus sent Count Maffei to London in January asking for help. Queen Anne and her government received Maffei very well, and financial support came. But before it was possible to organise any further military commitment, the news of the fall of Nice and Montmélian arrived. Now it was impossible to reach Piedmont by sea, or from Rhineland or Burgundy. There was only a possible route left: from the eastern Po valley.

The English funding became available in Venice as early as 1706, and was welcome. Eugene's correspondence reveals the usual hard situation of the army of Italy, even if it could be considered less catastrophic than in the past. The troop numbers decreased because the soldiers died, or deserted. This time it happened not due to lack of food, but because of how badly it was distributed. Moreover there were no uniforms or shoes, especially for cavalry, and without cash it was not possible to organise warehouses. Lastly the needed reinforcements were still en route; and the road from Prussia and central Germany was long.

On 24 February Eugene could more or less give Count von Reventlau the happy news that "with the last post I have already sent a letter for 200,000 florins on the English money that is expected in Venice", but forbade to use it, because it was up to him to let Reventlau "know how and when it will be employed".[1]

At the beginning of March he sent a letter for a further 100,000 ducats, from which – given the change fee – wrote the Prince, again to Reventlau, a month later, 80,000 florins had to remain

> for the purchase of provianda … Since through the mail today I sent to Mr. MG. and Chief War Commissioner Baron Martini a new bill for additional 100,000 ducats, and moreover I tell him that 80,000 of those florins are also to be *appliciren* to the purchase of provianda, so that with those two summs, 160,000 florins are devoted to the supply, not counting that *summa*, which the Commissioner of War

1 Prince Eugene to count von Reventlau, Vienna, 24 February 1706, rep. in "*La campagna d'Italia*", p.36.

Venice, and the *Bucintoro* dogal Ship.

> Messa has already received and which will amount to about 200,000 florins if not more, so it is finally to be hoped, that we shall achieve the planned establishment of the warehouses and you can do it immediately.[2]

Clearly the Imperial administration had not changed that much, thus when the Prince by mid April arrived in Rovereto, he found the usual situation: no bridge or pontoon crews, the warehouses were not yet organised, there was shortage of ammunition, the assets had not yet left Germany ... so he had to write to Victor Amadeus that he could hardly be ready before 20 May.

However at least his plan was ready. It was quite simple, and he had already explained it to his cousin:

> Meanwhile I have news of the Enemies intending to bring from Piedmont a great detachment in Italy to drive out our army in the mountains before all the troops have arrived, in order to be able to pull all their forces towards Turin, act defensively here and make the siege of this capital more comfortably, which enforces me to hold back the concentrated army and remain on a very difficult defensive as long as the army is assembled and the provisions are made. I believed my duty to notice Y.R.H. of this and of the fact that I will not neglect anything to act the faster that it will be possible and with vigour. I will form two corps, one in the Verona area and one in the Brescia area, and I will not leave anything out for the passage of the Po.[3]

Precisely because he was aware of the French movements, and knew that the Imperial troops had camped near Brescia, in Bedizzole, Eugene sent Reventlau an order to move immediately to the camp he occupied the previous December. It was not far, it was safer, and well connected to Trentino. But this was not done, and Vendôme took advantage of it. On the night of 18–19 April Vendôme led 58 battalions, and 67 squadrons – about 30,000 men – and on the 19th in the morning fell on the Imperialists, letting them flee near Calcinato.

The reason why Eugene's order was not completely executed is not very clear. In the report to the Emperor on the 20th he bypassed that fact as much as he could, writing that:

> in order not to be too troublesome, by now I want to omit to say most devoutly to You how things went in that unhappy action and how confusion occurred because the enemy came forward before that our men were gathered or that we had news of him.[4]

Actually it seems that Reventlau had to face a real uprising. The troops refused to move. Once more Austrian disorganisation caused a disaster. According to the contemporary eyewitness detail collected by Sanvitale, Eugene ordered Reventlau to move the camp, and Reventlau issued orders accordingly, but

2 Eugene to Reventlau, Vienna, 24 March 1706, rep. in *La campagna d'Italia*, p.38.

3 Eugene to Victor Amadeus II, Rovereto, 16 April 1706, rep. in *La campagna d'Italia*, p. 51.

4 Eugene to Emperor Joseph I, Gavardo, 20 April 1706, rep. in *La campagna d'Italia*, p. 57.

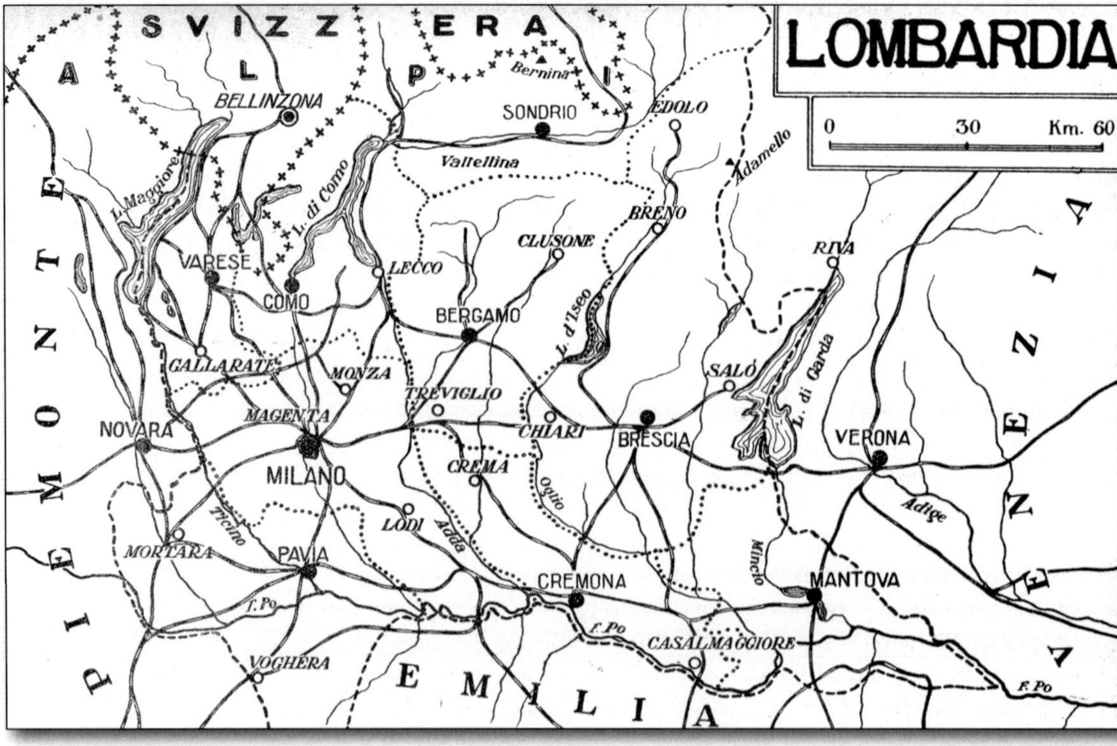

Map of the Lombardy Region.

"Several officers did not like to obey, and some Regiments did not even want to leave the Quarters", because they had no tents, and disliked the idea of sleeping outdoors, for in March in that part of Lombardy the nights were, and still are, cold, and wet and the temperature still drops easily below zero centigrade.

Anyway Reventlau obeyed as he could, and moved only 9,000 foot and 3,000 cavalrymen behind the Fossa Seriola, for the others refused to leave. That was not enough to watch the Fossa, but he did not have enough men to guard it all, precisely because several others had not moved. Thus, when Vendôme arrived he discovered the Fossa to be only half garrisoned, and attacked.

Meanwhile, Eugene was coming, but he was still very far away when he was told that the enemy had attacked, and that the Imperial troops had been beaten.

Casualties had been low: some hundreds of dead, and 1,200 prisoners. Eugene gathered his forces in Gavardo, moved back to Trentino, and then passed into the Verona area. In a sense he was back to 1701: he was on the Adige, and wanted to reach the Po. As he anticipated of Victor Amadeus, he wanted to cross the Po, and move to Piedmont marching upstream on the right side of that river. There was a good reason why. The tributaries of the Po from the right side are all torrential, so their stream in summer is smaller and their level lower than the rivers on the left side, coming from the big lakes and from the then existing Alpine glaciers.

The Army of the Two Crowns was mainly on the left bank of the Po, and leaning forward east. Had Eugene crossed the Po the enemies would lose a lot of time too, moving to the right bank of such an unfordable river, and would remain behind. Had the enemy decided to follow Eugene's march remaining on the left side, no problem at all: there were no bridges before Piedmont, thus they had no opportunity to harass his march.

Eugene had to start operations; and it seemed a repeat of the 1701 campaign, with some differences in favour of the French.

Knowing what Eugene could do, Vendôme had wasted no time. His soldiers had fortified the entire line from the mountains to the Po, with a palisade two metres high, protected by a deep moat. But they were not as many as needed to effectively watch that long fortified line, and when they had to garrison a group of forts around Verona and Legnago they lost almost all their initiative and mobility.

In the last days of June the troops from the Palatinate and Saxe-Gotha reached the Imperial army, and on 2 July Eugene received "news that the Duc d'Orléans and Marshal de Villars should come here and take command and that the duc de Vendôme must go to the Netherlands".[5]

On the 3rd he warned the Duke of Savoy that the expected reinforcements had arrived, and that he would do everything possible to reach Turin.

On the 4th in the morning he gave Colonel Battée orders about how to cross the Adige. Had the crossing succeeded, his intention was to go back to the Canal Bianco – the White Canal – in order to be able to reach the Po. From there, from Polesella, a 447 kilometre (278 mile) march to Turin was waiting for him.

5 Eugene to Joseph I, post scriptum to the report on 2 July 1706 from the camp of San Martino, rep. in *La campagna d'Italia*, p. 137.

16

The Great 1706 Siege of Turin

I: Preliminaries

As soon as he was appointed Caraglio issued restrictive orders concerning the population. First he practically forbade the entrance to the city, to prevent any spies getting in, and because it was known that the French would be ready to start generalised firing from 24 June. In fact, in the last week of June the artillery fire became really intensive. It killed many civilians, caused substantial destruction of civil buildings, and as said forced the evacuation of the whole inhabited area near the citadel.

The artillery of the place answered well. It destroyed enemy supplies, and gunpowder warehouses, caused serious casualties, and succeeded in putting out of order enemy cannons, 22 on 28 June alone. It was so successful that the French later admitted that by 30 June they had only 30 cannons still on duty, all the others having been destroyed by Piedmontese artillery. It was an additional reason why La Feuillade insisted so much in pursuing and chasing the Duke, but had no success.

Having left his capital to join the advancing Imperial army, Victor Amadeus escaped. His cavalry had protected his ride, stopping and delaying for the first time the French cavalry in Carmagnola on 22 June. The Duke reached Cherasco. La Feuillade did not try to attack, due to the city artillery protecting the Piedmontese cavalry. So, he decided to try to surround Victor Amadeus by crossing both the Tanaro and the Stura. He took the bulk of his troops and moved to the Tanaro, and committed Mauroy, with 1,000 cavalrymen and 300 grenadiers to Fossano, to cross the Stura river there. Notified by his own cavalry patrols, Victor Amadeus on 24 June set his forces in Bene, halfway between the two rivers. The Sabaudian Cavalry had neither field artillery nor infantry support, nonetheless it could delay the enemy movements until 29 June, then it had to withdraw to Cuneo.

Plan of the Streets and Fortifications of Cherasco.

Victor Amadeus then made a feint: he committed a column of 300 cavalry to Mondovì, and let rumours

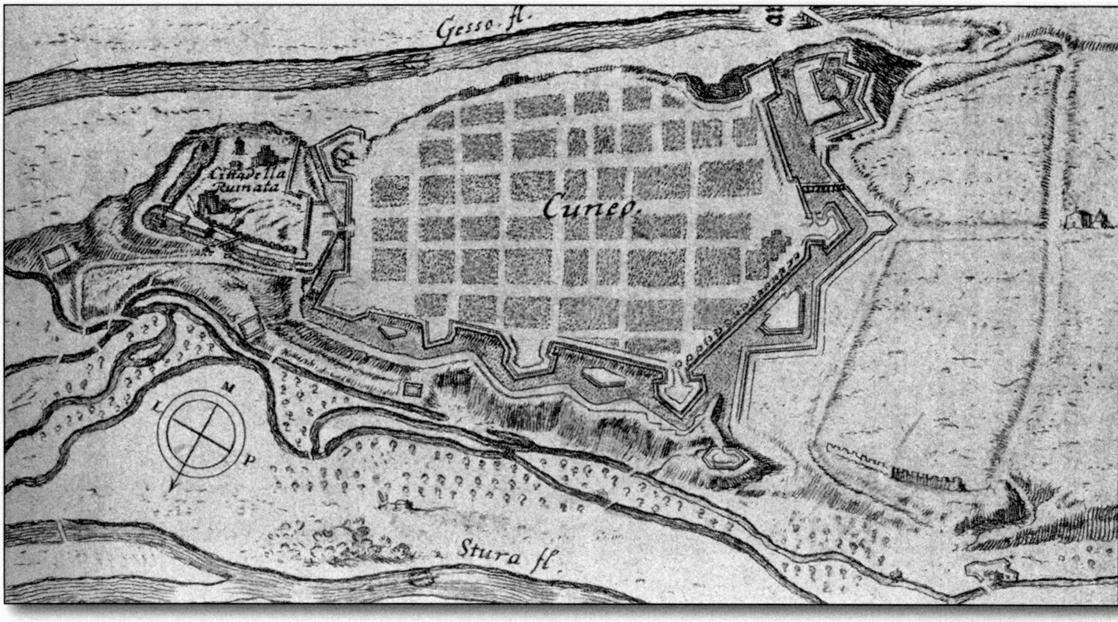

Plan of the Streets and Fortifications of Cuneo.

spread about his presence with them. La Feuillade trusted the rumours, sent 4,000 men to Mondovì and missed the Duke.

On 2 July the French realised their mistake and moved to Cuneo, a strong place, quite well protected. Nonetheless a standing defence did not fit Victor Amadeus' plans, so, he left a good garrison there and on 4 July left the city with 2,000 cavalry towards Saluzzo.

On 7 July the French – 40 squadrons, five battalions, and 20 cannons commanded by General d'Aubeterre – tried to engage the Duke while he was leaving Saluzzo. The Piemonte Reale regiment, in Ducal rearguard, reacted and the skirmish stopped the French for three hours in the town periphery. Then Victor Amadeus came back to relieve his rearguard and the French were rejected with 250 casualties. The Piedmontese lost 47 dead and 30 wounded.

The failure convinced La Feuillade that any further attempt to seize the Duke was useless. Thus, on 9 July he ceased pursuit. Victor Amadeus barricaded himself with 6,000 men in Val Pellice; and the French could do nothing but go back to Turin, and complete the operations to approach the citadel.

II: Starting the Siege

On 14 July the duel began. The garrison opened the dance by blowing up a mine in front of the so-called Arrow of the Beato Amedeo. Then the grenadiers of the Guards and the Imperial haiduks came out, and caused so much damage to the enemy earthworks that the French had to work 15 days to fix them.

On 18 July the artillery duels intensified, as well as clashes between the besieging, and besieged patrols.

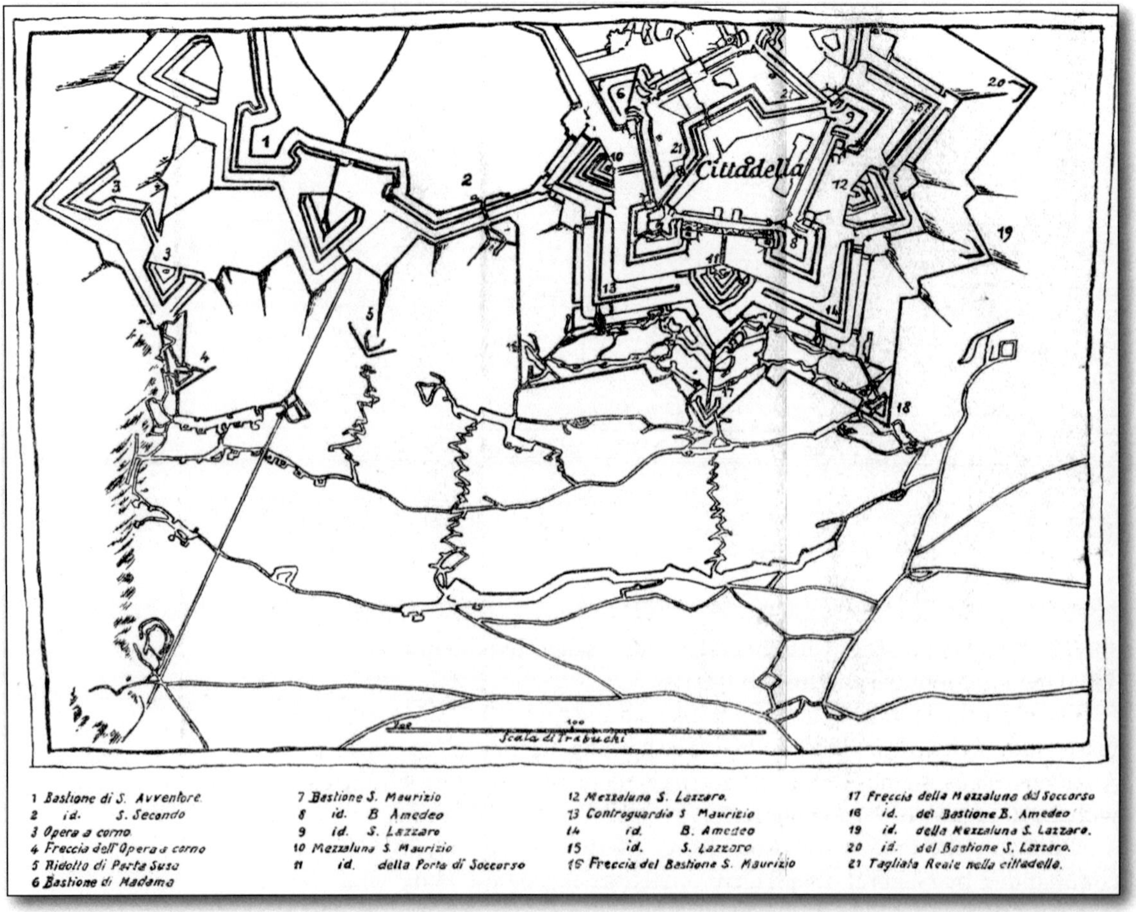

Siege of Turin. French and Spanish attacks on the citadel.

Meanwhile the besiegers' trenches were moving toward the three arrows of the small defensive works before the ramparts of San Maurizio and of Beato Amedeo, and the rampart of the Soccorso Crescent. In fact, the bastions and the walls in between had two forwarded fortified protections. Let us consider the citadel to be a pentagon, having a bastion as each point. That pentagon was protected by an external bigger fortified pentagon, which was in turn protected by an even bigger external pentagon. The inner pentagon was properly the citadel, whose walls were the highest. The most external pentagon had the lowest walls. They were triangle shaped – thus called "arrows". The fortified five pointed star between the external pentagon and the citadel was composed too of triangular, although slightly semicircular walls, called "half-moons", or "crescents", and by triangle-shaped defensive works just out of the bastions, as a sort of double-bastioned points, called counterguards. All these fortifications were known after the related bastion name, and the besiegers had to seize the half-moons first, then the arrows, and last the bastions if they wanted to enter the citadel. As we shall see, it was such a hard task that, when the siege ended, the besiegers had achieved practically nothing.

Back to the attack. In the night of 21–22 July the French–Spaniards stormed the San Maurizio, Soccorso and the Beato Amedeo arrows, which they had on their left, centre and right. In other words, they seized the most external pentagon. But on the next afternoon, 22 July, the grenadiers of the Guards, Saluzzo and Piemonte regiments, reinforced by Imperial troops, attacked and recaptured the Beato Amedeo arrow, and pursued the enemies into their trenches.

Unfortunately the French were changing the guard in those trenches, therefore they were twice as many as usual. and counter-attacked. They lost 300 dead and 33 prisoners, but succeeded in allowing the Austro-Piedmontese slowly withdraw and settle into the arrow. Disturbed by the fire of the French artillery, the Austro-Piedmontese retreated a bit more, just as much as needed to be out of range, but kept the arrow under their fire-range, to prevent any enemy attempt. Given the heavy casualties, the besiegers suspended any major action for the next dozen days.

Then on 3 August at night they seized by surprise the edge of the covered road in front of the three counterguards of Beato Amedeo, San Maurizio, and Soccorso. They were now holding the second pentagon, and were facing the bastions. On the 6th at night, supported by 56 cannons, they launched 20 companies of grenadiers, followed by many pickets, in a new attack on the covered road, and the three salients behind.

After a violent struggle they passed through, and rushed to the fortifications. The Soccorso Gate opened and, headed by the grenadiers of the Guards, two columns of grenadiers came out and counter-attacked. There was a furious hand-to-hand fight. The French–Spaniards collapsed, and quickly retreated. At dawn they tried a new limited attack to the crescent salient, and tried to seize it, but failed. The whole night cost them 300 men; the defenders only 80.

After five days, on 8 August, a further attack on the Beato Amedeo counter-guard was tried. The French set fire to its wooden protection and then tried to pass; but they were repulsed by the grenadiers of the Guards: half of the grenadiers fought, and half extinguished the fire.

The French then started setting fire to all the villas and country houses in the hills of Turin. In two days they burnt more than 150. Solaro wrote: "everybody sees with his own eyes the burning home belonging to him, and no longer waits to be notified by other people."[1]

The French infantry was proving ineffective, due to the ineffective artillery support. In fact the French batteries practically left the walls undamaged because, as has been said, the walls were not high enough to be targeted from a distance. Thus the French worked hard, and by 20 August they could finally set a siege battery in the only place the walls could be effectively hit from. It had to start firing on Saint Louis day, and would cause a dramatic disaster for the defenders, the French announced.

But while they were working the Ducal miners worked too, digging a tunnel until they were under the battery and setting three mines there. Then at 10:00 a.m. on 24 August, under Count Daun's eyes, the Piedmontese blew the mines. The battery vanished in a turmoil of smoke and earth, and 11

1 Solaro, op. cit. p.127.

cannons out of 14 were destroyed. Stunned by the explosion, disorganised, and blinded by the smoke, the French tried to escape but crowded toward the end of the trench, just under the Piedmontese positions on the bastion, and were massacred by cannons and rifles. And all this was purposely and nastily done just as the French generals were in church attending the mass celebrating Saint Louis day, the Sun King's name-day.

Mines and countermines exploded in the next 48 hours in the same area, and the besieged blew two more enemy cannons.

One hour after sundown on the 27th, after an intensive and very short artillery bombardment, the French infantry advanced. They stormed the counterguards and the crescent, killed all the defenders, and arranged a defensive line with gabions and wooden fagots they had brought along.

The Austro-Piedmontese grenadiers rushed in, and started firing. Volley by volley, in a few minutes the French situation turned for the worse. Decimated by the volleys, their attack could not be fed, because their reinforcements were stopped by the fire from the ramparts.

The French lost momentum and initiative whilst the Piedmontese grenadiers, led by Colonel Rocca, fought in the light of torches and enflamed fagots, and attacked twice: the second time they succeeded and seize the crescent back. The French advanced anew. They attempted to get the lost positions, and concentrated under the fortifications. But due to the restricted room they overcrowded, providing the defence with an excellent target, so the Piedmontese began shooting into the crowd. Solaro was there and reported:

> Such was the carnage we made that, in the joy of repulsing them, we could not prevent ourselves from mourning them. Those who approached the crescent were cut to pieces, those who mounted were practically all killed; the others, who supported them, were shot in the moat. This massacre was finally terminated by another even more horrible one: the great pile of goudrons,[2] illuminating balls, gunpowder bags, grenades and bombs at the extremity of the breach – since that we never had enough, and the soldiers asked always for more and more – caught fire. What an accident! Virtually all our soldiers were killed and many brave officers with them: the crescent appeared burnt out, the flames and the smoke touched the clouds. Grenades and Bombs: everything had exploded. This horrible explosion, this great blow of thunder stunned the defenders, astounded the attackers and made them both frightened.[3]

At that point, after a five-hour clash, the French renounced the possession of the crescent, and settled in the counterguards.

The night passed. Then, between 9:00 and 10:00 a.m. on 27 August, 400 grenadiers from the Guards, Cortanze, Saluzzo regiments, and from an Imperial regiment stormed and kept the counter guards. Enemy reinforcements arrived too late. Discouraged, they did not attempt to seize back the lost positions, and immediately withdrew. According to the

2 The "goudrons", "illuminanti" in Italian – "illuminating"– were halfspheres filled with asphalt, used to make light.

3 Solaro della Margarita, *Parte del manoscritto…* cit., from 26–27 August, p.129.

deserters, in the two clashes the French lost more than 1,000 grenadiers and 1,000 other soldiers, whilst the garrison lost 400 privates and 30 officers.

The Guards returned to the city, and went to San Carlo Square to acknowledge Our Lady for the success of their action.[4] In the meantime, such a "Pietas" in the city was echoed by a somewhat more common behaviour on the walls. During the day the garrison threw a lot of wood down into the moat and almost filled it. Then, in late afternoon, a little earlier than 5:00 p.m. the job was achieved and one hour later all that wood was set on fire. A wall of flames grew up, and the besiegers could not approach the walls. Thus, as Solaro wrote:

> Delighted by the besiegers' confusion, and spite, our Soldiers mocked them, willingly adding the mockery to the insults they had the habit to say each other in similar cases: 'Come' shouted to them aloud, "Come and dance at the sound of our oboes. Here are well-lit halls."[5]
>
> In the morning, from the top of our Towers and from the Redoubts on the Hill, the Enemy Camp was seen to expand and extend across the plain. The Deserters and the Prisoners confirmed to us that the Duke of Orléans had just arrived with a corps of Cavalry and that he was followed by the rest of his Army, with which he claimed to oppose to Prince Eugene, who advanced with powerful forces from Upper Monferrato towards Piedmont.[6]

On the following day a further wood fire was made in the moat, and the fire caused a French ordnance warehouse to explode, together with a battery nearby. Bodies, hats, rifles, clothes, all flew into the air. The paper sheets used for the cannons' gunpowder flew away and came down "letting us see a snowfall in the deep summer", as Solaro wrote. Seeing this, Daun was very happy and had money distributed to the bombers.

With a 22,000-man reinforcement from the army of Lombardy, the besiegers intensified their efforts to seize the city, also because Prince Eugene was approaching with the relief army and they risked to being caught in between.

III: The Duke and his Cavalry Outside Turin

As said, in the early days of July Victor Amadeus entered Waldensian Valleys and stood there, whilst his cavalry engaged the French in guerrilla warfare. Convoys were attacked and destroyed, and cavalry raids were made. Fast actions harassed the French posts and small garrisons and rendered their communications poor. The French had to commit 60 cavalry squadrons and 600 hussars to react and to protect their communications, whilst the Duke had no more than 2,000 cavalrymen with more or less 2,400 horses.

---

4 Normally in the evening the Regiments not committed on the walls met in San Carlo Square to pray the Rosary.

5 Solaro della Margarita, op. cit., 27 August, p.130.

6 Solaro della Margarita, cit., 28 August, p.131.

Anyway no clear information went around. On one hand secrecy was kept to protect Ducal initiatives, on the other hand, but for a few letters between him and Eugene, all the communications between the Duke and his allies were cut. So, from a foreign perspective the situation was not completely clear. The only clear thing was that Austria had to relieve Piedmont. Thus Sir Charles Hedges had to advise Lord Methuen that it was "absolutely necessary for his [Charles of Habsburg] interest in particular, as well as that of the whole Confederacy that the war in Italy be kept up, for should the Duke of Savoy be reduced and that war at an end, the French would then be at liberty to pour their forces into Spain."[7] But Austria too could do nothing now, it was all up to Eugene alone.

IV: Prince Eugene's March

On 4 July Eugene had split his army in different parts and left General Wetzel with 5,000 foot and 700 cavalry near Verona, to keep communications with Austria, and above all, to keep the route free to the incoming troops of the Prince of Hesse-Cassel.

Then he arranged five attacks: three were fake, and two real. The first had to occur in Rivoli. under the mountains. The second just beyond the Lazaretto of Verona. The third was above Legnago; the fourth was made in his sight against the bridge, and the French Forts of Castel-Baldo, and of Masi. The fifth was near Padua, at Rotta Nuova, at the Luscia, and surrounding area. The latter two were the real ones.

Colonel Battée's men had succeeded, and allowed Eugene to gather the troops between Castelbaldo and Badia Polesine and to prepare the march to the Canal Bianco.

Meanwhile, the French–Spanish command had been passed to the Duke of Orléans, who arrived in Milan on 11 July. The future regent of France[8] left the Count of Médavy on the Mincio with 17 battalions and 12 squadrons to face Wetzel and the incoming Prince of Hesse-Cassel. Eugene did not care. He forced the crossing of the Canal Bianco in the first half of July, marched to the Po, and crossed it on the night of 15–16 July. The French were bypassed. When they reached the Oltrepò of Ferrara, Eugene was already gone, for he had crossed the river at Serravalle, just beyond Crespino, at Polesella and at Occhiobello.

The Franco-Spaniards had more or less 2,000 men in that area, and they were scattered in small garrisons. So, Philip of Orléans crossed the Po at San Benedetto Po, and when on the river's right side, stopped on the canal called "La Fossa Parmigiana", and blockaded the road to Modena Eugene was supposed to take.

---

7 Hedges to Lord Methuen, on 11 June 1706, in PRO, SP, 104/207, fo. 109, reported in Hattendorf, op. cit., p.90.

8 Philip was the Duchess of Savoy's half brother, the eldest son of Duchess Anne's father's second wife: the Palatine princess.

Eugene crossed the Secchia and captured the garrison of Concordia. On 1 August he approached the enemy positions and found them impossible to be crossed quickly. Thus he extended his march to Carpi, seized that town after a two-day siege, and set there a garrison, warehouses and a hospital.

As we can see, until this day – 5 August – Eugene's march was not yet very fast; and he blamed the non-Austrian soldiers from the Empire. Those Germans had wagons in excess, far more than needed, and as Eugene wrote:

> If the *Auxiliares* were accustomed to suffer hunger like the Imperial troops, I would not care so much about the bread, but having to pass amidst enemy Fortresses in the uncertainty of finding bread, while the *Auxiliares*, if I missed the bread even for just one day, would no longer take a step.[9]

Yes, that was definitely preposterous: how could one manage a war properly if the troopers demanded to be fed daily? Did they think they were attending a picnic?

Once Carpi was seized, Eugene went ahead. He knew that it would have been better to secure Modena, but he simply had no time. And he also had another big issue: how would the enemy act? Eugene moved Wetzel's men, whom he left far behind on his back. They crossed the Mincio, and marched toward the Oglio, that is to say directly on Médavy's troops.

As soon as he was notified, Philippe behaved as Eugene expected: he left the area of Guastalla with all his troops, went back to the left bank of the Po, and marched to rescue Médavy. Doing so, he left Eugene free to go to Piedmont. Eugene issued very strict orders to keep discipline, seized Correggio, and on 9 August entered Reggio Emilia. The French, commanded by the Sieur de Narbonne, defended it for a few days then abandoned the walls and withdrew into the castle, where they finally surrendered at discretion on 14 August.

As soon as he was notified of the result of Wetzel's movements, and of the departure of Philippe d'Orléans from Guastalla, Eugene wrote to Daun on the same day: "Tonight after midnight I leave with the army and march to Parma."[10] Then he took the Via Emilia, and advanced. On 16 August, always worried due to the lack of autonomy of the German auxiliary troops, not that far from Parma, he notified Victor Amadeus that he had been forced to stop. Many Germans had fallen behind along the road and some had died, thus he stopped until the next day. He begged Victor Amadeus for "a good quantity of bread ready in the countries", and was in trouble due to the lack of water "since all these rivers are completely dry", thus he asked his cousin to have "the goodness to let me know what facilities I will find for the bread and in which way you can help me on your part, because after the State of Parma I will not find anything anymore."[11]

---

9 Eugene to Daun, camp of Carpi, 5 August 1706, rep. in *La campagna d'Italia*, cit., p.177.

10 Eugene to Daun, camp of San Prospero di Reggio, 14 August 1706, rep. in *La campagna d'Italia*, cit, p.192.

11 Eugene to Victor Amadeus, camp between the Enza, and Parma, 16 August 1706, rep. in *La campagna d'Italia*, cit., p.193.

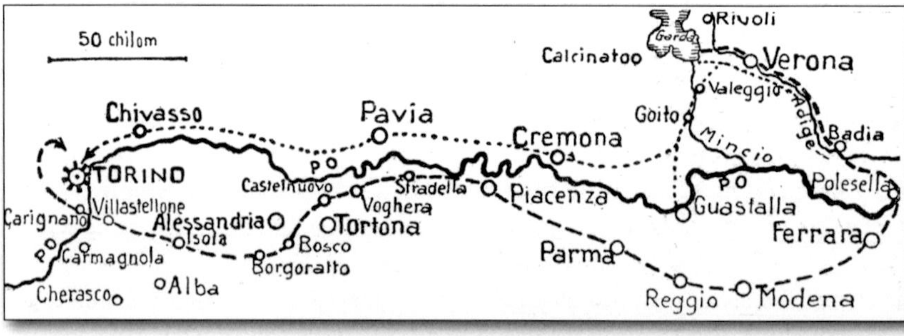

The respective marches. Prince Eugene's marked by long lines, Philip of Orléans' marked by short lines.

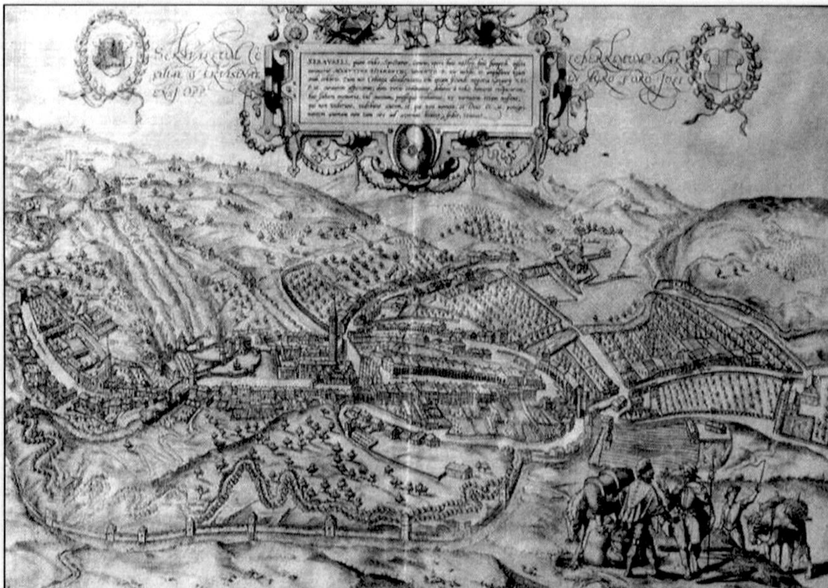

Drawing of Serravalle.

Preceded by the vanguard commanded by Baron Kriegsbaum, and by Old Dessau's Corps, Eugene advanced with his cavalry, followed by infantry, having on flanks security provided by Riedt's, Saint Amour's, and Eben's Corps. On 18 August Eugene was in Serravalle, and sent to Victor Amadeus the planned timetable to reach Nizza Monferrato on 29 August.[12] He respected it in full. On the 26th he wrote to the Emperor:

> tomorrow I will pass the Bormida, and, so, not only will the enemy no longer be able to make any remarkable opposition to my march up to Turin, but within two days he will have to decide whether he intends to continue or to leave the siege of the mentioned Turin.[13]

12 "Project: eighteenth August, Serravalle; nineteenth, between Fiorenzuola and Piacenza; twentieth, stop; twenty-first, between Piacenza and Castel San Giovanni; twenty-second, Stradella; twenty-third, Voghera; twenty-fourth, stop; twenty-fifth, Castelnuovo di Scrivia; twenty-sixth, beyond Bosco; twenty-seventh, Castelnuovo Bormida; twenty-eighth, stop; twenty-ninth, Nizza della Paglia", attached to the letter to Victor Amadeus sent on 18 August from Serravalle, rep. in *La campagna d'Italia*, cit., p.195.

13 Eugene to Joseph I, Bosco, 26 August 1706, rep. in *La campagna d'Italia*, cit., p.207.

On the 27th he announced his arrival to Victor Amadeus, saying that he wanted to: "come myself in person to Y.R.H., and to assure you at the same time of my profound respects, waiting for … your orders to know where I should find you, to take the right, and very necessary measures in such an important situation."[14]

On the same day the Imperial army crossed the Bormida at Borgoratto, and on the 29th the Tanaro in Isola d'Asti, pushing the vanguard until Villafranca. Leaving the heavy wagons and convoys, and the sick men behind in Alba, the army went on. At half past four in the afternoon of 29 August 1706, Eugene met in Villanova d'Asti a Piedmontese 200 cavalry escort, who accompanied him to Carmagnola to meet Victor Amadeus. A Piedmontese eyewitness reported:

> With great joy of the whole army we saw Lord Prince Eugene arriving at about 10 in the evening,[15] but he had been preceded by the Marquis of Prié who had already taken note of his arrival, and he had informed H.R.H. of the state of the army. The said R.H. went to meet him beyond Carmagnola and waited for him on foot on a green. The Lord Prince saw this while arriving, and set foot on the ground and went on to kiss him on the hand, H.R.H. withdrew it, and hugged him several times, then they went to the Camp.[16]

On 31 August the Imperial army arrived in Villastellone, just south of Turin, where they joined the Ducal troops, and "with a Royal volley of the Artillery, the very happy end of the long and fatiguing march was celebrated".[17]

A note: Eugene made 447 kilometres – or 278 miles – in 45 days, thus he seemed to have a 9.9 kilometre – 6.1 mile – daily marching average; not that fast, but fair in the contemporary standards. But we must subtract from these 45 days two days spent besieging and seizing Carpi, one day to seize Correggio, and five days to besiege and seize Reggio Emilia, a one-day stop on 16 August due to the excessively fatigued troops because of the heat, and three further stops on 20, 24, and 28 August. In other words his troops spent eight days in three different sieges, rested only four days – in August in Italy – and marched 33 days, covering in fact 13.54 kilometres, or 8.41 English miles per marching day. This was more than the standard. As said when speaking about eighteenth-century warfare, armies used to rest up an entire day every two or three days on the march. In this way, counting also the day of rest, an army was expected to march an average of 24.8 miles in four days, whereas Eugene's troops managed in this case, excluding the eight days spent in sieges, but including the four days to rest, to cover an average of 30.5 miles every four days. And this was remarkable – and different by the supposed "rules everybody respected" – not only because of the longer daily distance, but because of how long a time this speed was maintained.

14 Eugene to Victor Amadeus, camp of Castellazzo, 27 August 1706, rep. in *La campagna d'Italia*, cit., p. 207.

15 According to the peculiar Italian contemporary way to measure the time, based on daylight, it was 10:00 p.m, but according to our way, astronomically more correct, it was 5:00 p.m.

16 Carlo Giacinto di Roero, count di Guarene to his father, Camp of La Motta, 30 August 1706, rep. in Trabucco, op. cit., p.133.

17 *Vita e campeggiamenti*, cit., p.176.

17

The Dramatic, Amazing Last Week

I: Holding at Any Cost

Turin was now close to its end. It was short of ammunition, and the garrison was decimated by casualties, and far more by huge desertions.

In their letters to Eugene, both Victor Amadeus and Daun had underlined only two points: relief and gunpowder. Above all, the second was missing. The intensive fire by the city artillery consumed much more gunpowder than expected; and it was really hard to introduce a little into the city. It was not surprising that in August Eugene knew from Daun that, given the daily consumption, there was only gunpowder until 12 September, and then …

Not only for these reasons did the end of August see the interest of the two opposing parties focus on Turin as never before. Eugene was coming. Victor Amadeus came out from Val Pellice with the reorganised cavalry and gathered all the possible provincial militias and regular troops. Lastly the Duke of Orléans, once he had beaten Wetzel in Lombardy and forced him to withdraw, had preferred not to engage Eugene, and rushed to join La Feuillade.

As said, Philippe of Orléans's army reached Turin on 29 August, and had a nasty surprise:

> Monseigneur found the siege in an unsatisfactory state … everything languished there; no engineer or artillery officer capable of carrying out such a serious undertaking … no activity anywhere; the infantry weakened by fatigue and trench losses to the point that just two hundred men remained in each battalion.[1]

Philip's troops – 15,000 infantry, and 3,000 cavalry – enhanced anew the Two Crowns army to 44,000 men – 34,000 infantry, and 10,000 cavalry – and the siege area was divided into three sectors. The one from south to west, facing the citadel, from the left bank of the Po to the right side of the Dora

1 De Vault, op. cit., vol. VI, 1706, p.261.

remained under La Feuillade. The second, in the north, a rectangle between the Dora and its parallel river the Stura, from Lucento to the confluence of both the rivers with the Po, was under the Duke of Orléans. The last sector, the opposite semicircle, on the whole right bank of the Po, from south through east to north – that is the sector including the hills – was assigned to Albergotti.

On the evening of that same day, 29 August, whilst Eugene was reaching Nizza Monferrato, the Duke of Orléans wrote to the King: "The army of Prince Eugene has passed the Tanaro and the head has already joined the troops of Monseigneur the Duke of Savoy."[2]

That same night a French underground penetration failed. A Piedmontese sapper, Pietro Micca, died when he blew a mine, burying with himself a column of enemy grenadiers trying to enter through a tunnel. There was no direct eyewitness, but Solaro and a later chronicler, Father Antonio Maria Metelli reported:

> Around midnight from 29 to 30 August, four completely armored enemy grenadiers descended into the ditch of the Crescent, crawling unnoticed along the counterscarp and having suddenly reached the salient corner, reached the door through which one enters the gallery leading to the interior of the square." They were seen and killed by the sentinels "But ten or twelve more are following these, who ... let our small guard flee. So this group of daredevils would have penetrated the gallery in bulk" followed by a column of grenadiers "if one of our miners, seconded by another, had not taken the party to close on their face the door at the beginning of the staircase from the upper to the inferior gallery."[3] "The French tried with iron clubs to pull it down; but meanwhile a certain Pietro Micca, a miner of Andorno, nicknamed "Passapertutto" seeing that the guard who was in charge of the mine-stove did not hurry to set them on fire ... "[4] "...Get out of there – he says to him, catching him by the arm – you are longer than a day without bread; let me do it, flee! – Then he brings the too-short fuse to the end of the sausage[5] and set it on fire. The stove bursts and the poor man has less time than is needed to save himself, since he is found dead forty steps from the stair he had descended.[6]

It was a heroic action. Solaro late underlined that, had the French succeeded in entering the citadel, they would have been stopped by the wall – the "Royal cut" – dividing it in two parts, just to prevent any surprise. Maybe, it could be, anyway Pietro Micca did not think of it, and this should also be the first time that an Italian trooper was remembered in the contemporary official

2 Philippe d'Orléans to Louis XIV, camp in front of Turin, 31 August 1706, rep. in de Vault, op. cit., vol. VI, 1706, p. 271.

3 Solaro della Margarita, *Journal historique du siége de Turin*, cit., p.133.

4 Antonio Maria Metelli, *Torino assediato, e soccorso l'anno 1706, dedicato all'altezza reale di Vittorio Amedeo* 2 [Turin besieged and relieved the year 1706, dedicated to the royal highness of Victor Amadeus 2] (Parma, 1711), p.252.

5 It was a sort of long pipe made of tough tissue, containing mining explosive, and ressembling a sausage.

6 Solaro della Margarita, op. cit., p.133.

records, other that in memoirs and private journals, for, before that, only officers were remembered.

Having failed in this attempt, on 31 August one hour after midday, the French and Spaniards launched a second general assault. They made a feint on the side of the Po, hoping to attract a part of the garrison. Daun did not believe that area to be weak, and kept his troops concentrated. He was right. No fewer than 11 companies of grenadiers from the Lombardy army, supported by at least 5,000 fusileers and dragoons on foot, split into three columns and attacked. The surprise worked, and they stormed the three contested fortified works: the San Maurizio, and Beato Amedeo counterguards, and the Soccorso crescent.

Caraglio and Daun promptly rushed in. They called all the available reinforcements, and moved the reserve. All the available soldiers, from seven different regiments, led by General La Roche d'Allery, and by Colonel Schulenburg attacked the crescent, and the counter-guard of Beato Amedeo. But the most dramatic counter-attack was carried out by the Guards Regiment against the San Maurizio counter-guard. Led by Major General Baron of Saint-Rémy, with flags and rolling drums, between two wings of a crowd of silent, worried civilians, the Guards passed through the gate and came out of the ramparts. They advanced slowly to the counter-guard, while the top of the city walls were filled by the citizens who wanted to watch.

After a short exchange of shots with the enemy, the officers of the Guard gathered at the head of the column, raised their swords, and ordered: "Forward the Guards!" The Regiment shouted "Long Live Savoy!" and the enemy shouted in reply, "Long Live the King!"; and the Guards rushed at them at a brisk pace.

It was a terrible hand-to-hand fight. It lasted two hours, and then the French slowly lost their positions. They immediately reorganised and advanced again. But as soon as they approached, Daun ordered the blowing of the big mine prepared there underneath; the explosion made the whole city tremble and 300 French grenadiers literally fly in the sky. No one survived. It destroyed two enemy cannons and threw a third into the ditch. Then the grenadiers came out and let any survivors flee.

The cannon was pulled out of the ditch, and brought as a gift by the enthusiastic citizens to Count Daun.[7] Moreover, immediately afterwards, some letters dated the 25th arrived: the Princes of Savoy made known that they were very close, and that liberation was now a matter of days. Enthusiasm rose to the stars.

On that same evening, 31 August, the Duke of Orléans underlined to his uncle Louis XIV that, when he reached the army, he found only 150 men per battalion, the other being missing due to desertion, casualties, and sickness; and that there were only two cannons able to fire, out of the nine the breach battery had in origin. He added: "The army of Prince Eugene has passed the

7 It was presented with an inscription saying "Oppugnatori Gallo – in aggressione repulso – A Comite Virico Daun – Taurini propugnatore capto – anno 1706 die XXXI Augusti", "To the Gaul besieger – repulsed in the attack – by Count Virico Daun – defender of Turin, kept – in the year 1706, in the day 31 of August", cfr. Montù, op. cit., p.991.

Tanaro and the head has already joined the troops of Monseigneur the Duke of Savoy." Continuing, he proposed two possibilities: to stay, and wait within the circumvallation and countervallation lines for a possible enemy attack, or, given the risk of having communications with Lombardy or France cut off:

> give them battle, and there is enough to think that it would be lucky ... But the consequences of these two choice are so serious that I content myself to represent them to Your Majesty and I will not determine for one or the other choice if not after a precise order of Your Majesty.[8]

But Versailles was far away, and only on 6 September Louis would send an answer; and it would be too late.

The defenders were in good condition now, they perceived a happy end to be close. and mocked the enemy as much as they could. On 1 September, in the evening, Marquess Roero di Cortanze was on duty on the bastions. He went there accompanied by the band of the Guards to let them play throughout his stay. Hearing the music, a French officer from the opposite trenches asked him to make the band play the at that time popular tune "the Fooleries of Spain".[9] And the Marquess answered boldly that he would let them play a more updated one: "the madness of France."

Mengin wrote: "The capture of Turin seemed very delayed now, especially since the disaster of this second assault, combined with the next arrival of Prince Eugene, threw consternation among the troops." De Vault added: "Monseigneur the Duke of Orléans, in charge for the first time of commanding an army, did not dare in such critical circumstances to take the responsibility for a decision, and therefore on 1 September he summoned a council of war."[10] Marshal Marsin and generals La Feuillade, Chamarande, d'Estaing, Saint-Frémont, de Vibraye, Galmoy, de Murcey, and Albergotti attended. Philip of Bourbon proposed to gather the troops, get out of the lines, and engage battle. There was nothing else to do – he said – because the failure of the general assaults had shown the impossibility of a short-term fall of Turin, and the proximity of the Austro-Piedmontese army at least increased the difficulties of the siege itself. Had, moreover, the two Savoy cousins cut off communications with France or Lombardy, the result of the enterprise would have been in real danger. Therefore – the Duke concluded – the best solution was to get out of the lines and fight; also because, had the French won, the conquest of the city would immediately follow. Had the French lost, as things were, being already out of the circumvallation, they would have been in better condition for a withdrawal. According to Philip the victory was at hand, because the enemy – and here he was wrong – could not have more than 23,000 infantry and cavalry against the 44,000 French

8 Philippe d'Orléans to Louis XIV, from Turin, 31 August 1706, rep. in de Vault, op. cit., 1706, p.271.

9 Even if it seems now forgotten, that tune is still known, for it was used – in Handel's Sarabanda version – as Stanley Kubrick's *Barry Lyndon* main theme.

10 De Vault, op. cit., 1706, p.276.

and Spaniards. Actually neither could the Piedmontese provincial militias be calculated, for in his opinion it could not compete with the French–Spanish troops, nor the garrison of Turin, weakened by the siege and unable to leave in time to take part in a battle, and this was an additional mistaken statement. He supposed his reasons to be good, and well grounded, but he did not know the councils of war; not by chance, Eugene called them "the best way to do nothing."

In this case, all the other nine generals rejected the idea of a battle. According to them it was enough if they remained within the lines and pushed the siege on. The situation was not that desperate – Marsin said – to push them to such an initiative, and even if Monseigneur was the supreme commander of the army of Italy, he could not dismiss the siege without the King's permission. Philip had to accept, and the troops remained within the circumvallation.

II: Reconnaissance, Planning and Preparation

On 2 September Eugene and Victor Amadeus seized Chieri, and protected by a 1,200 cavalry and 500 infantry detachment went on reconnaissance to the top of the Superga hill.

Superga was at that time 10 kilometres from the city centre, whilst now is in fact in the periphery, just across the river. The hill is relatively steep, and at that time it was 712 metres above sea level, whilst now it is 672. It was the best observatory one could have at that time, and Eugene and Victor Amadeus could see the entire plain at their feet, intersected by the web of the French lines, just as if they were looking at a three-dimensional map.

They were both determined to engage a battle, but it was still unclear the best way. They had already discarded the idea of attacking from and on the hills, because the enemy fortifications between the hills and the city were too strong. Therefore only an attack in the plain remained – and that was why they climbed Superga – but against which enemy side?

The observation provided the solution. The part between the Dora and Po – the one commanded by La Feuillade – was surrounded by circumvallation, and countervallation, while the sector of the Duke of Orléans had the countervallation, but no circumvallation between the Dora, and the Stura, that was the point they could attack with some hope of success.

To tell the truth, the French generals – La Feuillade first – did not believe it possible to be attacked in that zone. The ground seemed poor for an army, and anyone attacking from there had no way to retreat. The mountains were behind, and in the case of a defeat the attacking army would have been smashed against those mountains and destroyed with no hope. Who would be so foolish as to risk that much?

Eugene decided to bring the army there. It meant to march along a wide circle, from south to north, passing through the west. A special corps had to support the manoeuvre: it had to come from south-east, and approach the enemy field fortifications on the opposite side, on the right of the Po. That would attract the attention of the French, who probably would not attack

Turin from Superga as Victor Amadeus and Eugene saw it on 2 September 1706 – the citadel lies on the opposite side of the city.

neither the right wing, nor the back of the large moving Austro-Piedmontese army until it had finished the crossing to the left bank of the Po. Then the special corps had to stay on the opposite side of the city. At last it had to approach the hills, acting as a deterrent against Albergotti, remaining close to him. In case there was an opportunity, the special corps had to ship a gunpowder and food convoy to Turin.

On 4 September the Allied army, 30,000 strong – 28,000 Imperial infantry and cavalry, and 2,000 Ducal cavalry – was split into three columns, crossed the Po to Carignano, and stopped on the small River Sangone, between Mirafiori and Beinasco. Meanwhile the special corps, commanded by the Count of Santena and more than 9,000 Piedmontese militia strong, followed a route diverging 45 degrees to the right, and moved from Carmagnola to Chieri. On the evening of the same day the French launched the last general assault on the citadel of Turin. They were repulsed with very serious casualties.

On the 5th the Austro-Piedmontese three columns continued their march towards Rivoli. They maintained the French circumvallation on their right, eight kilometres away. Their right column included the infantry, the left one the cavalry, the central column was composed of carriages and artillery. Basically it was the scheme adopted by Eugene in the march along the Roman Wall in Hungary, just before Zenta, nine years before. In case of attack, it would have allowed him to take position in battle order just by a simple turn to the right.

However the besiegers did not move, even if the day before the Duke of Orléans, still convinced like all his generals that Prince Eugene, and the Duke of Savoy would never dare to attack, had proposed again to go out and offer battle. But, once more, he got no result.

Eugene and Victor Amadeus March around Turin on 3–5 September 1706.

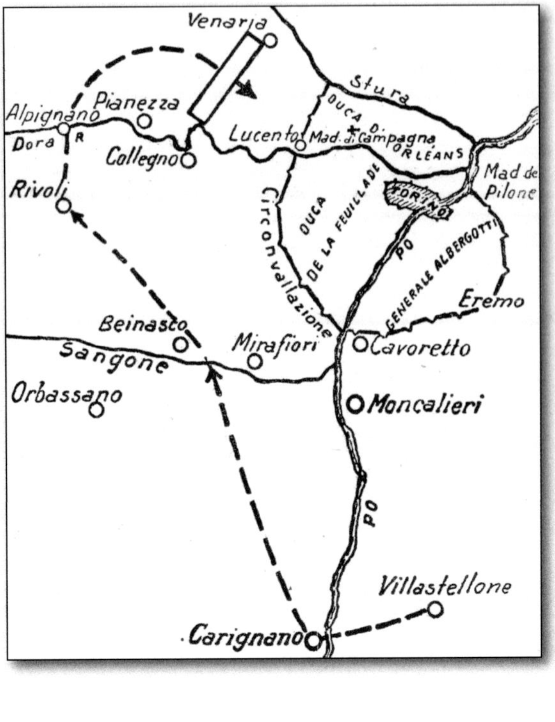

As the march proceeded, Eugene was warned that an enemy convoy of over 1,000 mules, escorted by 400 or 500 cavalry, was approaching Turin from Susa. He ordered Visconti to take two cavalry brigades – Monasterolo, and Falkenstein – and to capture it. Visconti accomplished the task. The escort was destroyed, and the convoy split into three parts. The smallest – 200 mules – managed to enter friendly lines. Another part of the convoy was taken, and the biggest escaped into the castle of Pianezza, garrisoned by the French. Being a castle, the cavalry was no longer needed and command passed to the Old Dessau, who surrounded the castle, heard its refusal to surrender, attacked, and let his grenadiers enter through a tunnel whose exit was in the basement. Then the Prussians seized the castle and the convoy, and destroyed the garrison.

This news of Pianezza depressed the French soldiers, and the generals had their first doubts. That could be the first act of the feared cutting of their communications, but it could also be something else. What had Eugene in mind? Where was he going? Perhaps it would have been better to close the section between Stura, and Dora by a circumvallation, thus orders were issued to begin the work on the following day, 6 September.

On 6 September 1706 the Allied army crossed the Dora at Alpignano, upstream of Pianezza, and settled between the Dora and the Stura, looking eastward and having the mountains on its back. It was now perpendicular to the extremity of the right wing of the Duke d'Orléans. Many other things happened on that day. On the other side of the Po, the Count of Santena approached the French lines from Chieri, and got the result Eugene wanted. "The Duke of La Feuillade, and Marshal of Marsin did not want to leave the hills fearing that the enemy from that part would rescue Turin."[11]

Old Dessau's Troopers Storm the Castle of Pianezza.

In Turin, Count Daun saw the fires lit on the hill of Superga to announce the forthcoming battle, and kept his operational corps ready. It was a matter of 2,100 men – 1,600 foot, and 500 cavalry – with six cannons: it would be the 34th sally since the beginning of the siege.

According to their orders, the French troopers dug a long circumvallation entrenchment between the Dora and the Stura, preparing an earth wall, neither very high or thick, with a shallow ditch. Meanwhile the artillery was to set 39 cannons there, that is to say a gun every 100 yards. La Feuillade ceded to insistent demands from the Duke of Orléans and Marshall Marsin, and gave them six battalions and 34 squadrons to strengthen their sector.

Three people wrote that day. In the camp in front of Turin, the Duke of Orléans was writing a letter to his uncle Louis XIV reiterating that he wanted to get out of the lines to attack:

> but these gentlemen, whose experience and preparation I have to trust more than myself, find so many and so important inconveniences in this idea, that it is not appropriate, during my fresh command, to take such a serious decision on my own opinion … and if we were so fortunate that the enemies would attack us, which I dare neither hope nor fear, I will procure just … not to give bad examples to your Majesty's troops.[12]

11 De Mauroy, rep. in Assum, *L'assedio ecc…*, cit., p.190.

12 Philippe d'Orléans to Louis XIV, from Turin, 6 September 1706, rep. in de Vault, op. cit., 1706, p.277.

In Versailles, Louis XIV was answering him:

> The letter I received from you, begun on the 30th of last month, and completed on 31st, tells me the difficult situation you are in, due to the conditions of the siege … You ask me for orders about what you have to do, and tell me that you believe that the only way to prevent the evils from which you are threatened … would be to give battle.
>
> Although I am, like you, persuaded that the result would be favourable, I think … that it is more prudent not to risk it … and to think only of preserving what remains of my infantry, and preventing the enemy from occupying the territories of the domination of Spain …
>
> When taking this decision, which seems obliged to me, it is not possible to continue the siege of Turin … what I write to you sufficiently authorises you to do what you consider most convenient for the sake of my service, and if you stop the siege, as I do not have reason to doubt, take all the necessary measures …[13]

But the long-awaited permission would come too late because, at the Venaria camp, Eugene wrote at that same time: "Tomorrow, God liking, we shall march against the enemy lines in the prescribed ways, and in the following order …"[14]

13 Louis XIV to Philippe d'Orléans, from Versailles, 6 September 1706, rep. in de Vault, op. cit., 1706, pp.285–6.

14 *Disposition pour la bataille de Turin, faite au Camp de la Venerie le 6 7.bre 1706*, [Dispositions for the battle of Turin, made at the Camp of Venaria on 6 September 1706] Vienna manuscript, rep. in D. Guerrini, *I Granatieri di Sardegna 1659–1900* (Rome, 1969), Appendix, p.743. It must be noted that the text reported by Guerrini has, in parallel, on two columns two of the four different versions of that order known up to now. The first is the best known, after the manuscript from Vienna Kriegsarchiv, in Italia 1706, IX, 12, which in origin was published by Mayerhofer and Komers. The second is in the less known manuscript 287bis in the Biblioteca Reale di Torino, published by the first time by Guerrini in the first edition of his book, in 1902. The third and the fourth appeared in 2006, thanks to research by Count Giuseppe Balbiano d'Aramengo, when preparing the celebration of the third centennial of the siege, and both resulted, after a careful compared analysis I was asked for, two versions of the Vienna manuscript, shortened, or slightly modified in the succession of the orders. I will report parts of the first two versions, and in the next chapter they will be identified as Vienna MS and Turin MS respectively.

18

The Battle of Turin

Eugene's orders for the attack stated that:

> An hour before the day, the cavalry will saddle without sounding the trumpet; infantry without rolling the drum will also be set for marching, and the whole army, at daybreak will be ready to march.[1]
>
> The infantry will have the vanguard, and all the Grenadiers will gather ahead the Prussian infantry …. The infantry will be in eight columns, so the two lines will form four columns each … all the Grenadiers will march before the Stillen Brigade; the field guns will be among the Battalions according to the distribution that will have been made … the cannons will be placed between the Battalions and the space from one Battalion to the next will be 20 or 30 steps.[2]
>
> The second line will do the same thing, but will leave larger intervals so that in the event of confusion the battalions of the 1st line may be reformed behind them, and also to let the cavalry pass when it will be necessary for them to act[3] … and nobody will shoot without having a positive order by his officer. After the enemy line has been taken, the Grenadiers and the first line will be in formation, until further notice, providing for the Cavalry gaps to pass through.[4]
>
> The squadrons of the 1st line will have a space of 15 to 20 steps from one to the next, and those of the 2nd line will have a space of 40 steps.[5]
>
> After that Infantry will have taken their place in the enemies' line, the Cavalry will pass through the openings that the Infantry will have left, and will settle to take advantage of the Enemy confusion: and in the event that they [the enemies] gather, [the cavalry] will charge immediately and pursue them with the Infantry to take away the time and the means to get back on track."[6]

---

1 *Disposition pour la bataille de Turin, faite au Camp de la Venerie le 6 7.bre 1706*, Vienna Ms, rep. in Guerrini, op. cit., p.743 The numbers 6 7.bre mean 6 September, being "Septem"ber, the seventh month according to the Latin calendar, thus shortened in post-Latin languages as Italian, and French in "7.bre".

2 *Disposition pour la bataille de Turin, faite au Camp de la Venerie le 6 7.bre 1706*, Turin Ms, rep. in Guerrini, op. cit., pp.743–744.

3 *Disposition pour la bataille de Turin,…*cit., Vienna Ms, rep. in Guerrini, op. cit., p 744.

4 *Disposition pour la bataille de Turin,…*cit., Turin Ms, rep. in Guerrini, op. cit., p.744.

5 *Disposition pour la bataille de Turin,…*cit., Vienna Ms, rep. in Guerrini, op. cit., p.745.

6 *Disposition pour la bataille de Turin,…*cit., Turin Ms, rep. in Guerrini, op. cit., p.746.

> The Hussars will march in front of the left wing on the main road and will already have the order about what they will have to do.[7] … The supply train and the sick will remain behind, and gather in front of the right wing, where they will obey the Major of the Old Guard following the orders by the Generals.[8]

Therefore, at dawn on 7 September 1706, that is to say shortly after half past five in the morning, "God liking", the Allied army marched "against the enemy lines in the prescribed ways" while the enemy was still asleep; and gave him an abrupt wake-up call.

> At six o'clock in the morning His Highness [the Duke of Orléans] was warned that the enemies were marching towards us in battle order. Monsieur de Marsin could not yet be persuaded that the enemies really wanted to attack us.[9] His Royal Highness disposed as best he could the few troops and sent orders to those closest to him to come; but they did not arrive in time.[10]
>
> I believe that there were not more than 16–17 battalions on the line when the enemies attacked it: the troops who could intervene arrived panting, and only when the enemies had already forced our right and entered our trenches.[11]

In total confusion the French troops of the northern sector rushed to their places, while requests for reinforcements were sent in great haste to La Feuillade. Eugene had not only taken the enemy completely by surprise, but also fulfilled the dream of every commander: with the same forces in the operational theatre – 44,000 French–Spaniards against about 42,500 Austro-Piedmontese – he got local superiority, and got it overwhelmingly: from 3 to 1 at the beginning, until 2 to 1 at the end. To his 30,000 men ready to fight – 24,000 infantry, 3,500 Imperial cavalry, and 2,500 Piedmontese cavalrymen and dragoons – the Duke of Orléans, and Marshal Marsin could oppose with only 8,000 foot, and 5,000 cavalry, who increased to 16,000 after the arrival of the 3,000 dragoons La Feuillade sent after their desperate dispatches.

Moreover, the French position was ugly also due to its location. The northern sector was in a sort of rectangle. It had on one short side the enemy, on the opposite side the Po, and as its long lateral sides the Stura and the Dora Riparia rivers. From the former to the latter, the road ran from Turin close, and parallel to, the Po. It crossed the Dora just outside the city, then it crossed the Stura and at last continued towards Aosta and Chivasso.

In short: the French position was a trap that one could leave only through three sides: through the bridge to Turin's Palazzo Gate, where the Allied garrison was; through the bridge on the Stura to Aosta and Chivasso; and

7 *Disposition pour la bataille de Turin,…*cit., Vienna Ms, rep. in Guerrinii, op. cit., p.745.

8 *Disposition pour la bataille de Turin,…*cit., Turin Ms, rep. in Guerrini, op. cit., p.744.

9 It was a sort of destiny: Marsin had been one of the commanding generals at Blenheim. There too the French did not expect the enemy to attack, there too the Allies appeared on the ground very early in the morning, and that was so surprising that no French or Bavarian general could believe to an attack until the Allies moved ahead. At Blenheim Marsin had been with the Elector of Bavaria, on the wing just against Eugene.

10 De Mauroy, rep. in Assum: *Eugenio di Savoia*, cit.,p.141.

11 De Chamarande to Chamillarti, rep. in Assum, *L'assedio..ecc*, cit. p.198.

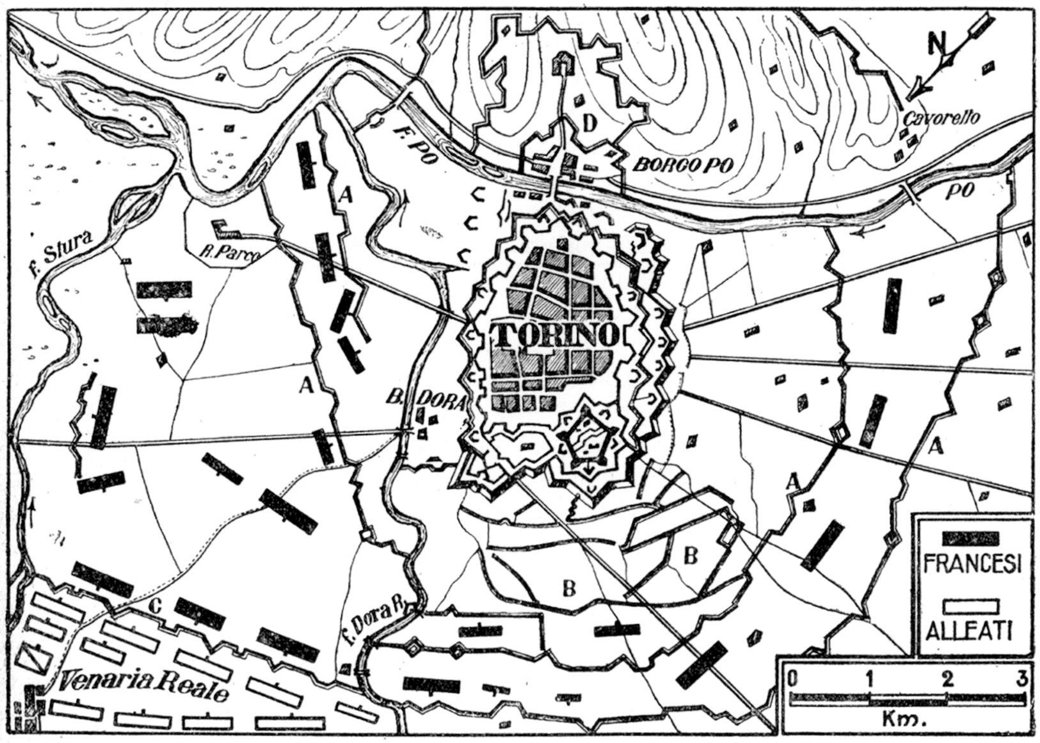

Battaglia di Torino (1706)
A, trinceramenti ossidionali francesi; *B*, apertura delle parallele; *C*, nuovo trinceramento contro l'esercito alleato; *D*, testa di ponte oltre il Po

Turin: a general view of the whole battle theatre. The incoming Allies are in the lower left corner.

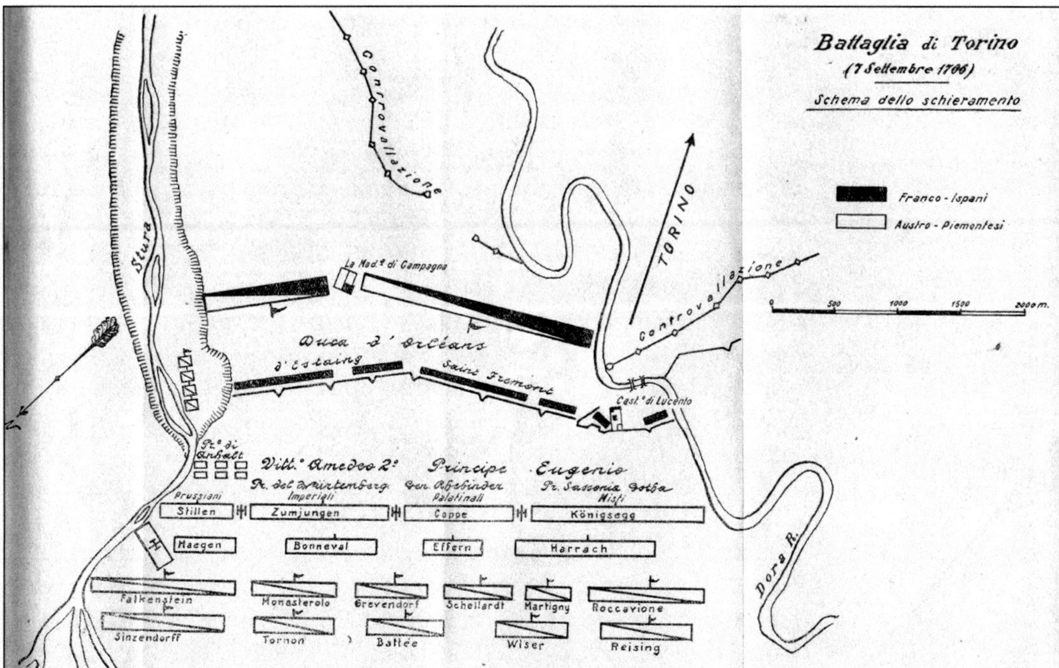

The Battlefield at Turin.

through the third and last bridge, crossing the Dora, near the castle of Lucento, a strongpoint of the French left wing, close to the first line.

Eugene's idea was very simple. He wanted to break through the enemy right wing, and with a semicircular movement like a broad swath from his left to his right, he wanted to leave only two choices to his enemies: to flee through the Lucento bridge before it was too late, or to have their back to the Dora. In short: he wanted to cut them the way to the bridge crossing the Stura, wanted to push them more or less on Lucento, and with the help of Daun's sally from Palazzo Gate, he hoped to open his way towards Palazzo Gate and break the blockade of the city.

The two armies spent the whole morning setting their lines. The Allied left wing had to pierce the enemy lines and rush to join the sallying garrison. That was why both Eugene and Victor Amadeus were there, and why the Piedmontese cavalry was concentrated there. Victor Amadeus, as was usual to him, advanced much faster than necessary, arrived within the enemy guns' range, and was forced to retreat slightly. It was still too early.

Between 11:00 a.m. and noon the Allied army became fully ready and stood, as Eugene had ordered, out of the range of the enemy cannons. Then Eugene, with his usual gesture, barely moved his right hand, silently giving the order: "advance". Under the concerned and wishful eyes of thousands of citizens crowding the terraces, the roofs, and the bell towers, and accompanied by the prayers to God of thousands of other citizens in their churches, the Allied soldiers advanced in squared order, rifles on their shoulders, under the fire of enemy infantry and artillery. Ten steps far from the enemy they stopped, aimed, and shot a deadly volley. Then, bayonets fixed, they attacked.

The first attempt by the German grenadiers and by the Old Dessau was repulsed by the French. They were supported by Hagen, and the Prussians started a new attack on their left.

More or less in that moment, the Imperial hussars reported to Victor Amadeus. The Stura at that time of the year was dry and shallow. They found the bed of the river passable and unwatched. Victor Amadeus let all the hussars, his household, and some grenadier companies go down into the river bed, along it, overpass the extremity of the enemy right wing, climb the bank on their side and behind them, and attack. The French right wing collapsed, and fell back in disorder.

Then the Imperial infantry split in two. A part converged to their right, and continued the attack against the enemy line. When doing so, a breach appeared in the Allied line, because the other part commanded by the Prince of Württemberg was pushing forward, and did not stop on the former enemy line as Eugene had ordered.

The French cavalry tried to exploit the situation, charged and tried to crush the Prussians, who were rescued by the volleys of two Imperial battalions, and by the former enemy cannons they had just seized in a redoubt. Eugene rushed in, settled the disorder, urged the sappers to widen the breaches in the field fortifications, and let Visconti's Imperial cavalry charge the French cavalry. While the enemy bullets killed a page and a valet around him, Eugene's horse was struck and he fell into a trench, and came

The Battle of Turin.

out immediately, untamed, muddy, and bloody, asking for another horse, and ordering another attack.

In fact the French cavalry had just gathered again, but was charged again by Visconti, by Langallerie with the second line, and by the Duke of Savoy, "who at the head of the dragoons and of the Piedmontese Guards fought ardently". The French cavalry was outnumbered, and overwhelmed. Its casualties were huge, and the survivors fled across the Dora, or across the Stura to Chivasso. Some fled towards Milan.

The French infantry realised they were no longer supported, and escaped also, trying to gather near, and around the small church of the Madonna di Campagna.

The French right wing was vanishing, then the drama of their left began. The French left relied on the Castle of Lucento, and was commanded by Philip d'Orléans and Marshal Marsin. Reinforced by the 3,000 dragoons sent by La Feuillade, until that moment they had held against General Rhebinder's and the Prince of Saxe-Gotha's attacks.

It had not been easy. Philip had been wounded in the hip and took three rifle shots in his armour, but wanted to stay and remained until, almost simultaneously, two things happened: the troops of the right wing still holding at the Madonna di Campagna were overwhelmed, and he and

Marsin were injured. Marsin was mortally hit. Philip was wounded in the arm so badly that this time he had to leave.

At that moment Eugene rode up and brought his men the good news about the prevailing Imperial left, and then led a new assault. This time the French trenches were seized. Then the Imperial lines opened like the two halves of a gate, and their cavalry charged: it was the end. The French collapsed and fled in disorder toward the Lucento bridge. The castle garrison, supported by dragoons, held and stopped the men of the Prince of Saxe-Gotha. This allowed the survivors of the French left wing to cross, but an additional disaster was coming upon them: Daun.

Daun had carefully followed the battle from the walls of Turin. Around noon, assessing that the best moment had arrived, he left the city through Palazzo Gate along with his 2,100 men, and six cannons. When he reached the battleground the French right, the closest to him, had already collapsed, thus he marched to Lucento and committed his cavalry against the castle, and along the Dora to cut off the retreating enemies. Then he set his 1,600 infantrymen behind the Franco-Spanish centre, just when it was retreating, and let them shoot.

Given the situation, the garrison of Lucento set fire to the warehouses. Then, pressed from all sides, it crossed the bridges over the Dora, and blew them. This temporarily stopped the Imperial advance, but cut off all the French from the centre and from the right wing. They were now between Daun, Prince Eugene, and the river: they could only surrender, and they did.

Meanwhile, under Turin, La Feuillade was still unaware of what was happening. He was fulfilling his daily duty by bombarding the citadel when, a bit after mid-day, the first fugitives came from the battlefield. Tattered, unarmed, untidy, and terrified, they rushed among La Feuillade's regiments spreading panic with the few things they knew, enhanced by fear: the bridges blown, Lucento lost, the army massacred, the enemy incoming. Rumours spread quickly and the troops under the city, fearing to be taken between the garrison and the arriving Austrians, disintegrated and fled, abandoning weapons, carriages and materials. The battle was over.

The first scattered Allied teams who reached Turin confirmed to the citizens the spreading uncontrolled rumours about victory. Their arrival also caused some surprises. For instance when, fatigued and affected by heat, some Prussians arrived, one of their officers:

> coming in through Palazzo Gate with his clothes in disorder, dirty due to dust, and blood, breathless, and burned by thirst, entered a cafe belonging to a certain widow Arignano, and, to the astonishment of the boys, of the owner, and of the client, he, almost out of mind, emptied water bowls furiously, and made a great crash of pots, and crystals ...[12]

He broke a huge quantity of glasses and bottles to drink faster, under the astonished eyes of the customers. Refreshed, and rested, he would later take

12 Domenico Carutti, *Storia del Regno di Vittorio Amedeo II* (Florence, 1863), p.299.

part in the solemn entrance of their Royal and Most Serene Highnesses, and the astonished coffee clients would recognise him: the Prince of Anhalt-Dessau.

Meanwhile Victor Amadeus and Eugene reached the hill called Mount Valentino, observed the enemy movements, and realised that a rapid and disordered retreat was occurring. A hasty council of war held by the surviving French generals who escaped the fight – the Duke of Orléans was barely on his feet, Marsin had been picked up on the field and was dying in a farmhouse, de Murcey had been captured, Albergotti was far away at his headquarters over the hills – decided to completely abandon the siege and retreat to Pinerolo. The two cousins of Savoy committed their cavalry against the columns in disorder, then, followed by all the allied princes, they solemnly entered liberated Turin around six in the evening, about an hour and a half before sundown.[13] They stopped in the Cathedral's "great square" – which is not that wide – and were received with a blessing by Archbishop Vibò in pontifical dress; then the Duke bade him start singing the Te Deum.

After the Te Deum, Eugene and Victor Amadeus inspected the citadel and finally – since they had not eaten anything since dawn – had dinner at Daun's residence, Graneri Palace. After dinner the Duke went back home, that is to say walked to the Royal Palace, not far, just at the back of the cathedral.

Meanwhile, military movements continued during the night. The French army continued to flow toward Pinerolo, harassed by the Austrian–Piedmontese cavalry. Another part, pursued by the Imperialists, retired that evening to the Hill district, not yet abandoned, because Albergotti continued to hold the position. But after midnight he too withdrew, so as not to be encircled by the Count of Santena's troops.

The next morning the first reports revealed a truly unexpected truth to the Allies. They knew they had achieved a great victory, but the liquefaction of the enemy troops turned it from tactical into a strategic victory, and the French flight to Pinerolo, far away from Lombardy, and from the only efficient army the Two Crowns still had, rendered that victory definitive.

---

13 According to an ancient tradition, when solemnly entering Turin the Prussians played the *Alte-Dessauer marsch* – the *March of the Old Dessau* – they adopted after an Italian song at Cassano in 1705. It is still a best-loved march, regularly played by German military bands, and regularly welcome by the public, due to the long, hard to play and virtuoso trumpet solo in its central part. Unfortunately, by a philological point of view that solo is completely fake. A Baroque era march followed rigid rules. It was composed according to the so-called ABA scheme. "A" was a first short tune, "B" was a second short tune differing from "A", then "A" – now becoming the second A – was played again. *The British Grenadiers* is a perfect example. Not by chance, when applying the ABA scheme, one realises the part of *Alt Dessauer* without trumpet to be just the original march. Apart from that, an infantry march was never played by trumpets, but by fifes and drums, because trumpets were for cavalry. Well, one could say, that was a cavalry march. No, it was not, and there is an additional evidence, As they were produced – handcrafted – at that time, and until deep into the second half of the eighteenth century, trumpets could not play tunes other than in Re maggiore – D-dur in the Anglosaxon way. A perfect example of what a D-dur tune sounds like, is the famous *Trumpet Voluntary*, by Clarke, long ago attributed to Purcell, whose title is *Trumpet Voluntary and March of the Prince of Denmark*. Those long extended sounds are the only way a trumpet in the early eighteenth century could play. Thus, when entering Turin, the Prussians played *Der alte Dessauer*, but not as it is played now, because they used only fifes, and drums.

Casualty figures provided evidence. The Allies lost 947 dead and 2,304 wounded,[14] that is to say, only 10 percent of their force on the battlefield, and 7.65 percent of the committed total force. The French–Spanish casualties, not considering the huge number of deserters, which is still unknown, were 2,550 dead, and 1,500 wounded. Then one had to add prisoners: 197 officers, and 5,210 soldiers, so, the total figure was 9,500 men, that is to say 59.5 percent of the committed force, and 21.5 percent of the total besieging army.

Moreover the French abandoned their warehouses, and the escorts of food, fodder, and weapons. They managed to burn only most of the gunpowder. Thus more than 4,000 mules, horses, and oxen were found, along with 220 guns – 164 cannons, and 56 mortars – and amazing quantities of ordnance.[15] Victor Amadeus got all, including the money the enemies left: 22,000 golden Louis, and four "jewels with portraits of the King" valued altogether a further 60,000 lire. Animals for train and cavalry, food, ordnance, cannons, money: the Ducal army could be reorganised, and fight again.

14 The garrison, excluding the eight city militia battalions, was reduced to 3,570 fit for duty, that is to say 187 officers, 134 sergeants and 3,249 corporals and privates, and 1,918 wounded. Piedmontese wounded were 1,889, Imperials were only 29. Dead were 1,584 (only 20 Imperialists died), but there were 1,992 deserters, according to Daun and Hackbrett, cit:, *tués, blésses et désertérs 5.120*. Including the militia there were 4,876 men fit for duty by the end of the siege.

15 According to Count Solaro della Margarita, who created a detailed list, the Piedmontese found 1,590 rubbi (14,660 kilogrammes) of gunpowder, 86,500 flints, 102,273 cannonballs, 1,689 cannon bombs, 1,590 howitzer bombs, 14,832 handgrenades, and 168 cannon beds.

19

The Conquest of Lombardy

Philip of Orléans at Pinerolo, to Louis XIV, 8 September 1706:

> I send a courier to Your Majesty to inform you that the enemies have relieved Turin. They attacked yesterday, 7 September, the line between the Dora, and Stura. This was how it had been possible to make it in twenty-four hours, because there was none when I arrived at the army.
>
> Since we could not put behind it more than a line of infantry, because it had not been deemed appropriate on the previous day to reduce the posts on the hills as I had recommended, the enemies broke the line, breaking our line in two.[1]

On the same day another courier gave Philip the letter by which his uncle and the King authorised him to stop the siege. In that moment the situation of the Duke of Orléans was disastrous. Due to casualties his men were reduced to a half. The only militarily still valid force was that of Albergotti, and the Allied threat persisted.

Indeed Victor and Eugene let General Martigny's cavalry brigade occupy and bar the ford of the Dora and Pianezza, to prevent the French from returning to the State of Milan. Additional cavalry continued harassing and attacking the French rearguards still streaming into Pinerolo, where food started lacking. In a few days the supply situation was so bad that the French had only grapefruit and nuts to eat, and the bread price inflated to seven Piedmontese liras.

The Duke of Orléans summoned a council of war, and they decided to cross the Alps and withdraw to Dauphiné instead of trying to join the army in Lombardy, for had they tried they were sure to be destroyed en route.

As soon as the French retreated beyond the Alps, Eugene and Victor Amadeus turned to the elimination of the remaining enemy strongpoints in Italy. They started from Piedmont. It was easy, because the destruction of the fortresses during the two previous campaigns left the French with no fortified support. So, thanks to the Piedmontese militia, they quickly recovered all of Piedmont, and ejected the enemy from the Aosta Valley and from the fort of Bard.

---

1 Philippe d'Orléans to Louis XIV, from Pinerolo, 8 September 1706, rep. in de Vault, op. cit., 1706, p.283.

The Fortifications of Pinerolo in the Eighteenth Century.

Then they went to Vercelli, detaching a corps to besiege Chivasso, which fell with its whole 1,000-man garrison in a few days. The same happened in Crescentino, while the Allied army seized all the warehouses and depots the enemies had in the area.

The next step was to Novara. The Milanese garrison was small, compared to the extension of the walls – 800 Italians, Spaniards and Swiss – and even arming the inhabitants it had no possibility to hold, so the Governor left the city on 20 September with all his men.

On 22 September, protected by 12 guns and some grenadier companies, the Allies crossed the Ticino river. On the 24th they were in Corsico, four miles from Milan. Old Vaudémont had already gone to Mantua, just leaving a couple of French battalions to strengthen the garrison of the castle.

Abandoned to itself the city administration surrendered after an invitation by Eugene's aide de camp, and on the 24th submitted the city to the Emperor. On 26 September 1706, at 5:00 p.m., the two cousins formally entered Milan, greeted with joy by the inhabitants.

The army remained in Milan a few days, just enough time to organise the new government, and blockade the castle. Eugene did not waste time arranging a full siege. He wanted not to fatigue his troops, and knew hunger would soon prevail upon the garrison's will.

The two cousins of Savoy continued their march towards the Adda, to force Médavy to abandon his positions between that river and the Oglio and to withdraw toward Mantua. Lodi was blockaded, and surrendered at the first call. Daun was then sent to besiege Pavia, whose 2,000 men seemed willing to hold. But after a few cannon shots, due to pressure from the population and the urban militia, the French commander preferred to lock himself in the castle. He left it the following day by capitulation with all military honours. The Imperialists found a full food warehouse, and a good artillery.

Since there were still many places to seize, and not that much time before it was time to go into winter quarters, the cousins shared the tasks. Victor Amadeus took care of Pizzighettone; Eugene besieged Tortona and Alessandria. The city of Tortona surrendered spontaneously, allowing the Imperialists to immediately blockade the citadel. Alessandria decided to hold out, but in mid October its gunpowder storage exploded; on 21 October the Governor, the Count of Colmenero, agreed to surrender and, indeed, passed into Imperial service.

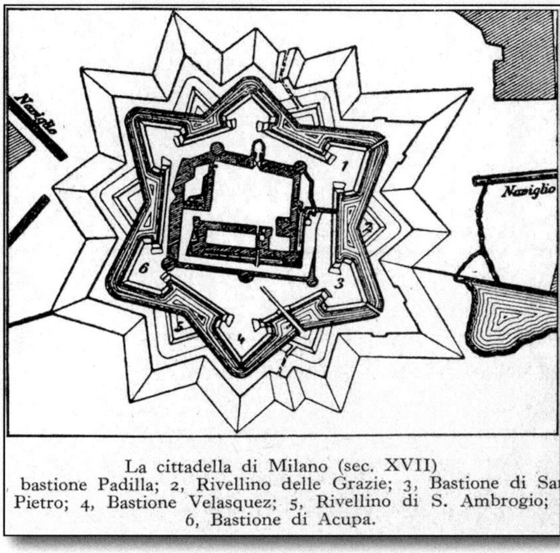

Plan of the Citadel and Castle of Milan.

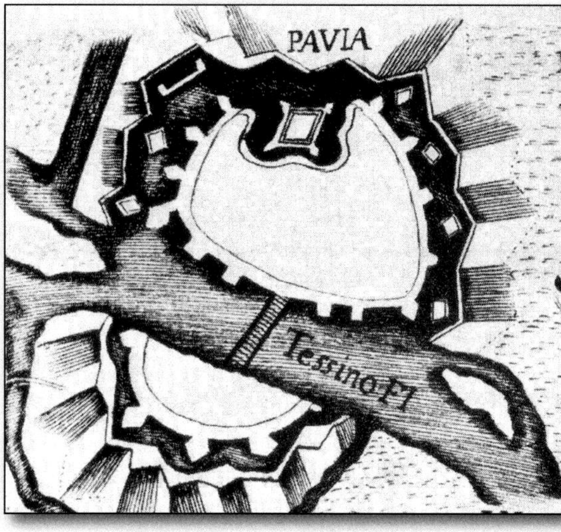

Plan of the Fortifications of Pavia.

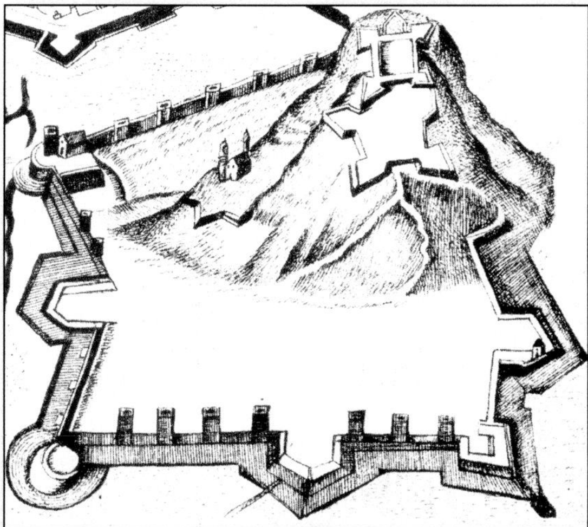

Plan of the Fortifications of Tortona.

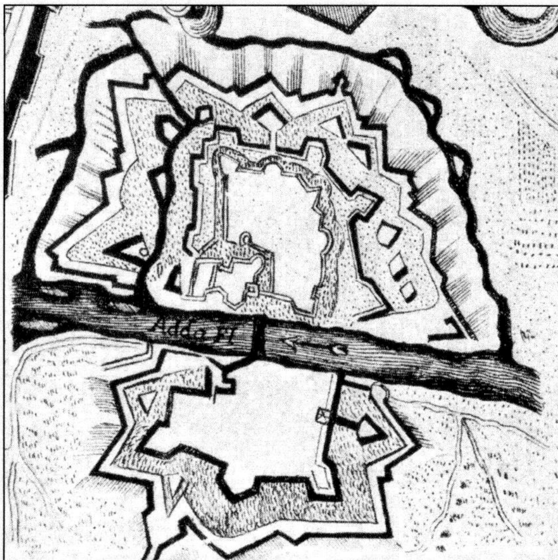

Plan of the Fortifications of Pizzighettone.

Victor Amadeus besieged Pizzighettone which, with the neighbouring fort of Gera, or Ghiara, d'Adda constituted perhaps the hardest obstacle in the whole of Lombardy, and took it on 29 October. He allowed the garrison to leave with military honours, and four cannons.

At the same time the Imperial generals seized all the other fortresses – Arona, Trezzo, the fort of Fuentes, Mortara – and sent cavalry teams downstream along the Oglio and in the Cremonese.

The news of so many disasters came to Louis XIV, and to the Duke of Orléans, and convinced them to try an offensive return to Italy. Philip gathered troops, weapons, wagons, animals, and 100 covered wagons, then summoned his generals to a council of war in Briançon. At first it was thought to land La Feuillade with some battalions in Liguria to rescue Tortona and retake Alessandria; but before it was possible to begin, Eugene had discovered the plan and settled in the area with huge forces. Moreover, Eugene foresaw also a possible attempt through Switzerland, if any, and when the Marquis de Vibray with 4,000 men tried to seize the Aosta Valley, generals Saint-Rémy and la Roche d'Allery cut him off. After a further examination of the situation, Louis XIV suspended any further move and summoned his nephew back to the court.

This news reassured the Austrian–Piedmontese command, and the fortresses continued to surrender. The citadel of Tortona was stormed on 28 November and the garrison was massacred, commanders included. Casale Monferrato, without walls since the end of the Nine Years' War, agreed with the Duke of Savoy the exit of the wounded and the sick before the beginning of the siege; then the garrison surrendered on 6 December, after 13 days.

Given the bad situation, on the opposite side of Lombardy the French evacuated Castiglione delle Stiviere and Guastalla, and locked themselves into Mantua, Ostiglia and the Serraglio, taking the winter quarters with supplies from Ferrarese and Venetia.

The Imperial army did the same. Eugene stationed the cavalry in the Cremonese, and Mantuan areas, ordered the blockade of the places still raising Philip V's flag, and delegated Wetzel to besiege Modena. That French garrison, as soon as it saw the Imperial troopers climbing the walls, entered the citadel and held out until February, when it surrendered to the Duke

Casale seized.

of Modena. Only the castle of Milan remained; and Eugene calmly took care. That fortress was imposing and well built, with two rings of walls – an ancient and a modern one, the latter with six bastions – a deep moat and well-stocked arsenals. It was short of food, however.

The governor, the Spanish Marquess de la Florida, refused to surrender and threatened to bomb the city if it did not supply him with food throughout the siege. Eugene allowed the city administration to negotiate. In exchange for a supply of wine, meat, and rice at a value of 2,000 doubles, they obtained a truce until 1 February and de la Florida's promise not to fire on the city had the castle been attacked only from the countryside or from the side of the gardens. On 1 February the truce expired, and was not renewed. Eugene notified the Marquess that it was useless to bomb Milan: had de la Florida done it, the citizens would not be able to provide him with food. Moreover, had he bombed it, de la Florida could be sure that as soon as the castle surrendered – something Eugene had no doubt about, as he said – he would have been treated as an arsonist, which implicitly meant to be hanged with his whole garrison.

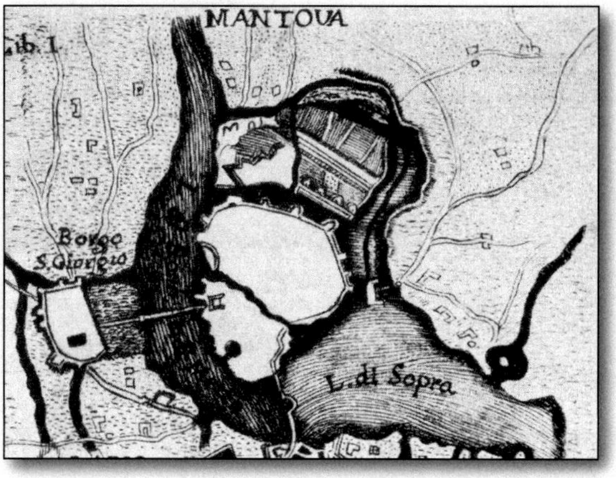

Mantua from above.

De la Florida was stubborn, and insisted. On 24 February he started firing. Eugene took his time. He began the approaches from the west side, where there were gardens, and a few houses, then replied to la Florida with artillery. He set more than 20 cannons in Santa Lucia facing the ramparts of Padilla, and Don Pedro. He put another battery against the inner enclosure commanding those ramparts, a third one against the so-called Torriani, three more batteries of mortars here, and there, and left Daun continuing the siege.

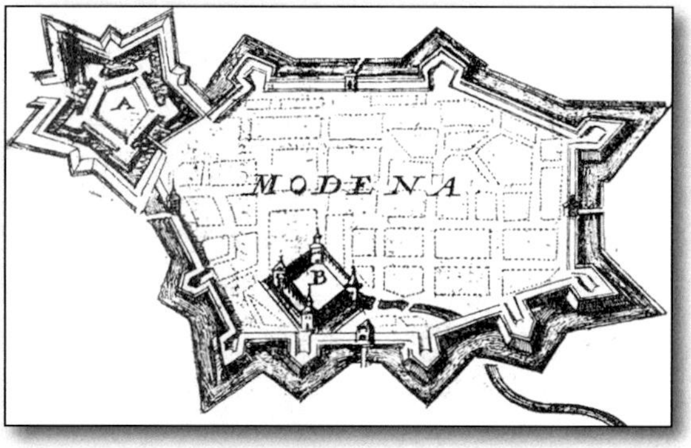

The Fortifications of Modena.

Eugene was in no hurry either because he was waiting for hunger to take effect, and above all because negotiations were underway for the evacuation of the French from Italy, and that would involve the fall of the Castle of Milan due to a good half – the French half – of the garrison leaving it.

And so it was. Louis XIV had such a need of troops in Flanders and in Spain that he did not think he could keep any in Italy. In mid December 1706 he ordered Saint-Pater to start talks with Prince Eugene. The talk turned into negotiations, and on 13 March 1707 the French plenipotentiaries Saint-Pater, and Javelier

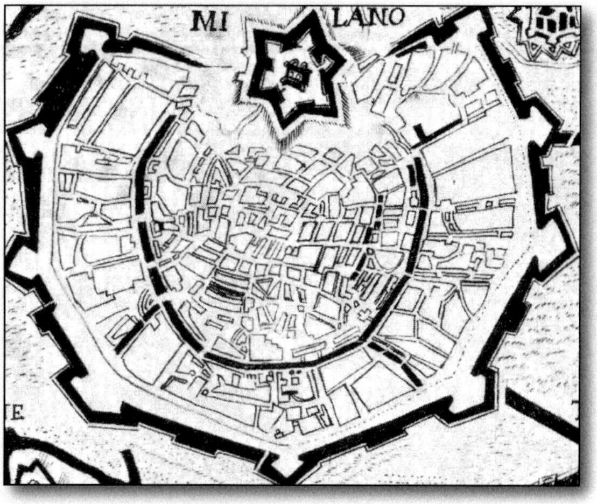

Plan View of Milan.

met their Imperial counterparts Daun and Schlick, and signed the treaty. According to it, the French had to leave the Castle of Milan, and the places and citadels of Mantua, Cremona, Sabbioneta, Mirandola, Valenza, and Finale Ligure. They had then to concentrate in Susa, carrying with them no more than 14 big-calibre and 24 field guns, with 50 shots for each of the former, and 40 shots for each of the latter.

They could take as much food as they wanted from their stocks, and sell the rest. Austrian and Piedmontese deserters enlisted in French units would be forgiven, and allowed to return to their original regiments. Lastly, there had to be an exchange of all the prisoners kept in Italy.

The treaty was extended to the Spaniards, and ratified by Vaudémont in Mantua on 14 March and by Victor Amadeus II on the 16th in Turin. As

Susa, Seen from the Citadel.

Eugene Presents Captured French Flags to Joseph I.

Charles III of Habsburg, King of Spain.

Emperor Joseph I.

expected, it provoked the surrender of the castle of Milan. Eugene had been appointed governor of Milan on 22 September, and took official possession of it in the name of Charles III of Spain.

It was not in Joseph I's name, because the "Pactum mutuae successionis" of 12 September 1703 directed that the Spanish succession had to go to Charles, whilst Joseph would receive the Empire, and the hereditary territories of the House of Austria. However, a previous secret agreement was added. It stated that the Duchy of Milan and the Marquisate of the Finale, being Imperial fiefdoms, had to be reunited to the Austrian domains, and thus had to pass to Joseph.

20

Planning Summer 1707: French Riviera[1] or Southern Italy?

Naples was a healthy portion of Spanish-ruled Italy and consistently a part of the late Charles II's inheritance. As we know, Philip V had held it since he became king. Now, in 1707, Emperor Joseph decided it was time to seize it.

We have seen how a first pro-Habsburg attempt in 1701 failed. Most of the noblemen involved in the plot escaped to Rome, and then some moved to Vienna and pressed and pushed on the court to let the Emperor attack Naples.

In winter 1701–1702 Leopold had already decided that he could do it. The Aulic War Council had tried to make him change his mind, but with no result. Thus the magician, the wizard able to solve every problem, to get big results with scanty assets had been asked: what about seizing Naples? Prince Eugene's answer was dry: he offered to resign. He absolutely refused to undertake such an idiotic expedition, but Leopold did not change his own mind: he wanted a detachment of the army of Italy to be sent to Naples. In January 1702 The papal nuncio in Vienna reported that it was possible "to deduce to that the resolution had been taken to make the decided detachment, no matter if Prince Eugene of Savoy protested against it until asking to be called back."[2]

Whatever Eugene said, Leopold insisted. According to him, Eugene had to commit Commercy and 10,000 men, along with an impressive artillery support: eight guns – six cannons and two mortars – later reduced to one falcon, and two mortars. No more guns were needed, because, because … oh, yes, "because the Marquess del Vasto is aware of artillery hidden in a certain Island", which were supposed to be enough to shell and seize "the castle" of Naples, the Emperor wrote. When considering that the name of the island remained unknown, and that Naples had four castles, instead of one as

1 The Riviera – the shore or coast – is the name generally given to the Mediterranean coast of France and Italy from west of Marseille to the harbour of La Spezia, east of Genoa. The French Côte d'Azur is part of the Riviera, and is called so only since the nineteenth century.

2 The nuntio in Vienna, Archbishop Gianantonio Davia to Cardinal Paolucci, Secretary of State, Vienna, 20 January 1702, in ASVa, *Nunziatura di Germania*, anno 1702.

Plan View of the Coast of Naples, and the City Layout.

the Emperor's letter said, one may only wonder how reliable the intelligence gathered in Vienna could be, and how successful a plan made upon it.

From Luzzara Eugene once more said no: it was impossible. He had not enough men, and a French reinforcement 4,000 strong was reported to have just landed in Naples. Leopold still argued. Eugene, one by one, sent seven letters to the Emperor, and received as an answer that His Majesty was very displeased at his stubbornness to not go to Naples, but it came with no real confutation of his reasons. Eugene thus replied underlining that if he in that moment, with no detachment sent to Naples yet, could not hold against the enemy, how will he be able to hold if the detachment left? No answer.

William III's death stopped the quarrel. In Vienna they were waiting for the announced Anglo-Dutch fleet committed to Mediterranean, and nothing more was said.

In 1703, and 1704 Eugene was in Germany, and Leopold did not suppose the Neapolitan task to be possible for anybody but Eugene, thus no pressure was applied. But, of course, as soon as things seemed to go better, that is to say in spring 1706, the Naples issue sprang up again.

In May 1706 Archduke Charles, supported by his brother the Emperor, started asking for an invasion of Naples. Eugene, as we know, was deeply engaged in the complicated operation to relieve Turin. Thus he carefully turned around the main question, simply not to give a clear negative answer, whose result would be a clear order to go south. He underlined how necessary a naval support was. He stressed that such a support could be provided only by the Maritime Powers. He was willing to do it, for sure, and, as soon as the naval support arrived, he would go. The Austrians could also commit troops other than Eugene's, he suggested, shipping the Croatian and Hungarian borderers from Trieste to Naples. Anyway, Vienna had to ask London and The Hague, but, surely neither the British nor Dutch had any intention to support such an expedition. The victory at Turin and the following conquest of Lombardy reopened the question. Charles wanted Naples, and Joseph backed him. Unfortunately, neither London nor The Hague wanted to commit a boat, a sailor, or a soldier, or to spend a penny to do it.

British plans were clear: the French Mediterranean fleet first. This meant Toulon, but Toulon could not be seized without an army, that is to say without the armies of the two Savoy cousins. Victor Amadeus did not reject the idea. He needed to secure his Alpine border, and to reconquer his lands across the Alps, thus any plan to cross the Alps sounded attractive.

If 1706 marked a turning point – if not "the" turning point – of the war, in autumn 1706 the general situation of the conflict was still unclear, although its trend was unfavourable to the Bourbons.

After Höchstadt Germany lay quietly asleep, thanks to the fortified lines of Stollhofen, and the Anglo-Dutch army led by Marlborough, was the magnet for every possible threat in Flanders. The Allied situation in Spain was good, but continued to be uncertain as long as French troops remained there. This problem had especially puzzled the English, and now they wanted to follow William III's mind: an attack to the French homeland would have the immediate result of recalling the French troops from Spain. One had only to decide where France had to be attacked, and there were several options.

Earlier, Marlborough had hypothesised an invasion of France through the valley of the Moselle river, but logistical problems made this option impractical. Another possibility was through Flanders, but this proved to be as impractical as the Moselle route. It was true that the Anglo-Dutch victory at Ramillies produced a French collapse and allowed the Allies to seize the fortresses of the Barrier, but it was also true that beyond the Barrier lay the great French fortified system organised and built by Vauban. No fewer than 40 strong places barred the way into northern France: It was impossible to lead an Allied army through them, and it was impossible to capture all of them. Thus, leaving aside a cross-Channel landing on the French coast, only one possibility remained: an invasion of France from the south-east, by way of Piedmont, just as had been done in the previous war.

It was not a new idea. William III had wanted it the first time during the War of the Grand Alliance, and in 1692 it had been done with a good result in terms of damage, but nothing in terms of strategy.

When London proposed the expedition anew in 1706 it was approved in Turin and Vienna, from both Eugene and Victor Amadeus, and from Joseph I and Charles III. However problems began when deciding how and when to launch the operation. The Austrians did not see it as their priority. They wanted Naples, and Vienna had several times requested Anglo-Dutch naval support for the operation. But Sir Cloudesley Shovell, the English commander of the Allied Mediterranean fleet, shared the strategic view of London and Marlborough, not that of Vienna and the Emperor. To his mind, the Allied fleet would be best employed supporting a land attack on Toulon, to destroy the French Mediterranean fleet, and open up the Near East to British commerce, all the way to the Dardanelles, Cyprus, and the Nile.

The Austrians were not opposed to the Toulon operation, but wanted to subordinate it to the conquest of Naples. The English, however, insisted that their idea should be given priority, and tried to bypass Vienna by going directly to Victor Amadeus. The Duke agreed to attack through the Alps, although he had some reservations about targeting Toulon rather than the Dauphiné. Anyway, since The Hague, and especially London, were going to pay a special contribution of 100,000 pounds – or 406,976.70 Piedmontese scudi, if we prefer – the Duke was not that hard to convince. Thus thanks to Admiral Sir John Norris, the English delegate with the Savoyard army, an Anglo-Piedmontese treaty was signed in February 1707, according to which London agreed to provide 40 first-class warships for the operation, along with the necessary auxiliary vessels to protect and supply the Piedmontese army in its march along the Riviera. The fleet had to transport ordnance, money, and supplies, and to carry troop reinforcements and evacuate the sick, and wounded. Moreover, the English agreed to back Victor Amadeus's territorial claims against Austria, foreseen – but not completely decided – by the alliance treaty of 1703. At the same time, Article 15 of the Anglo-Piedmontese pact absolutely ruled out any descent on Naples, considered for the moment as impossible and dangerous for the Allied cause.

Joseph I.

If anyone in London supposed the Emperor would accept it, he was sadly mistaken. Joseph had only one priority in mind: Naples and only Naples, and the other fronts were only secondary. The Habsburg brothers were grateful to their Anglo-Dutch allies, and especially to the Duke of Marlborough, for the victory at Ramillies, which had led to the acquisition of Spanish Flanders and its submission to His Catholic Majesty, Charles III of Habsburg, but they did not want to renounce Naples. The situation was also made tense by a crisis in Allied relations the previous year. Joseph I had rather unexpectedly offered Marlborough the general governorship of the Spanish Flanders, but this produced a negative reaction in the Netherlands. In the face of Dutch fury, Marlborough preferred to refuse the offer, thus arousing English anger against the Dutch and forcing Austria to reconsider its policy in the Low Countries. But this time Vienna stuck to its guns, and so did London.

Then, during this quarrel about Naples, London and The Hague received the news of the signing of the French–Imperial treaty allowing the former to withdraw their last 20,000 men from northern Italy. Clearly the British and Dutch felt betrayed by the Austrians, on whose cause they had expended so much blood and money, and who were now returning the favour by allowing substantial enemy forces to be redeployed against them in Flanders and Spain. Besides, given this kind of behaviour, who could be sure that Austria, once she had Naples, would not go on to try to conquer Sicily and Sardinia instead of helping her allies fight the common French menace?

The Maritime Powers now pushed on Vienna to secure her support for the Toulon operation. The Austrians were reminded that the Maritime Powers were ready to provide a fleet, and financial backing to support the

Duke of Savoy, and would be prepared to subsidise Imperial participation as well. In exchange, they "hoped" that Austria would agree to be "cooperative" about Toulon, especially given that Savoy had already agreed to help. As a matter of fact, the Maritime Powers knew quite well how difficult, not to say impossible, a successful attack on Naples would be without their naval support, while the French Mediterranean fleet could reinforce and resupply the Naples garrison. A victorious operation against Naples would be impossible without first neutralising the French Mediterranean fleet.

As the supreme Imperial field commander, it was up to Eugene to pronounce the last word. Eugene, however, was resolutely opposed to the idea of crossing the Maritime Alps and the Var River, and involving his army in a 110-mile march to Toulon, perhaps along narrow, winding coastal paths. Moreover, every previous invasion of France from the south had been a failure. In 1536 Eugene's and Victor Amadeus' ancestor Emperor Charles V,[3] backed by the Spanish and Genoese fleets, and with no opposition from the French navy, had been compelled to withdraw to Liguria with heavy casualties. At the end of the sixteenth century Eugene's and Victor Amadeus' great-grandfather, Duke Charles Emmanuel I, had tried to conquer the same region but without success, even if he had the support of part of the local population. When attacked, the French had always had time to put strong garrisons into the threatened places before retreating north the bulk of their army, burning and wasting everything behind them. They would halt their retreat near Lyon, where they could be easily supplied from the Rhône and Loire rivers and wait for the enemy to be exhausted, possibly speeding that up by raids on his flanks. On every occasion, the invading army had been forced to leave, pursued by the French who, descending from Lyon, were well-supplied from the Rhône as they proceeded down to Marseille and the sea.

Lord Peterborough.

Count von Daun.

Eugene knew well that, from a strategic point of view, the best choice was to come from the north-west of Italy, across the Alps to Savoy, and then onward to Lyon and – perhaps – to Grenoble. This route would have threatened central and southern France, and from there it would have been possible to march north to Franche Comté, the Vosges and the Rhine. But Eugene's option was not on the cards. The British wanted Toulon. But Toulon was never an easy target: attempts on the port would fail in 1746, and again in 1793. However, when Lord Peterborough told Eugene in 1707 how important the march on Toulon was to the British, and when Eugene recognised that the British and the Dutch wanted to pay for the some 20,000 Palatine, Hessian and Prussian troopers who were the bulk of his army in Italy, he grudgingly agreed to go along with the plan.

Nonetheless, as the Imperial commander, he now could no longer neglect his Emperor's will, thus he consented also to commit the famous "detachment to Naples", and appointed his best general to command it: count Lawrence Wierich von Daun.

3 Eugene's and Victor Amadeus' great-grandmother, Catherine of Habsburg, Duchess of Savoy, was Charles V's granddaughter.

21

Toulon 1707

I: Planning a Journey to the Riviera

The Toulon enterprise had a remarkable result, even if nobody seemed to realise it, and even if it was presented as a total failure. In his typical patriotic spirit Winston Churchill, writing more than two centuries later, blamed Eugene and the Piedmontese for everything. The Royal Navy, Churchill wrote, did all that was possible, not to mention impossible, but in 1707 Austria's "glorious warrior prince" was not up to the task because he did not understand naval and amphibious warfare. "Eugene," Churchill wrote, "was a land animal, a denizen of Central Europe. He did not understand the sea; what he knew of it he disliked and mistrusted. He had no comprehension of amphibious strategy."[1] Things, however, were rather different. In spite of Churchill's opinions, Eugene understood perfectly that military problem. Naval and land tactics are different, but strategy is the same everywhere, and Eugene knew very well what the result could or would be. Let us see what happened.

"The enterprise was kept very secret; but it began late because of the snow, which does not melt away early in the Apennine Mountains."[2] But had the snow melted earlier, it still would have been impossible to march south immediately. Actually, according to the agreements, the Allied army could move only in conjunction with the Anglo-Dutch fleet, which was supposed to arrive off the Riviera in May. Movement of the land force before that arrival was strictly forbidden, not to waste the surprise by revealing to the French the objective of the expedition. From March to April, Eugene and Victor Amadeus slowly led their troops out of winter quarters, stationing them on the Alpine passes and massing the main part of them in southern

1 Churchill, *Marlborough*, V, pp.276–277.

2 *Vita e campeggiamenti*, cit., p. 204. It may appear strange that the author refers to the southern part of the Maritime Alps as the Appenines. Actually, the name "Apennines" was – and is – used in Italy to designate mountains that separate parts of Italy from each other. In those times the south-western spur of the Maritime Alps were called this because they had to be crossed to go from Piedmont to the County of Nizza – Nice – which remained Italian until 1861, when it passed to France.

Victor Amadeus II.

Piedmont. As they hoped, this greatly puzzled the French. Which was the Allied task? Surely an invasion of France, but from which side? The best route would have been through Savoy, but if so, why were there troops on the other Alpine passes? Were the Allies preparing an attack against Provence? But, if so, why had they left so many troops in the north, near Savoy?

By the second half of June the French headquaters was totally disoriented. More than 40,000 men were gathered in Piedmont near the town of Busca.[3] They were clearly ready to invade France; but from which direction? Where should Tessé concentrate the 83 infantry battalions and 37 cavalry squadrons he had deployed to protect the Dauphiné, and hold Savoy? To the north? The south? But nothing moved, and for many good reasons.

One was the weakness of the Imperial forces in Italy, as some 8,000 men, and 14 cannon under Daun had been sent to attack Naples. The most important factor, however, was a series of French victories. The first was in Spain. On 25 April 1706 the Duke of Berwick won the battle of Almanza against the Lord Galway's Anglo-Portuguese army, pushing them back in disorder to Valencia. This defeat forced Shovell to land most of his Royal Marines to help Galway, and this delayed operations on the Italian front. Then, in May, Villars had launched a surprise attack on the Lines of Stollhofen, and by the 23rd had set his headquarters in Rastadt and seemed ready to seize the whole Western Germany. And Marlborough could do nothing, because his 90,000 men in Flanders had been pinned in place by Vendôme's army, 112,000 strong.

Eugene realised that, as things were, the only feasible thing was to attack from Piedmont across Savoy to Lyon, and the Franche-Comté. This would sever the French supply routes to Germany, and threaten the rear of their army in Flanders. But London did not change her mind about attacking Toulon because as Eugene wrote, the British Admiralty, although "unable to manage the war by land, won't let itself be persuaded and absolutely refuses to budge from its opinions."[4]

Both the calm reigning in Italy, and the French uncertainty about the target of the expected Allied invasion evaporated in June. On the 28th a French spy sent an apparently routine information to his masters: the Guards Regiment had moved from Rivoli to Cuneo. Immediately Tessé realised: the Guards were going south-west; the Guards always followed the Duke; so the Duke was going south-west. If that was the case, then the Allies must be

3 These included some 20,000 Imperial troops, 5,000 Palatines, 6,500 Prussians, 2,500 soldiers from Saxe-Gotha, and 7,000 Piedmontese.

4 rep. in Wolfgang Oppenheimer, *Eugenio di Savoia* (Milan: 1981), p.97.

planning to invade Provence and ... attack Toulon! Toulon, and the French Mediterranean fleet were the task! No matter that those guys in Versailles had always said that an invasion of Provence would only be a diversion! Helter-skelter, terrified that it could be already too late, "Marshal de Tessé, having discovered that the enemy goal was Provence, removed almost all of his infantry from the Alpine passes and sent it to Toulon."[5]

The Allied troops began to move. Too late, the English would say later. Actually, Lord Chetwynd, the British minister to Savoy, wrote to Marlborough that most of the officers thought that had they not moved so slowly during their march on Toulon, they would have accomplished a great result.[6] This was true, but the delay was due for the most part to the snow, and the English, rather than Eugene.[7] Given that it was a combined operation – as the English had insisted – the Imperial–Piedmontese army had not moved until the fleet arrived. But, because of the situation in Spain, Shovell's ships were a month late. It was only on 13 June 1707 that the first of the Allied 47 vessels, 16 smaller ships, and 60 transports came into view,[8] and the Allied army, some 30,000 strong, could advance across the mountains. Eugene's Imperial-Piedmontese force, which included most of the army's infantry and about half of its cavalry, was divided into four groups, marching a day apart from each other. This was necessary because the roads in the region were too narrow.

The first group – 26 infantry battalions and 600 cavalrymen – left Busca on 1 July and was joined by Eugene and Victor Amadeus en route. Nine days later, on a terribly hot day, the column descended the Roia Valley and liberated the County of Nice.

Casualties were light, as the French garrison at nearby Sospello surrendered almost immediately, and the remaining French troops in the vicinity retreated across the Var river, where they regrouped, waiting for a further attack. In the meantime Victor Amadeus had sent Colonel Cavalier with money, weapons, and ammunition to raise the Camisards in order to give Tessé some more worries, and hasten French evacuation of Provence. Having opened the route, the Allies advanced at San Lorenzo across the Var, near its mouth, under the cover of Anglo-Dutch naval gunfire. A pincer movement now took place. A newly-arrived Allied group attacked and engaged the enemy front, while the force that had seized Nice outflanked the French from the north, crossing the Var at La Tour du Puget, and falling on the enemy left wing. The attack drove off seven French regular battalions

---

5 *Vita e campeggiamenti*, cit., p.206.

6 Churchill, *Marlborough*, V, pp.282–283.

7 As Henderson in his *Prince Eugene of Savoy*, p.140, wrote: "This delay before the Allies began to march has frequently been invoked as the prime cause of the ultimate failure of the expedition, and English historians have not been sparing in their use of it as a stick with which to beat the Empire. But the facts scarcely support them. For so long as Eugen remained at Turin the French were in a quandary. They knew that some attack was coming, but they did not know where."

8 This was the number of vessels reported to the Habsburg Emperor by the Prince of Liechtenstein. According to Carutti, in his *Storia del Regno di Vittorio Amadeo II*, the Anglo-Dutch fleet consisted of only 30 men-of-war, 27 frigates and 45 transports, whilst according to Tessé (*Memoirs*, p.239). they were respectively 26 and 46.

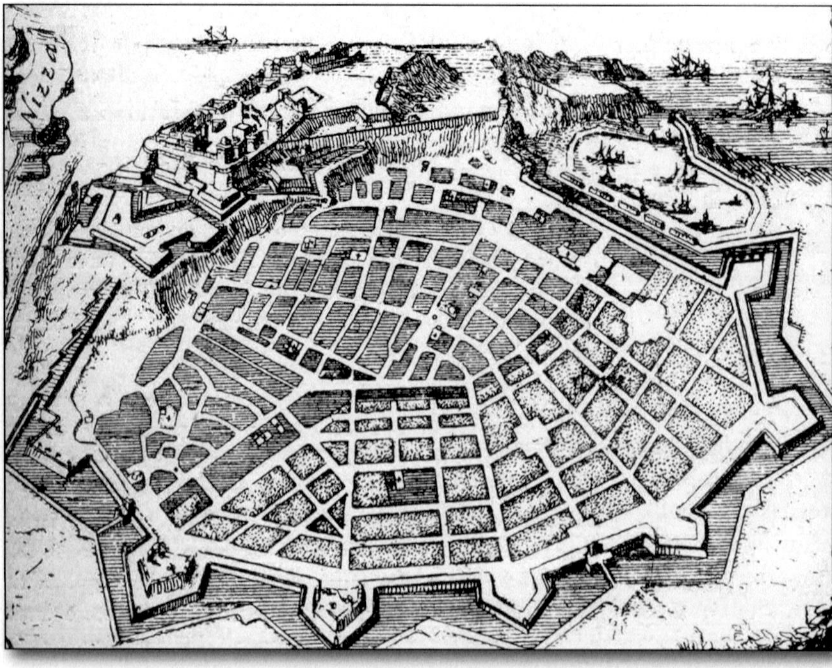

Plan of the Fortifications and Street Layout of the City of Nice.

and 4,000 militia and freed up the entire river bank. Meanwhile, 600 British marines landed at the mouth of the river from Admiral Norris' vessels, and forced the Marquess de Sillery to retreat to the west to avoid encirclement.

"The cities of Grasse and St. Paul offered their surrender. Here it proved necessary to put the ovens to work, to bake bread in abundance, the army having to march in enemy country, short of food, with so many people."[9] Now it was necessary to wait for the other two incoming Allied groups. By 15 July Eugene, and Victor Amadeus could restart their march, but the great heat made their progress painful. A 24-hour halt occurred in Cannes to let the troops rest, but half of the infantry collapsed on the subsequent march to Fréjus. It was only on 26 July that the vanguard of the Allied army appeared before the walls of Toulon.

The British grumbled about what they saw as the slowness of the march. Two centuries later Winston Churchill wrote that, after crossing the Var, the army was only 70 miles from Toulon, and as its artillery and baggage were ferried by the fleet, it should have taken only a week to reach Toulon instead of 15 days.[10] This statement is wrong on four counts. First, naval support was absent; it had been left behind because of the greater speed allowed by the army's chosen route. The second mistake was that this route was not a coastal one, as Churchill wrote, but through the interior. Actually, the army marched "through Cagnes, Fréjus, Arce, Pignan, Souliers [Cannes, Fréjus, Les Arcs, Pignans, and Sollies], along very steep paths, tormented by the heat, the forced pace, and shortages of food, and arrived on the 26th at the Valletta

9 *Vita e campeggiamenti*, cit., pp.205–06.

10 Churchill, *Marlborough*, V, p.282.

[La Valette du Var] before Toulon."[11] Churchill's third mistake was to reckon the time consumed by the march as 15 days, when in fact it only took 12; the army moved on 15 July and reached Toulon on the 26th. Finally, the march was longer than Churchill had calculated: 105 English miles, not 70.

It wasn't a slow march. As we said when speaking of logistics, at that time armies marched an average of 6.5–7.5 English miles a day and rarely more than nine. Thus, a march of 105 miles in 12 days was not slow. But – and look at the dates – more than 105 miles were covered in this 12 days. Eugene moved his troops from Biot on 15 July and his vanguard reached Toulon on 26th, covering more than 8.7 miles a day, perfectly in accord with the best contemporary standards. Moreover, we must remember that it was summer in southern France, and that the weather was intensely hot. In such cases, as we have seen when speaking of early eighteenth-century warfare, armies used to rest an entire day every two or three days on the march. In this way, counting the day of rest, an army was expected to march an average of 24.8 miles in four days. We have seen that in his August 1706 march to Piedmont Eugene's troops covered in fact an average of 30 miles every four days. Here they went faster: they covered an average of 34.8 miles in four days. Not only this was an outstanding performance, and an evidence of what I said when discussing the blind aprioristic application to the eighteenth century many historians make of Perjés' statements; it was also considered very fast by the French, who stated that they had little time to prepare the defence of Toulon.[12] The English, however, persisted in regarding the march to Toulon as having proceeded at a snail's pace.

All the King's horses and all the King's men – when available – rushed to Toulon. Sillery arrived with his troops retreating from the battle on the Var. Generals Saint-Pater and Dillon came in with 13 battalions. Then on 24 July Tessé himself arrived with 300 dragoons and more infantry, raising the number of battalions concentrated around the city to 41. In the harbour, navy officers removed the masts from their ships and flooded their holds, sinking them in the water to protect them from enemy cannonballs.[13] Meanwhile, Tessé's sappers worked feverishly outside the city, digging trenches and strengthening fortifications.

Toulon was dominated by mountains, in particular the peak of Sainte-Anne to the north.

> So, the first effort consisted in linking the city to the mountain by trenches, manned by six-thousand men. On top of the mountain, Tessé placed a large force of infantry. Twenty-six battalions, under the command of the Sieur de Gobrieant, were formed up in two lines behind the trenches. Their right covered the road to Toulon, while the left reached out to Mount Sainte-Anne, where another

11 *Vita e campeggiamenti*, cit., p.206.

12 De Vault and Pelet, op. cit., pp.111, 118, and, especially, *Mèmoires et lettres du Maréchal de Tessé, cit.*, II, chapter 11, pp.241–47.

13 The naval commander, the Marquis de Langeron, had under his command some 50 vessels, 800 navy officers of all ranks, 150 marines, 400 gunners and hundreds of other sailors, in addition to the crews of the vessels and galleys sunk in the harbour.

> French corps was in place. On the road to the west, to Marseille, two forces were deployed, one of eight battalions in front of Saint-Antony, the other, of sixteen battalions, closer to the sea near the Château de Mastici … [These and other camps around the city] were fortified, and strengthened with cannon, and enjoyed easy communication between themselves and the city. The Marshal, having organised everything, went to Aix, the capital of Provence, to put together another army from contingents sent in from many other provinces.[14]

II: Two Months at the Seaside

On 26 July Eugene and Victor Amadeus sent a vanguard of 300 grenadiers against the French defenders on top of Mount Saint-Antony, driving them off in disarray. From the nearby Croix-Pharaon heights, the generals could look down on the defences of Toulon. Their conclusions about the chances of a successful siege were not good. Toulon appeared well defended with field works, built on uneven ground. The city was commanded by Mount Sainte-Cathérine, which was at the vortex of a triangle whose base was the line Toulon–Sainte-Anne Camp. This camp, fortified and protected by 100 cannon, was the link between the city and the rest of France. Thus the key to seizing Toulon was Mount Sainte-Cathérine and the nearby Sainte-Anne Camp, and they were held by an experienced French army of some 20,000 men. The Savoy cousins:

> asked Admiral Shovell and other senior naval officers to come ashore to accurately observe the situation of the enterprise, in order to give an exact account of it to England and, meanwhile, to give their opinions about the actions to be taken next.[15]

The Allied council of war did not go smoothly. Eugene had no intention to look for trouble, because his advantage was only three to two over the French, who were also protected by fieldworks.

Moreover, the army assembled by Tessé was threatening his right flank, while to his rear the local militia was trying to cut his line of communications and his potential escape route. Shovell insisted on an attack. He told Eugene not worry about the militia to his rear, since the fleet was prepared to supply the army from the sea. Further, he said, in case of retreat, the cavalry could simply gallop away while the infantry could be taken onboard by the navy and shipped eastward, perhaps to Nice. Eugene was not convinced. Shovell's plans in case of retreat seemed superficial, since the fleet had up to that moment given little support to the ground troops; in fact "… the ships, because of the winds blowing off the land, could not reach the shore and thus were hampered in providing the soldiers with food and supplies."[16] The British, however, were unconvinced by Eugene's arguments and so a

14 *Vita e campeggiamenti*, pp.208–09.

15 *Idem*, p.209.

16 *Ibid.*

compromise solution was reached: the next day the Imperial–Piedmontese troops would attack Mount Saint-Cathérine. Once the position was taken, it would be transformed into an artillery emplacement, thus making it possible to shell Toulon from both land and sea. The results of the bombardment would determine whether or not it would be worth continuing the siege.

As agreed, on 30 July 1707 some 7,500 Allied foot commanded by generals Königseck, Rhebinder, Zumjungen and the Prince of Saxe-Gotha stormed the mountain. They drove off the French and seized the farms in the area, all under an artillery bombardment by the 100 French cannons in Sainte-Anne. The Allies agreed that the result was satisfactory, so, they quickly anchored their right flank on the seized position and prepared to bring ashore the heavy artillery to be used in the siege – 100 cannons and 40 mortars – and their ammunition.

It soon became clear that Eugene had been right when questioning the feasibility of the operation. Shovell's ships could off-load the guns and ammunition, but then they had to be carried for eight miles to the army camp and then, beyond that, to the foot of Mount Sainte-Cathérine. But this was only the beginning. The guns and ammunition had then to be carried up the mountain, along steep and narrow paths and under constant enemy fire. Thousands of men had to work widening and strengthening the roads, while thousands more dug the trenches for the outward parallel.

Since the area around Toulon could not provide enough wood and other materials for the ramparts, redoubts and gabions required for the siege, hundreds of men, wagons and horses had to be sent out to find them. Finally, after days of hard labour under the terrible sun of that very hot summer, the Allies were able to open fire with two batteries of mixed cannon and mortars, set on the side closest to the sea. Work to site the batteries on the peak of Sainte-Cathérine, meanwhile, inched forward.

The French garrison in Toulon responded with an intensive, if largely ineffective, fire. Lack of results from his artillery convinced the French to sally to break the siege. The sally was repulsed, and soon afterwards the Allies started firing with an additional 40 big guns, divided into two batteries. Their fire, anyway, did not damage the city that much.

The best solution appeared now to send the Anglo-Dutch fleet into the harbour, but since it was well defended by the forts of Saint-Louis and Sainte-Marguerite, the ships could not get close enough to fire effectively. Finally, on 7 August, the first parallel was completed. But it was clear that more time would be necessary before the Allies could start to progress toward seizing the city. And, once they had seized it, what then? The question had already arisen within the British cabinet, and there were few options. Holding the city against the French counter-offensive would be demanding. The Anglo-Dutch fleet could not be always there, so how could one support the Allied army garrisoning Toulon? Lord Sunderland had an idea: "there is no easier way of doing that, than by inducing the Venetians to enter into the alliance and to let us have some ten or twelve thousand of their troops."[17] What was

17 Lord Sunderland to Lord Manchester, 5 August 1707, Blenheim Sunderland Letter Book, I, p.89, rep. in Hattendorf, op. cit., p.96.

not said was that, once she had committed her army, Venice would probably have to commit her fleet also, to support her troopers and the whole Allied army, rendering the Anglo-Dutch squadron free to leave. What a pity that Venice was not that willing to join.

Seeking an alternative plan, Eugene carried out a reconnaissance in force to determine if was it possible to completely encircle Toulon. He quickly realised that this would not be possible. There were other discouraging developments. The French militia was continually harassing Allied foragers, and Eugene had to commit Colonel Saint-Amour's and Baron Felts' cavalry against the militia to keep open the road to the Var. Yet despite all efforts it proved possible to quicken the pace of the siege, and meanwhile French reinforcements were coming in from everywhere.

On 8 August Tessé re-entered Toulon with some 27 battalions and immediately began planning for a sally a week later:

> Thirty Grenadier companies and 27 battalions, about 10,000 French in all grouped into three corps, were ordered to march out of the city. The Sieur Dillon would command the left, the Marquis de Gobrieant the centre; and the Count of Monserò the right, facing the Germans.[18]

At dawn on 15 August the French attacked the Allied positions of La Croix-Pharaon and Mount Sainte-Cathérine. The Imperialists on the right were surprised and fled, having lost two positions and two guns. The Prince of Saxe-Gotha was killed. On the left the Prussians held, thanks in part to the arrival of two regiments of dragoons led by the Prince of Hesse-Cassel. Eugene immediately sent forward his reserves, stopped the French and recovered the lost positions, losing 800 Allied soldiers against 300 French. Still, the day was not a complete loss: that evening the fort of Sainte-Marguerite surrendered, leaving only one fort, that of Saint-Louis, to guard the harbour of Toulon. On the 19th the garrison of Saint-Louis escaped by sea, leaving behind 20 heavy cannons.

The Allied fleet could now approach the harbour. The shelling from land and sea soon began to wreak severe damage on the city. The news of this serious events hastened the efforts of the French to mount a defence. Berwick had already been ordered to leave Spain with 10 battalions of infantry and 600 dragoons, and was coming to Toulon. At the same time Vendôme had detached 12 infantry battalions and two cavalry regiments from his army in Flanders for the same purpose. With these men and other available forces, the French wanted to assemble a relief force under the command of the dukes of Burgundy and Berry, but this was no longer necessary: the Allies had decided to leave the siege of Toulon.

Day by day it had become increasingly clear that Eugene's doubts about the campaign had been correct. Victor Amadeus and Shovell wanted to continue, but after examining the situation and looking at what the future might bring, it was agreed by everyone that no more could be done. Toulon

18 *Vita e Campeggiamenti*, p.211.

could not be seized without a long siege, ultimately in the face of superior numbers. Enemy resistance was already increasing. It was time to leave before it was too late and the retreat was scheduled to begin on the night of 21 August. The fleet began to take on the sick and wounded, materials, heavy artillery and ammunition. Rear Admiral Sir Thomas Dilkes was given the task of bombarding the harbour.

Toulon Shelled in 1707.

III: Back Home

On the morning of 21 August the Anglo-Dutch fleet bombarded the quays and warehouses with roundshot and explosive shells. Tall pillars of smoke rose in the sky, and the roar of thousands of explosions could be heard throughout the day and into the night, saluting the Allied departure for Italy. By the light of the burning ships and warehouses, the Allied army left in five groups. Baron di Saint-Rémy commanded the vanguard, composed of grenadiers. The flanks were protected by cavalry units under Felts and Saint-Amour. Eugene in person commanded the rear, leaving behind him a vision of ruins, with a few abandoned and spiked cannons overlooking a desolated landscape.

The Allied army marched to the Var, devastating southern Provence in the best French style of that time. The retreat proceeded smoothly and rapidly but carefully. Saint-Rémy and his troops quickly reached the only dangerous passage – the gorge of Esterel – just before the French vanguard from the north, thus allowing the main body of the army to reach Nice safely on 31 August. A few days later the Anglo-Dutch fleet sailed to Spain and the Allied army crossed the Alps through the Col di Tenda. Still marching in five groups, a distance of one day from each other, the troops reached the Piedmontese camp of Scalenghe on 11 September and were in Turin on the 16th.

Getting information that the French garrison at Susa was still very weak, Eugene decided to seize it. He left Turin the next day, 17 September, with 10 battalions of infantry and 1,000 Imperial horse, leaving Victor Amadeus and the rest of the Piedmontese to hold against any possible French incursion from Provence. The attack on Susa was a complete surprise. The Old Dessau with the grenadiers in the vanguard swept the 3,000 French from the ramparts, forcing them to flee into the city and its citadel. Susa capitulated on 22 September and the French in the citadel surrendered on 3 October, after a five-day bombardment. Meanwhile, Eugene had detached General

The Valley and Citadel of Susa.

Zumjungen to seize the last remaining French strongholds in the Italian Alps, Chiomonte and the Fort de Catinat. The city was stormed under the cover of three batteries and taken on 29 September. Tessé tried to intervene but found Victor Amadeus barring the route.

IV: Wrong Comments, and Good Results

With the arrival of winter, the 1707 campaign in Italy came to an end and troops went to winter quarters. Then it followed a rising quantity of complaints about the campaign, especially from the British. It is not clear if this somehow affected the flow of British subsidies to the Empire, but what is clear is that Eugene did not receive all the money he needed once the campaign was over. In fact, on 26 November he was forced to raise a loan for 100,000 doubles in Milan, at an astounding rate of interest: two percent per month, and he could guarantee it with contributions the Emperor expected to receive – that is to raise – in 1708 from Imperial fief holders in Italy.[19]

The campaign in Provence had aroused in London a remarkable disappointment, and it was considered a failure. Toulon had neither been seized nor destroyed; southern France had not been occupied; the pressure on the armies in Flanders had not been lifted; and the whole Toulon undertaking

19 See the *Capitolazione per l'anticipo di 100,000 doppie dal sig. Calcino alle truppe imperiali comandate dal Serenissimo Principe Eugenio di Savoia* (Agreement for the advance of a loan of 100,000 doubes from Signor Calcino to the Imperial troops under the command of the Most Serene Prince Eugene of Savoy), concluded in Milan on 26 November 1707; handwritten copy in AUSSME, L 3, 8, *Stati Preunitari – Piemonte.*

had meant the loss of 10,000 soldiers and sailors, dead, wounded, sick, missing, and deserted.[20]

These complaints were misleading and wrong. From a strategic point of view matters did not turn out all that badly. The attack on Toulon had stopped the French fleet from coming to the aid of the Spaniards in Naples, with the result that Daun's army had no difficulty seizing the Kingdom. Also, by forcing the French to concentrate so many soldiers in Provence, the Allies stopped French operations on the Flemish and German fronts – as William III, and later Marlborough, always said – and, even more important, stopped them from exploiting the advantages gained at Almanza. In fact Berwick had been obliged to leave Spain quickly, when all that remained in front of him was a token Anglo-Portuguese army. Finally – but this was discovered only later – the French fleet had been destroyed. When the French had started to refloat their ships in the harbour, they received a horrific shock: although their ships had been sunk to protect them against enemy fire, it soon became apparent that Allied shot had smashed decks and hulls. The French navy was destroyed. Everything else, wharves and warehouses, could be rebuilt in a relatively short time, but not the ships. French maritime power was crippled. "The war of squadrons is finished ... Toulon is safe; but our Fleet is defunct."[21]

Albeit reluctantly and with much grumbling, ignoring what he had really accomplished, Prince Eugene had helped to deliver a mortal blow to France. But, following Churchill's lead, British historians never admitted it.

We will not go into details here, because I already, and successfully, did it in 2006,[22] but there is a long list of historians who completely misunderstood, and thus misassessed, the operational result.[23] Anyway, setting aside the factual mistakes – especially about the route – due to the reliance upon Churchill's work as a major source, was the campaign a success or not?

Let us make it clear. A tactical or strategic action may be considered successful only if, and when, it achieves the previously agreed goals. It is also true that it is necessary to have a clear idea about the final objective, and thus avoid confusing it with others of minor importance.

We have seen that, according to the British, the stated goal was to seize the city of Toulon and destroy France's naval capability in the Mediterranean. But this was just one objective, not two: in the British mind, the seizure of Toulon would have meant the neutralisation of the French fleet. We can object, however, that taking Toulon would only have deprived the French fleet of a good base, not of its ships. Marseille was close, and it could easily

20 Moreover, on 22 October 1707 (Old Style, that is to say on our 2 November) in the evening, four of five British vessels coming back from the Mediterranean were wrecked off the Scilly Isles. Some 2,000 British seamen lost their lives, including the 57-year-old admiral Shovell, whose body was later found on the beach.

21 Winston Spencer Churchill, *Marlborough*, V, p.290. Churchill quotes the French naval historian Charles de la Roncière, *Histoire de la marine française* (Paris: 1932), VI, p.395.

22 Ciro Paoletti, "Prince Eugene of Savoy, the Toulon expedition of 1707 and the English historians – a dissenting view", in *Journal of Military History*, vol 70, n. 4, October 2006.

23 The list of those who trusted Churchill and misassessed the operation includes David Chandler, John Hattendorf, J.H. Owen, Correlli Barnett, Nicholas Henderson, Christopher Storrs, and Derek McKay. In spite of having published in a world known and highly rated academic journal, there was no reaction to my article by any of the people concerned.

receive the French Mediterranean fleet. So, there is a question to be answered, in order to decide if the siege of Toulon – and, more generally, the whole campaign of 1707 – was successful or not: at the end of the campaign was the enemy fleet still a threat? Had it still an operational capacity or not? If yes, the campaign was a failure; otherwise, it was a success. As we have seen, at the end of the campaign the enemy fleet was no more a threat, thus, the campaign was successful, and the failure to seize Toulon was unimportant. As a matter of fact, it could be seen as an advantage. Holding the city against a sure French counteroffensive would have forced the Allies to manage an expensive defence, with heavy losses in both men, and money, as happened in 1793, when an English–Spanish–Sardinian–Neapolitan expeditionary force could not hold Toulon against the French.

The picture becomes even brighter if we look at the Toulon campaign from a grand strategic perspective. In order to relieve Toulon, the French had to stop their offensive in Spain, just when they were going to finally destroy the Anglo-Portuguese army after Almanza. Thus, thanks to the siege of Toulon, the Allies avoided defeat in another theatre. Furthermore, the effort to relieve Toulon weakened the French army in Flanders, where their numerical superiority was reduced by one third by the decision to commit troops to Provence. Indeed, it could be argued that if it had not been for the attack on Toulon, Marlborough might have received a year earlier the beating he got from Vendôme in 1708. Actually, during the early 1708 campaign, before the arrival of Eugene in Flanders, the French seized Ghent and Bruges, and threatened Allied communications to the Netherlands and the sea. Had French troops not been diverted to Provence, this might have occurred in 1707. But there is a difference: in 1708 the arrival of Eugene and his army saved the Allied situation in Flanders, and this would not have been possible in 1707 because Eugene was in Italy, and in southern France. And speaking of Italy, it should not be forgotten how the French gathering of forces around Toulon weakened their garrisons in Piedmont, allowing Eugene to seize Susa, Chiomonte, and Pinerolo the keys to the Alps, finally closing the door to northern Italy to the French. Last, it would be interesting to see how the sending of reinforcements to Toulon affected the prosecution of the French offensive in Germany, which ceased soon after the crossing of the Stollhofen Lines, and the conquest of Rastadt in May.

In conclusion, the attack on Toulon by Eugene, Victor Amadeus II and Shovell, despite the Eugene's reluctance to undertake it, stopped the French fleet from gaining a strategically definitive victory in the Mediterranean, avoided an Allied strategic defeat in Spain, allowed the Allies to gain complete control of the Alps, probably postponed – and practically allowed the Allies to resolve – the crisis in Flanders, while perhaps avoiding further French progress in Germany. Not so bad for a campaign the British considered – and many still consider – to have been a failure, only because it did not go exactly as planned.

22

Daun to Naples

I: Naples in the Early Eighteenth Century

'Naples' meant the Kingdom of Naples, which included the whole southern part of Italy, except for Sicily. The cities of Benevento and Pontecorvo too were excluded, due to their direct dependence on the Pope, but Naples held the Stato dei Presidii on the Tuscan coast, and a portion of the island of Elba.

The Kingdom was a little more than 85,700 square kilometres wide, that is to say, in British terms, as big as Scotland and Lincolnshire together. It was inhabited by roughly three million people, and was considered "healthy", thus everybody wanted it, due to its huge food production.

The Kingdom of Naples had practically no industrial production, other than that needed to fulfil internal demand: shipbuilding, food in general, wax, olive oil, wood, and wood-derived commodities. Textiles made in the Kingdom were not enough, and thus had to be imported. Export relied mostly, if not only, on raw materials.

The most of the small industrial production was for military purposes. Spanish military land power was centred on the Kingdom of Naples, which during the sixteenth and seventeenth centuries consistently provided the Spanish Habsburgs with great quantities of money and military manpower. When needed, more troops could be concentrated in Naples from Sicily and

Naples in 1713.

The Spanish Road: the Maritime Route from Naples to Finale.

occasionally Sardinia. If Spain had to commit them to Flanders or Germany, they marched northwards along the Adriatic coast, but normally they took ship in the Tyrrhenian Sea, and after an intermediate stop in the Stato dei Presidii they landed in the small coastal town of Finale, west of Genoa and south of Piedmont. Then they marched north to Germany and the Rhineland along their traditional route, the at that time famous Spanish Road, known in Italian as il Cammino di Fiandra.

As a consequence, the Kingdom spent a lot of money to keep the military organisation ready, and it was not an easy task. Moreover, when in the last quarter of the seventeenth century the stream of silver and gold from South America to Spain decreased, there was no way to maintain the Spanish military organisation in Naples other than relying more and more on only Neapolitan money. Consequently, in terms of money, situation was not good. Had it been independent, Naples would have been rich. Depending on Spain, it was not. Since the sixteenth century the Kingdom lost money every year, and men to feed the Spanish system. Men were needed to fight. Money was raised by taxes, and the expenses were made heavier by a further "present" to the King of Spain. Initially it had been a more or less occasional "gift", then in 1560 the gift became a 1,200,000 Neapolitan ducats[1] "donation", a present to be made every two years. It became harder and harder to gather that sum, because the Kingdom had to pay it no matter how bad the harvest, or how low the revenues of the nobles, and of the cities had been. The burden of the financial support to Spain, to the Spanish troops in northern Italy, and since 1690 to the Duchy of Milan to sustain the war, exhausted the Neapolitan treasury. When the Nine Years' War ended, there was almost no more money.

1 In English currency, in 1699 a Neapolitan ducat equalled four shillings and two pence, so 1,200,000 Neapolitan ducats meant 250,000 English pounds.

Bad financial conditions and heavy taxes played a major role in the 1701 plot. They did not trigger it, but convinced the organisers that the people could easily rise up. It did not happen, but after the failure of the plot general conditions did not improve, and that dramatically reduced the consensus. Moreover Viceroy Medinaceli in 1701 had an additional problem. The "present" was not that automatic. It was the result of a negotiation between the viceroy and the "Seats", that is to say a sort of Naples city council and Kingdom parliament, composed of many representatives of the nobles[2] and of one representative of the people. The Seats became less and less easy about money. If in August 1701 they still agreed on a 300,000 ducats present, later their consent was not that easy, and it happened because Madrid asked for even more money.

Eugene's victories in Northern Italy rendered the situation worse. The more the Austrians won, the more the Viceroy felt unsafe, due to the increasingly hostile attitude of the people. Poor daily living conditions were a reason why the Austrian supporters gathered consensus, but this was also a reason why that consensus increased in the lowest classes too. The common people suffered high prices, no money, expensive food, and all that was due to the Spaniards. And above all, the situation had worsened in recent years,

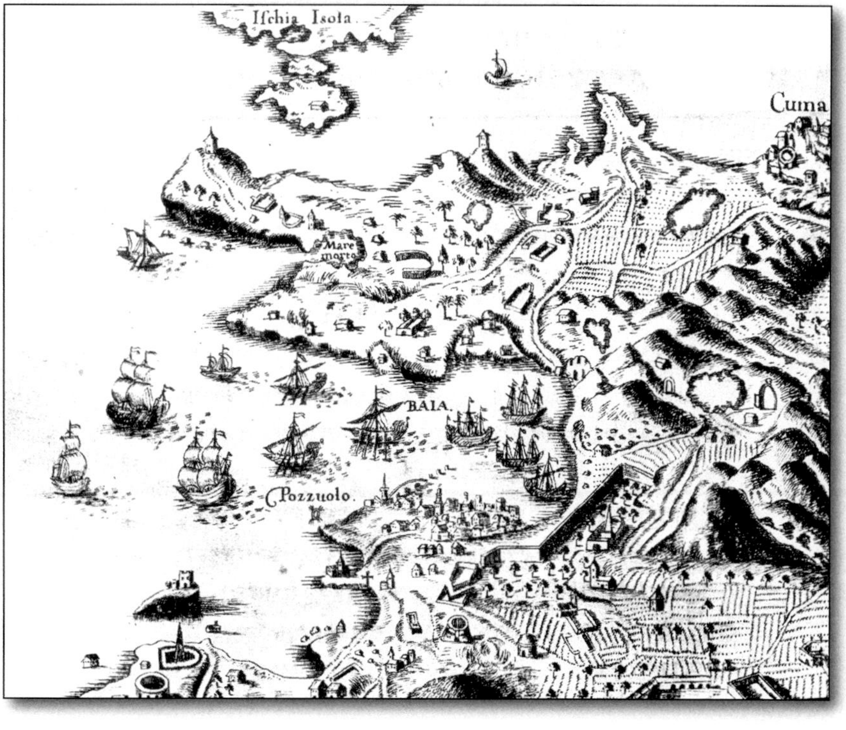

Imagined Arrival of Philip V in Pozzuoli in 1702, Greeted by the Neapolitan Galley Squadron.

2 The Neapolitan noblemen living in the city since the early Middle Ages met in halls, where they sat and discussed city and their own businesses. Each quarter had such a hall, which, due to its seats, was later called "seat", or "place". In the sixteenth century all the nobles of the Kingdom came to live in Naples and affiliated to one of the seats, which hence became a sort of House of the Lords shared in five parts. In 1701 there were five "seats" – Capuana, Nilo, Porto, Portanuova, and Montagna – and an "Elected of the People", that is to say a representative of the middle class, who could only report middle class complaints or questions, and could not make a proposal.

The Battle of Vigo Bay.

that is to say since Philip V became king. Hence people in Naples, and in other parts of Italy too, for example the Papal States, began looking at the victory of the Austrians as the dawn of a new era of peace, justice, and health, which simply meant not to risk starvation anymore.

When Philip V came to Naples in spring 1702 there were great expectations, but these were followed by great disillusionment.

Philip landed in Pozzuoli on 16 April, and left Naples on 2 June. When he reached Naples, on 17 April, a cannon on one of the five galleys of the Neapolitan fleet exploded during a gun salute for the King. This was considered an ill omen. When Philip went to the Cathedral on 18 April, San Gennaro's blood did not liquefy until late in the night, when the King was no longer in the church, and this was a very bad omen. But a bad omen has no consequence; facts have, and the facts were that Philip reduced to a half the tax on flour, cancelled the tax arrears due from the communities – which in the Kingdom were called "universities" – issued an amnesty, and left for the north. The result: pardoned prisoners made crime increase, and when the Kingdom was asked by the King for a 400,000 ducats gift it had to issue a new tax: additional 10 percent on real estate revenues. The situation could be quite well described by the old Italian way of saying: "It was better when it was worse."

Viceroy Juan Manuel Pacheco, Marquess of Villena and Duke of Escalona.

The Anglo-Dutch victory at Vigo Bay in October that same year was a disaster. Initially the news of the Spanish convoy shipping many millions in gold and silver from South America had been more than welcome. It meant at least a pause. If Spain received money from her colonies, probably it would no longer ask Naples for it. The subsequent news of the destruction of the fleet was not perceived simply as a defeat. It meant that Naples would be asked by Madrid for more and more money, but that money was now almost impossible to find.

The Kingdom was squeezed. The deficit had started in second half of the sixteenth century. By 1607 the Kingdom's debt was already 8,000,000 ducats, and the situation did not improve later.

In summer 1704 the total yearly state income was 1,602,837 ducats, and the annual deficit was 553,411 ducats. Additional money was needed to pay debts and fill the gap, and at last a threatening signal appeared. When in December 1704 Viceroy Villena asked the Seats for money, proposing a further five percent tax on wages, and revenues. the Seats were clearly unhappy. So during that meeting Villena told them that if Holland supported a foreign Prince – the Emperor – in his war, paying 20, 30, or 40 percent, how could the Neapolitans protest if the King asked for a mere 5 percent? And then a terrible answer came. The representative of the people, Gennaro d'Andrea answered: "Today Holland fights for her liberty, our case is different."[3] Such a statement could be understood in different ways, but everybody perceived it as meaning: "Holland fights for her liberties, we do not, because we depend on a foreign king." In an absolute kingdom, and in front of the viceroy, this was the maximum one could say without being hanged on the spot as a traitor. Never in the past had a Neapolitan – moreover a commoner – protested against the King of Spain, who had always been seen as the legitimate heir of the long-ceased Aragonese dynasty ruling the independent Kingdom of Naples until 1492. Occasionally people had protested against the Viceroy, as in 1647 and in 1701, but that had been the top. If it happened now, it meant the time was ripe for a change, and a change meant the fall of the Spanish rule. The question was whether Spanish rule was strong enough to defend itself in Naples, and it was not.

II: Naples' Troops

Before the Nine Years' War, Naples had 3,500 foot included in the so-called "Tercio Fijo" – standing third, or standing regiment – and 500 cavalry organised into nine light cavalry companies. There were 12 companies of Greek-Albanian "stradiotes" – soldiers – and a feudal militia. The latter was cavalry, and composed 19 companies of "men-at-arms", that is to say 15 cuirassiers, and four light cavalry companies, and each was 125 men strong on paper. The Viceroyal Guard was 257 strong: 107 spear-bearers, 70 halberdiers, and 50 Noble Guards.

The artillery was small. It included an artillery train, a foundry and an artillery school, with a master, 11 artillerymen, and 150 "pupils". The coasts were watched by a network of 330 watchtowers, garrisoned by 1,200 men.

Croton Castle.

3 Rep. in Giuseppe Galasso, *Napoli nel Viceregno spagnolo (1696–1707)*, vol. VII (Naples, 1972), p.325.

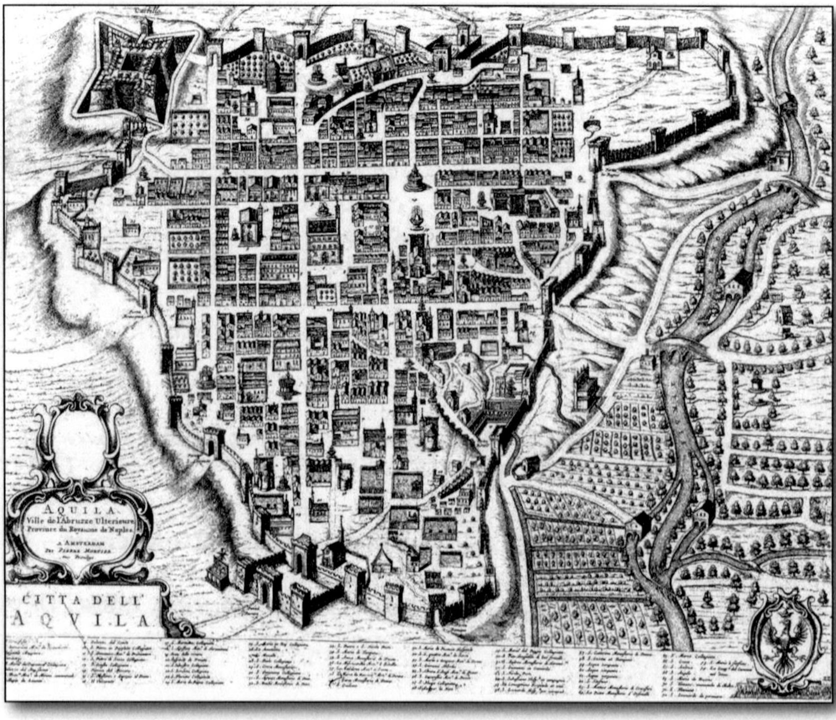

Plan View of Aquila.

By 1701 the Tercio Fijo was 52 companies strong, but normally kept 13 companies in the Presidii, and only 39 in the Kingdom. Half of the companies were in the capital. The others were in the most important fortresses, that is to say Ischia, Gaeta, Capua, Fondi, Aquila, Pescara, Bari, Barletta, and on the Tremiti islands. Other forts and castles were in Civitella del Tronto, Amantea, Catanzaro, Cosenza, "Cotroni", that is to say Croton in Calabria, Brindisi, Taranto, Monopoli, Gallipoli, Trani, Otranto, Manfredonia, and Monte Sant'Angelo, in Apulia. Enrolment in 1701 originated 14 infantry new companies, quartered in the arsenal.

As Naples was considered as being in danger after the 1701 uprising, during winter 1701–1702 a 10,000 men reinforcement came: 1,500 from Milan, 5,500 from Spain, and 3,000 from France. The Spaniards increased to 6,800 by June 1702, and up to 7,700 foot by the end of August 1703. It was not by chance. The Anglo-Dutch fleet appeared in the Tyrrhenian Sea that summer, and the Kingdom was supposed to be her target.

Then the situation became worse. The French troopers sometimes clashed with the Spaniards in Naples, and in 1705 many French, notably the Grancey and Dauphiné Regiments, embarked bound for Finale and Lombardy. In May 1706 other French troopers left, as well as the local French commanders, and when the news of Turin came, the Viceroy realised Naples was likely the next target.

In November 1706 infantry in Naples had 5,000 men divided into one Walloon and eight Spanish, battalions. A new enlistment was issued that autumn, but recruits had to be sent to Naples in chains and under escort, to prevent them escaping. However this more or less meant a further four Neapolitan battalions, thus the infantry had now a little less than 8,000 men in 13 battalions.

The cavalry in Naples increased slowly. In June 1702 it had 1,531 men, including 792 dragons, but only 551 horses. In August 1703 it reached its top, with 2,292 men and 1,046 horses, but soon decreased and on the eve of 1707 was some 2,000 strong.

It was just to enhance this small force that viceroy Villena summoned the Seats, and received the dry answer that "Holland fights for her liberty, our case is different." He hoped to gather 20,000 men, but needed money. After that, and after the refusal of any reinforcement from Sicily, he realised that he could do nothing more than hold the main fortresses: Gaeta, Naples, and Capua. Naples was too big, Capua too deep in the Kingdom, thus he concentrated all he could in the coastal fortress of Gaeta, because being on a peninsula linked to the mainland by a narrow strip of land, it could be defended easily and supplied and relieved by sea. Then he waited.

III: Wierich Daun Comes to Town

In spring 1707 Daun took 5,880 infantrymen and 2,222 cavalry[4] from the Austrian force in northern Italy. As Eugene complained in two letters to the Emperor, on 22 September, and 1 October 1707, it weakened the condition of his army; but there was nothing to do. This was Joseph's will, and this had to be made.

Daun's expeditionary force gathered at Finale Emilia, not far from Modena, marched south, and on 13 May entered the – neutral – Papal States. On 15 May Daun and the Imperial commissioner Count Schlick asked the Papal Legate of Bologna for food, wood, and fodder.

On the 18th, under the control of Papal troops, the Corps crossed Bologna. The Swiss Guards, the light cavalrymen, the bombers, and 200 volunteers watched the main buildings, whilst seven companies – three militia, three cavalry, and one regular infantry – reinforced by volunteers and police, patrolled the city and kept workers in the factories to prevent their likely rally in favour of the Emperor.

When in Faenza Daun committed General Wetzel to Rome, to discuss the Austrian troops' itinerary through the Papal States. Following Cardinal Grimani's advice, Daun left the Adriatic coast, crossed the Apennines in Umbria, and on 16 June encamped in Monterotondo, not far from Rome. The Pope closed eight city gates, and as in Bologna Papal troops not only watched the city, but patrolled the streets, to prevent any rally in favour of Austria. On 19 June Daun left the army and paid his visit to the Pope. The next day his army moved, passed around Rome at a distance, and along the Casilina road – the same used in 1944 by the Germans to feed the Cassino Front – reached Ceprano on the 26, and then crossed the Neapolitan border.

As said, viceroy Villena gathered all he could into Gaeta, including 40 bronze cannons from the Neapolitan castles, and put an observation cavalry

4 Other sources report his force to have been 5,294 foot, and 2,098 cavalry strong, with 400 artillerymen, 14 field cannons, a pontooner corps, and 100 men escorting the train, plus 680 non-combatants, and 59 members of the staff.

corps 1,500 strong, commanded by the Prince of Castiglione, along the Garigliano river. When the Austrians came, those cavalrymen were ordered to withdraw to Naples. The capital was now held by militia and police. Castiglione did not reach the city. He and his men entered Capua, to try to hold it.

On 27 June a British squadron composed of four men-of-war and three smaller ships appeared in the Gulf of Naples. Boats filled with happy citizens sailed and rowed to greet them. When they returned, those citizens were arrested, but at the same time the Seats refused Villena's last demand: neither a penny, nor a human life must be spent to defend a King who made nothing but scanty, and late arrangements to keep the Kingdom. Hence, on the next day, Villena left Naples by sea and the Neapolitan galleys shipped him to Gaeta. The British ships allowed them to pass.

On 4 July the Austrians besieged Capua. The garrison, 300 foot strong, surrendered at the first call. The same was made by the smaller garrison of Aversa. On the same day, after the Viceroy's departure to Gaeta, pro-Habsburg groups took the control of Naples. The Spanish garrison, now reduced to 1,400 men, was scattered among five different fortresses and castles, and when Daun entered the city on 5 July they agreed to surrender as soon as the Imperialists stormed the main castle and seized one of its gates. Then they turned their coat, passed into Habsburg service, and helped the Austrians besiege Gaeta, and Pescara. Meanwhile, the Prince of Castiglione had realised how bad the situation was, and had already left Capua with 600 cavalry before the capitulation.

Daun committed Imperial cavalry commanded by Carafa – he too a Neapolitan – to follow Castiglione. Castiglione still had his 600 men, followed by 190 nobles loyal to Spain. They tried to reach Apulia, but when

Tommaso d'Aquino, Prince of Castiglione; of the same family as St Thomas Aquinas.

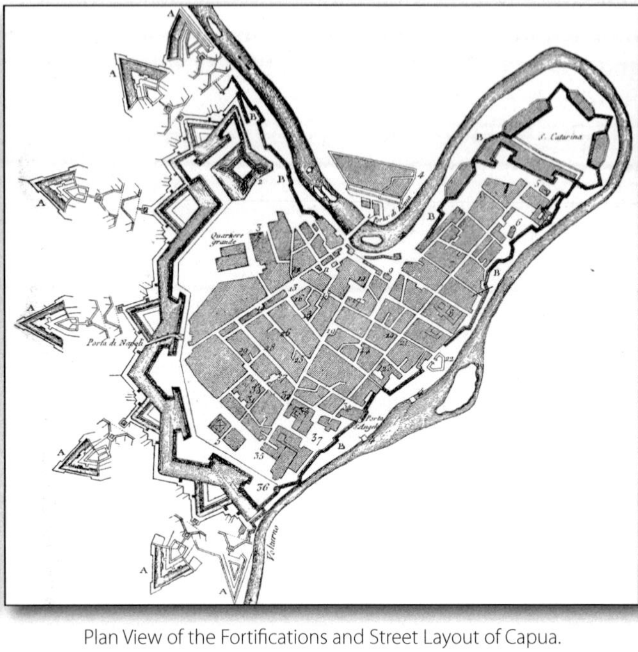

Plan View of the Fortifications and Street Layout of Capua.

Sant'Elmo Castle, Naples.

approaching the Apennine, in Avellino they found the route barred by the enemy. They turned west towards Salerno, still pursued by Carafa. Casualties and desertions weakened the column, and then the survivors were taken by the Austrians.

Once the Spanish cavalry was destroyed, Daun took care of Gaeta and Pescara. The latter was defended by the Duke of Atri, Gian Girolamo Acquaviva. He had 42 guns, 250 Spanish foot, 200 dragoons, and 250 cuirassiers. On 15 July General Wallis started the siege. On 28 August a truce was settled, but on 6 September the fight restarted. After a week, on the 13th, the Spaniards capitulated, even if they had still 4,000 balls, 450 gunpowder barrels, and food for a month more.

Daun started his operation against Gaeta on 22 August. Villena had 126 guns – 113 cannons, and 13 mortars – and 3,000 men, but only 2,500 were fit for combat.

On 30 September the Imperial artillery opened a breach. A Spanish infantry regiment deserted and the Imperial infantry stormed and pillaged

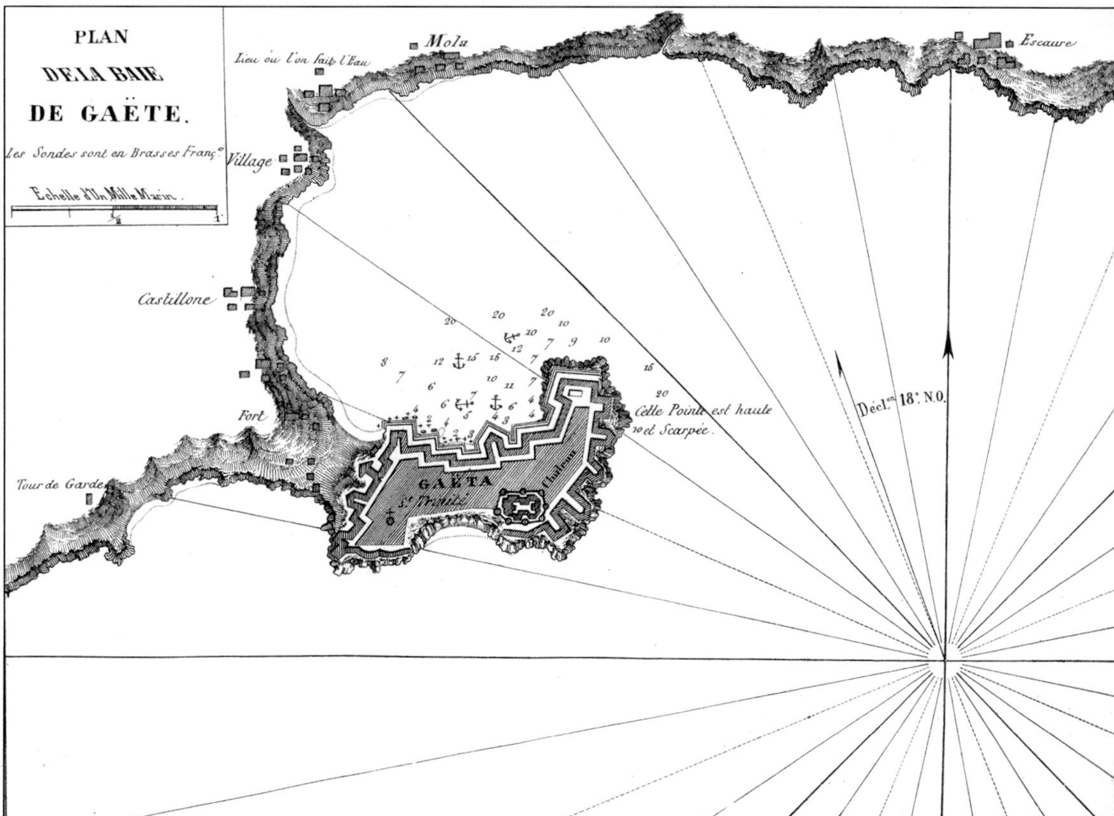

Map of the Fortifications and Coastline of Gaeta.

the city, whilst the Viceroy fled into Orlando's tower with 1,500 men. On the next day, 1 October 1707, he surrendered. The Austrians brought him back to Naples, where he had to walk in the streets along with his top officers, booed by the people.

Daun presented to Saint Gennaro's treasury the Spanish flags his troops kept, and sent a messenger to Vienna. The Emperor appointed him field marshal. Charles of Hasburg appointed him marshall, and governor of the arms. Then Daun left towards northern Italy, to join Victor Amadeus in the forthcoming 1708 Alpine campaign, whilst Cardinal Grimani was appointed Charles of Habsburg's Viceroy of Naples.

IV: Presidii and Sardinia

By the end of 1707, once Naples was seized, the Imperial troops moved toward the Presidii, and Sardinia. Sicily was left aside. It was too complicated to seize it. There was a remarkable French garrison supporting the Spaniards there, and Sicily was far south, but Presidi and Sardinia were weaker, and easier to seize, or at least so it seemed.

The Imperialists moved by land and by sea, on two convoys toward both the coastal towns and the islands, including Elba, comprising the Presidii.

The first convoy destined for the coast in December shipped an expeditionary force commanded by Wetzel, but bad weather forced them to stop in Civitavecchia, in the Papal States. They landed, and went on by land to Orbetello. The local population rose up against the King of Spain, whilst the local garrison, commanded by Marulli, had already officially switched to the Austrian side.

Spanish troops from the other forts were gathering to seize Orbetello, but Wetzel arrived on 20 December just in time to deter them, then moved ahead. On 23 December he took Talamone and Santo Stefano, where he left two garrisons before going back to Naples.

The other convoy was a British-provided one, and shipped General Wallis to Porto Longone, later renamed Porto Azzurro, on the island of Elba. On 8 January 1708 the British ships were ready to land the Austrians, but the Spanish governor of Porto Longone, Pinél, refused to surrender. Wallis blockaded the town and besieged Fajardo fort, whilst on the coast Marulli, from Orbetello, tried to seize Porto Ercole.

No matter how things were going in Porto Longone, on 19 January Wallis seized Piombino on the coast and obtained also its small dependancies on the Elba – Forte del Giogo, Torri di Rio, Marciana, and Campo nell'Elba – by surrender.

Nonetheless, Porto Ercole and Porto Longone still held. They had been supplied by French privateers, and held until spring. In May the Austrians tried a surprise attack on Porto Ercole, but the garrison sallied in advance, waited for the incoming enemies, and trapped them in a small valley. Casualties were so huge, and the result so bad, that the Spaniards forced the Austrians to leave Capoliveri, and Piombino too, and held them until the peace in 1712.

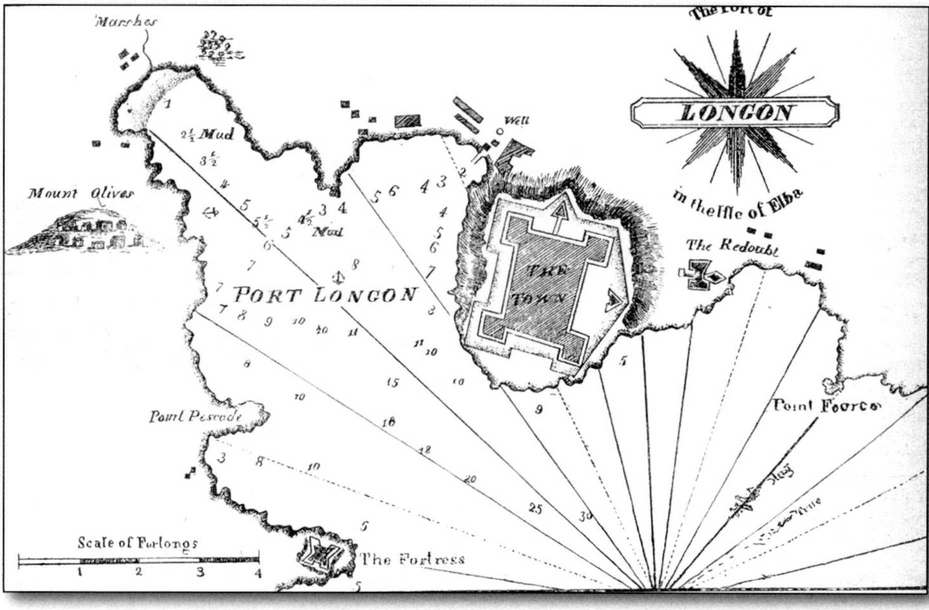

Map of the Fortifications and Coastline of Porto.

If Austrian business went not that well in the Presidii, Sardinia was a different story. Sardinia was poor, neglected by the Spaniards, and inhabited by roughly 300,000 people only, nonetheless it was a kingdom and a part of the Spanish inheritance Charles III was claiming, thus it had to be seized, and contacts were established with the Sardinian nobles supporting Austria.

In early August 1708 Sir John Leak's fleet landed in Cagliari an Imperial expeditionary force commanded by the Count of Sifuentes, a Spanish nobleman loyal to Charles III of Habsburg. Sifuentes demanded the Spanish viceroy, the Marquess of Jamaica[5] to surrender, got a refusal, and order his force to fire. A hundred bombs signalled the pro-Habsburg noblemen that it was time to act. They gathered all the men they found, excited them against the Spaniards, and rushed to the government palace. The Marquess of Jamaica withdrew into the castle with the garrison. The people opened the city gates to the Imperial troops, who entered Cagliari and besieged the castle. The Marquess capitulated and surrendered the whole Kingdom in a short while. So, the city was seized in a few hours, and the island a little after.

A Bastion at Cagliari.

According to the capitulation, the British vessels shipped the Marquess and his men to Cartagena, and then sailed to the conquest of Minorca and Port Mahon in September.

5 Pedro Manuel Colón de Portugal y Castro, Admiral of the Indias, Duke de Veragua and de la Vega, Marquess de Villemizar, and last (due to the English conquest in 1656) Marquess of Jamaica, was a descendant of Christopher Columbus.

23

The King, the Emperor, the Pope and the Grand-Duke

Seeing how badly things were going in Italy, the Bourbons tried to organise a League of Italian princes against the Emperor, but only Pope Clement XI tried to fight. There were reasons why. As soon as operations in northern Italy ended, the Emperor demanded the Duke of Parma, as a prince of the Empire, a 90,000 doubles contribution. Clement XI protested, not only because Parma was a subject of the Holy See, but also because the Duke found the money just selling the Ecclesiastic properties. Then Vienna gave Modena the feud of Comacchio. Comacchio was a small town near the Adriatic coast, commanding the southern part of the wide Po delta, that is to say the portion of the delta not belonging to Venice. Rome ruled Comacchio and considered it as its own property, it never having belonged to the Empire, thus the Pope declared anathema against the Empire. Unfortunately what had worked in the Middle Ages against Emperor Henry IV, did not work at all in 1708 against Emperor Joseph I, who in March officially reaffirmed Imperial supremacy over the whole of northern Italy and Tuscany.

This meant to deprive Rome of the feudal lordship just confirmed in 1701 on Modena, Parma, and Mantua after the respective dukes' requests. The next step was the Imperial order to the Papal Legates and garrisons to leave Parma and Plaisance, where they had been since 1701.

Clement had no real army, and was forced to accept, but refused to recognise Charles of Habsburg as the king of Naples. This was a legal question the Emperor had no way to argue. The Kingdom of Naples had been established by the Normans in the eleventh century just after, and only thanks to, a formal recognition by the Pope, who since then had been its supreme feudal Lord, thus Papal recognition was the legal ground for whomever wanted to be the king there.

And now Louis XIV intervened. As Montesquieu later resumed, he:

> wanted an alliance, according to which he would commit 12,000 soldiers and 3,000 cavalry without horses; the whole at the Pope's expense. The Duke of Tuscany had said: "Sir, I'm a cane which bends towards what one wants. Let me bend." The Pope on the other hand enlisted 25,000 soldiers; and certainly it would

The Adriatic Coast.

> have been easy to get back Naples and Milan … The King promised to the Pope 15,000 weapons for which the Pope had to pay.[1]

Actually Montesquieu was too fast in describing the situation. The Pope had been thinking about his own military situation since the eve of the war. After the survey made in February 1702, the problems affecting the Papal military remained unsolved, and Roman administration was much more concerned with small logistical issues than with strategic tasks or drilling problems.[2] The English Cabinet was notified as early as autumn 1704 that the French were encouraging the Pope to organise a league of the Italian Princes to support Philip V, but nothing happened.

In 1705 in Rome a specially tasked congregation discussed the military situation,[3] but no matter; whatever they could suggest, the core of the problem was at the same time political and religious, "and" military only in addition: how could the Pope balance himself between the two main Catholic dynasties without letting one of them organise a schism?

After the battle of Turin, the Imperial troops' presence in Lombardy became an increasing problem.[4] It was clear that the situation had to be considered, but, once more, whatever concession could be made to one side, the other would react on the religious level.

As soon as the situation worsened, the Pope tried to react. As usual, the problem had to be assessed and faced by a religious point of view first, then by the diplomatic side, and the military side with its financial aspects last. On 9 May 1707 the first problem appeared on the table: what to do if Cardinal Grimani asked for the Imperial troops bound for Naples to have passage through the Papal States?[5] And under which conditions could it be permitted or happen?[6] An arrangement was found, and Daun passed through.

On 28 April 1708 a tasked congregation met, and discussed what was going on in Ferrara and Comacchio. Within a few days, in May 1708, the question was dramatically open and Rome had to decide what to do.[7]

On 20 June a further congregation met,[8] and decided what to suggest the Pope do. They preferred to rely on precedents, but the most recent they could

---

1 Montesquieu, op. cit., p.208.

2 See in ASR fondo *Soldatesche e Galere*, Miscellanea, busta 657, the "Elenco dei letti forniti alle truppe dalle Comunità ed Ebrei alle Guardie di N.S" [List of the beds provided by the Communities and Jews to the Guards of Our Lord], on 14 August 1704, or the "Concessione dell'Armeria Vaticana" from 1701 until 1709.

3 ASR, fondo *Congregazioni Particolari Deputate 1600–1760*, T. 18, foglio 18, "Tassa del Milione".

4 ASR, fondo *Congregazioni Particolari Deputate 1600–1760*, T. 38, foglio 12, "Germanorum Militum".

5 ASR, fondo *Soldatesche e Galere*, Miscellanea, busta 656, number 3, "Verbale della congregazione del 9 maggio 1707" [Minute of the congregation held on 9 May 1707].

6 ASR, fondo *Soldatesche e Galere*, Miscellanea busta 656, number 2, "Questioni relative all'arrivo e passaggio degli Imperiali". [Questions related to the arrival and passage of the Imperialists].

7 ASR, fondo *Soldatesche e Galere*, Miscellanea, busta 656, number 4, "Invasione dello Stato Ecclesiastico anno 1708" A) "Invasione di Comacchio e del Ducato di Ferrara dalle Truppe Cesaree et Armamento dello Stato Ecclesiastico in Difesa 1708" [Invasion of Comacchio and of the Duchy of Ferrara by the Caesaren Troops and defensive armament of the Ecclesiastic State in 1708].

8 ASR, fondo *Soldatesche e Galere*, Miscellanea, busta 656, number 4, "Invasione dello Stato Ecclesiastico anno 1708" – 4) "congregazione del mercoledì 20 giugno 1708 sulle provvisioni economiche e d'armamento da farsi". [congregation on Wednesday 20 June 1708 about the

find was very old, from the Castro War in 1640–44. Anyway they relied on it, and on older ones, and here is the result: they had to enhance taxation first – as was done on 2 July – following the examples provided by Urban VIII's bull issued on 13 September 1643, ordering the commons to give the Holy Seat 3,600,000 Roman scudi per year, as well as the other bull issued by the same Pope on 12 April 1630 to find money for the troops.

The cardinals had known since 1705 that a million was probably needed[9] just to start, and now the Pope needed it to raise an army. The money was taken from the Papal treasury in Castel Sant'Angelo, the citadel of Rome.

Pope Pius V stored there in the late sixteenth century half a million golden scudi, equalling five million Roman scudi in 1708 currency. The later popes in the seventeenth century sometimes exploited that treasure, and in 1708 there was still barely a half, or at least so it was said.[10] The Pope took 300,000 scudi and the armament started. Thus conscription of "chosen men" by the commons of the state[11] was issued, and all the Papal subjects serving abroad were ordered to come back under the national flag.[12] Incidentally, whoever volunteered was accepted, especially Spanish and French deserters, who were supposed to be already drilled and skilled.

The recall of the Papal subjects from abroad aimed to gather as many experienced officers as one could. Actually there were not that many Papal subjects serving abroad, and above all the army could have the best officers, but how could they perform without experienced and well-drilled men? Well, perhaps not that much, but it is certain that they could have performed much better had politics not affected their actions, as we shall see.

A new military rule was issued,[13] wartime wages were regulated,[14] and cavalry increased.[15] Plans were made. At first in the summer the Cardinals calculated the financial support needed for a 20,000 men force, "Supposing

economic and weaponry provisions to be made]. This is a summary made later. The original text is missing, but one can realise what did the cardinals had in mind thanks to the list of the congregations, and acts reported in the minute.

9 ASR, fondo *Congregazioni Particolari Deputate 1600–1760*, T. 37, foglio 5, "Congregazione sulle Armi del 1705".

10 Ottieri, op. cit. vol. 3, Book 13, p.64.

11 ASR, fondo *Soldatesche e Galere*, Miscellanea, busta 656, number 4, "Invasione dello Stato Ecclesiastico anno 1708" – "Editto per la leva d'Uomini scelti da farsi dalle Comunità dello Stato Ecclesiastico" [Invasion of the Ecclesiastic state year 1708 – Rule for the levy of chosen Men to be made by the communities of the Ecclesiastic State].

12 ASR, fondo *Soldatesche e Galere*, Miscellanea, busta 656, number 4, "Invasione dello Stato Ecclesiastico anno 1708", Order to all the Papal subiects to repatriate, issues on 19 June 1708.

13 ASR, fondo *Soldatesche e Galere*, Miscellanea, busta 656, number 4, "Invasione dello Stato Ecclesiastico anno 1708" – "Capitoli e leggi da osservarsi per ordine espresso della Santità di Nostro Signore dagli Ufficiali e Soldati tanto di Cavalleria, e di Fanteria dell'Armamento fatto nelle presenti emergenze". [Chapters and rules to be observed due to an clear order by the Holiness of Our Lord by the Officers and Soldiers as well of Cavalry as of Infantry of the armament made in in the prsenet contigencies].

14 ASR, fondo *Soldatesche e Galere*, Miscellanea, busta 656, number 4, "Invasione dello Stato Ecclesiastico anno 1708" – lista delle paghe [list of wages, issued on 24 August 1708].

15 ASR, fondo *Soldatesche e Galere*, Miscellanea, busta 656, number 4, "Invasione dello Stato Ecclesiastico anno 1708" – "notificazione per l'aumento della Cavalleria" [Notification about improving Cavalry], on 29 September 1708.

Count Marsigli.

(as it is said) that O.L.[16] is in resolution not to invade the State of Milan, and the Kingdom of Naples, but only to be in condition to defend the Ecclesiastic State."[17]

Problems arose as the army was raised: even if one could find weapons, there were not enough beds for the troopers.[18] Corps too were a problem, for they were expensive, thus some of the noblest families organised, paid on their own, and offered regiments, such as the Ruspoli and Albani in Rome, and the Malvezzi in Bologna did.[19]

As said, the campaign went as bad as one could expect. On one hand the Papal army had no training and no experience, whilst the Imperialists had been at war for a generation against the most dangerous enemies of the period, the French and the Ottomans, thus no comparison and no competition was possible. Nonetheless, as said, the Papal troops would have not proved that bad had policy not so badly affected their actions.

General Marsigli, from Bologna, was appointed as the commander-in-chief. Marsigli successfully served for a very long time in the Austrian army in Hungary, the Balkans, and in Germany. He had been one of the most important members of the Austrian delegation headed by Prince Eugene at the peace negotiations in Carlowitz in 1699. At the eve of the Spanish succession crisis he besieged and seized Landau in 1702, but was later deprived of his rank due to the fall of Breisach im Brisgau. Actually he was only the deputy commander there. The city was commanded by Bavarian Count d'Arco when it was seized by the French. D'Arco and Marsigli suffered a military trial, were charged of not having well defended Breisach, and were declared guilty. D'Arco lost his rank, and his head, Marsigli only his rank. The news spread out in all the courts of Europe, and Louis XIV offered Marsigli to

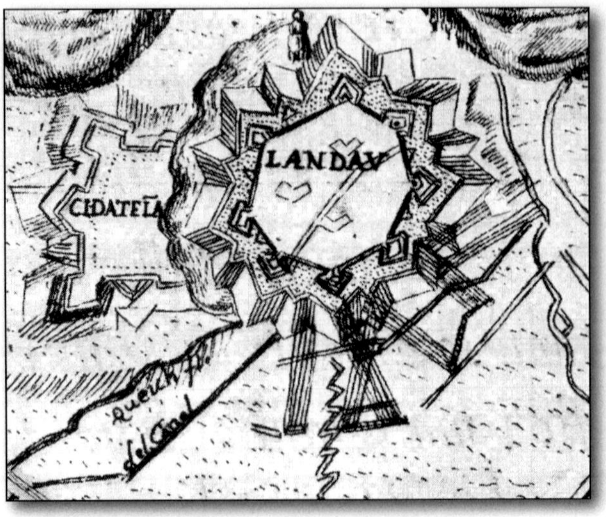

Landau Beseiged by Marsigli.

16 "O.L". means "Our Lord", and it is how I translated "N.S." – Nostro Signore – which was one of the usual ways to mention or to appeal the Pope at that time, the other being "Your/His Holiness", or also "The Holiness of Our Lord", "Our Lord" meaning the Pope, not God.

17 ASR, fondo *Soldatesche e Galere*, Miscellanea, busta 656, number 4, "Invasione dello Stato Ecclesiastico anno 1708" – Congregazione on a not mentioned day, probably in July, p.86.

18 ASR, fondo *Soldatesche e Galere*, Miscellanea, busta 657, see the "Elenco dei letti forniti alle truppe dalle Comunità ed Ebrei alle Guardie di N.S. à tutto maggio del 1708" [List of the beds provided by the Communities and Jews to the Guards of Our Lord throughout the whole of May 1708], and the "Memoriale sulla fornitura di letti alle Truppe" [Memoir about providing beds for the troops] on 10 October, 1708.

19 ASR, fondo *Soldatesche e Galere*, Miscellanea, busta 657, "accettazione della levata del Rgt Malvezzi", 8 September, 1708.

come to France. Thus he retired in Provence, and remained there a long time, almost until the Pope called him to arms.

Marsigli planned to concentrate 12,000 men in the Legations and put 4,000 more in Faenza, because it was the strategic hub for any operation in the plain of Aemilia, left 3,000 soldiers in Rome, and committed 2,000 cavalry to watch the Neapolitan border. In early September 1708 he had 9,000 regulars and 1,800 militia concentrated around Ferrara.

Since the first half of the seventeenth century the Papal State had organised a fortified system protecting its Aemilian border, whose main fortresses were Ferrara and Forte Urbano, near Bologna. Ferrara had a forward protection relying on Fort Stellata, near the Po, and on the Pontelagoscuro forts. Both had proved themselves quite well, and were strategically relevant during the 1640–44 war, thus Marsigli knew that if he could hold them, he could feel safe.

On 7 September, with a free corps, he started operations eastbound, attacking the towns of Argenta and Ostellato on his side of the Po. They were in Austrian hands, and were the first step to seize back Comacchio. He succeeded, and on 27 September he reached Comacchio with 1,800 men, but due to the situation preferred not to attack, and withdrew. The Austrians were gathering, and Marsigli did not want his not so reliable troops scattered.

In the first decade of October Daun had six cavalry and 16 infantry regiments. In Rome the cardinals planned to enhance the army with a further army corps 12,000 men strong, supported by 16 six-pounder field cannons. Each cannon had to be towed by three horses, whilst a fourth horse had to be kept as reserve, thus the artillery needed 64 horses. whilst 82 more horse and 496 oxen – 248 pairs – had to tow a supply train composed of 145 wagons.[20]

It was already too late. On 16 October the Austrians attacked Ostellato, north-east of Argenta, and halfway between Comacchio and Ferrara. Once attacked, the regular Papal troopers fled and left the militiamen alone, who bravely tried to defend the town, but 200 were killed in the combat and the town was stormed and sacked. Soon afterwards the Austrians stormed Goro, on the coast, whilst Marsigli withdrew again.

On 27 October Daun reached Bondeno. The garrison was short of ammunition. On the third day they had no more, and asked for supplies from Ferrara, but the Legate suggested they surrender.

Marsigli was in trouble. He was around Ferrara, and had the Po on the north and the Austrians now to the west in Bondeno and to the east in Ostellato, but his real problem was that Rome and Vienna started negotiating. This was reflected in contacts between Daun and the Papal Legate, who ordered Marsigli not to initiate anything. Then the negotiation with Daun went further, and the Legate ordered Papal Troops to leave Pontelagoscuro. The Austrians then besieged Fort Stellata, which had to surrender on 3 November. Marsigli had now no option but holding passively. Thus he left

20 ASR, fondo *Soldatesche e Galere*, Miscellanea, busta 656, number 4, "Nota dell'Artiglieria da Campagna con il suo treno per servizio d'un Corpo d'Armata di 12000 uomini" [Note of the Field Artillery with its train supporting a 12,000 men Army Corps], issued on 10 October, 1708.

5,000 men in Ferrara and 3,000 in Forte Urbano, locked himself in Ancona with 1,400, and sent the remaining 4,000 back to Rome.[21]

On 12 November the inactivity imposed by the Legate showed its results. Daun had only 9,000 men – foot and cavalry – but due to the Papal lack of initiative, they happily blockaded both Ferrara and Forte Urbano and started looting the country, for – how unusual for the Austrians! – they were short of food. They intercepted convoys bound to Ferrara, and distributed the main part of their forces in Romagna to winter quarters.[22]

By mid December the Imperial forces in the Kingdom of Naples started moving north. They crossed the Garigliano river and encamped in the Papal State to see out the winter. At the same time, in the north, Daun occupied Fano and Senigallia on the Adriatic coast of Romagna.

The Pope hoped for a French intervention, but things in Flanders went very badly and Louis XIV had bigger troubles to care about than Rome.

On 22 December the Emperor sent an ultimatum to Rome: if by 15 January 1709 at midnight the Pope had not retired the anathema, reduced the army to only 5,000 men, and allowed the Austrian troops to pass through the Papal States for the rest of the war, the Imperial offensive would increase, that is to say until it reached Rome.

Clement ordered the walls of Rome restored, concentrated nine infantry and three cavalry regiments in the city, issued a pardon to bandits volunteering into the army, ordered a period of penitence and fasting, and hoped for a miracle. Meanwhile, Daun moved along the Adriatic coast and occupied the town of Jesi.

No miracle occurred, no French came, and, one hour before the term expired, Clement agreed to undersign the Imperial conditions. The war was lost, and Austrian rule over Italy definitely affirmed for the next 150 years.

---

21 ASR, fondo *Soldatesche e Galere*, Miscellanea, busta 657, "danni subiti e spese fatte per il passaggio delle truppe pontificie" [Damages suffered and expenses made due to the Papal Troops' passage], concerning the cities and towns of Cantiano, Gubbio, Sinigaglia, Mondolfo, Fossombrone and Rimini.

22 ASR, fondo *Soldatesche e Galere*, Miscellanea, busta 656, "passaggio delle Truppe Cesaree per lo Stato ecclesiastico nel 1708" [passage of Caesarean Troops through the Ecclesiastic State], concerning the cities and towns of Cantiano, Gubbio, Sinigaglia, Mondolfo, Fossombrone, and Rimini, and busta 658 "Danni e spese patite dalle Comunità dello Stato ecclesiastico a causa delle truppe imperiali – 1709" [Damages and expenses suffered by the communities of the Ecclesiastic State because of the Imperial Troops]. The folder contains also the bills presented by the commons to the Papal Administration to be repaid for the food and accommodation provided to Papal troops withdrawing to Rome in late 1708.

24

Campaigning in the Alps

Victor Amadeus's financial situation had improved only since when the French were expulsed in 1706, but revenues remained affected until the liberation of Nice and Savoy, that is to say until the end of the war. Moreover, French pillaging caused a dramatic rise in wheat prices which by 1709, also due to the terrible 1708–09 winter freeze in Europe, reached a peak of five liras per measure, that is to say practically twice the 1700 price. The Duke decided to enhance the so-called "comparto dei grani" – share of the grains. This tax in origin was a three percent share of the harvest, and when practically doubled in the previous war, it had given the state 53,000 sacks of corn.

The year 1707 practically ended operations in Italy, and it was not by chance that the 1707–08 Piedmontese military budget absorbed some 7,268,000 liras.[1] As said before, revenues and incomes from taxes were still lower than in peacetime, for both Savoy and Nice were still in French hands, but recently occupied Monferrato "benefited" from the Savoyard presence and had the honour to contribute to Victor Amadeus' war budget, starting by paying the winter quarter to the Allied troops.

Financial exercise 1708–09 saw a further increase of military expenditure to 8,000,000 liras,[2] and revenues were still in a poor situation, even if the liberation of the Cisalpine territories made things less difficult than in the past. Nonetheless, also because of the shortages due to the terrible 1708 winter, in summer 1709 Victor Amadeus had to pay a lot of money to purchase wheat on neutral markets, as he did in Venice where he spent more than a million liras. Clearly that was not a present to his subjects: he sold them the purchased wheat and gained a million.

The British were still supporting him. Nothing had changed since Godolphin wrote to Marlborough in September 1707:

> Spain cannot be supported this winter without Prince Eugene, and some troops from Italy and Italy cannot be made useful next year to the Common Cause, but by putting the Duke of Savoy at the head of an Army to act offensively against

1 Prato, op. cit., p.260.

2 Prato, *idem*.

> France ...When these things are well provided for France will be less able to have any great superiority either upon the Rhine or in Flanders.[3]

Victor Amadeus' 1708 objectives were limited, even if strategically important. He simply wanted to remove the French from the upper Dora, and Chisone valleys, seizing Perosa, Fenestrelle, Exilles and, if possible, Briançon, that is to say all the Alpine passes acceding Italy. The plan was simple. The Duke wanted to enter Savoy through the Cenisio, and the Piccolo San Bernardo. Lyon had to appear as his task. As soon as the enemies concentrated there, ducal troops would turn south, and back, towards the Upper Dora Valley, marching directly to Oulx and Cesana. The next step had to be against the fortresses of Exilles and Fenestrelle, with the besieging corps protected by the concentration of all the available troops between those fortresses and the enemy manoeuvring mass.

Victor Amadeus gathered 23 ducal and 31 Imperial battalions, officially totalling 32,345 infantry and 1,261 cavalry, and collected 30,000 sacks of wheat in Morges, on Lake Geneva. In mid April he seized 1,500 mules, contracted the purchasing of a further 4,000, and scattered everywhere bold and boasting rumours of the enormous war contributions he was going to impose in Lyon as soon as he seized it. The French were concerned. Louis XIV cared so much about the Alpine front, that he committed there his other best general, Villars, who tried to gather as much information as he could.

Meanwhile Victor Amadeus split his army in two columns. The smaller – 3,345 foot and 350 cavalrymen – was commanded by Schulemburg, who advanced through the Aosta Valley and Tarantasia up to Moutiers. Victor Amadeus prepared to perform all the feints he planned. Along with the strongest column – 29,000 infantry, and 911 cavalry – and followed by 3,000 mules, on 16 July 1708 he entered the Moriana, committing the vanguard ahead to La Chambre. Considering this movement, adding it to the well-known presence of the warehouses, and to the magazines set up near Geneva, and given the presence of Schulemburg in Moutiers, the Savoyard army seemed effectively moving ahead towards Lyon. To confirm this impression, Victor told everybody how he was willing to make an offensive. He made great preparations, setting up additional warehouses everywhere. Then, suddenly, following his plans, he let Schulemburg's column join him south through the Encombres Pass, gathered up all the other detachments but the vanguard, turned back and secured the Roue hill. Last, all his men crossed the Roue pass, and went to besiege Exilles.

On 1 August Villars realised he remained with 73 battalions and 17 squadrons in front of a vacuum, or almost. That was a problem because, according to him, the protection of the Dauphiné depended on the conservation of Savoy. Had the fortresses Victor Amadeus was going to besiege fallen, the French return to Italy was impossible. On the other hand, Allied raids in the Dauphiné would be possible, and easy. Villars asked for

3 Lord Treasurer Godolphin to Lord Marlborough, 7 September 1707, Blenheim MSS, A2–23, rep. in Hattendorf, op. cit., p.91.

reinforcements. but the situation in Flanders was so complicated that he got far less than he was looking for: only nine battalions and eight more squadrons.

Actually he had a favourable five to three ratio, but only on paper, because his troops were scattered between the Dauphiné, the Lyon area, and Savoy, and they had to be concentrated first. On 2 August Villars decided not to use 27 battalions to relieve all the threatened fortresses. He preferred to reduce damage, and moved to Briançon, ordering another incoming 16 battalions to move to Montgenevre as soon as they arrived. They came only on 9 August.

At the same time, Victor Amadeus had happily begun the sieges of Exilles – on 6 August – and Perosa. The former was defended by 600 men, the latter by 500. On 9 August the Duke was notified that Villars entered Briançon with 60 battalions and 25 squadrons, thus he ordered Schulemburg to take five battalions and occupy the heights of Exilles, to prevent the enemy from passing any aid to the fortress.

On 11 August Perosa surrendered. In the afternoon, the opposing vanguards clashed in Cesana. The Allies lost 150 dead, the French something more, and massed at the bottom of the valley on the left of the Dora. During the night Victor Amadeus let general Rehbinder's corps move to the Pragelato Valley, in order to blockade the road from Fenestrelle. Then he recalled to Oulx the bulk of his troops, and on the 12th sent them to Salbertrand, reinforcing the position of San Colombano. That protected the back of the troops besieging Exilles, and the next morning, 13 August, Exilles surrendered. Villars was notified that day.

Now the Duke had to seize Fenestrelle and committed the bulk of his troops to support Rehbinder at Balbotet, where they arrived on the 15th. On that same day Villars moved towards the Assietta hill, and found the route barred by four Allied battalions. He ordered widening and repairing of the roads to allow passage for the cannons needed to support the attack, but this took time. Then he sent further five battalions to the Albergian pass, but Victor Amadeus heard about it, and committed there seven of his. When on the morning of 17 August the French reached the Albergian, they found the Allied battalions already entrenched, waiting for them.

Villars left aside any other attempt, and waited to see what next: the arrival of reinforcements, or Fenestrelle's surrender? The surrender came on 31 August, and marked the end of the 1708 campaign in the Alps.

The French defeat in Flanders, and Vendôme's misfortune at Versailles after Oudenarde caused a rotation of generals. Villars was moved to Flanders, and the Duke of Berwick arrived in the Alps. This English general was not as brilliant as Villars, nonetheless he was skilled, and knew the art of warfare.

The 1709 campaign started with great projects. According to the Allies, their army was to enter Savoy, go upstream along the Rhône, reach Franche-Comté and join the Imperial army on the Rhine. Louis XIV communicated this to Berwick, who had more or less the same forces Villars had the previous year: 84 battalions, and 30 squadrons. Berwick thoroughly studied the morphology of the likely operational theatre, and deployed his troops along a crescent, with the centre further ahead then the wings. This had to force Victor Amadeus ' troops – wherever they wanted to go – to move outside along the arc of a circumference, whilst Berwick would move faster, manoeuvring on internal lines along the chord of the same arc. He put the extremity of his right wing on the Mediterranean, between San Lorenzo del Varo and Antibes, set the centre at Tournoux, relying on a strong entrenched camp containing also the supplies, and stretched his left wing to Barreaux, where he relied on another entrenched camp.

That year Victor Amadeus left the command to Daun, and to Rehbinder. They came across the Alps from Mount Cenisio between 8–10 July, tested the French line here and there, and through Arc arrived in Moutiers on the 26th. On the 27 they engaged in a fight. It ended victoriously on the 28th. The Allied troops broke through two enemy resistance lines in the gorges of Nôtre Dame of Briançon, due to a harsh vanguard action by all their grenadiers. This opened the way to Conflans, which the Allies reached having engaged and beaten the enemy again at Cervins, capturing three flags, and more than 300 prisoners. However Daun, hearing the non-positive trend of Imperial operations on the Rhine, and notified about the defeat of Rehbinder's corps in Briançon which rendered the Allied conjunction in the Rhineland impossible, opted to return to Italy, and ended the campaign.

1710 came. At the end of June the Austrian army arrived in Piedmont, commanded by the Count of Harrach. Victor Amadeus assumed the supreme command, and once more sent ahead a corps commanded by Schulemburg towards the Aosta Valley, whilst he moved to Susa with the bulk of the army. Berwick too reached his army at the same time, and occupied the same positions he had the previous year.

On the night of 6 July Victor Amadeus crossed the Moncenisio. On 9 July he sent detachments to reinforce and cover some sectors, and on the 10th he seized Moutiers. Then, given the French positions, he was not able to pass into Moriana, and camped in Tarantasia. Meanwhile, Schulemburg attacked an enemy corps in Conflans. This allowed the Allied army to advance, and commit detachments to liberate Annécy, and other places. Berwick retired to the camp of Barreaux and left free passage for the Allies, who took Miolans on 24 July and on the 27th Rumilly and Chambéry, where they encamped.

Now Victor Amadeus could no longer advance if he did not take Barreaux first. But fodder was scarce, and it was August, that is to say on the mountains it was late and the weather would soon make communications hard, due to rain and snow. It was not possible to take winter quarters in Savoy, thus the Duke decided to leave, and on 8 August, he moved towards Italy, ending the campaign. Besides, news was coming to him about solid diplomatic negotiations between England and France. From London they asked him about an exchange between the crown of Savoy and that of Spain, so, it was better to stay in Turin, and follow events closely. He knew his military war was over, and his diplomatic war was starting again.

No matter the restrictive orders the next British commander in Flanders, the Duke of Ormonde, would get, in London the new Tory government headed by Lord Saint John knew the British army had to look as bellicose as usual. Thus in February 1711 Saint John urged the British ambassador in Piedmont, Peterborough, for a diversion from Savoy into south-eastern France:

> Many advantages would result to the Common Cause from such a measure. Spain would be relieved; our Army in Flanders would be able to penetrate further into enemy's country and France would be in no condition to act offensively on the Rhine and to penetrate one side into the Empire, whilst the King of Sweden does the same thing on another.[4]

Emperor Charles VI.

Then a political turmoil occurred. On 17 April 1711 Emperor Joseph I died and his brother Charles, Archduke Charles, Charles III King of Spain, became the Holy Roman Emperor. Had Austria won the war, this meant the union of the Spanish Empire with the Holy Roman Empire in a powerful compact that had not existed since Charles V's abdication in January 1556. What to do? Go ahead with the war, of course, London said, but only to exploit it as a means to getting a more remarkable diplomatic strength. Thus the operation had to be pushed ahead, especially in Italy, where nothing seemed to occur.

In May, Saint John underlined to the new English ambassador to the States General: "If the French should reinforce their Army on the Rhine from Dauphine, we ours from Flanders, and the Duke of Savoy remain in a state of inaction, our condition would be bad indeed."[5]

At the same time the instructions to the British ambassador in Vienna mentioned once more a diversion to be made from Piedmont into France: "You will urge the situation of our affairs in general both in Flanders and on the Rhine as well as in Spain, and show that there is no scheme so likely to give an immediate ease to the War in all parts, and particularly in Spain, as a vigorous diversion on the side of Piedmont."[6]

Well, all this was nice and fine, had Victor Amadeus not been aware of the secret talks going on between England and France. No matter how warlike the British attitude and instructions could appear, whoever knew something about warfare could easily realise that, as things were, such a war could be ended only by a negotiation or it would last a century more. Thus it was clear that these British instructions aimed more at creating diplomatic pressure on

4 Lord St. John to Lord Peterborough, on 13 February, 1711, in PRO, SP 104/40, rep. in Hattendorf, op. cit., p.92

5 Lord St. John to Lord Raby (soon to be created Lord Strafford, on 29 June that year), 8 May 1711, in PRO, SP 84/241, fo. 107, rep. in Hattendorf, op. cit., pp.92–93.

6 Instructions to ambassador Charles Whitworth, issued on 29 May 1711, in PRO, SP 104/214, fo. 209, rep. in Hattendorf, op. cit., p.93

France through operations, than achieving a military goal, no matter how important it could be.

By the end of the war, sums were performed in Turin. In total the war cost 211,100,000 liras, of which 43,200,000 – that is to say 20.46 percent – came from loans and debts. Revenues lost between 1703 and 1710 due to the French occupation rose to 26 million liras. The gap had been in theory covered by subsidies providing a bit less than 49 million in the same period. But subsidies often arrived so much later than promised that, when signing the peace, Victor Amadeus still had to receive one million liras from Amsterdam and four million from London, that is to say more or less 50,000 scudi from the Netherlands and 200,000 from England, whose payment "to be made in advance" was four months late. Thus the actual figure of the subsidies received by Piedmont did not exceed a little more than 43,000,000. Anyway, due to rumours in the wind, and to the huge expenditure made, Victor Amadeus knew that it was time to sit, and see.

25

Utrecht

The Anglo-French talks had started long before, and achieved nothing. But soon after Joseph I's death, and Charles of Habsburg's accession to the Imperial throne, the problem came back on the table. The settlement, if any, now depended far more than before on the aftermath of the war, and that aftermath had just changed dramatically. Britain did not intend to present the Emperor with all the Spanish-held countries, otherwise the situation would be the same as in 1701, just differing in the family name of the enemy: Habsburg instead of Bourbon. French–British talks continued, and the little that was rumoured in The Hague was enough to scare the States General.

As is known, after long inconclusive talks the Anglo-French negotiations really resumed in spring 1712, and resulted in Great Britain's military separation from the other Allies. It might have seemed like a French success, but in fact it was Britain's. London wanted to avoid the reconstitution of a power as the late Charles V had, and wanted to control the militarily and commercially strategic points in areas she considered important.

The other concerned parties each had quite a wealth of requests, and did not seem willing to drop them, unless under heavy pressure or hearing adequate counter-offers. London wanted to settle the quarrel quickly, but without losing the results she could expect after more than 10 years of war. Versailles had to get out of the conflict as soon as possible, and with the least amount of damage. A possible agreement was found between Britain, and France. Now it depended on the other concerned parts: what did they want to do?

Turin entirely had interest in settling the question at the best price, and before the others found a separate agreement, leaving Savoy alone facing France. As for the fate of Austria: the Netherlands demanded the Barrier, Prussia wanted Upper Gelderland, and official recognition of royal rank for the Hohenzollern; Portugal looked for border changes in the colonies; the German princes demanded the most disparate things; the Emperor wanted all the Spanish inheritance. That was the reason why, at the end Austria was left alone.

Austrian demands meant a confrontation with England. In fact, leaving aside what for Vienna was the heart of the matter – that is to say a Bourbon on the Spanish throne claimed by Charles VI – from the English point of view

Philip V.

the ideal king of Spain had to be a trusted, faithful British ally, militarily not strong, therefore incapable of managing a policy not dependent on London, and willing to grant British trade the opening of the world markets belonging to Spain.

Charles of Habsburg was already too powerful, and after all it was known how selfish the Habsburgs were – and he proved to be far more selfish than any other – thus he was no longer a suitable candidate. As things were, now Philip V was a match, but there was always the risk of French interference, as seen in 1701.

It is easy to realise why British policy now looked for an agreement with the French. It depended on how much Louis XIV and Philip V would accept the British proposals; and this seemed much more likely than having the same proposals accepted by Charles VI. Still hoping that Philip V could decide to leave the throne, Lord Saint-John planned a complicated ballet, with an exchange between the crowns ending with Philip getting southern Italy, Charles VI being indemnised in various ways, and Victor Amadeus II being crowned king of Spain. This was the ideal solution for Britain, because Victor Amadeus enjoyed both the sympathies of Queen Anne, as a relative, and of the British government, thanks to the enthusiastic reports Lord Peterborough sent about him.

Actually, to be sincere, Peterborough was so enthusiastic because he fell in love with Victor Amadeus' natural daughter, later legitimised. Besides, the Duke of Savoy had good cards. He was a legitimate heir to the crown of Spain, and he was accepted by Britain due to personal reasons, and thanks to his military weakness, which would render Spanish domains de facto dependent on London commerce. Lastly, Victor was a friend neither of France, nor of Austria, and – which at that time counted very much in the eyes of the British – had not only shown tolerance towards the Waldensians, but he had also engaged in bitter disputes with Rome on jurisdictional matters, which for Protestants was the best thing a Catholic sovereign could do.

And what did he think of such an exchange? He hesitated. The throne of Spain, or as foreseen by another hypothesis the thrones of Naples and Sicily, involved the cession of his hereditary states; and beyond the "ifs" and the "buts", Victor would miss his Piedmont, and was too Italian to leave without regrets. When in 1710 that possibility had been suggested the first time, he remained in doubt. Regarding that possibility he ordered his advisor Pietro Mellarède, at that time in Holland for the ongoing negotiations, "that you take the opportunity to reason about it with Prince Eugene (in time, however, that it will not endanger its achievement) to probe his feelings, being this such a great transplant of the House, and then to provide to us an exact account."[1] Nothing occurred, because when the letter arrived in Holland Eugene already left for the front, and Mellarède had not been able to follow him, but the issue was still pending.

And was Austria available for peace? Not so much. The so-called "specific requests" advanced by Vienna could be summarised in three words: "all or nothing", and, of course, "nothing" meant the continuation of the conflict to the bitter end.

From Holland both Sinzendorff and Eugene had flooded the Hofburg with reports and letters whose content was always the same: it was necessary to meet the British and Dutch positions to find a common line; Austria risked being abandoned. However there was nothing to be do done, as Charles did not want to hear.

When in early April 1712 the project to give Victor Amadeus the Spanish crown made its way, Imperial ambassador Wratislaw reacted in the most pragmatic way and prepared an indemnity plan: the Emperor would get the Savoyard States in exchange for Spain. And what did Charles do? He became furious and rejected the project, thus eliminating any possible negotiation his ambassadors could undertake within the peace congress.

Still, in spring 1712, not caring about the Habsburgs, Saint John arrived a step away from the goal. Louis XIV wanted to cease supporting his grandchild, and had Philip V agreed to leave Madrid, the war was over. But destiny let its axe fall on men's decisions. In 10 months death repeatedly struck the House of France, bringing to the grave all Louis XIV's heirs but two: the great-grandchild Louis, Duke of Anjou (the future Louis XV), and Philip V. And what if the little, and sickly, Duke of Anjou had not survived? Who would inherit the crown? The cadet branch of Orléans, that is to say Philippe d'Orléans, or the last survivor of the main branch, Philip V?

The question was very serious. The ghost of the union between two powerful crowns reappeared.

Saint John demanded Philip V choose whether to stay in Madrid or pass to France. To be ready for every possibility, Saint John called to London Count Annibale Maffei, Victor Amadeus' plenipotentiary in Utrecht. He had to be on the spot if the Duke of Savoy was designated king of Spain, in case Philip chose France.

In spite of the offer of Naples, Sicily, and Savoy, had he opted for France, on 29 May 1712 Philip chose Spain. That was a first issue decided. Thus on 17 June, Saint John could at least submit to the British Parliament the general conditions for peace, and obtained the Parliament's consent. Finally the real work to settle the war began.

---

1 H.R.H. Victor Amadeus II to Pietro Mellarède, Turin, 14 April 1710, rep. in Carlo Contessa, *I regni di Napoli e di Sicilia nelle aspirazioni italiane di Vittorio Amedeo II di Savoia* (Turin:1933), p.73.

In the same period the Duke of Ormonde received the famous and blamed "restrictive orders", stopping the British participation in the fighting. This, together with the diplomatic situation, put the Netherlands in trouble. Denain cut the legs to every further Dutch ambition to go ahead, and the news of the closer and closer contacts between London and Versailles made Heinsius accept the negotiations.

On one hand, now Saint John accelerated negotiations with the French, fearing that Heinsius would start separated talks. On the other hand, the Dutch accession to the negotiations made all the Allies realise that to be their last chance to join the winner's side, otherwise they would remain alone against France. Thus the ambassadors of Portugal, Prussia, and Savoy let Britain and the Dutch know that their masters were willing to make peace.

At this point London had still two important questions pending. The commercial problem was to be resolved through various agreements, including the monopoly of the slave trade – "the Asiento" – throughout Spanish Americas, but the Mediterranean situation was still in progress. To the eyes of a Maritime Power, such as Britain was, the keys to the Mediterranean were two: Gibraltar and Sicily. The first was already British but the second was not, and had not even to become British. It would be too demanding and expensive to keep Sicily against the Imperial, and French claims.

It was better to apply to Sicily, on a smaller scale, what had been planned for Spain, that is to say, to put Sicily in the hands of a weak sovereign, a faithful ally to London, and not friendly to Versailles, and Vienna. Hence the Royal Highness of Victor Amadeus II was the best choice. Choosing him meant to control the Mediterranean, obtain the House of Savoy's perpetual gratitude, fulfil the promises to enhance him to the royal rank, make Queen Anne happy, and ensure British commercial rule of the whole Mediterranean, due to the commanding central position of Sicily. Last, holding Sicily would be on the Savoyard budget, not on the British one.

It may seem narrow-minded and chauvinistic to dedicate so much room to questions relating to Savoy and Italy, but it is not, because they had the same wide room at that time, and even more during the following Rastadt peace conference, and the consequent discussions in Baden. Moreover, all the Italian States sent their representatives to Utrecht, but only the Savoyard delegation was recognised with the right of taking an active part in the negotiation, due to the committment in the war, and the meetings occurred between France, Britain, the Netherlands and Savoy only.

The assignment of Sicily to Savoy was as important for Britain as it was for the Emperor. When it was clear that Charles would not accept either that, or any other solution, London proceeded straightforward on her way, regardless of what Vienna could say or do.

How did it go? One of the three Savoyard representatives, Pietro Mellarède, was looking for compensation or rewards for Savoy, and found an open door in London: the Queen's door. On 9 May 1712, that is to say 20 days before Philip V chose Spain, Mellarède reported to Turin:

> The queen of England told many persons she trusts, that she had been engaged in conscience to give a considerable enhacement to the House of Savoy, for she

> [the Queen] deprived her [the House of Savoy] of the hope of the Crown of Great Britain due to the Catholic princes exclusion her [the Queen's] Parliament did to the succession to the said Crown, whilst she [the House of Savoy] had the main right to demand it.[2]

It was not yet a matter of Sicily, only a matter of reward. On 15 June 1712 the idea of Sicily started appearing in public, although implicitly. On that day Queen Anne addressed the Parliament and said that Sicily would not be given back to Spain, for its assignment was still pending; then, after a few mentions of Prussia and Portugal, she mentioned the Duke of Savoy and said that he behaved so well, contributing so much to the common cause, that she was working to let him have the major benefits.

Victor Amadeus was aware, but very doubtful. On 23 June Bolingbroke told Count Maffei that by no means would Britain accept Austria getting both Naples and Sicily.[3] Then Lord Strafford wrote to Turin confirming it, and Lord Oxford said that Philip V would cede Sicily only to Savoy. Then Lord Bolingbroke officially told the French of the Queen's will, underlining that giving Sicily to Savoy was a basic condition to start real peace talks. Had Sicily not been given to Savoy, the war at sea would not stop, the British army would not leave Spain, and the conference in Utrecht would never start real negotiations.

Torcy tried to put on the table something for the Elector of Bavaria. Anne did not care. She committed Bolingbroke to Paris to make the truce. He had to settle the formal renunciation of the Spanish Bourbons to France and the right of Savoy to the Spanish succession according to Philip IV's last will, but – the Queen told him – Bolingbroke must do that only if Louis XIV gave Sicily first. Before leaving London, Bolingbroke said to Maffei: "When it was a matter of the interests of England the Queen sent to Paris only Prior, now that those of the duke of Savoy are concerned, she finds fine to commit me, and this must let you realise how much does she care."[4] Of course it was not only a matter of Savoy, the main issue was the enhancement of the two months truce signed on 17 July, into a real truce, nonetheless it was right that Anne focused on Sicily and Savoy.

On 21 August Bolingbroke and Torcy settled the main points, including giving Sicily to Victor Amadeus, plus some other questions related to Savoyard territorial gains to be discussed in Utrecht. Then the truce was announced and the real negotiation started. On their side, the Savoyard diplomats had clear instructions, and did their best. "The Savoyards have committed themselves to get Sicily, and now they have great hopes of being able to get it,"[5] the Tuscan ambassador reported to Florence.

---

2 President Mellarède to Duke Victor Amadeus II, from London, 9 May 1712, rep. in Carutti, "Diplomacy", vol. III, p.429, footnote 1.

3 Count Maffei to Duke Victor Amadeus II, from London, 24 June and 27 July 1712, rep. in Carutti, "Diplomacy", vol III, p.430.

4 Count Maffei to Duke Victor Amadeus II, from London, 12 August 1712, rep. in Carutti, "Diplomacy", vol. III, p.431.

5 Marquess Carlo Rinuccini to His Most Serene Cosimo II, granduke of Tucany, Utrecht, 8 September 1712, rep. in Moscati, p.61.

Jean-Baptiste Colbert, Marquess de Torcy.

Versailles accepted the proposal, also because the cession of Sicily did not imply any direct threat to her own Alpine border, and in fact was no great loss to Philip V.

The news of the incoming Anglo-French agreement put the fait accompli in front of Charles VI, and Austria began to bend. In February, Vienna sent London her proposals for a global agreement. France reacted, saying that the Austrian plans about Bavaria could not be accepted. Elector Maximilian had to be reinstated in all his states. This meant forcing the Empire to pardon he who, according to Charles, was a traitor of the German cause. Above all, it meant finding compensation for the Palatine Elector, who had to lose the portion of Bavaria he received as a reward for his military aid to the Allies in Flanders. It was a problematic issue.

Here the French believed they could play safe, and flat. They knew Britain to be anxious to obtain peace, and were confident of British support against Austrian resistance, thus they raised the bar, and became the defenders of the Italian princes.On 22 March Sinzendorff announced that he could accept the general agreement if France put aside those last requests about the Italian princes. This put the French diplomats in a serious embarrassment. They could not withdraw from their positions, especially considering that each Italian prince had his own envoy in Utrecht, and in any case the French were sure to succeed, so they said no. To Austria that was not a negligible issue. The royal titles to Savoy and to Hohenzollern were not things one could take lightly. They were dangerous and threatening changes, including serious consequences affecting the north and south of the Empire. The enhancement of the Hohenzollerns from the rank of king "in" Prussia to that of king "of" Prussia meant that their rank had to be recognised and accepted as equal to the only kings existing in the whole Empire until that moment, namely the Habsburgs, who, just to keep their title of King of Bohemia had fought the bloody Thirty Years' War. With the rise to the status of king "of", that is to say, of kings recognised worldwide, the Hohenzollerns began the long journey that resulted in expelling the Habsburgs from Germany in 1866, and in unifying Germany under their sceptre in 1871.

The recognition of the royal crown to Victor Amadeus was not less dangerous. It meant rendering completely autonomous a dynasty who had asked the Emperor for the formal investiture of the States of Savoy until a few years before. That dynasty had accepted her position as a vassal of the House of Habsburg, but now? Although ruled by Emperor Frederic II of Hohenstaufen in the first half of the thirteenth century, Sicily had never been a part of the Holy Roman Empire, and a King of Sicily was by no means a subject of the Emperor. Moreover, the Duke of Savoy was a dangerous man, who would stop only if and when he had gathered the whole Italian peninsula under his sceptre, a game easier to a king as he was going to become than to a duke as he was now.

Lastly, if it was hard to have to accept changes in the hierarchy of the Empire, it was intolerable to see France continuing its usual Richelieuan policy, letting discontent raise, and supporting the claims of all the small landowners of the Po Valley. That could not be tolerated, and Sinzendorff opposed: no concession, either for Italy, or for Bavaria. He would stay in Utrecht until the treaty, if any, was signed, hoping for some change at the last moment, then it would be war.

Louis XIV Ratifies the Peace of Utrecht.

Nobody cared. Once the discussions on trade and customs were completed, on 15 March, Lord Bolingbroke let Torcy know that Britain was ready to sign. On 11 April 1713, after offering Austria one last opportunity to join, the conflict that bloodied the world for more than 12 years ended.

At 2:00 p.m. the treaties of peace and trade between France and Britain were signed. Immediately afterwards Savoy signed. Then, at 8:00 p.m., Portugal. At 11:00 p.m. Prussia signed and, two hours after midnight, the Dutch plenipotentiaries too.[6]

Charles VI tried to prevent Victor Amadeus' signature, but the Duke underlined a not so small detail: the Emperor still had a debt of nine million to pay, for no supply by Piedmont to Imperial troops had ever been paid since the start of the alliance. Could he pay now, on the spot? This solved the problem.

On the next day the cannons thundered once more, and the couriers rushed off to their respective capitals to announce:

> Let it be known to all present and future, that having pleased to God after a very long and bloody war to inspire to all the Powers that are interested, a sincere desire for peace, and for the restoration of public tranquillity, the negotiations begun in Utrecht after the care of the most serene and powerful Princess Anna, by the grace of God Queen of Great Britain, were, due to the prudent conduct of this Princess, brought to the point of the conclusion of a general peace; to which, wishing to contribute the most serene and most powerful Prince Louis XIV, by the grace of God Most Christian King of France and Navarre, who during the present war has always sought the means to restore the general peace of Europe; and His Royal Highness Victor Amadeus II, by the grace of God Duke of Savoy and Monferrato, Prince of Piedmont, King of Cyprus etc. desiring to contribute to a work so healthy ... they gave their full powers to negotiate, conclude and sign the peace.[7]

6 This was the Treaty with France, and did not include Spain. Spain ceded Sicily on 10 June and signed the peace with Britain and Savoy on 12 July 1713. In June 1714 Spain settled the peace with the United Provinces, and signed the peace with Portugal only in February 1715.

7 Treaty between Savoy and France; Premise, rep. in Moscati, cit., p.125 and following.

Fireworks in London to Celebrate the Peace of Utrecht.

On 14 May 1713 all the ratifications had been received at Versailles, and on the 17th Louis XIV let his ministers announce:

> LET IT BE KNOWN to all those to whom it will compete, that a good, firm, stable and solid Peace, with a whole and sincere friendship, was made and agreed between the Most High, Most Excellent and Most Powerful Prince LOUIS, by the grace of God King of France and Navarre, our Sovereign Lord; the Highest, Most Excellent and Most Powerful Princess ANNE, Queen of Great Britain; the Most High, Most Excellent and Most Powerful Prince FREDERICK WILLIAM, King of Prussia; the Most High, Most Excellent and Most Powerful Prince VICTOR AMADEUS , Duke of Savoy; and the Lords General States of the United Provinces of the Netherlands, their Vassals, subjects, Servants, in all their Realms, Countries, Lands and lordships of their obedience.[8]

Te Deums, feasts, celebrations and ceremonies marked those days and buried with their pomp, and their noise the memory of the mourning, and the pains that stained the previous 12 years.

The war was over and all the contenders, a rare case, seemed to come out more or less happy.

France lost very few territories, which in the past she had stolen from the Dukes of Savoy, and was guaranteed, Philip V remaining King of Spain, tranquillity on the Pyrenees. Spain lost its Italian possessions, and Flanders; but her sovereign was, at least at the moment, happy enough to have saved the throne and the colonies not to pay too much attention to the rest. It could last also a dozen years, or less, in case of rain. In fact it lasted four.

By now Austria held the Duchies of Mantua, and Milan, Orbetello, and the State of the Presidii, the Kingdoms of Naples, and of Sardinia, and the Spanish Flanders: not that bad, but not enough. The Dutch had the permission to garrison their Barrier in what was now Austrian Flanders, as a guarantee against possible aggressions from the south. The King of Prussia received the Upper Gelderland and was recognised as the King of Prussia, the Duke of Savoy got the Monferrato, taken from the Gonzaga (who had been charged for felony in 1708, and deprived of their states by the Diet of the Empire), the Langhe, the Valsesia, the Lomellina, Varallo, Casteldelfino, Alessandria, Oulx, Fenestrelle in exchange for Barcellonette[9] to the French, and the crown of the king of Sicily, which however was not recognised by Charles VI. Therefore Victor Amadeus got much more than he had been promised in the 1702 negotiations, since he obtained a real kingdom.

8 *Ordonnance du Roy de France pour la liberté du Commerce tant par Terre que par Mer, Donnée à Marly le dix-sept May 1713*, rep. in Marius Topin, *L'Europe et les Bourbons sous Louis XIV* (Paris:1868), p.397.

9 The Treaty of Utrecht stated that where the water flowed from the top westward, was France; and where it went eastward was Savoy's. This part of the Treaty of Utrecht was never abolished and is still active. After the cession of Savoy to France in 1861, the same conditions were applied to the new French–Italian border. This means that the top of Monte Bianco, the White Mountain, the highest mountain of Europe, is half-French and half Italian. French maps – and others maps copied from the French ones – show the top as owned by France, and are completely wrong.

He achieved a huge political result. For the first time the ambassadors of Savoy had been admitted in full equality with those of the Great Powers, to discuss the problems of the Continent, and of the world. The Savoyard state had entered the European political system as a protagonist. This lasted until 1814.

Thanks to London, the House of Savoy was now the Royal House of Savoy. Shipped to Sicily by vessels rented in Genoa and escorted by a British squadron, in December 1713 Victor Amadeus was crowned king of Sicily in Palermo.

He was now one of only 11 kings in Europe,[10] and the only one in Italy. His prestige was great and his House was considered the most important referee in Italian affairs. After Emmanuel Philibert's restoration in 1560, this was a second turning point, and the first step on the route of Italian unity under the House of Savoy.

10 No matter how many kingdoms existed in Europe, the European kings were those of Britain, Denmark, France, Poland, Portugal, Prussia, Sicily, Spain, Sweden, and the Emperor as king of Bohemia and of Hungary, plus the Czar of Russia.

Colour Plate Commentaries

Plate 1 – Duke Vittorio Amedeo II of Savoy, Turin, 7 September 1706.

There are many images relating to Victor Amadeus during the battle of Turin, most of them made long after the decisive battle that freed the Duchy's capital from the Franco-Spanish siege. Written sources, in particular the diaries of the 1706 campaign, report that the Duke wore the uniform of the *Guardie del Corpo* (Life Guards), with the usual officer attributes, including the corselet in back polished steel. The figure shown here is a reconstruction after the portrait by the school of Giovanni Battista Curlando (private collection), and Francesco Ludovico Soleri's *Diario manoscritto* containing his *giornale dell'assedio di Torino*. In the painting the Duke is portrayed carrying the collar of the *Annunziata* order, which here has been removed.

Plate 2 – Savoy-Piedmont: Dragoon Regiment *Genevois*, private, 1706; Cavalry Regiment *Piemonte-Reale*, trooper 1704–09.

Until 1774, the uniforms of the Savoy-Piedmontese (and later Sardinian) dragoons were marked by the red coat, which was introduced as early as 1696. The dragoon regiment of *Sua Altezza Reale* had cuffs, lining, waistcoat and breeches of dark blue cloth, while the regiment *Piemonte* had them in light grey. Tin buttons and white shoulder braids were the same for all the regiments. The Piedmontese cavalry, especially the dragoons, appeared very similar to the French, except for the azure cockade on the tricorne. With the change of alliance, which took place on 24 October 1703, the Piedmontese dragoons replaced the cloth bonnet, which was substantially identical to those of the French dragoons, with the tricorne in order to differentiate them from their enemies. (Reconstruction after Emilio Grimaldi, 'Un secolo di uniformi per i dragoni di Piemonte (1690–1798)', published in *Armi Antiche*, 1963)

The two cavalry regiments maintained the coat colours received in the 1690s: light grey with red facing for *Piemonte Reale* and dark blue for *Savoye*. Under the coat, the trooper wore waistcoat and breeches in natural leather. Saddle covers were in red cloth for both units. In 1712, the regiment *Savoye* received permission to wear the red cravat, in order to commemorate the episode of the unknown regimental courier who, before dying from a throat injury, brought the Duke the good news of the relief of the besieged Turin. (Reconstruction after Rodolfo Puletti and Franco Dell'Uomo, *Piemonte Cavalleria: 1692–1992*, published by the regiment Piemonte Cavalleria, 1992)

Plate 3 – Savoy-Piedmont: Infantry Regiment *Aosta*, NCO 1701–1705; Infantry Regiment *Monferrato*, grenadier, 1704.

The Piedmontese infantry, as well the cavalry, appeared very similar to the French infantry. The light grey coats and even the NCOs' partisans were manufactured after French models. In this regard, between 1699 and 1703 the uniform for the Duke's army had been manufactured in Lyon. The most important change in infantry clothing occurred in 1702, when the distribution of the waistcoat was definitively approved for all regiments. The introduction of this item served the dual purpose of better protecting the soldier in the winter months and saving the coat, which in ordinary services was kept in the quarters. In this way, at least in the intentions of the ducal treasury, the coat could last beyond the two-year period established until then. A further improvement in the equipment for the infantry soldier was the distribution, always every two years, of a pair of leather breeches in the summer and a pair of cloth ones in the winter. All these introductions also served to differentiate the regiments, which were previously identified only by the color of cuffs and stockings. The fur cap became standard for grenadier rank and file after 1702. (Reconstruction after Enrico Ricchiardi, 'Le prime uniformi e stendardi dell'Esercito ducale sabaudo 1671–1713', in *Armi Antiche*, 1988–1989. Grenadier uniform, dated 1704–06 preserved in the Turin Civic Museum Pietro Micca. Battle scene from the table of Prinotto relating to the siege of 1706, collection of Palazzo Reale Turin)

Plate 4 – Savoy-Piedmont: artilleryman, 1706–11; senior commander, 1709–14.

The Piedmontese artillery continued to dress in dark blue throughout the course of the War of the Spanish Succession. The heroic action of Pietro Micca helped to preserve the information regarding the uniform issued to the artillery in these years. The Civic Museum of the siege of Turin, dedicated to the brave Piedmontese miner, preserves a complete artillery uniform dating back to the period of the siege. It is difficult to establish to what extent this uniform is to be considered authentic, however most authors consider it reliable. The second figure wears the dress reserved to major commanders after 1700, as for the blue coat with red facing of the Duke's Foot Guards. (Painting by anonymous, possible portrait of Giuseppe Maria Solaro della Margarita, private collection, Turin)

Plate 5 – Savoy-Piedmont: Infantry Regiment *Guardie*, grenadier 1709; Infantry Regiment *Savoye*, fusilier, 1712–15.

The regiment of Foot Guards maintained the traditional dark blue coat with red facing, but some changes were introduced in 1702, such as the white-laced buttonholes, and after 1707 the high fur cap in Austrian style. The queued hair tied with a black strap appears in the same period in the army of Savoy-Piedmont for soldiers and NCOs. In 1710 the Foot Guard received the coat tailored in 'Prussian style' with the reverse on the breast in scarlet red. The dark blue waistcoat did not change, but now received the laced buttonholes. Between 1710 and 1712, the new 'Prussian' coat gradually replaced the old one in all the infantry regiments. Gaiters of waxed canvas were also issued to the infantry already in the early of the century. After 1709, swords and sabres were carried only by the Guards and grenadiers of the national regiments, while the privates of national and provincial regiments and battalions had just the bayonet. (Reconstruction after Enrico Ricchiardi, 'Le prime uniformi e stendardi dell'Esercito ducale sabaudo 1671–1713', in *Armi Antiche*, 1988–1989)

Plate 6 – Savoy-Piedmont: Infantry Regiment *Hackbrett* (Valais), fusilier 1712-14; Infantry Regiment *Reding* (Valais), officer 1704.

The Duchy of Savoy also resorted to foreign mercenary infantry during the War of the Spanish Succession, and at the end of the conflict Victor Amadeus II still had five infantry regiments, mostly Swiss and German. Among with them there was also one infantry regiment recruited in the Republic of Valais. The history of this unit is quite troubled. In 1704, the regiment's colonel Johann Franz von Reding was in command of the fortress of Bard; the garrison included several companies of the regiment Reding, and the Duke and his Allies trusted in the resistance of the garrison. Instead, when the Franco-Spaniards besieged Bard, the colonel offered to surrender and passed into French service. The unit was reconstituted with recruits from a second Valais regiment, entrusted to a new colonel and finally became *Hackbrett* in 1712. (Reconstruction after Enrico Ricchiardi, *Il Costume Militare Sabaudo*, Turin 1989. Battle scene from the table of Prinotto relating to the siege of 1706, collection of Palazzo Reale Turin)

Plate 7 – Papal States: Infantry Regiment *Ruspoli*, fusilier 1708; Infantry Regiment Serlupi, ensign 1708.

Information on the uniforms of the Papal army raised in 1708 to face the Imperialists comes mostly from written sources and archive documents relating to the formation of the regiments. Infantry regiment *San Martino* wore light grey coats with red facings and stockings, and white metal buttons; regiment *Colonna* had had dark blue coats with yellow cuffs and lining; *Serlupi* had grey-white coats with dark blue cuffs and brass buttons, while the officers wore dark blue with white facings. Grenadiers had the bearskin cap with the bag in the facing colour, and the front with the Papal coat of arms. Written sources give details also on the uniforms of cavalry and dragoons. *Autanne* cuirassiers had dark blue coats with red facing, waistcoat and breeches, tin buttons with silver buttonholes, white metal cuirass, black tricorne laced with yellow-gold and azure-yellow cockade, and silver braids on the right shoulder of the coat; the *Fasanini* Dragoons wore red with green facings and dark blue waistcoat and breeches; the *Balbiani* Dragoons were also in red coats with green waistcoat and breeches, and brass buttons; the *Albani* Dragoons were dressed in red coats with brass pointed white braids on the right shoulder, azure cuffs, lining, waistcoat and breeches, brass buttons and red French-style red dragoon cap with dark blue brim embroidered with the Pope Clemente XI Albani's coat of arms.

None of these descriptions are supported by an iconographic source. The only significant exception is represented by the painting by an anonymous artist preserved in Palazzo Ruspoli, depicting the *Ruspoli* infantry regiment in the spring of 1708. Although the painting shows numerous details regarding uniforms and ensigns, mysteriously a written source from a contemporary eyewitness gives a completely different description. While in the painting the regiment appears dressed in red with light grey facing and waistcoat, the chronicler reports the following:

> This morning the Marquis Ruspoli distributed the uniforms to the soldiers of his regiment. All divided into companies with their officers arrived at the Monte Cavallo palace to take the blessing, lined up in the courtyard of the Bonelli palace in SS. Apostoli, where the marquis lives. The officers have a golden steel half moon (gorget) under the coat, and they are armed with French-style half-pikes. The uniform of the soldiers was of fine yellow cloth with blue facing, with waistcoat and stockings of a similar colour; silver-edged headgear with blue and white ribbon, black cravat, yellow breeches and fine cow leather shoes. In addition to this, the Marquis distributed a shirt, under-breeches and a pair of stockings to each soldier.'

(Reconstruction after Francesco Valesio, 'Diario di Roma: 1708–1728', *I Cento libri*, volume 4, *di Diario di Roma* (Roma: Longanesi, 1978), pp.150–151)

Plate 8 – Duchy of Parma and Piacenza: Infantry Company *Guardia Irlandese*, fusilier 1704-12; Grand Duchy of Tuscany fusilier 1708–14.

Following the successful action performed in Cremona by the Irish infantry in French service, in November 1702, the Farnese court, which sided with the Franco-Spaniards, decided to form its own company of soldiers destined for the Duke's life guard recruiting soldiers from Ireland. The company was under the command of the Irish Captain O'Gill and Lieutenant Hervey as vice commander, and comprised 1 ensign, 1 chaplain, 3 sergeants, 5 corporals, 5 vice corporals, 6 oboes, 2 drums and 92 soldiers, amongst whom, however, there were also some Germans, English, French, Swiss and Italians from other states. The commander of the company was the best-paid officer of the small army of the Duchy. The company was licensed in 1733, and in Parma it was known as *i Rossi* because of the colour of the uniforms. (Reconstruction from Mario Zannoni and Massimo Fiorentino, *L'Esercito Farnesiano dal 1694 al 1731* (Parma: Palatina Editrice, 1981))

With the regulations of 1707, known as *Regolamenti, Ordini e Privilegi delle Milizie Toscane*, the Grand Duke Cosimo III reorganised all his regular troops, and as for concerns the uniform, the document includes some illustrations depicting soldiers taken from a French military exercise manual published in 1696: *L'Art Militaire François* illustrated by Pierre Giffart. Iconographic evidence confirms that the Tuscan infantry wore uniforms designed on the pattern of the French Foot Guards like the models coming from Giffart's manual, except for a lesser use of lace. The French influence in matter of military dress continued in Tuscany until the 1750s.

Ensigns

Plate 10

Savoy-Piedmont: above, *Reggimento delle Guardie* colonel colour, 1714; below, *Reggimento delle Guardie*, possibly ordinance colour, lost at Vercelli in 1704.

Plate 11

Savoy-Piedmont: above, possibly Infantry Regiment *Nice*, company colour capured at Vercelli in 1704; below, Infantry Regiment *Fucilieri*, ordinance colour lost at Ivrea in 1704.

Plate 12

Savoy-Piedmont: above, Infantry Regiment *Savoye*, ordinance colour lost at Vercelli in 1704; below, Infantry Regiment *Piemonte*, ordinance colour lost at Ivrea in 1704.

Plate 13

Savoy-Piedmont: above, Valais Infantry Regiment *Reding*, ordinance colour lost at Bard in 1704; below, possibly Swiss Infantry Regiment *Alt*, ordinance colour lost at Ivrea in 1704.

Plate 14

Savoy-Piedmont: three ordinance colours possibly belonging to provincial infantry regiments, 1705–06.

Plate 15

Papal States, 1708: above, Infantry Regiment *Serlupi*, company colours over Infantry Regiment *Ruspoli*, company colours; below, Dragoon Regiment *Fasanini,* colonel cornet.

The infantry colours are a reconstruction after a contemporary account relating the mobilisation of the Papal army in 1708. These sources describe the Papal ensign in crimson red or azure with Pope Clemente XI Albani's coat of arms and the usual devices with keys and mitre; the colonel's ensigns were in white. On the corner, there was the coat of arms of the colonel proprietor. Further information concerning the Papal ensigns refers about the six regiments raised in the *Legazioni* of Ferrara and Bologna, which had white ensigns with the Albani coat of arms with crimson red edging, while the colonel's flag was in full white. Dragoon regiment *Fasanini* received ordinary companies' cornets in red crimson and in white for the colonel's company, each with the Papal coat of arms.

Plate 16

Painting illustrating the review of the Infantry Regiment *Ruspoli* in Rome, in 1708. Collection of the Ruspoli Palace (with the kind permission of the Ruspoli family). See the commentary for plate 7 for further details.

Bibliography

Albera, Marco, *La zuppa dopo l'assedio. La notte del 7/8 settembre 1706 a Palazzo Graneri della Roccia*, in Mola di Nomaglio, Gustavo – Sandri Giachino, Roberto – Melano, Giancarlo – Menietti, Piergiuseppe, *Torino 1706: memorie e attualità dell'assedio di Torino del 1706 tra spirito europeo e identità regionale – Atti del convegno, Torino 29 e 30 settembre 2006*, 2 vols , (Turin, 2006), (onward "Mola – Sandri – Melano – Menietti" *Torino 1706 proceedings*), vol. I..

Albertan Min, Massimo, *L'assedio di Ivrea del 1704*, on "Rivista Italiana Difesa", anno XXVII, n. 6, giugno 2008.

Ales, Stefano, *Insegne militari preunitarie italiane*, (Rome, 2001).

Amoretti, Guido – Menietti, Piergiuseppe, *La cittadella e le mura di Torino*, in Sandri Giachino, Roberto – Melano Giancarlo – Mola di Nomaglio, Gustavo (edited by), *Catalogo della mostra Torino 1706: l'alba di un Regno*, Torino, Il Punto, 2006., (onward Sandri – Melano – Mola, *Torino 1706 Catalogue*).

Amoretti, Guido – Menietti, Pierluigi, *Riscoperta e valorizzazione del forte torinese detto Pastiss*, in, Amoretti, Guido – Petitti, Patrizia, *La scala di Pietro Micca 1958-1998*, (Turin, 2000).

Amoretti, Guido – Petitti, Patrizia, *La scala di Pietro Micca 1958-1998*, (Turin, 2000).

Amoretti, Guido, *L'assedio e la liberazione di Torino*, in "Sandri – Melano – Mola" (edited by), *Torino 1706 Catalogue.*

Amoretti, Guido, *La battaglia di Torino nel contesto della storia italiana ed europea*, in *1706-2006, verso il terzo centenario dell'assedio e della battaglia di Torino*, acta of the conference held on May 24th 2003, Turin, 2004).

Amoretti, Guido, *Museo Pietro Micca e dell'Assedio di Torino del 1706*, (Turin, 1989).

Anibaldi Ranco, Marco, *Cartografia numerica delle opere di difesa e assedio di Torino del 1706 georeferenziata sulla cartografia tecnica regionale al 10.000*, in Mola – Sandri – Melano – Menietti" *Torino 1706 proceedings Année 1701: Liste des Troupes que l'Angleterre et les Etats des Provinces Unies payent de ce côté de la mer*, s.i.,.

Anquetil, Louis Pierre, *Vie du Maréchal duc de Villars*, 4 vols, (Paris, 1734).

Antonielli d'Oulx, Fabrizio – Reviglio della Veneria, Maria Luisa, *Cenni sugli ordini reali e militari francesi, sabaudi e imperiali all'assedio di Torino*, "Mola – Sandri – Melano – Menietti", *Torino 1706 proceedings*, vol. I.

Assum, Clemente, *Eugenio di Savoia*, (Turin, 1935).

Assum, Clemente, *L'assedio e la battaglia di Torino (1706)*, (Turin, 1926).

Atto col quale il Duca di Savoia Vittorio Amedeo II accetta il Trattato concluso fra la Regina Anna d'Inghilterra ed il Re di Prussia per cui quel Re invia in Piemonte contro la Francia un Corpo d'ottomila uomini sotto gli ordini di S.A.R., fatto al Campo di Crescentino il 27 dicembre 1704, in Solaro della Margarita (edited by), *Traités publics de la Royale Maison de Savoie avec les puissances étrangères depuis la paix de Chateau Cambresis jusqu'à nos jours* onward *Traités*, Vol. II, (Turin, 1836).

Atto di cessione del Reame di Sicilia fatta dal Re di Spagna in favore di S.A.R. il Duca di Savoia, in Solaro della Margarita (edited by), *Traités*, Vol. II, (Turin, 1836).

Baggio, Silvia – Marchi, Piero, *Miscellanea Medicea*, (Rome, 2002).

Balbiano d'Aramengo, Giuseppe, *L'assedio di Torino nei documenti di Giuseppe Maria Solaro della Margarita*, "Mola – Sandri – Melano – Menietti", *Torino 1706 proceedings* vol. II.

Banks, John, *The history of Francis Eugene prince of Savoy*, (London, 1741).

Barberis, Walter – Merlotti, Andrea – Riccardi di Netro, Tomaso, *I Savoia: storia di una dinastia*, in Castelnuovo, Enrico (edited by), *La reggia di Venaria e i Savoia – arte, magnificenza e storia di una corte europea*, (Turin, 2008).

Barberis, Walter, *Le armi del principe – la tradizione militare sabauda*, (Turin, 1988).

Barnett, Correlli, *The first Churchill: Marlborough soldier and statesman*, (New York, 1974).

Barone, Enrico, *I grandi capitani dell'età moderna*, (Rome, 1982).

Barrera, Francesco – Magnaghi, Agostino, *Il forte di Exilles tra storia e progetto*, in, Amoretti, Guido – Petitti, Patrizia, *La scala di Pietro Micca 1958-1998*, (Turin, 2000).

Barton Thomas – *Campagna miravigliosa or An exact journal of the Imperial Army's Advance into, and encampement in Italy under the command of Prince Eugene of Savoy, with the several Actions and Recounters betwixt Them and the French and the Spaniards, by an officer of the German Army*, (London, 1702).

Baudrillart, Alfred, *Philippe V et la cour d'Espagne*, 5 vols, (Paris, 1890-1901).

Bellerive, chevalier de, *Histoire des campagnes de Monsieur le Duc de Vendosme*, (Paris, 1715).

Benatti, Paola, *Paesaggio e territorio al tempo della battaglia di Luzzara, 15 agosto 1702*, in Bugada, Giorgio (edited by), *Storia e luoghi di una battaglia: Luzzara e Riva di Suzzara*, (Luzzara, 2004).

Bérenger, Jean, *Une décision stratègique: l'acceptation par Louis XIV du testament de Charles II d'Espagne*, in «Revue internationale d'Histoire Militaire», n.° 82, 2002, Paris, Comité International des Science Historiques – Commission Internationale d'Histoire Militaire, 2002.

Bérenger, Jean, *Storia dell'impero asburgico 1700-1918*, (Bologna, 2003).

Bernardini, Rodolfo, *Breve storia del Sacro Militare Ordine di S. Stefano papa e martire dalla fondazione a oggi e dell'istituzione dei Cavalieri di Santo Stefano*, (Pisa, 1995).

Bersani, Stefano, *Storia del cardinale Giulio Alberoni*, (Piacenza, 1861).

Bertarelli, Guido, *Le Alpi Marittime*, on "Le vie d'Italia", anno XL, n. 9, settembre 1934.

Bertin, Pierre, *Le fantassin de France*, (Paris, 1988).

Bertotto, Silvio, *Torino 1706: luci sull'assedio dagli archivi comunali e parrocchiali del Torinese*, "Mola – Sandri – Melano – Menietti", *Torino 1706 proceedings* vol. I.

Bertrand, Louis, *Luigi XIV*, (Milan, 1962).

Berwick – Fitz-James, James, duca di Berwick, *Mémoires du Maréchal de Berwick*, in *Collection de Mémoires pour servir à l'histoire de France, depuis l'avénement de Henri IV jusqu'à la Paix de Paris conclue en 1763 ; avec des notices sur chaque auteur, et des obsérvations sur chaque ouvrage*, par messieurs A. Petitot et Monmerqué, (Paris, 1828).

Berwick, James fitz-James, duke of, *Mèmoires du Maréchal de Berwick écrites par lui-meme*, 2 vols, Paris, Moutard, 1780.

Bevilacqua, Paolo – Petitti, Paola – Zannoni, Fabrizio, *L'assedio sotterraneo*, in "Sandri – Melano – Mola" (edited by), *Torino 1706 Catalogue*.

Bevilacqua, Paolo – Zannoni, Fabrizio, *Le "gallerie di Emanuele Filiberto". Breve storia di un luogo comune*, "Mola – Sandri – Melano – Menietti", *Torino 1706 proceedings* vol. I.

Bevilacqua, Paolo – Zannoni, Fabrizio, *Mastri da muro e piccapietre al servizio del Duca: cronaca della costruzione delle gallerie che salvarono Torino*, (Turin, 2006).

Birlic Nolano, Giovanni, *Historia della vita di Carlo V duca di Lorena e Bar, generalissimo delle truppe imperiali*, (Venice, 1699).

Black, Jeremy, *Britain as a military power 1688-1815*, (London, 1999).

Black, Jeremy, *War and warfare in the Age of Louis XIV: the global context*, in *the Projection and Limitations of imperial Powers, 1618-1850*, edited by Frederick C. Schneid, serie History of Warfare, no. 75, (Leiden-Boston, 2012).

Blackly, W., *The diplomatic correspondence of the Right Hon. Richard Hill, (L.L.D., F.R.S., &c., &c.), envoy extraordinary from the Court of St. James to the Duke of Savoy, in the reign of Queen Anne: from July 1703, to May 1706*, 2 Voll, (London, 1845),.

Bluche, François, *Louis XIV*, (New York, 1999).

Boccaletti, Massimo, *Salvate la Sindone!*, "Mola – Sandri – Melano – Menietti", *Torino 1706 proceedings* vol. II.

Boeri, Giancarlo – Brandani, Massimo, *L'esercito pontificio del 1708-1709, Cavalleria*, on "Panoplia", year II, n. 7, 1991.

Bolognini, Daniele – Ciferri, Elvio, *L'assedio di Torino negli scritti di Serafina Brunelli*, "Mola – Sandri – Melano – Menietti", *Torino 1706 proceedings* vol. II.

Bonino, Giovanni, *Repertorio di musiche del tempo di Luigi XIV in uso presso unità militari partecipanti (sui due fronti) all'assedio e alla battaglia di Torino del 1706*, "Mola – Sandri – Melano – Menietti", *Torino 1706 proceedings* vol. I.

Bonnet, Philippe, *Ercole Negro et Vauban à Fort Barraux et ses environs*, in, Amoretti, Guido - Petitti, Patrizia, *La scala di Pietro Micca 1958-1998*, (Turin, 2000).
Bosso, Davide, *L'occupazione francese di Chivasso, luglio 1705 - settembre 1706*, "Mola - Sandri - Melano - Menietti", *Torino 1706: conference*, vol. I.
Botta, Carlo, *Storia d'Italia continuata da quella del Guicciardini sino al 1789*, 10 vols, (Paris, 1832).
Bovio, Oreste, *Bandiere e araldica militare*, in *Le fonti per la storia militare italiana in età contemporanea*, (Rome, 1993).
Bovio, Oreste, *Le bandiere dell'esercito*, (Rome, 1981).
Bozzola, Annibale, *Giudizi e previsioni della diplomazia medicea sulla Casa di Savoia durante la guerra di successione spagnuola*, (Turin, 1914).
Breve cenno delle principali operazioni militari svoltesi nelle Valli Pellice, Chisone, Germagnasca e Dora Riparia, ms in AUSSME, L 3 - 8.
Breve e succinto giornale del memorabile assedio di Vercelli (1704), ms in AUSSME, L 3 - 11.
Brezzi, Paolo, *La diplomazia pontificia*, (Milan, 1942).
Brignoli, Marziano, *Savoye bonne nouvelle*, (Milan,1989).
Broglie, Emmanuel duca de, *Catinat, l'homme et la vie 1637 - 1712*, (Paris, 1902).
Bugada, Giorgio (edited by), *Storia e luoghi di una battaglia: Luzzara e Riva di Suzzara*, (Luzzara, 2004).
Bulferetti, L. - Costantini, C., *Industria e commercio in Liguria nell'età del Risorgimento 1700-1861*, (Milano, 1961).
Bussy Rabutin, Roger de, *Lettres de Messire Roger de Rabutin comte de Bussy*, 7 voll, (Amstrerdam, 1738).
Caciagli, Giuseppe, *Lo Stato dei Presidi*, (Pontedera, 1992).
Caizzi Bruno, *Industria e commercio della Repubblica Veneta nel XVIII secolo*, (Milan, 1965).
Calascibetta, Nadia, *Il beato Sebastiano Valfrè: un percorso iconografico attraverso i secoli*, "Mola - Sandri - Melano - Menietti", *Torino 1706 proceedings* vol. II.
Campagna delle Alpi nel 1708, ms AUSSME, L 3.
Campagne del Principe Eugenio di Savoia, 21 vols, (Turin, 1889-1892).
Canale, Michel-Giuseppe, *Nuova istoria della Repubblica di Genova, del suo commercio della sua letteratura dalle origini all'anno 1797*, (Florence, 1860).
Capitolazione per l'anticipo di 100.000 scudi dal sig. Calcino alle truppe imperiali comandate dal Serenissimo Principe Eugenio di Savoia, del 26 novembre 1707, copia manoscritta in AUSSME, L 3, 8, Lavori Svolti.
Cappellini, Antonio, *Genova repubblica*, (Genoa, 1949).
Carmelitane Scalze di Moncalieri, *Nel cuore di una città assediata, una seminatrice di speranza*, "Mola - Sandri - Melano - Menietti", *Torino 1706 proceedings* vol. II.
Carolus Sextus...Eugenio, Principe di Savoia e Piemonte, marchese di Saluzzo....Essendo sempre stata la nostra maggior applicazione..., regolamento della questione del Finale, ms. ASG Archivio Segreto F 257 (Finale), done in Milan, on 22nd december 1711.
Carolus Tertius Dei gratia Hispaniarum & c Rex...Eugenio, Principe di Savoia e Piemonte, marchese di Saluzzo....Ancorché secondo il tenore del proclama..., against the deserters, Milan, Regia Ducal Corte, per Antonio Pandolfo Malatesta stampatore regio camerale, 20th November 1707.
Carutti, Domenico, *Storia del regno di Vittorio Amedeo II*, (Florence, 1863).
Carutti, Domenico, *Storia della diplomazia della Corte di Savoia*, 7 vols, (Turin, 1879),.
Casirati, Alberto, *Vittorio Amedeo II, il "Grande Re"; gli albori d'Italia in un regno lungo e difficile nell'Europa del XVIII secolo*, "Mola - Sandri - Melano - Menietti", *Torino 1706 proceedings* vol. I.
Casoni, Filippo, *Dell'Istoria di Lodovico il grande*, 2 vols, (Milan, 1706).
Cassi Ramelli, Antonio, *Evoluzione dell'architettura fortificata*, in Natali, Aurelio, *Castelli e fortificazioni*, (Milan, 1974),.
Castagno, Gianguido, *Maria Bricca tra storia e leggenda*, "Mola - Sandri - Melano - Menietti", *Torino 1706 proceedings* vol. II.
Castagnoli, Pietro, *Il cardinale Giulio Alberoni*, 3 vols, (Rome, 1929).
Castelnuovo, Enrico (edited by), *La reggia di Venaria e i Savoia - arte, magnificenza e storia di una corte europea*, (Turin, 2008).
Catinat, de la Fauconnerie Nicolas de, *Mémoires et correspondance du maréchal de Catinat*, (Paris, 1819).
Cénat, Jean-Philippe, *Les débuts d'une la carrière militaire hors du commun : l'ascension du marquis de Chamlay, conseiller militaire de Louis XIV (1672-1678)*, in «Revue internationale d'Histoire

Militaire», n.° 82, 2002, Paris, Comité International des Science Historiques – Commission Internationale d'Histoire Militaire, 2002.

Cerino Badone, Giovanni – Campagnolo, Francesca – Lucini, Mauro, *Bandiere nel fango*, (Turin, 2004).

Cerino Badone, Giovanni, *1700-1713: la Guerra di Successione Spagnola sulle Alpi, l'attacco e la difesa del fronte alpino 1707-1713*, in "Sandri – Melano – Mola" (edited by), *Torino 1706 Catalogue*.

Cerman, Markus, "*Rural economy and society*", in *A Companion to Eighteenth-Century Europe*, (edited by Peter H. Wilson), (London, 2008).

Cernuschi, Enrico, *Venezia e l'Islam*, on "Rivista Marittima", anno CXXXVI, May 2003.

Churchill, Winston Spencer, *Marlborough*,(Verona, 1973).

Cipolla, Alfonso – Moretti, Giovanni, *"Diroccata con apoteosi": il mito di Pietro Micca attraverso il teatro*, "Mola – Sandri – Melano – Menietti", *Torino 1706 proceedings* vol. II.

Cipolla, Carlo M., *Storia economica dell'Europa preindustriale*, (Bologna, 2002).

Ciravegna, M., *La Corte di Savoia durante l'assedio di Torino (1706)* , on "Rassegna storica del Risorgimento", anno XXVI, fascicolo IX, settembre 1939.

Clark, G. N., *War trade and trade war 1701-1713*, on "The Economic History Review", Vol. 1, n. 2, jan 1928.

Coccon, Gino, *La Venezia di Terra (1381-1797)*, (Venice, 1985).

Coda, Costantino (edited by), *Ragguaglio giornale dell'assedio di Torino cominciato li 13 maggio 1706 e liberazione del medesimo seguita li 7 settembre del medesimo anno*, (Turin, 1980).

Coda, Maria, *I Micca: una famiglia del ceto popolare entrata nella storia grazie all'eroismo di Pietro Micca*, "Mola – Sandri – Melano – Menietti", *Torino 1706 proceedings* vol. II.

Colapietra, Raffaele, *Napoli e Vienna nel primo Settecento: linee interpretative recenti*, on "Cultura e scuola", anno XXXI, n. 123, luglio-settembre 1992.

Colletta, Pietro, *Storia del reame di Napoli*, (Milan, 1989).

Colmuto Zanella, Graziella, *Territorio e fortificazioni: confini e difese della Gera d'Adda*, (Bergamo, 2003).

Concina, Ennio, *Le trionfanti armate venete*, (Venice, 1972).

Condizioni sotto le quali le Corone di Francia e di Spagna offrono d'evacuare le piazze della Lombardia, in Solaro della Margarita (edited by), *Traités*, Vol. II, (Turin, 1836).

Coniglio, Giuseppe, *I Vicerè spagnoli di Napoli*, (Naples, 1967).

Contessa, Carlo, *I Regni di Napoli e di Sicilia nelle aspirazioni italiane di Vittorio Amedeo II di Savoia (1700-1713)*, (Turin, 1933).

Conti, Giuseppe, *Firenze dai Medici ai Lorena*, (Florence, 1993).

Convention faite et conclue sur l'approbation de S.A.E. et de LL.HH.PP., à la Haye ce 27 mai 1707 déterminant le Contingent Palatin pour la Guerre de Succession d'Espagne en 1707.

Convenzione fra S.A.R. il Duca di Savoia e S.M. Britannica per il commercio di Sicilia e d'Inghilterra, fatta ad Utrecht l'8 marzo 1713, in Solaro della Margarita (edited by), *Traités*, Vol. II, (Turin, 1836).

Convenzione fra S.A.R. il Duca di Savoia e S.M. il Re di Francia per una cessazione d'armi piena ed intera, fatta ad Utrecht il 14 marzo 1713, in Solaro della Margarita (edited by), *Traités*, Vol. II, (Turin, 1836).

Corino, Pier Giorgio, *Il forte della Brunetta, mito della fortificazione sabauda*, in, Amoretti, Guido – Petitti, Patrizia, *La scala di Pietro Micca 1958-1998*, (Turin, 2000).

Corpas Rojo, Francisco, *La financiación de los ejércitós en el marco de la guerra civil: Aplicación al caso de la guerra de sucesión en España (1701-1714)*, in Acta of the XXX Conference of the International Commission of Military History, (Rabat, 2005)..

Cortelazzo, Manlio, *Venezia, il Levante e il mare*, (Pisa, 1989).

Costantini, Claudio, *La Repubblica di Genova nell'età moderna*, (Turin, 1991).

Courtilz de Sandraz, Gratien de, *La guerre d'Italie, ou mémoires du compte d'****, (Cologne, 1703).

Crescenzi, Andrea, *Profilo storico della Leva*, on "Bollettino dell'Archivio dell'Ufficio Storico", anno IV, n. 7/8, gennaio – dicembre 2004.

Cronaca di Castelmella, anni 1702-1706, in Guerrini, Paolo, *Cronache bresciane inedite dei secoli XV-XIX trascritte e annotate*, Vol V°, (Brescia, 1933)..

Cros, Bernard, *Du siége de 1707 aux lendemains de l'alerte de 1746: évolution des fortifications de Toulon*, in, Amoretti, Guido – Petitti, Patrizia, *La scala di Pietro Micca 1958-1998*, (Turin, 2000).

D'Artanville, *Memoirs of Prince Eugene of Savoy*, (London, 1716).

Da Mosto, Andrea, *Milizie dello Stato Romano, 1600-1797*, in "Memorie Storiche Militari", (Rome, 1914).

Dal Pane, Luigi, *La finanza toscana dagli inizi del secolo XVIII alla caduta del Granducato*, (Milan, 1965).

Dal Pane, Luigi, *Lione Pascoli e la vita economica dello Stato Pontificio nella prima metà del Settecento*, on "Rassegna storica del Risorgimento", anno XXIII, fascicolo X, ottobre 1936.

Dassano, Fabrizio – Albertan Min, Massimo, *L'assedio di Verrua del 1704-1705*, on "Rivista Italiana Difesa", anno XXI, n. 6, giugno 2002.

Datta De Albertis, Giulia, *I favolosi Mancini*, (Milan, 1969).

Dattero, Alessandra, *Governatori delle piazzeforti e organizzazione militare nella Lombardia austriaca del primo Settecento*, in *Frontiere e fortificazioni di frontiera*, (Florence, 2001).

Daun, Philipp Lorenz Wierich, conte von, *Lettere a S.A.R. Vittorio Amedeo II duca di Savoia*, appendice X a, Manno, Antonio, (edited by), *Relazione e documenti sull'assedio di Torino nel 1706*, in "Miscellanea di Storia Italiana", Turin,1878.

De Candido, Mara, *Il porto di Villafranca*, in "Sandri – Melano – Mola" (edited by), *Torino 1706 Catalogue*.

De Candido, Mara, *L'attesa del confronto finale*, in "Sandri – Melano – Mola" (edited by), *Torino 1706 Catalogue*.

De Riencourt, Simon, *Histoire de Louis XIV*, (Paris, 1695).

de Vault, François-Eugène, *Mémoires militaires relatifs à la Succession d'Espagne sous Louis XIV, extraits de la correspondance de la cour et des généraux par le lieutenant général de Vault*, ed. Jacques G. Pelet-Clozeau, 10 vols. (Paris, 1835-62).

De Vecchi di Val Cismon, Cesare Maria, *Vittorio Amedeo II ed il beato Sebastiano Valfré*, on "Rassegna storica del Risorgimento", anno XXII, fascicolo VI, giugno 1935.

Decisione degli Arbitri nominati in conformità del Trattato d'Utrecht sulle differenze fra S.M. il Re di Sicilia ed il Principe di Monaco, in Solaro della Margarita (edited by), *Traités*, V vol., (Turin, 1836).

Decisione dei Commissari nominati sulle differenze fra il Duca di Savoia e S.M. l'Imperatore per l'interpretazione ed esecuzione del Trattato della lega dell'anno 1703, fatta a Milano il 27 giugno 1712, in Solaro della Margarita (edited by), *Traités*, Vol. II, (Turin, 1836).

Dedé Romagnoli, Luigina, *Quarant'anni di vita bresciana – Dalla pace di Candia ai trattati di Utrecht 1669-1713*, (Brescia, 1984).

Del Re, Niccolò, *La Curia romana – lineamenti storico-giuridici*, (Rome, 1952).

Della Regina, duchessa, *Sette italiane alla corte del Re Sole*, (Rome, 1955).

Dellepiane, Riccardo – Giacomone Piana, Paolo, *Le leve corse della Repubblica di Genova dalla pace di Ryswick al trattato di Utrecht (1697 – 1713)*, in "Studi e documenti di storia ligure", (Genoa, 1996).

Di Lascio, Claudio, *Il destino di un cadetto: Giuseppe Amico di Castellalfero dall'arte della guerra a fautore delle arti*, "Mola – Sandri – Melano – Menietti", *Torino 1706 proceedings* vol. II.

Di Vittorio, Antonio, *Gli Austriaci e il Regno di Napoli, 1707 – 1734*, (Naples, 1969).

Diaz, Furio, *Il Granducato di Toscana – I Medici*, (Turin, 1987).

Diehl, Charles, *Une république patricienne: Venise*, (Paris, 1931).

Distinta Relazione del Diario dell'Assedio della Città, e Fortezza di Gaeta, presa à forza dalle gloriosissime Armi di S.M. Cesarea il dì 30 settembre 1707, sotto il Supremo comando di S.E. il Sig. Generale Conte di Daun, (Naples, 1707).

Dondi, Giorgio, *Le artiglierie all'inizio del Settecento*, in "Sandri – Melano – Mola" (edited by), *Torino 1706 Catalogue*.

Doria, Paolo Mattia, *Massime generali e particolari colle quali di tempo in tempo hanno gli Spagnoli governato il Regno di Napoli*, (Naples, 1973).

Duboin, Carlo, *Raccolta per ordine di materia delle leggi, cioè editti, patenti, manifesti ecc. emanati negli stati Sardi sino all'8 dicembre 1798*, 29 vols, (Turin, 1816 – 1869).

Dubreton, J.Lucas, *La vita quotidiana a Firenze ai tempi dei Medici*, (Milan, 1991).

Duffy, Christopher, *The military experience in the age of reason*, (Ware, 1998).

Dumont – Rousset, *Memoirs of the lives and conduct of those illustrious Heroes Prince Eugene of Savoy and John Duke of Marlborough*, (London, 1742).

Dumont, *Histoire militaire du Prince Eugène de Savoye, du prince et Duc de Malborough et du Prince de Nassau Frise*, (The Hague, 1729).

Dumoulin, *Recueil des campagnes des divers maréchaux de France*, 20 vols, (Amsterdam, 1761-1773).

Elias, Norbert, *La società di corte*, (Bologna, 1980).

Estratto dagli Ordinati della città di Torino, (archivio civico di Torino, Registro n.° 236, anno 1706 e 237, anno 1707), in, Manno, Antonio, (edited by), *Relazione e documenti sull'assedio di Torino nel 1706*, estratto da "Miscellanea di Storia Italiana", (Turin, 1878), pagg. 489-499.

Faldella, Giovanni, *Gesta ed Eroi del Tempo antico*, (Turin, 1910).

Fea, Pietro, *L'assedio di Torino del 1706*, (Rome, 1905).

Ferguson, Niall, *Empire – the rise and demise of the British world order and the lessons for global power*, (New York, 2003).

Ferioli, Alessandro, *Luigi Ferdinando Marsili filosofo del mare*, on "Rivista Marittima", Anno CXXXIX, n. 8/9, agosto/settembre 2006.

Ferrari, Daniela, *La battaglia di Luzzara: appunti di ricerca tra le fonti archivistiche*, in Bugada, Giorgio (edited by), *Storia e luoghi di una battaglia: Luzzara e Riva di Suzzara*, (Luzzara, 2004).

Ferrari, Guido, *Vita e campeggiamenti del Serenissimo Principe Francesco Eugenio di Savoja, on premo comandante degli eserciti Cesarei, e dell'Impero*, (Naples, 1754).

Fieldhouse, H.N, *St. John and Savoy in the War of the Spanish Succession*, in "The English Historical Review", Vol. 50, n. 198 (April 1935), pp 278-291.

Forbin, comte de, *Mémoires du comte de Forbin*, in *Collection de Mémoires pour servir à l'histoire de France, depuis l'avénement de Henri IV jusqu'à la Paix de Paris conclue en 1763; avec des notices sur chaque auteur, et des obsérvations sur chaque ouvrage*, par messieurs A. Petitot et Monmerqué, 2 Tomes, (Paris, 1828).

Forte di Fenestrelle,la grande muraglia piemontese, (Turin, 2006)..

Francovich, Carlo, *Storia della Massoneria in Italia dalle origini alla Rivoluzione francese*, (Florence, 1989).

Frischauer, Paul, *Il principe Eugenio*, (Milan, 1935).

Galasso, Giuseppe, *Napoli nel Viceregno spagnolo (1696-1707)*, (Naples, 1971),.

Gariglio, Dario, *1706: l' assedio di Torino*, (Turin, 2006).

Gariglio, Dario, *Battaglie alpine del Piemonte sabaudo*, (Collegno, 1999).

Gariglio, Dario, *Le sentinelle di pietra – fortezze e cittadelle del Piemonte sabaudo*, (Cuneo, 1997)..

Gasca Queirazza, Giuliano, *Il capitano valdese Rouzier, prospettive di apprestamenti militari ai valichi delle Alpi occidentali di confine alla metà del Settecento*, in, Amoretti, Guido – Petitti, Patrizia, *La scala di Pietro Micca 1958-1998*, (Turin, 2000).

Genta Ternavasio, Enrico, *Cenni sull'attività politica e diplomatica tra Sei e Settecento*, "Mola – Sandri – Melano – Menietti", *Torino 1706 proceedings* vol. I.

Ghietti, Nicola, *Carmagnola 1706: riflessi della guerra su una città di provincia vicina alla capitale*, "Mola – Sandri – Melano – Menietti", *Torino 1706 proceedings*,.

Ghietti, Nicola, *Carmagnola 1706: riflessi della guerra su una città di provincia vicina alla capitale*, "Mola – Sandri – Melano – Menietti", *Torino 1706 proceedings*,.

Giacomini, G.B., *Cronaca dei fatti accaduti nella riviera di Salò e contorni dopo la morte di Carlo II delle Spagne*, in.

Giacomone Piana, Paolo – Dellepiane, Riccardo, *Militarium – fonti archivistiche e bibliografia per la storia militare della Repubblica di Genova (1528-1797), della Repubblica Ligure (1797-1805) e della Liguria napoleonica (1805-1814)*, (Genoa, 2004).

Giacomone Piana, Paolo, *Il colonnello Giovanni Battista Fenoglio: un ufficiale di Ventimiglia nella Guerra di Successione Spagnola,* in "Intemelion", n.° 4, 1998.

Giannone, Pietro, *Storia civile del Regno di Napoli*, 5 Vols, (Milan, 1844).

Giarelli, Francesco, *Storia di Piacenza, dalle origini ai nostri giorni*, (Piacenza, 1989).

Giglio, Vittorio, *Milizie ed eserciti d'Italia*, (Milan, 1927).

Girelli, Giovanni Antonio, *Cronaca di Erbusco (1701-1707)*, s.i., rep. in photocopy, from the Brescia City Library.

Gisondi, Francesco Antonio, *Innocenzo XII – Antonio Pignatelli*, (Rome, 1994).

Glauco, *Le buone armi del ministro Alberoni*, on "Storia Illustrata", anno III, n. 4, aprile 1959.

Gobetti, Roberto, *Le armi bianche all'inizio del Settecento*, in "Sandri – Melano – Mola" (edited by), *Torino 1706 Catalogue*.

Gracia Rivas, Manuel, *Aspectos econónomicos del apoyo sanitario en el ejército y la Armada de España, durante el reinado de los Austrias (siglos XVI-XVII)*, in Acta of the XXX International Conference of the Iternational Commissiono f Military History, (Rabat, 2005).

Grilletto, Renato, *La Valle del Chisone e la fortezza di Fenestrelle*, on "L'universo", anno LII, n. 5, sett. – ott. 1972.

Grilletto, Renato, *La viabilità nella Valle di Susa e la fortezza di Exilles*, on "L'universo", anno LI, n. 4, lug. – ago. 1971.

Grilletto, Renato, *Notizie storico-geografiche sulla sub-valle di Bellino (Valle Varaita)*, on "L'universo", anno LIX, n. 2, mar. - apr. 1979.

Guarnieri, Gino, *I Cavalieri di Santo Stefano*, (Pisa, 1960).

Guerrini, Domenico, *I Granatieri di Sardegna 1659-1900*, (Rome,1962).

Guerrini, Paolo. *Cronache bresciane inedite dei secoli XV-XIX trascritte e annotate*, Vol V°, (Brescia, 1933).

Guichonnet, Paul, *La Savoia e la Guerra di Successione di Spagna*, "Mola - Sandri - Melano - Menietti", *Torino 1706 proceedings* vol. I.

Hakbrett, Karl, *Rélation du siége, défense et libération de la ville et citadelle de Turin, dressée par un officier de la garnison sur les mémoires tirés du journal du Général Daun*, in Manno, Antonio, (edited by), *Relazione e documenti sull'assedio di Torino nel 1706*, estratto da "Miscellanea di Storia Italiana", (Turin, 1878), pag. 386-475.

Hanlon, Gregory, "*The Italian States*", in *A Companion to Eighteenth-Century Europe*, (edited by Peter H. Wilson), (London, 2008).

Hanlon, Gregory, *The twilight of a military tradition: italian aristocrats and european conflicts, 1560-1800*, (London, 1998).

Hattendorf, John B., *England in the War of the Spanish Succession*, (Newport, 1978).

Haussonville, conte d', *La duchesse de Bourgogne et l'alliance savoyarde sous Louis XIV*, (Paris, 1898).

Henderson, Nicholas, *Prince Eugene of Savoy*, (London, 1964).

Histoire des campagnes de Monseigneur le duc de Vendosme, (Paris, 1715).

Horric de Beaucaire (edited by), *Recueil des instructions données aux ammbassadeurs et ministres de France - Savoie-Sardaigne dès origines jusqu'en 1748*, (Paris, 1898).

Howard, Michael, *La guerra e le armi nella storia d`Europa*, (Bari, 1978).

Il Corpo degli Ingegneri dell'Esercito, (Florence, 2007).

Ilari, V.- Boeri, G.C. – Paoletti, C., *Tra i Borboni e gli Asburgo: le armate terrestri e navali italiane nelle guerre del primo Settecento (1701-1732)*, (Ancona, 1996).

Istituto Comprensivo 2 – Suzzara, *Una grande guerra in un piccolo paese: storia politica, militare e territoriale*, in Bugada, Giorgio (edited by), *Storia e luoghi di una battaglia: Luzzara e Riva di Suzzara*, in Bugada, Giorgio (edited by), *Storia e luoghi di una battaglia: Luzzara e Riva di Suzzara*, (Luzzara: 2004).

Istituto Secondario Superiore "A. Manzoni" – Suzzara, *La battaglia di Luzzara*, in Bugada, Giorgio (edited by), *Storia e luoghi di una battaglia: Luzzara e Riva di Suzzara*, (Luzzara, 2004).

Jörgensen, Christer - Pavkovic, Michael F. - Rice, Rob S. - Schneid, Frederick C. - Scott, Chris L., *Fighting techniques of the early modern world AD 1500 – AD 1763 – equipment, combat, skills, and tactics*, (New York, 2007).

Jori, Ilio, *Eugenio di Savoia*, (Turino, 1941).

Kamen, Henry, *How Spain became a world power 1492-1763*, (New York, 2003).

Kamen, Henry, *Philip V of Spain*, (New York - London, 2001).

Kennedy, Paul, *The rise and fall of the great powers – economic change and military conflict from 1500 to 2000*, (New York, 1988).

Klingenstein, Grete, *L'ascesa di Casa Kaunitz*, (Rome, 1993).

L.C.D.C. (Bousquet), *Histoire de François Eugène prince de Savoie et de Piémont, marquis de Saluces*, 2 vols, (London, 1739).

La Colonie, Jean Martin de, *Mèmoires de monsieur de la Colonie, maréchal de camp des armées de l'Electeur de Bavière*, 3 vols, (Utrecht, 1738).

La Hode, *Histoire de la vie et du regne de Louis le Grand*, 3 vols, (Franckfurt - Basel, 17409.

La Lande, P. A., *Histoire de l'empereur Charles VI*, 6 vols, (The Hague, 1743).

La Motte Yves Joseph - La Martinière Antoine Augustin Bruzen de, *Histoire de la vie et du régne de Louis XIV roi de France*, 5 vols, (The Hague, 1740).

Labarre, Carole, *La frontière franco-savoyarde: trois exemples de frontières fluviales XV – XVIII siècle*, in *Frontiere e fortificazioni di frontiera*, (Florence, 2001).

Lamigue, Isaac, *Histoire du Prince d'Orange et de Nassau*, 2 vols, (Leuwarde, 1715).

Lemire, Beverly, "*Manufacturing, markets, and consumption*", in *A Companion to Eighteenth-Century Europe*, (edited by Peter H. Wilson), (London, 2008).

Leoni, Antonio, *Ancona illustrata*, (Ancona, 1832).

Lettres Patents du Roi de France qui admettent les renonciations du Roi d'Espagne, du Duc de Berry et du Duc d'Orléans, factes à Versailles le mois de mars du 1713 Rinuncia di Monsieur il Duca d'Orléans alla Corona di Spagna, fatta a Parigi il 19 novembre 1712, in Solaro della Margarita (edited by), *Traités*, Vol. II, (Turin, 1836).

Levron, Jacques, *La vita quotidiana a Versailles nei secoli XVII e XVIII*, (Milan, 1990).

Libert, Giancarlo, *Gli Olivero e l'assedio del 1706: vicende di una famiglia e delle sue proprietà*, "Mola – Sandri – Melano – Menietti", *Torino 1706 proceedings* vol. I.

Ligne, Charles-Joseph Lamoral, principe de, *Mémoires du prince Eugène de Savoie écrites par lui-même*, (Paris, 1811).

Liste des Troupes de Son Altesse Électorale Maximilien Emanuel de Bavière, avec les Milices régimentées et régulières en 1703. s.i.

Liste ou établissemens de tous les Corps qui composent les 20.000 hommes dont la Reine de Grande Bretagne et les États Généraux sont convenus d'augmenter leurs troupes en 1703. s.i.

Lo Faso di Serradifalco, Alberico, *Il ceto dirigente del Ducato di Savoia fra il 1703 e il 1706: traccia per un dizionario biografico*, in "Sandri – Melano – Mola" (edited by), *Torino 1706 Catalogue.*

Lo Faso di Serradifalco, Alberico, *Il ruolo della nobiltà piemontese nelle campagne di guerra 1703-1706*, "Mola – Sandri – Melano – Menietti", *Torino 1706 proceedings* vol. II.

Lodolini, Armando, *Le finanze pontificie e i "Monti"*, on "Rassegna storica del Risorgimento", anno XLIV, fascicolo II-III, aprile – settembre 1957.

Longhena Mario, *Il conte L.F. Marsili: un uomo d'arme e di scienza*, (Milan, 1930).

Lupano, Alberto, *1706: i Savoia a Casale*, "Mola – Sandri – Melano – Menietti", *Torino 1706 proceedings* vol. I.

Lupo, Maurizio, *Spade e sabri dell'armata di Vittorio Amedeo II di Savoia*, "Mola – Sandri – Melano – Menietti", *Torino 1706 proceedings* vol. I.

Lynn, John A., *Recalculating French Army Growth during the Grand Siècle 1600-1715*, on "French Historical Studies", vol. 18, n. 4 (Autumn 1994), pp. 881-906.

Lynn, John A., *The other side of victory: honorable surrender during the wars of Louis XIV*, in *the Projection and Limitations of imperial Powers, 1618-1850*, edited by Frederick C. Schneid, serie History of Warfare, no. 75, (Leiden-Boston, 2012).

Macaulay, Thomas Babington, *Storia d'Inghilterra dall'avvenimento al trono di Giacomo II*, 2 Vols, (Turin, 1852).

Maffeo, Camillo, *Il sistema bastionato nei secoli XV-XVIII e gli ingegneri militari italiani*", on "Rivista Storica", anno II, n. 4, 1996.

Mandelli, Maurizio – Sala, Edoardo – Testa, Francesco, *La battaglia di Cassano – protagonisti, storia e vicende umane della battaglia del 16 agosto 1705 e della Guerra di Successione Spagnola in Lombardia*, (Cassano d'Adda, 2005).

Mandelli, Maurizio, *La battaglia di Cassano del 16 agosto 1705*, on "Studi Storico-Militari 2006", (Rome, 2008).

Mandrou, Robert, *Luigi XIV e il suo tempo*, (Turin, 1990).

Manno, Antonio, (edited by), *Relazione e documenti sull'assedio di Torino nel 1706*, estratto da "Miscellanea di Storia Italiana", (Turin, 1878).

Manno, Antonio, *Bombardamento di Torino*, appendice V a, Manno, Antonio, (edited by), *Relazione e documenti sull'assedio di Torino nel 1706*, estratto da "Miscellanea di Storia Italiana", (Turin, 1878), pagg. 509-518.

Manno, Antonio, *Cannoni di nuova invenzione*, appendice XII a, Manno, Antonio, (edited by), *Relazione e documenti sull'assedio di Torino nel 1706*, estratto da "Miscellanea di Storia Italiana", (Turin, 1878), pagg. 569-571.

Manno, Antonio, *Notizie sui Bertola*, appendice VIII a, Manno, Antonio, (edited by), *Relazione e documenti sull'assedio di Torino nel 1706*, estratto da "Miscellanea di Storia Italiana", (Turin, 1878), pagg. 531-538.

Manno, Antonio, *Provvedimenti finanziari*, appendice XI a, Manno, Antonio, (edited by), *Relazione e documenti sull'assedio di Torino nel 1706*, estratto da "Miscellanea di Storia Italiana", (Turin, 1878), pagg. 564-578.

Manno, Antonio, *Testimonianze sul Micca*, appendice IX a, Manno, Antonio, (edited by), *Relazione e documenti sull'assedio di Torino nel 1706*, estratto da "Miscellanea di Storia Italiana", (Turin, 1878), pagg. 539-548.

Manucy, Albert, *Artillery throught the Ages*, (Washington, 1985).

Manuele, Pierangelo, *Il Piemonte sul mare,* (Cuneo, 1997).

Martin Moreno, Ana, *Philip V*, (Madrid, 2000).

Massara, Gian Giorgio, *Le cascine sono occupate; bruciano a centinaia i casini e le ville*, "Mola – Sandri – Melano – Menietti", *Torino 1706 proceedings* vol. I.

Massonat, Claudio, *Ricordi storici delle Alpi Marittime* ms in AUSSME L 3.

Mauvillon, Eléazar, *Histoire du prince François Eugène de Savoye, Généralissime des Armées de l'Empéreur et de l'Empire*, 5 vols, vols 1 and 4 in Vienna, 1741 and 1770; vols 2, 3 and 5 in Amserdam, 1740.

Mazzoglio, Peter John – Anibaldi Ranco, Marco, on *ssistenze dell'assedio di Torino del 1706. Edifici e tracce delle opere di difesa e di assedio ancora esistenti nel territorio torinese*, "Mola – Sandri – Melano – Menietti", *Torino 1706 proceedings* vol. I.

Melon, Jean François, *Essai politique sur le commerce*, (s.i., 1736).

Menegazzi, Claudio, *Luigi XIV*, (Verona, 1980).

Menietti, Piergiuseppe, *Così vivevano*, in "Sandri – Melano – Mola" (edited by), *Torino 1706 Catalogue.*

Menietti, Piergiuseppe, *Dare un volto all'eroe. L'iconografia di Pietro Micca tra invenzione e celebrazione*, "Mola – Sandri – Melano – Menietti", *Torino 1706 proceedings* vol. II.

Menietti, Piergiuseppe, *Pietro Micca e gli altri eroi dell'assedio*, in "Sandri – Melano – Mola" (edited by), *Torino 1706 Catalogue.*

Millot, Claude François Xavier, *Mémoires politiques et militaires pour servir à l'histoire de Louis XIV et de Louis XV, composé sur les pièces originales, recuillies par Adrien-Maurice, duc de Noailles, maréchal de France & ministre d'Etat*, (Paris, 1777).

Mola di Nomaglio, Gustavo – Sandri Giachino, Roberto, *I Savoia sotto attacco*, in "Sandri – Melano – Mola" (edited by), *Torino 1706 Catalogue.*

Moncassoli Tibone, Maria Luisa (edited by), *1706-2006, la battaglia di Torino, memorie ritrovate*, (Turin, 2006).

Montesquieu, Charles Louis de Secondat baron de, *Viaggio in Italia*, (Bari, 1971).

Montù, Cesare Maria, *Storia dell'Artiglieria Italiana*,7 vols, (Rome, 1934).

Morandi Carlo, (edited by), *Relazioni di ambasciatori sabaudi, genovesi e veneti (1693 – 1713)*, (Bologna, 1935).

Morandini, Cesare, *L'anti-Ormea: il marchese Fontana di Cravanzana e l'impresa al servizio dello Stato*, in Merlotti, Andrea (edited by), *Nobiltà e Stato in Piemonte: i Ferrero d'Ormea – atti del convegno*, (Turin, 2003).

Moscati, Ruggero, *Direttive della politica estera sabauda da Vittorio Amedeo II a Carlo Emanuele III*, (Milan, 1941).

Mugnai, Bruno – Cristini, Luca, *L'esercito imperiale al tempo del principe Eugenio di Savoia 1690-1720 – La fanteria*, 3 vols, (Bergamo, 2010).

Mugnai, Bruno, *L'esercito imperiale al tempo del principe Eugenio di Savoia (1690-1720), parte II: la cavalleria*, 2 vols, (Bergamo, 2013).

Mugnai, Bruno, *La guerra di Comacchio: 1708*, in "Studi Storico-militari 1999", (Rome, 2000).

Muratori, Lodovico Antonio, *Annali d'Italia dal principio dell'era volgare sino all'anno 1750*, 13 vols, (Naples, 1870).

Muratori, Ludovico Antonio, *Delle antichità estensi ed italiane*, 2 vols, (Modena, 1740).

Nasi, Roberto, *Le azioni della cavalleria durante l'assedio di Torino del 1706*, (Collegno, 2006).

Naulet, Frédéric, *Pierre Surirey de Saint-Rémy et les mémoires d'artillerie*, in « Revue internationale d'Histoire Militaire », n.° 82, 2002, (Paris, 2002).

Nicolini, Fausto, *L'Europa durante la guerra di successione di Spagna*, 3 Vols, (Naples, 1937-1939).

Noailles, Adrien, duca di, *Mémoires politiques et militaires, pour servir à l'histoire de Louis XIV et de Louis XV, composées sur les pièces originales recuillies par Adrien Maurice duc de Noailles, maréchal de France et ministre d'Etat*, par l'abbé Millot, in *Collection de Mémoires pour servir à l'histoire de France, depuis l'avénement de Henri IV jusqu'à la Paix de Paris conclue en 1763; avec des notices sur chaque auteur, et des obsérvations sur chaque ouvrage*, par messieurs A. Petitot et Monmerqué, Tomes LXX-LXXIII, (Paris, 1828).

Ogliaro, Mario, *Un'eclissi per il Re Sole: ambiguità diplomatiche e intrighi delle corti europee alla vigilia dell'assedio di Torino del 1706*, "Mola – Sandri – Melano – Menietti", *Torino 1706 proceedings* vol. I.

Olmi, Giuseppe, *Medicina, eserciti e battaglie prima e dopo lo scontro di Luzzara*, in Bugada, Giorgio (edited by), *Storia e luoghi di una battaglia: Luzzara e Riva di Suzzara*, (Luzzara, 2004).

Oppenheimer, Wolfgang, *Eugenio di Savoia*, (Milan, 1981).

Ortholan, Henri, *Le prince Eugene et le duc de Marlborough, exemple d'une coopération militaire réussie*, in, Amoretti, Guido – Petitti, Patrizia, *La scala di Pietro Micca 1958-1998*, (Turin, 2000).

Ossian de Negri, Teofilo, *Storia di Genova*, (Milan, 1974).

Ostwald, Jamel, *The "decisive" battle of Ramillies in 1706: prerequisites for decisiveness in Early Modern Warfare*, on "Journal of Military History", vol. 64, n. 3, July 2000.

Ottieri, Francesco Maria, *Istoria delle guerre avvenute in Europa e particolarmente in Italia per la Successione alla Monarchia delle Spagne dall'anno 1696 all'anno 1725*, 4 vols, (Rome, 1753).

Paghe dell'artiglieria dal marzo 1699, ms AUSSME, ex AST. Ms. 129.

Paghe e spettanze dell'artiglieria, del 1708, handwritten copy in AUSSME, L 3, 8, Lavori svolti.
Paghe e spettanze di pace e di guerra, del 1701 – 1713, handwritten copy in AUSSME, L 3, 8, Lavori svolti.
Pagliucchi, Pio, *I castellani del Castel Sant'Angelo di Roma*, 3 vols, (Rome, 1928).
Paleologo Oriundi, Federico, *I Corsi nella Fanteria Italiana della Serenissima Repubblica di Venezia*, (Venic, 1912).
Palmas, Clara, *Il patrimonio architettonico*, in *1706-2006, verso il terzo centenario dell'assedio e della battaglia di Torino*, acta of the conference held 24th May 2003, (Turin, 2004).
Paoletti Ciro, *Logistica e assedi delle guerre del settecento*, on "Panoplia", anno VII, n. 27 – 28, agosto – dicembre 1996.
Paoletti, Ciro, "War 1688-1812", in *A Companion to Eighteenth-Century Europe*, (edited by Peter H. Wilson), London, 2008).
Paoletti, Ciro, *7 settembre 1706: battaglia e assedio di Torino*, on "Rivista Militare", anno CL, n. 6, nov. – dic. 2006.
Paoletti, Ciro, *A military history of Italy*, (Westport, 2007).
Paoletti, Ciro, *Capitani di Casa Savoia*, (Rome, 2007).
Paoletti, Ciro, *Dal Ducato all'Unità – tre secoli e mezzo di storia militare piemontese*, (Rome, 2011).
Paoletti, Ciro, *Errori d'impostazione storiografica e nuova valutazione dell'assedio di Tolone e della campagna sabauda in Provenza del 1707*, in *Studi storico-militari 2001*, (Rome, 2004).
Paoletti, Ciro, *Eugenio di Savoia*, a paper presented to the IV International Conference *Fonti e fatti della Successione Spagnola: 1705 – 2005*, Cassano d'Adda, 16 Ottobre 2005.
Paoletti, Ciro, *Gli Italiani in armi – cinque secoli di storia militare nazionale 1494-2000*, (Rome, 2001).
Paoletti, Ciro, *Il capovolgimento di fronte di Vittorio Amedeo II*, a paper presented to the II International Conference *Fonti e fatti e della Successione Spagnola: 1703 – 2003*, Rome, 18 november 2003.
Paoletti, Ciro, *Il cardinale i duchi, la strega – vita del cartinale Alberoni*, (Rome, 2021).
Paoletti, Ciro, *Il principe Eugenio di Savoia*, (Rome, 2001).
Paoletti, Ciro, *Il quadro generale del 1704 e Eugenio a Hochstädt*, a paper presented to the III Conference *Fonti e fatti della Successione Spagnola: 1704 – 2004*, Rome, State Archive, 1 December 2004.
Paoletti, Ciro, *Il quadro generale e le operazioni del primo biennio*, a paper presented to the I Conference *Fonti e fatti e della Successione Spagnola: 1700 – 1702*, Rome, 23 November 2002.
Paoletti, Ciro, *Italy in Louis XIV's grand strategy*, a paper presented to the 3rd Gunther Rothenberg Memorial Seminar, High Point, University, North Carolina, November 8th, 2008.
Paoletti, Ciro, *Italy, Piedmont and French anti-Habsburg strategy, 1690-1748*, in *the Projection and Limitations of imperial Powers, 1618-1850*, edited by Frederick C. Schneid, serie History of Warfare, no. 75, (Leiden-Boston, 2012).
Paoletti, Ciro, *Le armi e le Chiavi: storia militare degli Stati Pontifici nell'Età Moderna e Contemporanea*, (Rome, 2020).
Paoletti, Ciro, *Prince Eugene of Savoy, the Toulon expedition of 1707 and the English historians- a dissenting view*, on "Journal of Military History" , vol 70, n. 4, October 2006.
Paoletti, Ciro, *Storia dei trasporti militari italiani dalle origini all'Unità*, on "Studi storico-militari 2007", (Rome, 2009).
Paoletti, Ciro, *Un cas de financement prolongé des activités belliques: l'alliance entre l'Angleterre et la Maison de Savoye (1688-1861)*, in Acta of the XXX International annual conference of the International Commission of Military History, (Rabat, 2005).
Parallele de la paye en temps de paix et de guerre, ms AUSSME, ex Uff. soldo 1701-1713.
Pastor, Ludwig von, *Storia dei Papi nel periodo dell'assolutismo – vol. XV – 1700-1740*, (Rome, 1933).
Pellegrino, Giuseppe, *Il passaggio delle Alpi Trentine da parte del Principe Eugenio di Savoia*, on "Rivista Militare italiana", anno II, n. 9, settembre 1928, anno VI E.F.
Perini, Sergio, *La difesa militare della Terraferma veneta nel Settecento*, (Sottomarina, 1998).
Perrone di San Martino, *Guerra della successione di Spagna*, ms, AUSSME L 3 Stati Preunitari, Piemonte – Studi particolari, 6.
Petitti, Patrizia, *Il "sesso imbelle": cenni intorno alla partecipazione delle donne alla difesa di Torino nel 1706*, "Mola – Sandri – Melano – Menietti", *Torino 1706 proceedings* vol. II.
Petitti, Patrizia, *La scala di Pietro Micca 1958-1998*, (Turin, 2000).
Pevitt, Christine, *The man who would be king – the life of Philippe d'Orléans, regent of France*, (London, 1997).

Pezzoni, Giovanni, *Istoria dei fatti accaduti nel paese di Palazzolo scritti l'anno 1811 da me Giovanni Pezzoni*, (Palazzolo sull'Oglio, 1987).

Picchio, Carlo, *Filippo V sul trono di Spagna*, in *I Borboni in Italia*, numero speciale di "Storia illustrata", anno XV, n. 95, ottobre 1965.

Pieri, Piero, (edited by), Principe Eugenio di Savoia. *La Campagna d'Italia del 1706*, (Rome,1936).

Pieri, Piero, *L'evoluzione dell'arte militare nei secoli XV, XVI, XVII e la guerra del secolo XVIII*, in "Nuove questioni di storia moderna", (Milan, 1966).

Poddine Rattu, Rossana, *Biografie dei Viceré sabaudi del Regno di Sardegna (1720-1848)*, (Cagliari,2005).

Pognisi, Emilio, *Vittorio Amedeo II e la campagna del 1708 per la conquista del confine alpino*, (Rome, 1936).

Preto, Paolo, *I servizi segreti di Venezia*, (Cles, 2004).

Price, J. L., "*The Dutch Republic*", in *A Companion to Eighteenth-Century Europe*, (edited by Peter H. Wilson), (London, 2008)..

Provvedimenti finanziari presi durate l'assedio di Torino, (estratto da A.S. Torino, Archivio Camerale, Sessioni camerali 1705-1707, n. 52), appendice XIII a, Manno, Antonio, (edited by), *Relazione e documenti sull'assedio di Torino nel 1706*, estratto da "Miscellanea di Storia Italiana", (Turin, 1878), pagg. 572-577.

Puletti, Giorgio, *Genova Cavalleria*, on "Rivista Militare", anno CXXX, n.1, gennaio-febbraio 1986.

Puletti, Giorgio, *La cavalleria italiana*, on "Rivista Militare",anno CXXV, n. 4, luglio-agosto 1981.

Puletti, Rodolfo, *Caricat! - tre secoli di storia dell'Arma di Cavalleria*, (Bologna, 1973).

Puységur, Jacques François de Chastenet, marquis de, *L'Art de la Guerre par principes et par règles*, 2 vols, (Paris, 1749).

Quandoquidem morto sine liberis... Trattato della Grande Alleanza contro la Francia, fatto all'Aja il 7 settembre 1701, in Solaro della Margarita (edited by), *Traités*, Vol. II, (Turin, 1836).

Quazza, Romolo, *La formazione progressiva dello Stato sabaudo*, (Turin, 1942).

Quincy, Charles Sevin marquis de, *Histoire militaire du regne de Louis le Grand, vol. 6° 1708-1711*, 7 vols., (Paris, 1726).

Rapport, Michael, "*France*", in *A Companion to Eighteenth-Century Europe*, (edited by Peter H. Wilson), (London, 2008).

Rati, Armando, *La battaglia di Luzzara*, (Mantova, 2003).

Ravet, Bruno Guglielmotto, *In soccorso del Duca: lettere inedite del Principe Eugenio pubblicate da Luigi Cibrario*, "Mola - Sandri - Melano - Menietti", *Torino 1706 proceedings* vol. I.

Redaelli, Alberto, *Le grandi battaglie della storia bresciana*, (Brescia, 1980).

Regia Deputazione per gli Studi di Storia Patria per le antiche provincie e la Lombardia, *Le campagne di guerra in Piemonte (1703-1708) e l'assedio di Torino (1706) - studi, documenti, illustrazioni,* vol VI, (Turin, 1912).

Regolamento delle piazze di Quartiere d'inverno , di quali gioiscono gli Uffiziali di fanteria regolati a ss 10 caduna ed a R 1 di fieno caduna il giorno, come anche del contante che godono li Bass'Uffiziali e soldati come infra, in vigore dal 12 dicembre 1701 almeno al 1748, ms in AUSSME.

Regolamento stabilito da S.A.R. per le tappe, del 3 agosto 1700, in *Istruzioni ai Commissari di guerra del 9 febbraio 1751*, rip. in Duboin, *Raccolta...*, vol XXIX, pag. 969.

Reichard, Hans Ottokar, *Guide de l'Italie 1793*, (Paris, 1971).

Reineri, Maria Teresa, *Anna Maria d'Orléans, regina di Sardegna, duchessa di Savoia*, (Turin, 2005).

Relazione della liberazione di Torino, appendice XIV a, Manno, Antonio, (edited by), *Relazione e documenti sull'assedio di Torino nel 1706*, estratto da "Miscellanea di Storia Italiana", (Turin, 1878), pagg. 576-589.

Renée, Amédée, *Les nièces de Mazarin*, (Paris, 1856)..

Ressman, Claudio, *Il prezioso smeraldo dell'ammiraglio, on* "Lega Navale", anno CXVIII, n. 5, settembre-ottobre, 2015.

Ressmann, Claudio, *Duemila morti per un piccolo errore di navigazione*, on "Rivista Marittima", anno CXL, n. 1, gennaio 2007, pag. 189.

Ricaldone, E. Aldo di, *Annali del Monferrato 951-1708*, (Turin, 1972).

Ricchiardi, Enrico, *L'esercito ducale sabaudo negli anni dell'assedio*, in "Sandri - Melano - Mola" (edited by), *Torino 1706 Catalogue*.

Ricchiardi, Enrico, *L'esercito ducale sabaudo nel 1706: organizzazione, uniformi, bandiere*, "Mola - Sandri - Melano - Menietti", *Torino 1706 proceedings* vol. I.

Riccioli, J.L., *Le problème du passage des cours d'eau au XVIII siècle*, in *La révolution militaire en Europe (XV - XVIII siècles)*, (Paris, 1997).

Richelieu, Louis François Armand de Vignerot du Plessis, duc de, *Mémoires*, (Paris, 1890).
Rinuncia di Filippo V Re di Spagna alla Corona di Francia, confermata il 9 nomvembre dalle Cortes, fatta al Buen Retiro il 5 novembre 1712, in Solaro della Margarita (edited by), *Traités*, V vol., (Turin, 1836).
Rinuncia di Monsieur il Duca d'Orléans alla Corona di Spagna, fatta a Parigi il 19 novembre 1712, in Solaro della Margarita (edited by), *Traités*, Vol. II, (Turin, 1836).
Rinuncia di Monsieur il Duca di Berry alla Corona di Spagna, fatta a Marly il 24 novembre 1712, in Solaro della Margarita (edited by), *Traités*, Vol. II, (Turin, 1836).
Rivoire, Mario, *Luigi XIV il Re Sole*, (Milan, 1970).
Roberti, Giuseppe, *Vittorio Amedeo II, duca di Savoia, e le potenze nemiche o neutrali durante il secondo periodo della guerra in Italia per la successione di Spagna (1703-707)*, in *Le campagne di guerra in Piemonte (1703-1708) e l'assedio di Torino (1706) – studi, documenti, illustrazioni*, vol VI, (Turin, 1912).
Robio, Maurizio, conte di Montemarzo, *Notizie estratte dal cerimoniale della R. Corte di Savoia esercìto e registrato per ordine di S.A.R. da me conte di Montemarzo Mauritio Robio Maggiordomo di detta A.R. dali 26 ottobre 1703 sino per tutto l'anno 1709*, in, Manno, Antonio, (edited by), *Relazione e documenti sull'assedio di Torino nel 1706*, estratto da "Miscellanea di Storia Italiana", (Turin, 1878), pagg. 483-488.
Roimanmotier, R. May de, *Histoire militare de la Suisse et celle des Suisses dans les differens sérvices de l'Europe*, (Lausanne, 1788).
Rombaldi, Odoardo, *Aspetti e problemi di un secolo di governo estense a Modena e Reggio Emilia (da Alfonso IV a Rinaldo I – 1658-1737)*, (Modena, 1995).
Ronco, Mauro, *L'assedio di Torino del 1706: un episodio del tradimento del regno di Francia ai danni della Cristianità*, "Mola – Sandri – Melano – Menietti", *Torino 1706 proceedings* vol. I.
Rosa, Vincenzo, *Memorie storiche di Palazzolo*, in Guerrini, Paolo, *Cronache bresciane inedite dei secoli XV-XIX trascritte e annotate*, Vol V°,(Brescia, 1933).
Rosati, Antonio, *La relazione del generale Marsigli dell'agosto 1709*, a paper presented to the International Conference "Le Armi del Sovano", Rome, State Archive, March 2001.
Rosingana da Piovà, *Giornale dell'assedio di Torino*, in Manno, Antonio, (edited by), *Relazione e documenti sull'assedio di Torino nel 1706*, estratto da "Miscellanea di Storia Italiana", (Turin, 1878), appendice IV, pagg. 500-508.
Rossi, Anton-Domenico, *Ristretto di storia patria, ad uso dei Piacentini*, (Piacenza, 1832).
Rossi, Giovanni Felice (edited by), *Cento studi sul Cardinale Alberoni*, Vol I e II, (Piacenza, 1978).
Rota, Ettore, *Storia politica d'Italia – le origini del Risorgimento*, (Milan, 1938).
Rousset de Misy, *Istoria del Cardinal Alberoni, dal giorno della sua nascita fino ai principi del 1719, con aggiunta di quanto è seguito fino a' 22 marzo del 1720*, 2 vols, (Amsterdam, 1720).
Ruffi, Giuseppe, *Relatione della guerra dell'anno 1701 e Rovina di Castel Coati*, in Guerrini, *Cronache bresciane inedite dei secoli XV-XIX trascritte e annotate*, Vol V°, (Brescia, 1933).
Russo, Flavio, *Ingegno e paura*, (Rome, 2005).
Russo, Flavio, *Vigliena: autopsia d'un fortino*, in "Studi Storico-militari 1999", (Rome, 2000).
Sabatini, Gaetano, *La spesa militare nel contesto della finanza pubblica napoletana del XVII secolo*, in, Cancila, Rossella (edited by), *Mediterraneo in armi*, (Palermo, 2007).
Saint René Taillandier, *La Princesse des Ursins*, (Paris, 1926).
Saint-Simon, Louis de Rouvroy duc de, *Mémoires* (*Mémoires complets et authentiques du Duc de Saint Simon*), 20 Vols, (Paris, 1840).
Saitta, Antonio, *Messina antispagnola*, (Messina, 1974).
Saluzzo, Alessandro conte di, *Histoire militaire du Piémont*, 5 vols, (Turin, 1818).
Salzano, Michele Tommaso Vincenzo, *Corso di storia ecclesiastica dalla venuta di Gesù Cristo ai giorni nostri, comparata colla storia politica dei tempi*, (Rome, 1861).
Sandi, Vettor, *Principj di storia civile della Repubblica di Venezia dall'anno di N.S. 1700 fino all'anno 1767*, 4 vols., (Venice, 1769).
Sandri-Giachino, Roberto, *Un suddito sabaudo ambasciatore straordinario a Vienna e Commissario imperiale in italia: Ercole Turinetti di Priero*, "Mola – Sandri – Melano – Menietti", *Torino 1706 proceedings* vol. II.
Santi-Mazzini, Giovanni, *La macchina da guerra dal Medioevo al 1914 – La macchina da guerra nel Medioevo – metamorfosi della macchina da guerra*, in *Militaria: storia, battaglie, armate*, 12 vols (Milan, 2006), vol. 3.
Santi-Mazzini, Giovanni, *La macchina da guerra dal Medioevo al 1914 – Metamorfosi della macchina da guerra*, in *Militaria: storia, battaglie, armate*, 12 vols, (Milan, 2006), vol. 4.

Savarino, Renzo, *Forme, forza e limiti della dimensione religiosa in una città assediata: figure significative, classi sociali ed eventi collettivi nella Torino del 1706*, in "Mola - Sandri - Melano - Menietti", *Torino 1706 proceedings* vol. II.

Scala, Edoardo, *Intendenti, commissari ed amministratori egli eserciti sabaudi*, in *La guerra del 1866 e altri scritti*, (Rome, 1981).

Schalenberg, Marc, "*Towns and their inhabitants*", in *A Companion to Eighteenth-Century Europe*, (edited by Peter H. Wilson), (London, 2008).

Sconfienza, Roberto - Del Monte, Dario - Simoncini, Roberto, *Gli eserciti all'inizio del Settecento*, in Sandri Giachino, Roberto - Melano, Giancarlo - Mola di Nomaglio, Gustavo (edited by), *Torino 1706 Catalogue.*

Sconfienza, Roberto, *Fortezze e piazzeforti quadrilatere in Piemonte: modelli ed esempi tra XVI e XVII secolo*, in, Amoretti, Guido - Petitti, Patrizia, *La scala di Pietro Micca 1958-1998*, (Turin, 2000).

Scuole d'Applicazione d'Arma, *L'Arma di Artiglieria - Cenni storici*, (Turin, 1965).

Segre, Arturo, *Negoziati diplomatici della Corte Sabauda colla Corte di Baviera dalle origini al 1704*, in *Le campagne di guerra in Piemonte (1703-1708) e l'assedio di Torino (1706) - studi, documenti, illustrazioni,* vol VI, (Turin, 1912).

Sella, Domenico - Capra, Carlo, *Il Ducato di Milano*, (Turin, 1984).

Sella, Domenico, *Lo Stato di Milano in età spagnola*, (Turin, 1987).

Seren Rosso, Rossella, *La difesa di un transito alpino: il vecchio e il nuovo forte di Bard*, in, Amoretti, Guido - Petitti, Patrizia, *La scala di Pietro Micca 1958-1998*, (Turin, 2000).

Serra, Maria Teresa, *Echi di guerra nelle Valli di Lanzo*, "Mola - Sandri - Melano - Menietti", *Torino 1706 proceedings* vol. I.

Signorelli, Andrea - Signorelli, Ugo, *La loro ora più bella: l'assedio di Verrua*, in, Amoretti, Guido - Petitti, Patrizia, *La scala di Pietro Micca 1958-1998*, (Turin, 2000).

Signorelli, Bruno, *Giovanni Battista Gropello ministro di Vittorio Amedeo II e suo plenipotenziario durante l'assedio di Torino (giugno-settembre 1706)*, "Mola - Sandri - Melano - Menietti", *Torino 1706 proceedings* vol. II.

Sirtema van Grovestins, Carel Frederick, *Histoire des luttes et rivalités politiques entre les Puissances Maritimes et la France durant la seconde moitié du XVII'siècle*, 8 vols, (Paris,1853-1855), vols. 3, 4, 5, 6 and 7.

Sistema politico universale delli Ducati di Parma e Piacenza, in, Di Noto, Sergio (edited by), *Le istituzioni dei ducati parmensi nella prima metà del Settecento*, (Parma, 1980).

Slicher van Bath, Bernhard.Hendrik, *Storia agraria dell'Europa occidentale (500-1850)*, (Turin, 1972).

Snyder, Henry L, *The formulation of Foreign and Domestic Policy in the reign of Queen Anne: Memoranda by Lord Chancellor Cowper of conversation with Lord Treasurer Godolphin,* in "The Historical Journal", vol. 11, n. 1 (1968).

Sodini, Carla, *Frontiere e fortificazioni di frontiera della Repubblica di Lucca durante l'Età Moderna*, in *Frontiere e fortificazioni di frontiera*, (Florence, 2001).

Solaro della Margarita, Clemente (edited by), *Traités*, 5 vols, (Turin, 1836).

Solaro della Margarita, Giuseppe Maria, *Journal historique du Siege de la Ville et de la Citadelle de Turin l'Année 1706. Avec le veritable Plan*, (Amsterdam, 1708).

Solaro della Margarita, Giuseppe Maria, *Manoscritto preziosissimo del Conte Giuseppe Maria Solaro della Margarita Maggiore Generale d'Artiglieria che contiene l'Originale del suo Journal historique du Siege de la Ville et de la Citadelle de Turin en 1706*, (a cura di Ciro Paoletti), (Turin, 2006).

Soleri, Francesco Lodovico, *Giornale dell'assedio di Torino*, in, Manno, Antonio, (edited by), *Relazione e documenti sull'assedio di Torino nel 1706*, estratto da "Miscellanea di Storia Italiana", (Turin, 1878), appendice IV, pagg. 500-508.

Spini, Giorgio, *Storia dell'età moderna*, 3 vols., (Turin, 1971).

Stefanoni, Carlo Antonio, *Cronaca cremonese (1701-1712)*, a photocopy, no indications.

Stolberg-Stolberg, Franz zu, *I brandenburghesi a Torino nel 1706*, "Mola - Sandri - Melano - Menietti", *Torino 1706 proceedings* vol. II.

Storia di Brescia, promossa e diretta da G. Treccani degli Alfieri, (Brescia, 1960).

Storie di Senzastoria, Catalogue of the Exhibition held in Brescia, (Brescia 1980).

Storrs, Christopher, "*Iberia: Spain and Portugal in the Eighteenth century*", in *A Companion to Eighteenth-Century Europe*, (edited by Peter H. Wilson), (London, 2008).

Storrs, Christopher, *War, diplomacy and the rise of Savoy, 1690-1720*, (London, 1999).

Sunto cronologico dei fatti militari succeduti nel Ducato di Savoia durante le campagne del 1703 e 1705, ms AUSSME.

Susane, A., *Histoire de l'artillerie française*, s.i.

Susane, A., *Histoire de l'infanterie française*, s.i. 5 vols.

Susane, A., *Histoire de la cavalerie française*, s.i. 3 vols.

Symcox, Charles, *Vittorio Amedeo II e l'assolutismo sabaudo 1675-1730*, (Turin, 1989).

Symcox, Geoffrey, *L'età di Vittorio Amedeo II*, in Galasso, Giuseppe, a cura di *Il Piemonte Sabaudo – stato e territori in età moderna*, (Turin, 1994).

Tabacco, Giovanni, *Lo stato sabaudo nel Sacro Romano Impero*, (Turin, 1939).

Targe, Jean-Baptiste, *Histoire de l'avénement de la Maison de Bourbon au trone d'Espagne*, 6 voll, (Paris, 1772).

Tarizzo, Francesco Antonio, *L'arpa discordata*, (Turin, 2006).

Tarizzo, Francesco Antonio, *Ragguaglio istorico dell'assedio, difesa e liberazione della città di Torino*, (Turin, 2006).

Tassoni Estense, Alessandro, *Eugenio di Savoia*, (Milan, 1939).

Tessé, *Mémoires et lettres du Maréchal de Tessé, contenantes des anedoctes et des faits historiques inconnus, on r partie des regnes de Louis XIV et de Louis XV*, 2 tomes, (Paris, 1806).

The German and French Journals of the late Campaign in Italy confronted together, Taken from the Italian Diary, Printed at Vienna by the Emperor's Command and the Paris Gazette, (London, 1701).

The History of Francis Eugene, Prince of Savoy, (London, 1742).

The history of the remarkable siege of Toulon, Attacked by the English and Dutch by Sea, and the Prince Eugene and the Duke of Savoy by Land, in the year 1707, (London, 1746).

The Life and military actions of His Royal Highness Prince Eugene of Savoy, with an account of his death and funeral, (London, 1739).

The military history of the late prince Eugene and of the late duke of Marlborough, 2 vols, (London, 1739).

Thesaurus Geographicus, a new book of Geography, or a compleat description of the Earth, (London, 1695).

Thomazi, A., *Les flottes de l'or – histoire des galions d'Espagne*, (Paris, 1956).

Thompson, Andrew C., "*Diplomacy and the great powers*", in *A Companion to Eighteenth-Century Europe*, (edited by Peter H. Wilson), (London, 2008).

Topin, Marius, *L'Europe et les Bourbons sous Louis XIV*, (Paris, 1868).

Torcy, *Mémoires du Marquis de Torcy pour serivir à l'histoire des négociations depuis le Traité de Riswick jusqu'à la Paix d'Utrecht*, in *Collection de Mémoires pour servir à l'histoire de France, depuis l'avénement de Henri IV jusqu'à la Paix de Paris conclue en 1763 ; avec des notices sur chaque auteur, et des obsérvations sur chaque ouvrage*, par messieurs A. Petitot et Monmerqué, 2 Tomes (Tomes LXVII and LXVIII of the collection), (Paris, 1828).

Tosti, Amedeo, *Vittorio Amedeo II – il primo Re Sabaudo*, on "Rivista Militare italiana", anno VI, n. 11, novembre 1932, anno XI E.F.

Trabucco, Carlo, *La volpe savoiarda e l'assedio di Torino*, (Turin, 1978).

Traité de Ligue entre S.A.R. Victor Amé II Duc de Savoie d'une part et les Rois de France et d'Espagne de l'autre pour la conservation de la paix en Italie, fatto a Torino il 6 aprile 1701, in Solaro della Margarita (edited by), *Traités*, Vol. II, (Turin, 1836).

Trattati ed articoli segreti d'alleanza fra S.A.R. Vittorio Amedeo II Duca di Savoia e l'Imperatore Leopoldo II per continuare la guerra contro la Corona di Francia, fatto a Torino l'8 novembre 1703, in Solaro della Margarita (edited by), *Traités*, Vol. II, (Turin, 1836).

Trattato d'alleanza fra S.A.R. il Duca di Savoia etc. da una parte e S.A.S. il Duca regnante di Wurtemberg dall'altra, fatto a Stoccarda il 27 aprile 1711, in Solaro della Margarita (edited by), *Traités*, Vol. II, (Turin, 1836).

Trattato ed articoli segreti d'alleanza fra S.A.R. Vittorio Amedeo II Duca di Savoia e gli Stati Generali della Province unite dei Paesi Bassi, col quale S.A.R. accetta il Trattato della Grande Alleanza contro la Francia del 7 settembre 1701 e gli Stati Generali ratificano il Trattato concluso a Torino l'8 novembre 1703 fra S.A.R. e l'Imperatore Leopoldo, fatto all'Aja il 21 gennaio 1705, in Solaro della Margarita (edited by), *Traités*, Vol. II, (Turin, 1836).

Trattato ed articoli segreti d'alleanza fra S.A.R. Vittorio Amedeo II Duca di Savoia e la Regina Anna d'Inghilterra contro la Francia, fatto a Torino il 4 agosto 1704, in Solaro della Margarita (edited by), *Traités*, Vol. II, (Turin, 1836).

Trattato ed articolo separato di pace ed amicizia fra Vittorio Amedeo II Duca di Savoia e il Re di Francia Luigi XIV, per il quale il Re restituisce al Duca di Savoia il Ducato di Savoia e la Contea di Nizza, fatto ad Utrecht l'11 aprile 1713, in Solaro della Margarita (edited by), *Traités*, Vol. II, (Turin, 1836).

Trattato ed articolo separato di pace fra il Duca di Savoia ed il Re di Spagna, per il quale il diritto di successione alla corona di Spagna è riservato a S.A.R. e gli è ceduto il Reame di Sicilia Rinuncia di Monsieur il Duca d'Orléans alla Corona di Spagna, fatta a Parigi il 19 novembre 1712, in Solaro della Margarita (edited by), *Traités*, Vol. II, (Turin, 1836).

Trattato fra la Regina Anna d'Inghilterra ed il Re di Prussia per cui quel Re invia in Piemonte contro la Francia un Corpo d'ottomila uomini sotto gli ordini del Duca di Savoia, fatto a Berlino il 28 novembre 1704, in Solaro della Margarita (edited by), *Traités*, Vol. II, (Turin, 1836).

Trevelyan, George Macaulay, *Storia d'Inghilterra*, 2 vols, (Milan, 1973).

Vaj, Camillo, *Il sistema fortificato di Chivasso e Castagneto. Luglio 1705, la presa e l'occupazione di Chivasso. I piani d'attacco francesi e i registri dell'archivio storico della città, per una lettura dell'assedio che salvò Torino, attraverso nuovi documenti inediti*, "Mola - Sandri - Melano - Menietti", *Torino 1706 proceedings* vol. I.

Valente, Pompeo, *Relazioni diplomatiche di Vittorio Amedeo II, duca di Savoia, coi Cantoni Svizzeri e colla Repubblica del Valllese durante il secondo periodo della guerra in Italia per la successione di Spagna (1703-1707)*, in *Le campagne di guerra in Piemonte (1703-1708) e l'assedio di Torino (1706) - studi, documenti, illustrazioni*, vol VI, (Turin, 1912).

Valente, U., *Intorno a Vittoro Amedeo II*, on "Rassegna storica del Risorgimento", anno XXVI, fascicolo XI, novembre 1939.

Vaughan, D.M., *Campaigns in the Dauphiny Alps: 1588-1747*, in "The English Historical Review", Vol. 28, n. 110 (April 1913), pp 228-242.

Verani, mag., *Ponti gettati sui fiumi dell'alta Italia nella guerra della successione spagnola (1701-1713)*, ms, AUSSME.

Verrua - Lami, Lucio, *L'amante del Re - la Signora di Verrua*, (Farigliano, 1994).

Vibò, Michele Antonio, *Lettera al papa del 6 ottobre 1706*, in, Manno, Antonio, (edited by), *Relazione e documenti sull'assedio di Torino nel 1706*, estratto da "Miscellanea di Storia Italiana", (Turin, 1878), pag. 479-482.

Vico, Giambattista, *La congiura dei principi napoletani del 1701*, (Naples, 1971).

Viglino Davico, Micaela, (edited by), *La piazzaforte di Verrua*, (Turin, 2001).

Viglino Davico, Micaela, *Le difese verso levante del Ducato sabaudo*, in, Amoretti, Guido - Petitti, Patrizia, *La scala di Pietro Micca 1958-1998*, (Turin, 2000).

Villabianca, Benedetto Emanuele e Vanni, marchese di, *Diario e narrazione istorica de' tumulti successi in Palermo nel 1708,*, in, di Marzo Gioacchino, (edited by) *Diari della città di Palermo*, (Palermo, 1872), vol. XII.

Villars, Luis Hector, duca de, *Mémoires du Maréchal de Villars, écrites par lui-méme*, in *Collection de Mémoires pour servir à l'histoire de France, depuis l'avénement de Henri IV jusqu'à la Paix de Paris conclue en 1763; avec des notices sur chaque auteur, et des obsérvations sur chaque ouvrage*, par messieurs A. Petitot et Monmerqué, Tome LXIX, (Paris, 1828).

Viriglio, Alberto, *Cronache dell'assedio di Torino del 1706*, (Turin, 2006).

Vistarino Giacobazzi, Leontine di, *Enrichetta d'Este Farnese duchessa di Parma*, (Milan, 1941).

Vistarino Giacobazzi, Leontine di, *Passioni e scandali nel primo Settecento romano*, (Milan, 1959).

Voltaire, *Le siécle de Louis XIV*, (Paris, 1792).

Warren, Odoardo (edited by), *Raccolta di piante delle principali città e fortezze del Gran Ducato di Toscana*, (Prato, 1979).

Wheeler, Dennis, "*Eighteenth century history and the European environment*", in *A Companion to Eighteenth-Century Europe*, (edited by Peter H. Wilson), (London, 2008).

Wheeler, James Scott, *The making of a world power - war and the military revolution in seventeenth century England*, (Phoenix Mill, 1999).

Williams, Henry Noel, *A rose of Savoy*, (London, 1910).

Wilson, Peter H., "*The Empire, Austria, and Prussia*", in *A Companion to Eighteenth-Century Europe*, (edited by Peter H. Wilson), (London, 2008).

Young G. F., *I Medici*, 2 Vols, (Florence, 1934).

Zangheri, Renato, *L'imposta sul macinato nella finanza degli stati italiani fino all'Unità*, on "Rassegna storica del Risorgimento", anno XLIV, fascicolo II-III, aprile - settembre 1957.

Zannoni, Fabrizio, *Le fonti documentarie del Cisternone della Cittadella in relazione con il dato archeologico*, in, in atti del convegno del 24 maggio 2003, Torino, Lions Club Torino Castello, 2004.

Zannoni, Fabrizio, *Le ricerche in corso*, in *1706-2006, verso il terzo centenario dell'assedio e della battaglia di Torino*, in atti del convegno del 24 maggio 2003, Torino, Lions Club Torino Castello, 2004.

Zannoni, Mario – Fiorentino, Massimo, *L'esercito farnesiano dal 1694 al 1731*, (Parma, 1981).

Zavarella, Carmine, *Evoluzione storica della razione militare dall'antichità a oggi*, in *Studi storico-militari 2002*, (Rome, 2004).

Zilli, Ilaria, *Lo Stato e i suoi creditori: il debito pubblico del Regno di Napoli tra '600 e '700*, (Naples, 1997).

Zorzi, Alvise, *La Repubblica del Leone, Storia di Venezia*, (Milan, 1980).